REVOLUTIONARY
FORGIVENESS

REVOLUTIONARY

Essays on Judaism, Christianity,
and the Future of Religious Life

FORGIVENESS

MARC H. ELLIS

Baylor University Press
Waco, Texas

Library of Congress Cataloging-in-Publication Data

Ellis, Marc H.
  Revolutionary forgiveness : essays on Judaism, Christianity, and the
future of religious life / Marc H. Ellis.
    p. cm.
Includes bibliographical references (p.).
  ISBN 0-918954-75-4
  1. Judaism--20th century. 2. Christianity--20th century. 3. Ellis,
Marc H.--Relations with Catholics. 4. Catholics--Biography. 5.
Holocaust, Jewish (1939-1945) 6. Catholic Foreign Mission Society of
America. I. Title.
  BM565 .E389 2000
  296.3--dc21
                                              00-010524

Cover design by Joan Osth.

Printed in the United States of America on acid-free paper.

My precious son Aaron,

As you become a son of the commandments, I bequeath to you fragments of a great tradition and my own flawed witness. Thank you for the evening prayers and those difficult words of gratitude we pray—to be bound and yet called to be free. I wish you in abundance the traits of your namesake—leadership, compassion, and wisdom. Always search for the covenant. The covenant awaits hidden among peoples that are foreign to you and in places that you are not supposed to be. Practice revolutionary forgiveness in your personal and public life. Do not despair. The future is open to your word and testimony. It is not too late.

For the sake of Zion, I will not be silent,
For the sake of Jerusalem, I will not be still.
                                              Isaiah

Contents

Foreword

WHEN MY FRIEND AND COLLEAGUE Marc Ellis invited me to write a fore-
word to this collection of essays, I believe he did so knowing my strengths
and my limitations: I am a storyteller and a teacher, not a theologian, historian, or scholar of religion. And so it is within those parameters that I
would like to approach Marc's life and work, through stories.

Let us begin with a tale related in the pages of famed Nazi-hunter
Simon Wiesenthal's "The Sunflower," a short fable told of a concentration
camp inmate—Wiesenthal himself—and a dying S.S. man who sought forgiveness from Wiesenthal as a representative of the Jews he killed.
Wiesenthal is appalled and conflicted by this entreaty, and further, he is
aware of his own imminent death. His response to the entreaties of the
dying man—and later to the S.S. man's mother, when he encounters her
and she speaks of the virtues of her dead son—is silence.

The well-known story ends with a direct appeal to the reader: What
would you have done had you been in my shoes? The responses given by
noted writers, theologians, and victims of crimes against humanity in the
second half of the book are instructive, because they demarcate the terrain of repentance, atonement, justice, and forgiveness as seen by members of many faiths, although most interestingly—for our purposes—
Judaism and Christianity.

The Jews—among them Rabbi Abraham Joshua Heschel, Cynthia
Ozick, and Alan Berger—insist that Wiesenthal rightly refused to forgive
his enemies; the Christians—among them Theodore Hesburgh, Martin
Marty, and Edward Flannery—insist that one must forgive, even in such
grievous circumstances. It is—as noted explicitly by Jewish writer Dennis
Prager in his own response to "The Sunflower"—a mark of the differing
attitudes toward religion and even toward the problem of evil in the world
held by Jews and Christians, and it is one that has haunted the world.

In the Jewish tradition, of course, justice is paramount. The Torah admonishes in Deuteronomy, "Justice, justice you shall pursue." Likewise, the Later Prophets Micah and Amos emphasize the importance of justice in passages placing justice at the heart of the relationship with God and beseeching the people of Israel to let justice roll with the force of mighty waters. Within the Christian tradition, although we too should be animated by a concern for justice—Archbishop Desmond Tutu reminds us that for Jesus, as a Jew, "God's liberation would have to have real consequences in the political, social, and economic spheres or it was no Gospel at all"— forgiveness has become the paramount value. Jews may believe Christians have no concept of justice, and they certainly cannot conceive the enormity of the Holocaust, since it was, in large part, fueled by Christian anti-Semitism; Christians, for their part, may believe that whatever horrific things the Jews endured in years past, now they should forgive and forget. They should live in the present.

Do we forgive those who hurt us, who herd us into concentration camps or try to confine us to ghettos, who treat us as something less than human? Do we carry those offenses in our memories forever? Or do we vow to remember them not and refuse to treat others as we have ourselves been treated?

Hard questions, and Wiesenthal and his respondents do not always resolve them.

But in Marc Ellis's new collection of essays we see a fearless Jewish thinker working to understand and to explicate the meaning of some of the seminal events of our age: the Holocaust, the formation of a Jewish state in Palestine, the warfare between the Jews and Arabs of the region, and the effects of Christianity on the world, both positive and negative. Because he is a Jew, his understanding of the Holocaust and the problems of Israel/Palestine are central to his identity; because he has lived and worked for most of his adult life in Christian institutions, his understanding of liberation theology and forgiveness have also become part of him.

Rodger Kamenetz, author of *The Jew in the Lotus* and other books on Jewish spirituality, has said that in the Jewish tradition, the great rebbes are always storytellers, that the rebbe looks at you and tells you the story you most need to hear to be healed. In that tradition, Marc is telling a story of radical forgiveness in book after book, essay after essay, speech after speech, and although his message is not always popular with those who hear it, it may indeed be the story they most need to hear to be healed.

Greg Garrett
Santa Fe, New Mexico
July, 2000

Preface

IN THE PAST TWO DECADES Marc Ellis has established a remarkable record of creative ethical and theological thought in the context of some of the most controverted issues of our time. Starting with his early books on his experience at the Catholic Worker (*A Year at the Catholic Worker*, 1978; reprinted by Baylor University Press in 2000) and his pioneering exploration of Jewish liberation theology (*A Jewish Theology of Liberation*, 1987), Ellis has emerged as a thoughtful and prophetic voice who seeks to think between the boundaries: between Judaism and Christianity, between religiosity and secularity, without giving up his own roots and identity in the Jewish tradition. The 1990s saw a series of major monographs from him. These included *Beyond Innocence and Redemption: Confronting the Holocaust and Israeli Power*, 1990, *Ending Auschwitz: The Future of Jewish and Christian Life*, 1994, *Unholy Alliance: Religion and Atrocity in Our Time*, 1997, and *O' Jerusalem: The Contested Future of the Jewish Covenant*, 1999.

This new volume, *Revolutionary Forgiveness: Essays on Judaism, Christianity, and the Future of Religious Life*, is a kind of Ellis "sampler," tracing autobiographically something of his journey and exploring key themes that make up pieces of the full vision that he is seeking. The first section of the book, "A Jew Among Christians," is an engaging recapitulation of his years from graduate school to teaching at the Maryknoll School of Theology where he directed their program on Justice and Peace in the 1980s.

In these essays Marc Ellis brings before our eyes his year at the Catholic Worker, with its sights and smells of poverty, as well as its self-sacrificial piety. We journey with him in his studies at the Jesuit Marquette University where he followed his mentor from Florida days, William Miller, and completed Miller's own work on Peter Maurin. We are then introduced to the world of the Maryknoll order and school, with its "macho" commitment to danger in the poverty-stricken and revolutionary zones of the world, together with its silenced alienation from the internal realities in its own precincts.

Through his work with Maryknoll, Ellis deepened his global understanding in journeys through Latin America and then through major areas of Africa and Asia. In this sequence of journeys Ellis is ever the participant observer, immersing himself in intense learning experiences of new worlds, while at the same time remaining an outsider, a Jew among Christians. He learns to live between boundaries, between worlds, as one who identifies with and experiences the sufferings and fears of those whose lives he enters, while at the same time quietly noting the contradictions, the pomposities and sadnesses, the signs of impending death, invisible to them. In this process he develops a unique multi-linguality, rooted in a capacity to be with others, to see the world from their side, without being absorbed into and obliterated by those other worlds, always maintaining a sense of his own identity and difference.

The development of this multi-linguality will be deeply tested but also profoundly expanded in the next stage of his journey, which he alludes to in the next two sections of the book. (The detailing of this stage is a task he leaves for a subsequent book, *Practicing Exile: A Journey of Struggle and Hope.*) This is his entry into the contested realities of Palestinians trapped and surviving amid endless efforts at erasure within the expansionist Jewish state of Israel. Here Ellis comes back to the questions of his own cultural and religious identity as an American Jew, even as he enters into and learns to experience what the Jewish state has meant and means for that people who it continually tries to erase, the Palestinians.

Ellis realizes intuitively that after Auschwitz *and* after the empowerment of the state of Israel as a world nuclear and economic power, in alliance with the American superpower, the meaning of Jewish identity at the end of the 20th century can only be discovered through solidarity with the Palestinian people. Here he makes a key parallelism between the question of Christian and of Jewish identities after the Holocaust. Just as Christians cannot go back behind the Holocaust, but can't go forward, except in solidarity with their victims, the Jewish people, so Jews today cannot go back behind Auschwitz and Israeli (and American Jewish) power to a world of innocence as subversive marginals in a Christian Europe.

That world is over, erased by the Holocaust. But the empowerment of Jewish survivors through American and Israeli state power at the expense of the Palestinians, means that Jews cannot go forward except in solidarity with their victims, the Palestinian people. By "going forward," a favorite Ellis term, he does not mean simply "carrying on," which can always be done with access to wealth and power, but finding a new way to live authentically, ethically, in mutuality with others, seeking justice and the common good.

In exploring this parallelism of solidarity of Christians with Jews and Jews with Palestinians, Ellis became a "heretic" not only in the established Jewish world sold out to state power, but also to those "liberal" Christians who believed they should pay the price of guilt and repentance for the Holocaust in uncritical adulation of the state of Israel. Their repentance was expressed in compliance with establishment Jewish self-definitions that presupposed a "Constantinian Judaism" in alliance with the state, Israeli and American. This connivance of Jews and Christians to support their mutual power agendas, and to stifle both Jewish and Christian critics, Ellis, in his earlier work, labeled "the ecumenical deal." With a characteristic sense of integrity, perhaps intuited before it was fully articulated, Ellis stepped firmly into this "heresy" that would make him a pariah in the world of establishment Judaism and its Christian collaborators.

Far from pulling his punches, Ellis has taken each effort to silence and marginalize his insights as a new revelation of the truth of his intuition. In volume after volume, as well as in key essays in this collection, he explores the contradictory dialectics that demand an endless preservation of a past reality of innocent victimization, even to the preservation of Auschwitz itself as a monument, in order to cover up and silence the culpability of an empowered present. Instead of remembering Auschwitz in order "never, never again" to allow such atrocities to go on without outcry, Auschwitz is remembered and remembered again in order to stifle the cries of Palestinians as their houses are blown up, their land confiscated, their children maimed with so-called "rubber bullets."

No one has explored with such depth and trenchant insight this convoluted double-think that dwells on past atrocity in order to stifle outcry against new atrocities committed by those very people who seek to clothe their new power and victimization of others with the garments of their past powerlessness and victimization. Yet in this volume, as well as in his 1999 book, *O' Jerusalem*, Ellis is partly emerging beyond this prophetic critique of bad faith. He seeks to make clear how this very critique itself is grounded and must be grounded in the renewal of authentic faith, or what he calls here "living the covenant in a time of colonialism and evangelization."

This phrase is borrowed from the experience of Latin Americans, Asians and Africans, whose evangelization into Christianity was itself a series of acts of violence against their pre-colonial identity and their lands, carried out in the context of European colonialism. This pairing of colonialism and evangelization alerts us to the questionable meaning of such evangelization with a sensitivity that ties Jewish and third world experience together. Evangelization here is the cultural dimension of imperialism and colonialization.

Although Jews have mostly rejected and many third world people have accepted this evangelization, both have experienced the violent underside of Christian proselytizing. But false proselytizing does not only come from Christianity; it comes from all kinds of state religion masquerading as bearers of salvation. To seek authentic covenantal community, we must resist these various forms of evangelization that seek to rape our souls and teach us to embrace the ideology of our violators.

In a key central section of the book, Ellis explores the twin questions of covenantal life in a time of colonialism and evangelization and what it means to live in exile. Exile is a heavy-laden term in Jewish theologizing of their historical experience. Historically it means exile from the "promised land," to live among gentiles, as a stranger and often a persecuted one. On a deeper level it means the exilic condition of the whole creation separated from God and in a state of "galut" or exile, awaiting a new communion of God and humanity.

Ellis implicitly rejects the first meaning of exile, since the modern 'return' to the homeland has not created a real home of justice and peace, as its Zionist founders hoped, but has turned the indigenous Palestinian people into exiles, both within their own land and throughout the world. In creating a return based on violence and expulsion of the other people of the land, Zionists make their own return into an exile from their authentic traditions of ethical living foundational to the covenant with God. Those who claim to have overcome the exile have created a far deeper exile, an exile from the very soul of the Jewish tradition.

Ellis sees exile as a condition of all those who seek authentic covenantal existence. The institutions of synagogue and church, which claim to carry this message and identity, have deeply sold out to state forms of religion and persecute the prophets. Yet at the same time they carry the message itself and thus generate in spite of themselves their own prophetic critics, such as Marc Ellis himself. Thus those who seek authentic covenantal life, a life in justice-seeking community, are paradoxically in exile from the very communities who claim to bear this identity. Their religious services become difficult to sit through, for the hypocrisy and denial is blatant, once one has become sensitized to the contradictions between word and reality. The prophet is lonely, partly cut off from his (her) own people, and Ellis writes as one who feels deeply this loneliness of the prophet.

Yet while lonely, the prophet is not alone. He (she) has a host of brothers and sisters, from the Jewish and Christian communities, as well as those alienated from other religious traditions and from the secular world with its promises of progress and social transformation. These exiles, each engaged in their journeys of meaning and justice seeking, cross each other's paths, share each other's lives. In the struggle for true peace based on justice in Israel-Palestine, Israeli Jews, Western Jews, and Palestinians in the land and in the West meet each other and begin to work together around shared agendas. They start to create common stories of their struggles together. They become a new covenant community.

Ellis's vision of a covenantal community in the context of resistance is an ecumenical one. It brings together Jews and Christians, secular and religious people, in their common search for justice and meaningful life. It is in this context that new tradition is forged. For Ellis, covenantal community is not given "once-for-all" by God and then transmitted historically by institutional vehicles. These institutional vehicles are endlessly corrupted, creating their alliances with unjust power. Constantinian Christianity sold out the vision of Jesus as a prophetic Jewish teacher seeking renewal of the covenant in his context of Roman colonization and evangelism. The followers of the one crucified by Roman power transformed themselves into allies of Roman power. In our time those seeking the end of Jewish exile and persecution have transformed themselves into allies of the state of Israel and the United States in a new imperial system.

Thus covenant must be continually rediscovered, reinvented, by those alienated and in exile from colonialist systems and their religions. In this deep meeting with others engaged in a similar question for meaning and justice, new covenantal communities are created, new stories told. At the same time, these stories are connected with the older stories. They are recognized to be the continuation in new contexts of the older struggles; of the Jews in exodus, of the Jesus community in its conflict with Jewish and Roman authorities. A midrashic process takes place that adds to the scriptures, that provides new texts for theological reflection in the context of new communities. In Ellis's view, the Christian story of its betrayals of its vision through violence becomes a part of the history that should be told in Christian worship assemblies. The Jewish story of the Holocaust, and of Israel, of the ambiguities of new empowerment after destruction, also becomes new texts to challenge and question the meaning of Jewish identity now.

God, for Ellis, is not a *deus ex machina* orchestrating this whole process. Rather faith in God is generated in the process of exile, truth and justice-seeking, and the meeting of fellow travelers. God becomes present in this meeting together of seekers in fidelity to the truth and commitment to the possibility of a better human community. In Christian language, Christ becomes present in the meeting of believers: "wherever two or three of you are gathered together, there am I in the midst of you." Ellis's hopes for a future Judaism, a future Christianity, beyond the breakdown and death of the present compromises with power, lie in these meetings of exiles and their forging of bonds of solidarity together.

The third section of the book explores a variety of aspects of these quests of exiles. Ellis also analyses the contradictions of those who create new exile by trying to shore up present systems of power. There are those who seek to prolong the presence of the Holocaust, even as they destroy its ethical seriousness by making it a tool of power. There are those, like Gillian Rose and George Steiner, who cross over into or hover on the edge of Christianity, even as they seek of make sense of Judaism, and there are Christians who move to Judaism out of the same quest. There are the failed efforts of the Vatican to repent of the Holocaust, even as they display their inability to really repent and admit of a sinfulness that is not just of individual Christians, but of the church itself. There are the modern Jewish prophets, Martin Buber and Abraham Heschel, partial failures in their own time to confront the issues of Israeli empowerment, and yet preserving a testimony to an ethical faith beyond Constantinian Judaism.

These explorations are tied together with the theme of "revolutionary forgiveness" which provides the title of the whole collection. "Revolutionary forgiveness" comes from a book authored by Episcopal feminist theologian, Carter Heyward (1987). Heyward took a group of students to Nicaragua in the midst of the Sandinista struggle against the contras, expecting to find great anger against them as Americans. Instead they found a deep gratitude and an embrace of those from the United States who reached out in solidarity with the Nicaraguan struggle.

Ellis envisions a similar possibility of the meeting of those on opposite sides of many struggles, of first and third world, Israelis and Palestinians, who come together in solidarity. Revolutionary forgiveness is that acceptance and embrace that those suffering from colonial violence extend to those from the colonizing communities who reach out in solidarity. But revolutionary forgiveness is not an a priori commandment. It doesn't happen in the abstract. One cannot forgive those who have not repented. Rather it is the acknowledgment by those who have been oppressed of a praxis of repentance on the part of those who reject the oppressive violence of their own people.

Such repentance is expressed in a critique of oppression and in a crossing of boundaries. Israelis cross the "green line" during the Intifada, and join in solidarity with Palestinians who are resisting occupation. It is in that praxis of repentance, the crossing of boundaries, the risk of rejection by both sides of those who refuse their own people's wrongdoing, that the miracle of revolutionary forgiveness happens. It cannot be assumed or demanded. It can only happen as a free gift, a gratuitous recognition by the oppressed of the authenticity of those who engage in repentant outreach. In this interchange a community of faith and struggle is born. It is this vision of community beyond state religions and their colonizing power plays that Ellis strains his eyes to glimpse in his quest for the "future of Jewish and Christian life."

Rosemary Radford Ruether
June 2000

Acknowledgements

GATHERING A COLLECTION OF MEMOIRS and essays is easy and difficult. It is easy in the sense that the material is already written. It is difficult because they must be brought together in a way that makes sense to the reader and has a coherency for the author. That these essays were written over a five year time span, 1995-2000, simplifies the task. These writings come from a time and place that is contemporary with its publication and timely for the issues addressed herein.

Most thought represents borrowings and synthesis and these meditations are no exception. Even the title has been borrowed. The concept of revolutionary forgiveness first was articulated by Carter Heyward, the Episcopal priest and professor, and a group of seminarians at Episcopal Divinity School in Cambridge, Massachusetts, in a book that recorded experiences and reflections from their journey to Nicaragua in 1984. Its title is *Revolutionary Forgiveness: Feminist Reflections on Nicaragua* and was edited by Carter Heyward and Anne Gilson. In these pages we discover a people willing to differentiate Americans and American foreign policy, the latter seeking to destroy the Nicaraguan revolution that had, through struggle and suffering, overturned decades of dictatorship. The willingness of the Nicaraguan people to welcome this delegation from the United States was predicated on the following understanding of forgiveness: not as a static or pious plea to forget the past but a willingness to confess *and* embark on a new relationship of justice and peace. This is what makes forgiveness revolutionary. From the moment that I read of this understanding until today, revolutionary forgiveness is a dynamic presence in my life and thought—as a Jew in relation to Christians and Germans, as a Jew seeking a shared homeland for Jews and Palestinians. I borrow this title as a gesture of respect and with gratitude to those who originally formulated the term.

I thank those at Baylor University Press who approached me about republishing my first book *A Year at the Catholic Worker* and accepted my proposal for publication of these essays. I think here especially of Dr. Greg Garrett, Dr. David Holcomb, and Ms. Janet Burton. It has been a pleasure working with all of them as they continue to expand the press. I also want to thank Dr. Derek Davis, director of the J. M. Dawson Institute of Church-State Studies at Baylor University, for continuing to support my work and for creating an atmosphere that is welcoming of my new Center for American and Jewish Studies. In this regard I also thank Janice Losak, for her contributions to the Center, and the students, Jason Berman and Beau Egert especially, for their support and leadership in our inaugural conference.

Chancellor Herbert Reynolds has been especially forthcoming in his ongoing support of my own work and the work of the Center. His retirement from Baylor symbolizes the passing of an era of Baptist life. I am grateful that I have come to know him and through him part of the Baptist world that holds its values as proudly and fiercely—one might even say as stubbornly—as the Jewish world I was born within and affirm. I count him, as many others do, among the figures of Christian life in the twentieth century worthy of discussion and emulation.

I have also had the great pleasure of meeting with and becoming friends with Bernard Rappoport, a Jewish businessman who has spent a great amount of his energy and wealth in supporting progressive causes in Waco and around the world. Now in his eighties, he continually embarks on new projects. He is a reminder of how Jewish life used to be and perhaps could be again.

Finally, I want to thank my family—Ann, Aaron, and Isaiah. They remind me of the importance of love and friendship and provide a sense of place and belonging in the world.

REVOLUTIONARY
FORGIVENESS

Introduction

As THIS BOOK GOES TO PUBLICATION my eldest son, Aaron, is entering his final preparations to become a bar mitzvah, a son of the commandments. At thirteen he is growing physically and intellectually into adulthood. Entry into adulthood has never been easy, and certainly this is true today. As a Jew in the United States he is privileged, belonging to a people recognized for its contributions to society and civilization. He is free of many of the obstacles and persecutions that have befallen Jews in the past. Aaron is thus privileged in the world. He takes for granted the affluence he experiences. His future, like the future of most American Jews, is filled with promise.

Yet this promise is shadowed by the Holocaust, an event not so far in the past to lack import for him, and Israel, a contemporary and evolving reality. The suffering of the Holocaust remains a benchmark for Jews, while Israel is called upon for reasons of identity and pride. Yet both of these events have changed in their meaning over the last decades. When I was growing up in the 1950s and 1960s, the Holocaust was yet unnamed, a horrific event of mass death that one could not confront. Israel was a small pioneering state that also remained in the background, its relevance to Jewish life in America not yet discerned. Today the Holocaust is used more and more as a shield against accountability; Israel has devolved into expansionism and religious division. Christians and Christianity also provide a changing field of interpretation and relationship. When I was young, the history of anti-Jewishness lingered on even in America, and the Christian world, though no longer openly hostile, was foreign in symbol and culture. Aaron has grown up in a very different atmosphere, where Christians and Christianity are only marginally different from Jews and Judaism and where adolescent bonding occurs around sports, music, and television.

In this changing world, what does it mean to be Jewish? If there is a distinctiveness about being Jewish, how can that be defined? What does it mean to become a son of the commandments? Reviewing Jewish history and its contemporary manifestations in a loving and critical way makes questions as significant as answers. Can Jewish identity be formed around questions, especially questions asked about the direction of Jewish life and even about the relevance and existence of God?

As I started these preparations with Aaron some years ago, I was very conscious of being his father and teacher. As the process continued and his knowledge and self-awareness increased, I understood more of the difficulties of these positions and, over time, began to assume a more peer- like stance with him. Or rather, I began to simply share with him my own journey and questions about life and Jewishness. When he asks me about biblical stories that strike him as violent and unconscionable, I agree with his sensibility and tell him that I reject this violence as coming from God. When he asks me if I believe that God created the world, an affirmation that we make on Shabbat, I respond that I do not know for sure. When he asks why we pray, a devotion that we share each night before we sleep, I throw the question back to him. "What do the prayers mean for you?" I ask, knowing that the importance of prayer for me has grown over the years without a direct or even communicable reason.

As I deflect the questions to him, I remember the lines in our prayer that strike me daily: thanking God for making us Jews and calling us to be free. Why do we thank God for giving us a particularity and what does that particularity mean in our world—in the context of Jewish history, coming after the Holocaust and after Israel? Why does God call us to be free? And what does freedom mean, especially in the context of being Jewish? What is the relationship of being bound *and* free? Does being bound allow a certain freedom? Does being bound sometimes take precedence over being free, while at other times freedom is the path? How do we understand this relationship, judge its parts or even priorities? Does God decide or do we? Who is God? Who are we?

In these pages are some of my offerings to Aaron and to others who might through reading of another journey glean their own questions and possibilities. For what do I have to offer—what do any of us have to offer—if not our own journey? For me, the central element of that journey has been the struggle to be faithful, to history in its broadest contours and to my own people in our particularity. Of course it is difficult to know where the broader and more particular aspects of anyone's journey begin and end. Do we even know what part of our journey is bequeathed and what is fashioned individually?

As I come to the end of my fifth decade of life, for the first time I am beginning to look to the past as much as to the future. Even as I am traveling into the future, I have already been somewhere; I am becoming still, but not from nothing or nowhere. Thus I find my writing combining memoir and future, as exemplified in the first two sections of this book The first, "A Jew Among Christians," was begun in 1995 as the Maryknoll School of Theology was being closed. It traces my journey from my college years to my first teaching position at Maryknoll, roughly covering the years 1970-1988. These years were exhilarating, with teachers like Richard Rubenstein, the difficult and deep Jewish Holocaust theologian, author of the provocative and now classic *After Auschwitz: Radical Theology and Contemporary Judaism,* and William Miller, the eccentric and fascinating Catholic intellectual and historian, biographer of Dorothy Day and the Catholic Worker movement. It was during these years that I spent time at the Catholic Worker in New York City and had the privilege of coming to know Dorothy Day and Daniel Berrigan. I experienced first hand the poor and destitute in the United States, an experience I was wholly unprepared for and which has stayed with me to this day.

It was also during these years that I came to be at Maryknoll, teaching and traveling in the missionary world. During this time I experienced the world of liberation theology in its diverse manifestations and met such luminaries as Gustavo Gutierrez. It was also a time of martyrdom, as the Maryknoll world was struck with the political repercussions of siding with the poor and the oppressed. During these years I began to confront in my own life the experience of the Jewish Holocaust and the newly empowered world of my own people in Israel, thus the complexities of this shift from powerlessness to power used against the Palestinian people. This gave birth to a Jewish theology of liberation, a theology that continues to evolve today.

Section two of the book, "The Future of Jewish and Christian Life," was written during my first months after arriving at Baylor University in 1998, and represents a consolidation and expansion of my work on contemporary Jewish theology. My early writing explored the dynamic of Holocaust and Israel and how the lessons of the Holocaust called us as a people to respect the rights of Palestinians. Initially, this respect demanded a cessation of the occupation of Palestinian lands in the West Bank and Gaza and the emergence of a Palestinian state alongside Israel, with Jerusalem as a shared capital. Over time I began to realize that a deeper issue was at stake: justice and dignity remained at the forefront as the need for confession and reintegration of Palestinians with Jews in the Holy Land also emerged. The Oslo peace process, begun in 1993, highlighted the possibilities and limitations of my evolving understandings. A Palestinian state was assured and Palestinians had been recognized. But what was left of Palestine?

The Oslo process acknowledged the fact of the Israeli victory and the Palestinian defeat and sought to enshrine that reality in permanent borders. Widely celebrated around the world, this process brought me to another level of dissent within the Jewish community. Could it be that after the Holocaust we would emerge not only empowered but also as victors, lording it over a segmented and defeated people, whose only solace was a state so divided by Jewish settlements, access roads, and military areas, that many refer to that state as a bantustan? This entire history poses the question of Jewish history and continuity, even the covenantal affirmation at the heart of Jewish life. For when a Constantinian Judaism arrives, a Jewish religiosity that links with power and the state, then the Jewish tradition, *at least as we know and inherit it*, is over. What then is the future? Is there a Judaism beyond its present Constantinian incarnation? If so, how will Judaism be practiced and will that practice be identifiably Jewish? So many Jews have been lost to the Jewish community over the years. Will they return from exile or is another community forming, what I call the new diaspora, that these Jews will affirm as their own?

In this new diaspora Jews encounter people from different cultures and religions, especially exiles from Constantinian Christianity. Christianity has its own evolving history, one that features legitimating unjust power and resisting that power. Christianity's relationship to the Jewish people is evolving. Today ecumenism is the watchword, but I ask if this ecumenism is Constantinian in its focus. Christians have finally accepted Jews and Judaism as authentic and independent. Yet it seems that in the process of acceptance a deal has been struck to discipline the subversive elements of both Christianity and Judaism. If Jews must ask what it means to be Jewish after the Holocaust and Israel, Christians must ask what it means to be Christian after Constantinian Christianity and a renewed Christianity that contains many of the same elements of previous Christian world views though now shorn of specific institutional power. Do the Christian exiles in the new diaspora ask the future of their Christianity alone? Or do they ask these questions, paradoxically and ironically, with dissenting Jews?

There are many twists and turns here, including the fascinating historical life of Jesus, the tradition that gave birth to him, and the movement that carried faith in him into the world. Is Jesus the dividing line between Jews and Christians? Jesus read the Hebrew bible as his own and the explosive witness he evolved from his tradition continues to attract those on the other side of power. Jesus' bible, the one Jews read today and the only bible Jesus had or needed, is a series of historical and prophetic testimonies. Are these same testimonies being spoken and lived by other people in our time? Does the continuity of prophetic witness spell the end of the traditions Christians and Jews claim and the creation of a broader tradition of faith and struggle that is contextual and explosive? A major question, then, is the role of tradition in embracing a radical practice of fidelity, while limiting it at the same time. I ask if a new alliance of those within these traditions and those exiled from them may come together for a renewed journey of fidelity in the twenty-first century.

A series of essays makes up the final section, "The Future of Ecumenical Religiosity." I begin with an analysis of recent Holocaust writing, focusing especially on Daniel Goldhagen's controversial best-seller *Hitler's Willing Executioners: Ordinary Germans and the Holocaust.* There has already been much critical work done challenging the accuracy of Goldhagen's historical claim that the driving force of Nazi Germany was an "eliminationist" anti-Jewishness rather than a matrix of factors, including anti-Jewishness but also the punitive nature of the treaty of Versailles, the depression years, World War I, and advanced technology. My essay instead is about Goldhagen's reception by the elite Holocaust scholars, an almost brutal one by any standard, and the representation of the Holocaust by Jewish and German scholars in an era of Jewish empowerment. My own experience of traveling to Auschwitz and speaking on the issues of Israel and the Palestinians provides a base for understanding the complex interweaving that speech and writing about the Holocaust has become. Does Goldhagen's book remind us of a time when Jews were weak and helpless rather than empowered, and do Jews prefer this self and public understanding of victimization precisely because this is not our condition today? Have Holocaust historians turned the writing and teaching of the Holocaust into a field of inquiry that has its own status and reward structure, which one enters with fear and trepidation? I wonder how we can discuss the Holocaust, even have open warfare about interpretations relating to it, as if nothing has happened in Jewish history since the liberation of the death camps.

In the fall of 1997, I was asked to present a paper at a symposium in honor of Edward Said. The symposium was held at the University of Windsor in Windsor, Canada. The occasion was important, as this most interesting and provocative Palestinian intellectual was dying. I took this occasion to honor Said, but also another interlocutor of Jewish life, the sociologist of Jewish life John Murray Cuddihy. One of the themes of this essay is the need for those outside Jewish life to interact critically with us in the same way that Jews have interacted critically with Christian life. In the 1960s and 1970s Cuddihy functioned as an interpreter of the Jewish journey into modernity. So many Jewish intellectuals were involved in this journey—the political philosopher Karl Marx, the founder of psychoanalysis Sigmund Freud, and the groundbreaking anthropologist Claude Levi- Strauss. Though most commentators understand these intellectuals as essential to the foundations of modernity, Cuddihy alerts Jews and others to the less obvious agenda: guiding a people defined outside of gentile enlightenment society into the center of modernity. In one sense, these intellectuals did this through thoroughly novel understandings of the political, psychological, and anthropological world; at the same time that they turned mainstream understandings of the world upside down, they also provided an entry point for the difficult Jewish journey into modernity. For, as Cuddihy sees it, this journey for Jews was essential and costly, gaining status and affluence but leaving behind culture and community.

Yet this is only part of Cuddihy's analysis, for his later work is involved with Jews who invoke the Holocaust and morality in relation to Israel. According to Cuddihy, Jewish intellectuals provide a cover for the Jewish journey, not unlike their predecessors. The change, however, is crucial: the Jewish community is now empowered and the protection offered the Jewish journey into the latter half of the twentieth century involves the oppression of the Palestinians. Here Edward Said becomes important, as I understand Said to function not only for his own people, perhaps fulfilling the role for Palestinians that earlier Jewish intellectuals fulfilled for the Jews of Europe, but also to provide an intimate critique of what Jewish military power, legitimated through intellectual and moral values upheld by Jewish thinkers and commentators, is actually doing. By being brutally honest about the change Jews have undergone—the movement from being victims to being the oppressor—Said challenges Jews to live up to their own values or drop the moral facade and argue simply from the perspective of raw power.

Cuddihy and Said therefore bridge a gap in Jewish life: in the case of Cuddihy, the role of the critic who understands from outside; in the case of Said, one who has been exiled from his own homeland by Jewish power. Crucial to both is the absolute avoidance of anti-Jewishness, so though sometimes charged with this fault, the accusation fails to resonate. From their perspectives, both analyze the Jewish world in a way that most Jews cannot. In this way both become important to the Jewish future. For without critical analysis of the Jewish world outside the expected framework, how can Jews look again at the history we are creating? How can we check our assertion of morality with the reality of Jewish power?

Said's importance to Jewish history presses the Jewish community to understand that Israel is not innocent and that the future of Jews and Palestinians cannot be separate. In some ways, he responds to the conundrum that Daniel Goldhagen presents. We can lecture Germans about their historic refusal to integrate Jews into their life and society but only if we can hear lectures about our contemporary refusal to integrate Palestinians into our future.

In 1997, I was also asked to deliver a paper at a conference at Marquette University in honor of Dorothy Day. It was the centennial of her birth, and I returned to Marquette with fond memories. As a doctoral student their in the late 1970s, I studied with William Miller, who wrote on Dorothy Day and the Catholic Worker movement. It was here, too, that I wrote the biography of the co- founder of the movement, Peter Maurin. I have always been intrigued by the Catholicity of the Worker and its ecumenical character, especially its fascinating relationship with the Jewish people. In many ways, the Worker had broken ground on the labor and the racial fronts, speaking forcefully from the 1930s onward of the need to recognize the dignity of labor and people of color.

As intriguing is the groundbreaking discussion of Jews and Judaism, especially as the world descended into the dark days of World War II. I explore a startling series of contradictions, or so they seemed at first blush. For example, on the political scene, the Catholic Worker adopted a pacifist stand during World War II. And yet the Worker understood and reported early the plight of the Jews in Europe. They immediately argued for the admittance of all Jewish refugees from Nazi Europe into the United States. Another example: during this most difficult time, the Catholic Worker asserted the centrality of the Jews to Christian history—after all Jesus was born as a Jew and grew up within the Jewish tradition—and for contemporary Christianity, so that any offense done to a Jew was also an offense done to Jesus. At the same time that these understandings were presented in word and pictorial representation in its newspaper, the Worker also argued for the need of Jews to convert to Christianity. To be sure, this was less boldly declared but it was held nonetheless. Thus a dialectic ensued of affirming Jewishness, even the Jewishness of Christianity, and the completion of Jewishness in the acceptance of Christianity.

After the war and with the coming of Vatican II in the 1960s, the Worker maintained its emphasis on the authenticity of Judaism and the integrity of Jews, but dropped the desire to convert Jews to Christianity. At the same time, however, critical thought in relation to Jews waned. In the 1930s and 1940s there was, at least to many Jews, another contradiction: the Worker supported the acceptance of all Jewish refugees into America, but opposed Zionism. The opposition to Zionism rested on several counts, not the least of which had to do with Christian supporters of the Zionist movement who might be more comfortable with Jews living in a far away place. Zionism was also criticized for its proposed militarization of the Jewish tradition. If the voice of Jesus could not be heard above the clamor of a militarized Christianity, how would the voice of the prophets be heard above a militarized Israel?

My essay on Gillian Rose and George Steiner continues this exploration of limitations and interlocutors with Judaism and Jewish life. Gillian Rose was a Jewish philosopher who died of cancer in 1995. I met Gillian at Auschwitz in 1992 and respected both her thought and her person. In the last weeks of her life, Gillian converted to Christianity. George Steiner is a pre-eminent literary critic and philosopher whom I have admired and written about. Though Jewish and a forceful commentator on the Holocaust and Israel, perhaps the most known and respected of Jewish writers who can be defined as anti-Zionist, I have found many leanings toward Christianity in his writing.

The initial impetus for this essay was Gillian's death and her conversion. What should Jews make of this conversion? This led to a broader question of the limits of contemporary Jewish life and how many Jews—Steiner to be sure, but also figures like Viktor Frankl, Anne Frank, Edith Stein, Simone Weil, and Etty Hillesum, some of whom survived the Holocaust years while others did not—embraced their Judaism while broadening it into spheres prohibited by the Jewish tradition and contemporary commentators on Jewish life. Conversion here is obvious, at least in the common use of the term, but is there a deeper sense to the religious search than simply a change of faith communities? Only Rose and Stein changed religious affiliation: were these other Jews Christian, or was something else occurring that is yet unnamed?

It is fascinating that Jewish writers like Lawrence Langer and Cynthia Ozick—even in an earlier period, Martin Buber—condemn those Jews who search beyond the confines of Jewish life *as they have been defined* even as they themselves also open Jewish life to new currents of thought and activity. Why are certain searches declared off limits and other searches seen as authentically Jewish? Who defines which searches are appropriate and which are not? Especially in times of personal and communal distress, why is the prohibition upheld by those who live in comfort and relative safety? Why does the Jewish tradition declare boundaries that are consistently crossed and violated by Jews themselves? My own sense is that the time has come to question our understandings of conversion at their deepest philosophical and religious roots.

"Other Teachers, Other Paths," is a review essay I wrote in 1999 for *Perspectives in Religious Studies* on recent books on Martin Buber and Abraham Heschel. Buber and Heschel were born in Europe; both had to flee Nazi Germany. Buber landed in Jerusalem, Heschel the United States. Both explored aspects of Jewish life that continue to generate creative thought and disputation. Buber and Heschel are both important to my teacher, Richard Rubenstein, in a fascinating, negative way. Rubenstein feels that Buber's politics were utopian. During the Nazi era, Buber sought a regeneration of Jewish spirituality and in Jerusalem he argued for a Jewish rapprochement with Arabs. Over all, Buber was a communitarian socialist and Rubenstein argues that he idealized politics to the point where unjust power had little opposition. Heschel was Rubenstein's teacher at Jewish Theological Seminary: his invocation of the beauty of Jewish life and his mystical approach to God and the commandments disturbs Rubenstein. How can one hold to this view of reality during and after the Holocaust?

In some ways Rubenstein is right: Buber and Heschel, though living beyond the Holocaust years and being extremely influential even today, were formed before and remain pre-Holocaust thinkers. Yet it is precisely here that their value may be found. In a post-Holocaust period where Jewish power is developed and asserted, and where the fragmentation of Jewish life is also in evidence, does the power and its use itself increase the fragmentation that comes with the Holocaust? Buber and Heschel have much to say to us. I focus here on Buber's hidden circle of prophets, an understanding that for Buber comes from Isaiah, and Heschel's sense that while educated in a German university, his primary learning and grounding is Jewish. It is important that both Buber and Heschel experienced the world of Judaism and the secular university, as they, like most contemporary Jews, were able to move in both worlds. Their Judaism does not make sense without the interpenetration of the two worlds. Perhaps Jewish life is coming full circle and needs pre- and post-Holocaust thought to come into a new configuration.

The preceding essays suggest a revision of Jewish thought and a new encounter in the world. "On Revolutionary Forgiveness" is the place where I ask the question again, as I did in the essays "On the Threshold of the Twenty-First Century" that make up section two of this book. Originally written for a conference of the Baptist Association of Philosophy Teachers at the New Orleans Baptist Theological Seminary in 1998, the title of the essay, as the title of the book itself, is taken from a book some years ago that described a visit by seminarians from Episcopal Divinity School to Nicaragua. The delegation was led by the Episcopal priest Carter Heyward in 1984 during the time of the United States-financed war against the revolutionary Sandinista government. When the visitors asked why the Nicaraguan people accepted Americans so beautifully when the American government was causing so much suffering, the response was a separation between the people who wanted justice and those who wanted oppression. The former could be forgiven because they were working against injustice and wanted a future were justice is the norm. Hence the forgiveness given is revolutionary: confession and the agreement to struggle to a new way of life.

When I read this book I immediately wrote Carter Heyward, who was one of the first respondents to my Jewish theology of liberation years earlier. Could this concept be expanded to Jews in relation to Palestinians? Would Germans be able to experience this in relation to Jews? Had a certain kind of revolutionary forgiveness already occurred in the West between Christians and Jews after the Holocaust? Could revolutionary forgiveness be the key to the ending of many of the world's conflicts? Could it also present an internal theological reckoning, pointing toward a path that overcomes historical divisions and places the resources of fidelity before us as a joint inheritance?

In my own life, the struggle to be faithful has been influenced by people who come from different geographic, cultural, and religious backgrounds and time periods. But the issue is much broader: Should we be denied the strength and witness of others because a barrier has been set in place for reasons that are not our own? The practice of the covenant is at stake, because the covenant is free and travels where it will. Though religions often claim the covenant as their own, injustice and the covenant cannot consort together. When religion legitimates injustice, the covenant is found elsewhere. Can we have access to the covenant, can we seek and embrace the covenant, if those who have practiced the covenant historically and in the present are cut off from us? Could the practice of revolutionary forgiveness make the covenant more available in our time?

The Catholic church has been culpable in the oppression of Jews and Jewish life. Since Vatican II, the church has steadily made progress in its understandings of Judaism and its relations with the Jewish community. Yet each step toward reconciliation has been fraught with difficulty, sometimes evoking anger from Jewish leaders when Catholic leadership felt they were taking major steps toward healing. The main sticking point has been the Holocaust, seen by Jews as a culmination of the anti-Jewishness exhibited through much of Catholic, and by extension, Christian history. In 1998, a further step was taken with the publication of the church document *We Remember: A Reflection on the Shoah.* In some ways this document previewed the millennial pilgrimage of the Pope to the Holy Land and the documents and liturgy held just before his pilgrimage.

As I write in an essay prepared for the Schmidt Lecture on Jewish-Christian Dialogue at Spalding University in Louisville, Kentucky, the confessional stance of the Catholic church as it enters the new millennium should be taken seriously, both for its boldness and its limitations. Emotions are high on both sides, to be sure: Jews feeling that the entire history of Christianity, at least insofar as it relates to Jews, must be exposed and acknowledged; the Catholic hierarchy, at least the Vatican hierarchy, feeling the need to confess the sins of Christians while protecting the truths of Christianity and the place of the church in the promulgation of that truth. Thus the confessions tend to be significant and limited, raising questions as to whether the confession itself is strategic rather than heart-felt. Is the confession of the church an example of revolutionary forgiveness or the asking of a forgiveness that allows the assertion of innocence to be reclaimed? Does the confession move to the very heart of salvation, thus expanding the possibility of salvation beyond its present strictures or is the memory of the Holocaust being used to prepare the world for a new movement of evangelization?

Memory as prophetic moves beyond the confines of church confession. The challenge is whether the memory of the Holocaust will be used as a bridge of solidarity toward all those who are suffering in the present. The German Catholic theologian Johannes Baptist Metz is important here, as is the possibility that Jews will ask of ourselves what the Pope is asking of the church: Are we willing to confess our sins vis-a-vis Palestinians and demand that a new history of justice and equality be pursued? Or do we seek to keep the memory of the Holocaust as a strategic option of preserving our innocence while pursuing our own agendas?

"On Worship and Proclamation" began as a short lecture to a class on worship at the George Truett Seminary at Baylor University in 1998 and

was expanded when in 1999 I was asked to speak at the first annual conference of Religion and Literary Art, also at Baylor. By this time I had been
traveling among Christians for almost three decades. From the early
years of my journey, I have been struck by the significance of worship for
Christians; I have experienced nothing like it among Jews. Though I have
become more overtly religious in my later years, I remain peculiarly
unmoved by official religious ceremonies. My prayer life has significantly
expanded, with morning and evening prayers on a daily basis and Friday
Shabbat prayers. These prayers are typically said alone and with family,
most often not in a synagogue, though at times and under the right circumstances, synagogue worship can be beautiful. My prayer life also
includes Zen sitting in the morning, a discipline that I have found important to my focus. For some reason, silence has always been essential to
my being. This, too, is done alone, without religious ceremony and without accompanying Buddhist ritual or cosmology.

In my reflection, I realize, at least in retrospect, that my eclectic
prayer life is part of my search for a practice requisite to my own personality and needs in the context of the times in which I live. Like most Jews,
I have pieced together a post-Holocaust spirituality from fragments inherited from history and found within contemporary life. At least in my case,
the development of a practice occurred within my struggle to be faithful
as a Jew. This struggle came to a new level, and the need for a practice
came to be more important, as the demands on my public life increased
and the need for strong words and forceful argument became clear in the
late 1980s, the peak years of the Palestinian uprising. I embarked then
on an intense amount of travel, speaking engagements, and writing. How
could I keep my focus and health, mental and physical, when the travel
wore on me, and when I was either pronounced a prophet or a traitor,
sometimes on the same day, by those who either elevated or demeaned
me beyond reason?

The practice I developed at the time, one that continues to evolve,
combined parts of my own journey in dialogue with the Jewish tradition
and other traditions that I have come into contact with and which for
some reason speak to me. For me, this practice represents a discipline
rather than an ontology, a grounding rather than the "truth." It is across
boundaries, as my life has been lived, but its significance is for my own
life. I spoke of this discipline in the class on worship as an invitation for
seminarians to develop their own practice, or at least think critically
about how they pray and worship. In my lecture at the conference, I
emphasized that the practice each one of us develops is crucial to the
word and activity that we can contribute to the world. What is it that we
proclaim? Do we have a right to that proclamation? Where is that proclamation grounded? In a post-Holocaust Jewish life, after the establishment and expansion of Israel, proclamation, like worship, is bound to be
fragmentary. Does this lessen its power or, because of an unrelenting

honesty, increase its power as a witness to the possibility of a life and society beyond what we know today?

Recently a student, after having read this essay, questioned my propensity to cross boundaries. For a moment I was unable to form an answer to his query. Another student perceptively replied, "Professor Ellis crosses boundaries in order not to cross other boundaries." When I asked that student, an interesting and questioning evangelical Christian, to name the boundary I would not cross, he replied, " You cross boundaries in order not to cross what for you is the ultimate boundary, the militarization of Judaism, Jewish tradition and Jewish culture." I was stunned by his insight into my own journey. I wondered if he had unlocked the key to my eclectic spiritual discipline and to my ecumenism. Has my journey among others been part of my resistance to the reformulation of Jewish life into an assimilation that is Constantinian, one that bows before the state and power? Is my discipline a way of surviving this Constantinian formulation of Judaism, a way of practicing Judaism in exile?

My last essay on Jewish leadership serves as an epilogue. For many years I have been given honorific titles, without request and often against my wishes. The two are prophet and rabbi, for me the highest titles possible, but only if they are lived at the intensity that is demanded of them. Prophet and rabbi are disturbing in their grandeur: prophets are reserved for the Hebrew bible, safely past and exegetically available. We study the prophetic tradition and read from the words of the prophets within the context of a safe and known religiosity. Rabbis are ordained by Jewish seminaries; they study texts and engage in pastoral counseling. Rabbis marry the young and bury the dead. They defend the Jewish community against anti-Jewishness and increasingly against Jewish dissidents. And yet both the prophetic and rabbinic traditions are places of witness and power, providing the possibility of wisdom and justice. Are these places to be given over simply because their potential is unused or even abused?

Twice in my life I have witnessed the living tradition of the prophets in a rabbinic setting. My rabbi in Croton-on-Hudson, Michael Robinson, is one. As a Southerner, he demonstrated for civil rights of African Americans; as an American, he opposed America's involvement in the Vietnam war and refused to pay taxes for the development and deployment of nuclear weapons. It is unusual for a rabbi to have his automobile repossessed for failure to pay taxes, but this happened to Rabbi Robinson. He is also non-Zionist, neither for nor against the creation of the state of Israel, but ready to speak out against Israeli policies that are unjust to Palestinians, policies, he often points out, that also demean Jewish history and practice.

The other rabbi was Marshall Meyer who was educated at Dartmouth and Jewish Theological Seminary. After his rabbinic ordination, he accepted a pulpit in Buenos Aires, Argentina. Meyer resisted the

Argentine dictatorship of the 1970s and 1980s, often accompanying the Women of the Plaza searching for their disappeared loved ones. I met Meyer in the 1980s at a conference in honor of his teacher, Eugene Rosenstock-Hussey. Rosenstock-Hussey, a convert to Christianity from Judaism, had been a friend and dialogue partner with Franz Rosenzweig, perhaps the most famous and influential Jew to have pondered conversion and ultimately embraced his Jewishness. Meyer had suggested me as a lecturer at this conference, which was held at Dartmouth in 1988, and when I saw him there, he showed me his heavily underlined copy of my book *Toward a Jewish Theology of Liberation.* I traveled to meet him several times in the years that followed, including at his synagogue in New York City. I always found Meyer accessible and open. I came away from our discussions refreshed and invigorated. When several years later Meyer died, I felt a significant loss.

In the main, however, the rabbinic establishment has been woefully inadequate to the questions that confront us as a people. I wonder if that very inadequacy has encouraged the naming of people like myself as a rabbi. Is it a subconscious desire to hear words of critique and justice from a Jewish leader that encourages this appellation? Is it a sense that there must be Jews speaking for the oppressed—especially those suffering under Jewish power—because the Jewish tradition demands it? Whatever the reason, the title has been applied to me so often that in the end my demurrals have lost force. In the last few years, some aspects of my journey have opened me to parts of the tradition and my place within it. Clearly I have been formed within the Jewish tradition. Should it surprise me that my own being can be found there, even to the point of self-expression and archetype?

Beyond the personal is a communal question and ultimately a challenge to the future. What is Jewish leadership in a time when conscientious Jews are unwelcome in the mainstream of the Jewish world? What is it to be a Jewish leader as many Jews travel into exile? I ask what Judaism and Jewishness might look like in the new diaspora that is forming in our time. In the new diaspora, what will Jewish leadership be like? Will there be rabbis? What will the qualifications be for serving in that capacity? Since most Jews in exile and the new diaspora are committed to values central to the Jewish tradition but secular in their orientation, what kind of rabbinic speech will make sense to them?

The epilogue represents a personal and communal struggle of affirmation in a time of great crisis. In some ways the world is always in crisis and certainly Jewish life is no stranger to that. Paradoxically, for Jews the twentieth century has been a time of incredible desolation and jubilation. The Holocaust and Israel are formative events of unparalleled magnitude in the shortest of time periods, one following on the heels of the other. The movement from powerlessness to power is so incredible as to almost defy the imagination and the consequences continue to unfold.

On the threshold of the twenty-first century, the call of Jewish life is often trumpeted in the *before*, nostalgia for the kind of Jewish life that existed before the Holocaust, remembering the Holocaust as central to Jewish identity, and basking in the innocent empowerment of the fledgling state of Israel. The *after* is much more difficult. Jews of the twenty-first century come *after* the Holocaust and Israel, a most difficult place to start within. For the *after* is always fragmentary and up for grabs; definitive responses in the language of tradition are elusive even as they are promulgated by establishments whose security and power come from another place and time. Those who are aware of this situation exist in limbo, unable to use the language of the past and as yet without a language to form a new identity.

This is the challenge and the burden. But it is also the opportunity presented in all traditions: to be faithful to the times in which we live. The reflections in this volume are one attempt among others to search out and express that fidelity as the twenty-first century takes shape.

Part I

A JEW AMONG CHRISTIANS

1

On the Letters of
Thomas Merton and Rosemary Ruether*

I FIRST MET ROSEMARY RADFORD RUETHER in 1985. As director of a graduate program at Maryknoll, I invited her to give a series of lectures on feminism to a summer gathering of sixty students from around the world. It was our fifth summer session and she was the first prominent theologian to be invited, available, and who agreed to be with us. Because of her prominence, I hesitated to invite her at all; Maryknoll, a Catholic missionary order known for its publication of the works of emerging third world liberation theologians, lacked the prestige of the university lecture circuit.

Our students were of varying ages and academic abilities. Rather than degrees and theories, for the most part they were searching for religious values to reinforce their activities on behalf of justice. Though they combined experience and intelligence and even sometimes academic credentials, they were suspicious of degrees and prestige. For them the academy often masked with abstract language systems that reinforced oppression. So it was no certainty that a theologian of Rosemary's stature would appreciate such students and feel our invitation worthy of consideration.

But she responded immediately and, to my surprise, in a most personal way. For as it turned out, Rosemary had read my first book, a diary of my stay at the Catholic Worker some years earlier, and her letter accepting my invitation commented favorably on the book. I was delighted that she was coming to Maryknoll, and excited that a person of her stature knew something about me.

---

*The quotations in this section come from the following books: *At Home in the World: The Letters of Thomas Merton and Rosemary Radford Ruether*, ed. Mary Tardiff. Maryknoll, NY: Orbis, 1995; and *Thomas Merton: The Hidden Ground of Love; Letters*, ed. William Shannon. New York: Farrar, Straus, Giroux, 1985.

I awaited Rosemary's arrival with anticipation and when, some months later, I finally met her, I was quite nervous. After waiting most of the afternoon for her to arrive at Maryknoll, and realizing that there was likely a delay of indefinite duration at the airport, I left for home to rest, instructing a secretary to call me immediately when Rosemary arrived. Since I lived near Maryknoll, within minutes of her arrival I was back there myself, knocking at her door. I stood in the deserted corridor a few minutes, anticipating an imminent response and, head bowed to the floor, rehearsed a way to introduce myself.

Then Rosemary opened the door. As I raised my head, it became clear that Rosemary had just emerged from the shower, for she was dressed in a type of mini-robe, tousling her just-washed hair with a towel. The complete absence of any formality startled me, and the various introductions I was musing over evaporated. In their place I mumbled an apology and told her I would return later; Rosemary laughed, told me to wait a minute, and emerged from the room a few moments later fully dressed.

I recalled this experience as I read her correspondence with Thomas Merton. Merton, of course, was a Catholic monk whose entry into the monastery is recalled in his autobiographical bestseller *The Seven Story Mountain*, which appeared in 1940. In this brief correspondence, which began in 1966 and ended just two years later, only months before Merton's untimely death, we see the older, more established Merton grappling with Rosemary's almost relentless (though not without compassion) critique of the Catholic church and the monastic vocation he lived so fully. What calls to mind my meeting with Rosemary is that two decades earlier than her appearance at Maryknoll, she already had the free spirit and anchored sensibility that disavowed, even defied pretense.

It is clear from these letters that Merton was in the midst of a vocational crisis in the broadest sense: what he was meant to do and be in the world and how the disparate elements of his own being could reach a relative harmony, both within the context of a church and a world in which he lived, and to which he had responsibilities. Merton here pictures himself as a person more and more removed form the church and from even his monastic—that is local—community.

Merton sees his fame as pressing in upon him so that his public persona is inhibiting a continually evolving person. He is no longer the Trappist monk who entered the Abbey of Gethsemani, or even the monk of the 1950s and early 1960s who symbolized for the American church and beyond the possibility of Catholic renewal. In fact, his fame outside the abbey, what he represents to so many—including his commitment to the broader ecumenical religious reality and movements for justice around the world—is as constrictive as the internal church structures that limit the number of visitors Merton can welcome and the travel he can undertake.

Rosemary is clearly impatient with Merton's crisis. For example, Merton's complaints about restrictions imposed by his abbot seem to her almost childish. As an adult, Merton's problem is accepting and living within a structure that allows this arbitrary use of power. Merton's reluctant but tangible acquiescence to this authority reinforces the isolation that Rosemary sees as foundational to his growing crisis. It is in this mix of life and community that Merton can move toward the next stage of his life.

Merton disclaims that his complaints are about his monastic vocation, instead insisting they are only about particular elements of monastic life and authority. To Rosemary, the disclaimer is a disingenuous avoidance of the real problems. In a letter in February 1967, she writes: "You say that you have no trouble with your vocation, but, if that is really true, maybe you should be having some trouble with your vocation. I love the monastic life dearly but today it is no longer the eschatological sign and witness of the church. For those who wish to be at the 'kingdom' frontier of history, it is the steaming ghetto of the big city not the countryside. . . . Perhaps you have gone as far as you can in the hermitage direction; you are running out of fat from previous community contact, and need renewal in a period of service."

For Rosemary, Merton's personal situation is tied to the overall place of monasticism in the web of Christianity. This cuts closer to Merton's dilemma, for in his own correspondence and letters, even when distancing himself from institutional life, Merton hopes that monastic renewal will facilitate his own personal renewal. In response to a February letter, Merton writes in the same month: "I have the usual agonia with my vocation, but now, after twenty-five years, I am in a position where I am practically laicized and de-institutionalized and living like all the other old bats who live alone in the hills in this part of the country, and I feel like a human being again. My hermit life is expressly a lay life. . . . Also, I try as best I can to keep up valid and living contacts with my friends who are in the thick of things, and everyone knows where my real 'community' is." In March, Rosemary responds with perhaps her most scathing critique of monastic life and Merton's choice to remain within it: "All monasticism rests on the mistaken confusion of creation with this world, and so they suppose by withdrawing in some symbolic fashion from creation that they are leaving the world. But creation is precisely not the world but its antithesis, and so what they do is essentially the opposite of salvation. . . . Isn't it evident to you that everything you were saying about the bureaucracy and dehumanization of the monastic institution is precisely the very essence of 'this world,' the purest expression of the powers and principalities? You have not withdrawn into heaven, you have withdrawn from creation into hell!"

In this intellectual and emotional exchange between Rosemary and Merton, more than their ideas and personalities meet and clash; the entire edifice of Vatican II Catholic renewal in Europe and America is put to the test. Having entered during World War II celibate monastic solitude as the most traditional and highest calling of Catholic life, Merton is struggling to reclaim and transform the essence of Catholic spirituality and practice in the post-Vatican II era.

In this he mirrors the very Catholic generation that he has come to symbolize. Merton realizes that the symbolization has lost its content and that in fact his identity is more and more found outside even the post-Vatican II church. "I am simply browned off with and afraid of Catholics. All Catholics, from Ottaviani to DuBay, all down the damn line," Merton writes in January 1967. "There are a few Catholics I can stand with equanimity when I forget they are Catholics and remember they are just my friends, like Dan Berrigan and Ed Rice and Sister Mary Luke and a lot of people like that. I love the monks, but they might as well be in China. I love all the well-meaning good people who go to Mass and want things to be better and so on, but I understand Zen Buddhists better than I do them, and Zens understand me better. But this is awful because where is the church, and where am I in the church?"

Merton responds to his question with a further query: "Is the Church a community of people who love each other or a big dog fight where you do your religious business and seeking, meanwhile, your friends are somewhere else?" In late March, Merton again draws connections to people outside the church and his relation to the church: "Right now I am working on Faulkner and also writing on Camus and am, I suppose, again sneaking out the back door of the church without telling myself that this is what I am doing."

Rosemary affirms this existence outside the Roman Catholic structure as she worships and works within St. Stephens, an ecumenical Episcopal church in Washington, D.C. Here again we find her concretely taking the steps that Merton chooses in his intellectual and affective life, but is unable to do in actuality. To Merton's question about the church as community or religious business, Rosemary responds that her choice to affiliate with a non-Catholic parish is "unhappy" but necessary. In fact, at St. Stephens, Ruether finds a community that she can "believe in, among people who have a common faith with me, where I can participate and have a communal being, where I can contribute something and where my contribution is valued."

Rosemary is clear on leaving the "dead" structures behind: "Fringe existence in the dead parochial structure proved to be too soul destructive. . . ." On the other hand, by working within a participatory community structure, the "future ceases to be blocked, the road opens up ahead, the soul expands, not in a paltry sense of egoism, but in the sense of a plant with a place to flower." To be sure, Rosemary experiences with Merton the pain of a failed church and what is left behind. Still "one can only work where one can and hope that these various points of one intentionality will converge at some new point beyond the present."

For many Christians involved in renewal in the 1960s, Roman Catholic and Protestant alike, institutional structure and personal affiliation took on a secondary role to emphasis on the poor and the oppressed. Although there was loss, perhaps this new vantage point would be the place of convergence. Among Catholics in particular there grew an emphasis on identifying with the poor and on voluntary poverty as the essence of Christian life. As Merton is "sneaking out the back door of the Church," he is more identifying with the poor and simplifying his own life, thinking that perhaps a monk's life can at least witness to the possibility of doing both.

Here Rosemary responds in as emphatic a tone as her previous discussion of Christianity and monasticism. In a July 1967 letter, she undercuts this way of identifying with the poor as another illusion: "In actuality you only share the external appearances of economic deprivation with the poor hillsman who has no running water, and likewise with the ghetto poor. But actually there is nothing in common between you and them for the simple reason that they have to be there and you don't. You can dress up and walk into a hotel, and they won't throw you out. You have the knowledge and skill to handle the larger world of our society, and that is precisely what they lack. No one would really confuse a Catholic Worker type with a real ghetto person, and no one would really confuse you with a real impoverished hillbilly. You may identify with them, but they do not identify with you."

Though their correspondence is often contentious, even at times abrasive, the important themes that Rosemary and Merton are discussing with such passion are held in common. Both are seeking to work through the illusion of religious life and commitment—a solitude contained in authoritarian religious structures; a church that creates its own mythology to mask another more oppressive reality; a range of personal choices and commitments that seek to rescue and renew the faith and faith community to which one is committed and seeks to continue and deepen. Yet the shared themes and questions identifiable as Catholic in language and content should not mask the chasm already developed before and widening within this brief correspondence.

As noted in her introduction to the volume, Rosemary initiated the correspondence with Merton as a "genuine Catholic intellectual peer" with whom she could be "ruthlessly honest" about her own questions of intellectual and existential integrity. The issue was simple, at least to her: Whether it was possible to be a Roman Catholic and at the same time a person of integrity. Previous discussions with other Catholic peers—leaders of the renewal movement in the church—had left her with a deep sense of disappointment, because to Rosemary's mind the critical questions of integrity were glossed over. Though Rosemary does not say so explicitly, clearly Merton failed her test as well: "I see Thomas Merton and myself somewhat like two ships that happened to pass each other on our respective journeys. For a brief moment we turned our search lights on each other with blazing intensity. Then, when we sensed that we were indeed going in different directions, we began to pass each other by."

When I visited with Rosemary again at Maryknoll during the summer of 1989, her personality seemed largely unchanged. She evinced that strength and spirit that I had found in her correspondence with Merton. Yet the church surroundings, already changing in 1966 and 1985, had by the summer of 1989 changed even more.

Of course, the buildings and landscape were the same, beautiful and well-tended; it was the internal aspects of Maryknoll that had changed so radically. Since the time of my arrival in 1980, Maryknoll had lost more than a third of its members through retirement, death, and attrition. As there were so few new vocations, another third of Maryknoll would be lost in the next decade.

Soon after Rosemary's first visit to Maryknoll, the seminarians, few in number to begin with, were transferred to Catholic Theological Union in Chicago. In May 1995, the School of Theology was officially closed. The dormitory rooms once used by seminarians and students from around the world were being renovated to house retired Maryknollers. The Maryknoll nursing home was filled to capacity, and soon the entire building, which once promised life, would be a very large and modern nursing home. Maryknoll, like many other Catholic religious orders, traditional and renewed, was preparing for its death. Though the summer program was now truncated in its intensity and scope, the heavy hand of religious authority continued to present itself. When word was received by Cardinal John O'Connor of New York that Rosemary Ruether was to be part of the summer session, he tried, unsuccessfully, to prevent her from lecturing there.

It was in this context of the impending death of Maryknoll—and, by extension, the end of the post-Vatican II church—that I read the Merton-Ruether correspondence. Clearly Merton's vague hope of infusing the institutional and dogmatic aspects of Catholicism with new life and integrity had failed. The institution continues, but its main task seems focused on burying the dead, saying the Mass, and preserving funds to ensure a continued life-style for the ever-decreasing community members.

New life is found elsewhere. This is symbolized by Rosemary herself; as one of the most accomplished Catholic intellectuals of our time, one whom Merton accepted as an equal almost thirty years earlier, a professor at the Protestant, Garrett-Evangelical Seminary, she has never taught, let alone been asked to teach, at a Catholic seminary or university. Of course, the list of pre-eminent exiled Catholic professors is lengthy, and moves well beyond Rosemary herself. One thinks here of Elizabeth

Schussler-Fiorenza and Charles Curran as part of a flowering of Catholic intellectuals in effect barred from Catholic institutions.

In their correspondence Rosemary, a lay woman, is interacting with Merton, a monk-cleric, in a religious institutional framework. In fact this lay-cleric dialogue was not unique, but was an oft- used instrument in post-Vatican II Catholic renewal. The laity in general prodded the religious to become more relevant to contemporary life; the religious provided a tradition and an institutional structure that helped the laity see their changing life in a Catholic modality. The church could thus bestow its blessing on that which was already inevitable.

Yet even at the height of this renewal Rosemary is already moving beyond the solidarity of lay/cleric, for she sees it as a new mystification that inevitably the church will claim as its own, stripping it of its radical edge and hence of its efficacy. For can a renewal that leaves the underlying institution fundamentally intact be one of honesty and integrity? Or docs it simply for the sake of self-preservation tinker with the forms of worship and community, while leaving the designated "essentials" in place?

Just decades later this dynamic of lay-cleric, laity-institution has broken down. Rosemary's insightful critique and Merton's grappling as he exits "through the back door" is hardly relevant today. Those who carry on this discussion are mainly former clerics and religious who have already left the institutional church or those lay people formed in the era of Vatican II. Clerics and religious who remain and guide Catholic institutions now—especially Catholic universities—are on the verge of retirement; their control has waned considerably and the Catholic content of these institutions is more form than substance. Clearly there is more discussion in Catholic universities about "excellence in education" than about defining their inherent Catholicity.

Yet within this dynamic an important question is posed: Does the dialogue between Rosemary and Merton gain its depth and intensity because the tradition and its main institutional carriers exist, even as their worth is being debated? In essence, does this dialogue make sense because of the tension that both theologians experience between ideal and reality, and do both gain strength and focus precisely in that struggle where hope and disappointment co-exist? Looked at from this perspective, the loss of Catholic institutional life that both Rosemary and Merton, albeit in different ways, foresaw, signals the end of the Catholic intellectual tradition that both, again in different ways, exemplify. Catholic intellectuals formed in the struggle with the failings of the church may disappear as quickly as the institutions of the post-Vatican II church. Once renewal leaves a reformist terrain, the church cannot serve as a training ground for a future generation of people committed to the institutional church.

This may be true as well for Catholic intellectuals, for the deconstruction of the church tradition accomplished within a living church leaves less reason to continue for the next generation. The rebellion of one generation is simply assumed as an accomplished fact by the one that follows. This latter generation then faces a different agenda of concerns and tensions. Could it be that just as Rosemary found her peers disappointing—that is, found them engaging issues that she had already moved beyond—future generations might find Rosemary and her peers likewise disappointing?

The danger is that the next generation will lack the depth of the previous generation, which at least grappled with a tradition it found wanting. Both Rosemary and Merton understood the loss involved in the attempt to think and live a life of integrity. To subsequent generations even the anger of loss is distant, and the heated debate that also represents a love and a commitment can become a cool superficiality, a wandering without a home, thought without depth or insight.

There are those who blame theologians like Rosemary for the demise of the Catholic church in the West. Perhaps Merton, had he lived longer, would today have been blamed as well. Though it is impossible to know for certain, Merton may have one day boldly walked out of the church he was already leaving by the back door. Perhaps he, like Rosemary, would today be traveling in a similar direction, hoping to converge at some "new point beyond the present." Surely that new point is beyond the Catholic church—and for that matter beyond the other Christian denominations, the synagogues, and the mosques— and to blame "misguided" theologians, "hedonistic" atheists, "militant" feminists, is to miss the essential point of their critique. Such condemnation seeks only to further remystify a church that has too long a history of complicity with suppression, injustice, and atrocity.

Rosemary identifies it correctly in her letters to Merton; the position that the church is above and in judgment of history is in reality reversed. History ultimately judges the church, which is born and acts within history. At the conclusion of her first book, *The Church Against Itself*, parts of which she shared with Merton and which was published during the period of their correspondence, Rosemary writes: "Sonte cathedrals, jeweled monstrances, and infallible doctrines are false reflections of the value and fidelity of God. The eternal promise of God is entirely different from this sinful mode of preciousness and longevity. Rather the cultural forms of the church reflect their faith in God's fidelity to the extent that they can freely recognize the fallibility and ephemerality of themselves as expressions of it. The truly renewed church must be one which has allowed the spirit to exercise its searching judgment upon this cultural failure." In Rosemary's analysis it is the pretense to infallibility and longevity that undermines the very claims of the church. She, along with others, is only an articulate messenger of a fate sealed by the continual failures of the church in history.

It is important to see, however, that Rosemary is more than a critic bashing an institution that over time is almost helpless before the tribunal of history. She, and again perhaps Merton would be with her today on this, is involved in creating a point of convergence—or rather points of convergence—faithful to the struggle toward community in the present. By de-centering the church, Rosemary envisions people gathered together to struggle with the questions, crises, and opportunities that arise across differences and boundaries. Significant bonding takes place within this struggle, a bonding and struggle which may be either hindered or helped by stories and symbols emanating from traditions, including, without being privileged, her own Catholic tradition. Rosemary's radical sensibility is found in this simple reversal that begins with critique and ends in creative formulations. Rosemary writes in a recent book, *Gaia and God*: "The goal of this quest is earth healing, a healed relationship between men and women, between classes and nations, and between humans and the earth. Such healing is possible only through recognition and transformation of the way in which Western culture, enshrined in part in Christianity, has justified such abomination." If there is any role for the church, or indeed any other tradition and institution, it is to be in service to this goal of healing.

2

Meeting Daniel Berrigan

MY INTRODUCTION TO THE CATHOLIC WORLD—indeed to Rosemary Ruether herself—predated my time at Maryknoll. It began in the early 1970s, my college years, in Tallahassee, Florida, where I was introduced in thought and then in person to aspects of Catholic history and contemporary reality.

I was introduced to Graham Greene and Walker Percy, both contemporary Catholic novelists, by Lawrence Cunningham, a professor who is an ex-priest and whose expertise includes the life and literature of Francis of Assisi. Both Greene and Percy, though in very different styles, articulated a Catholic sensibility of tragedy and hope beyond the doctrines and dogmas of the church. I heard the Catholic sociologist and, yes, another ex-priest, Gregory Baum, as well as Michael Novak, then a leading lay Catholic liberal before his conversion to conservative Republican politics. Both spoke of openings to deeper realities nourished by Catholic insights. I also heard Rosemary lecture to a small group of students and professors. The differences evidenced in her correspondence with Merton were also found in relation to Baum and Novak and to some extent to Greene and Percy.

While Baum and Novak were broadening the Catholic ethos emphasizing inclusion rather than restriction, and Greene and Percy were tracing elements of tragedy and beauty in a meaningful cosmos, Rosemary was clearly engaged in battle. I had never encountered the word "feminism" before, but the reaction of the students and my professors made it clear to me that the path Rosemary was taking had implications beyond the Catholic world to which I was being introduced.

I remember that some faculty members were negative, even hostile toward her. There were remarks about her Catholicity and also about her sexuality. One professor, a teacher of mine, thought her anger to be related to a lack of sexual fulfillment. I was puzzled by this connection, and no doubt a little naive in the area of sexuality itself; I thought it odd, even out of character, for a teacher of mine to suggest such a link, especially one who had expressed a similar, and similarly justified, anger toward Christianity. And were not all my teachers, almost all of them former priests, ministers, and rabbis, fleeing from the very institutions that Rosemary was critiquing?

The details of the debate these Catholic thinkers were entwined in were of course beyond my ability to analyze. Their discussion of scripture, of church tradition, of theology, introduced to me a new vocabulary and a vast and almost incomprehensible world. As a Jew, I could enter this world only as I might learn a new language, by piecing words and culture together slowly, immersing myself beyond my immediate ability to grasp the whole and hoping day by day to understand a bit more.

For the most part, though, I began to understand, through encounters I could only later place in perspective. One such encounter was with Daniel Berrigan, a Jesuit priest who in protesting the Vietnam War had run afoul of the law. He had been jailed on numerous occasions and even had gone underground to publicize his opposition to the war. Berrigan's opposition was political in scope but religious in its essence; often as not he expressed this opposition in religious and poetic language, calling on God and the power of conscience to limit violence and the power of the state. Like Rosemary, Berrigan had corresponded with Merton, but unlike her had met with him on a number of occasions. Berrigan was part of Merton's inner circle, prodding him on the issues of war, non- violence and church renewal.

All of these issues were in the air when Berrigan arrived in Tallahassee, and his celebrity status occasioned an editorial by the *Tallahassee Democrat* questioning his invitation to speak at the university. The local church was under pressure to disassociate itself from Berrigan's views. The night before his arrival I heard a fellow Jesuit, visiting at the university parish, respond to queries about Berrigan's imprisonment by stating that jail was indeed the appropriate place for him.

I was asked to be a student host for Berrigan in the few hours before his address to a gathering of students and faculty. So there I was, alone with a famous (and to some infamous) Catholic priest, driving into the beautiful countryside surrounding Tallahassee. We stopped at a park where cypress trees rose from swamp; it was spring and the air was filled with the fragrance of flowers and new growth. Berrigan commented on the beauty of the countryside and inquired about my own background. When I told him I was Jewish, Berrigan recalled his recently deceased friend, Abraham Joshua Heschel, a Jewish theologian who emphasized the prophets and the task of calling humanity to a sense of community and justice. When I mentioned that Heschel was at the university just months before his death and that he had looked extremely tired at the time, Berrigan was silent, as if observing a moment of reverence.

I recall many aspects of Berrigan's visit. Sitting on a walkway constructed within a cluster of cypress trees, Berrigan spoke at length about his first visit to the Middle East and how his meeting with Yassir Arafat was interesting and unsettling. It was clear that Berrigan was torn on the issue: on the one hand, he was sympathetic to the suffering of European Jews, a suffering sanctioned and sometimes encouraged by his own church; on the other hand, he was sympathetic to the plight of Palestinians in the refugee camps he had visited. To Berrigan, Arafat was an enigmatic figure, charismatic yet prone to a militant rhetoric Berrigan abhorred.

I had recently returned from Israel, which I had visited in 1973 during my junior year abroad. By chance the Yom Kippur War had broken out while I was visiting, and I spoke to Berrigan about the eerie quality of being in the middle of a war. I could relate to Berrigan's sympathy with the Palestinian refugees, though on a very different level of experience and understanding. For staying in youth hostels and wandering around the country, I had observed the tremendous difference in power between Israeli Jews of European background, who seemed to carry the same culture as I did, and Palestinian Arabs, who were treated as foreigners, even in a land that they had once called their own.

I glanced at my watch and mentioned to Berrigan that we needed to start back so as to arrive in time for the faculty-student colloquium at which he was to speak. Since I was entrusted to host Berrigan and to return him at the appointed hour, I became alarmed when he responded that he was enjoying my company to the point of preferring it to his speaking engagement. At first I laughed at his preference, then realized that he was not only enjoying his time with me, but that he was also relativizing the importance of commitment to the faculty who had devised his itinerary.

As our discussion continued (while I attempted to steer Berrigan, physically and psychologically, into the car) it became clear that professors often saw it as their duty to lecture him in the proper role of the priest and on the importance of upholding governmental authority. Berrigan relished meeting with interested students who were seeking a path, and he was wary of the credentialed academy whose authority, at least in his view, was often silent in the face of oppression and death.

This, no doubt, was a harsh judgment, and as I cherished my professors, it was difficult for me to contemplate such a thought, let alone accept it. Surely our arrival, ten minutes late and with a grand entrance, heightened the already-tense atmosphere. After Berrigan finished speaking, Richard Rubenstein, a Jewish professor associated then with the radical "death of God" theology that had emerged in the 1960s, began to refute Berrigan's emphasis on non-compliance with unjust power and non-violence as strategies for life. Rubenstein cast Berrigan's position as a utopic enterprise that could lead to anarchy and religious zealotry.

Rubenstein's response was insistent, even at times harsh; neither of the two men made eye contact, and when Rubenstein finished his statement, Berrigan merely continued speaking as if Rubenstein's words had been spoken in a language he did not understand. It was strange to see the always-powerful Rubenstein treated as if his words were a bombastic interruption with little relevance to the subject at hand.

I saw in Berrigan then, even within my limited understanding of the Catholic tradition, what I would witness later in my Maryknoll years when I invited Berrigan to address our students on various occasions: a certainty of vocation and vision that sought the center of Catholic life through personal witness. It was almost as if he, along with others, could penetrate the encrusted layers of Catholic piety and, in so doing, cause to emerge a fidelity to God and to history. I felt there was, appropriately for Berrigan, a poetic ring to this fidelity and in some ways a conspiratorial air as well—an updated Jesus-and-the-apostles sensibility with symbolic acts that baffled and challenged the accepted wisdom and authority of the age. In this sense Berrigan relished his role as priest played against type, a free spirit, poet, protestor, agitator in the Temple, now transplanted to the church.

Surely Berrigan's relationship with Merton plays on this theme of going to the center of the tradition by subverting the expectations of the powerful. Unlike Rosemary, Berrigan's correspondence with Merton lacks confrontation on the issue of the church and vocation. Instead, he takes on a brotherly sensibility of advice and mutual support. When they first met in August 1961, Merton records in his journal finding Berrigan an "altogether winning and warm intelligence, with a perfect zeal, compassion and understanding." For Merton, Berrigan captured the "spirit of the church . . . a hope I can believe in, at least in its validity and its spirit."

During the period of Merton's correspondence with Rosemary, Merton was busy advising Berrigan, mostly through critical questions, on his increasing willingness to directly confront elements of the Vietnam War apparatus, which at the same time brought confrontation with church superiors. For example, Merton advises Berrigan that the problem of authority and obedience has to be handled with "delicacy and understanding" lest real renewal give way to an explosion of a "lot of emotional power pent up in lay people and just ordinary frustrated religious." Rather than systematic and concentrated change, this would result in a "big bang and a lot of fallout"; the debris would simply serve as decoration for an unrenewed church.

Still, Merton recognized the call of conscience within the challenge of church renewal. In his advice in April 1967 regarding an invitation for Berrigan to accompany a group to Hanoi bearing symbolic medical gifts, Merton cautions Berrigan to be clear about his intentions and only then to proceed: "There will be plenty of people standing by you . . . what will come?" Merton writes "The Holy spirit will take care of that. But be careful of the way people will exploit it: this is no Sunday picnic. In short, Dan, if you think this is it, then go ahead. And let them heave you out. And don't worry about the consequences: but just watch yourself in the mushroom cloud that follows, be sure in all things you are really trying to do it in God's way as a real Jesuit (because sometimes the real ones are the ones outside of the organization)."

The previous month, Merton wrote to Berrigan about an idea he had had to hold together his diverging views about the church, church authority and vocation. Merton proposed a gathering at the monastery of "extreme" people to discuss on the most radical level the future of prophetic and monastic community and if monasticism was even a tolerable Christian concept anymore. To argue against monasticism, Merton suggested Rosemary Ruether; to be for some continuity with traditional monasticism would be Merton himself. Berrigan would be, at least in Merton's mind and for this discussion, a "free-floater."

Upon meeting Berrigan I immediately had that same sense of him: a free-floater, yes, but one who had commitment. I was meeting so many religious people at the time who seemed tied and bound, almost as if their faith was at the expense of their freedom. As Merton recognized, Berrigan was different—free and yet at the same time close to the earth. His challenge to authority was wrapped in an intricate play of sign and symbol. However, as he moved closer to his target, his aim was swift and sure. Our late arrival, the grand entrance, his handling of Rubenstein were both impromptu *and* calculated, as if we were in a theater where stage and action were centered, decentered, and centered once more.

3

Living with Dorothy Day and the Poor

SIX MONTHS LATER I MET BERRIGAN AGAIN, though this time in a decidedly different setting. After graduating college I had decided to volunteer my services at the Catholic Worker house in New York City. I came to know of the Worker just after my first visit with Berrigan, through William Miller, who taught me at Florida State University and who was the biographer of the movement. In the spring of my senior year a series of discussions on the Worker were held which I attended faithfully. Though it would have been difficult for me to articulate at the time, I was searching for a way of life, and the Worker sensibility appealed to me. The Catholic context of the Worker's vision was still somewhat foreign to me; the search for a spirituality in the context of justice moved me deeply.

Thus I embarked, flying from Miami to New York, arriving at what I understand in retrospect to have been the ungodly hour of 1:00 a.m. With suitcase in hand, I walked twenty blocks from the bus stop to East First Street and rapped lightly on the windows of an apartment address I had been given. The apartment was directly across the street from St. Joseph's House of Hospitality, the main Worker community where people were sheltered and the hungry fed.

When I awoke early the next morning, I saw the line for soup and bread already growing. Over the next year I would learn many of the names behind the faces I looked out upon that first morning, and even some of the stories that brought so many to this line. That first morning, however, it was impossible for me to differentiate one person from the next. I saw a suffering humanity which I had read about and now wondered whether I wanted to touch, or ultimately to be touched by.

It was during this year that I met Dorothy Day, the woman I had read so much about and who was spoken of in such reverential terms. Berrigan had mentioned her to me as someone I should meet and get to know; Miller, as her biographer, spoke often about Dorothy (as she was called by everyone), and in such a familiar manner that I felt like I knew her already. It was indeed strange to meet a person to whom you had first been introduced in print, larger than life and in a biographical mode that brought you to intimate terms before you had ever met.

But by this time Dorothy's privacy was already a relic of the past and I was just one more interloper in the movement she had helped create and lived within. She, like Merton, had become an icon of Catholic renewal and she and Merton formed an important axis around which renewal turned. In the eyes of the vibrant post-Vatican II church, the monastic vocation opening to the world and the prophetic voice emanating from the poor brought the faithful, indeed the faith itself, into focus. Merton was just recently deceased and so lived on, perhaps even in an exaggerated way, in the Catholic imagination; Dorothy, now in her seventies, presented a living, almost legendary fidelity over the decades.

Dorothy's commitment to the poor by living and working with them and her outspoken criticism of injustice were balanced, one might say enhanced, by a spirituality of journey and longing. For Catholics who felt their faith to be abstract and institutionalized in irrelevant church structures, Dorothy represented a grounding of faith and practice that invited others to join. Catholics came from all over the world to meet her, to thank her, and sometimes to kneel before her. Indeed, the line to meet her at times could be almost as long as the soup line that continued to form outside the Worker each morning.

At first I witnessed these processions of the poor and the seekers as an outsider, wondering if and where I fit in this world. It was confusing in its particularity, as Catholic culture and spirituality were foreign to me, and confusing also from the broader social and political perspective. Could spirituality, even broadly considered, address the plight of the growing legions of poor? The centrality of Dorothy and the Catholic Worker tended to increase this confusion for me. Could one older woman, whose energy was waning and whose mind often wandered, living in a small house of hospitality where "radio Jimmy" lounged in his bathrobe during the day and slept on a desk at night, and where "Sister Jeannette," dressed in a military outfit and heavy makeup, uttered a continual and outrageous repertoire of dirty jokes and raucous commands, actually hold the key to the future?

I slept on the fifth floor of the house in a kitchen with another man who drank most of the day and read newspapers during the evening. Outside the kitchen was a floor with fifteen beds, always full each night, a few with "regulars" who lived in the house and the rest with men who came for a night or two and then disappeared into the city. The bathroom that served our floor was often in use and dirty; my kitchen mate solved this problem by periodically urinating in a jar that he kept by the side of his bed.

The noises in the city were difficult to get used to, especially the frequent police and fire sirens that dominated the night. The smells of the Lower East Side were foreign to me; the odor of the homeless men as I served soup on the ground floor or in the basement on cold days, as I sat with the men before they ate, and even on the floor where I slept, was pervasive, sometimes nauseating, until, like the sirens, they became part of life's rhythm. After a while, leaving the environs of the Worker became almost as disorienting as the initial entry into Worker life. What at first seemed like a cultural escape essential to my survival, visiting the Metropolitan Museum of Art, for example, soon appeared too antiseptic and fake. In the end the question of escape became relativized. Clean, uplifting, trendy, artsy New York was as difficult to experience as the poverty of the Bowery.

That I belonged to none of these worlds in which I was now enmeshed was in itself, again in retrospect, a profound lesson. My growing collection of books, bought in used bookstores and borrowed from others at the Worker—and stored in the unused kitchen oven above my bed—functioned as a way of deepening my knowledge of the Catholic world I had entered and of the sources that had fed the Worker itself. Included here was Dorothy's autobiography, *The Long Loneliness*, which was written in the 1950s with a style and beauty that made it a compelling story decades later; a collection of Peter Maurin's *Easy Essays*, prose poems that articulated for many, and especially Dorothy, the direction of a committed life; the French Catholic philosopher Jacques Maritain's *Integral Humanism*, which attempted to harmonize Catholic philosophy and humanism so as to protect philosophy from abstraction and humanism from a dehumanizing secularity; Simone Weil's haunting last letters on the possibility and impossibility of her conversion to Catholicism, published posthumously as *Waiting for God*. Last, but not least, my collection also included several works of Thomas Merton: *The Seven Story Mountain* and his more recent works, *New Seeds of Contemplation* and *Conjectures of a Guilty Bystander*, as well as Merton's *Asian Journal*, which he began to write on his fateful last journey and was published after his death.

My diary notebooks are full of quotations I copied from these books. From the postscript to Dorothy's autobiography: "The most significant thing about the Catholic Worker is poverty, some say. The most significant thing is community, others say. We are not alone anymore, But the final word is love. At times it has been, in the words of Father Zossima, a harsh and dreadful thing, and our very faith in love has been tried through fire." From a letter of Weil in which she discusses her difficulty in accepting her encounter with Christ: "Yet I still half refused, not my love but my intelligence. For it seemed to me certain and I still think so today, that one can never wrestle enough with God if one does so out of pure regard for the truth. Christ likes us to prefer truth to him because, before being Christ, he is truth. If one turns aside from him to go toward truth, one will not go far before falling into his arms." And from Merton's diaries: "Duty of contemplative life—(Duty's the wrong word)—to provide an area, a space of liberty, of silence, in which possibilities are allowed to surface and new choices—beyond routine choice—become manifest. To create a new experience of time, not as stoppage, stillness, but as 'temps vierge'—not as a blank to be filled or an untouched space to be conquered and violated, but to enjoy its own potentialities and hopes—and its own presence to itself. One's *own* time. (not dominated by one's own ego and its demands.) Hence open to others—*compassionate* time (rooted in the sense of common illusion and in criticism of it)."

I took these quotes to heart because they spoke to my questions—overcoming loneliness in community, wrestling with rather than simply affirming God, silence as a place of openness and invitation. From a traditional sensibility, of course, I was gleaning and synthesizing, at times creating an eclectic spirituality. In truth, of course, I was just at the starting gate reading those who had struggled with tradition. But where was I to start, if not where others had left off?

The authors who attracted me had themselves began in a similar way: Dorothy, Weil, Merton were all converts in one way or another and within this conversion had continued to evolve through life experience and insight. Surely the least important act of their conversion was changing their formal church affiliation, in Dorothy and Merton's cases from Protestant to Catholic, and the most intriguing, Simone Weil's refusal to convert, for she had chosen to love those peoples and culture whom the church had excluded or condemned. What took hold of me, what I wanted to explore in my life, was somehow encapsulated in one of Weil's last letters: "We are living in times that have no precedent, and in our situation universality, which could formerly be implicit, has to be fully explicit. It has to permeate our language and the whole of our way of life. Today it is not nearly enough to be a saint, but we must have a saintliness demanded by the present moment, a new saintliness, itself also without precedent."

I thought then, and wonder today, if those whom I was reading and in some cases meeting in person were part of this new saintliness, which Weil in her letters describes as the "exposure of a large portion of truth and beauty hitherto concealed under a thick layer of dust" and as almost equivalent to a "new revelation of the universe and of human destiny." Clearly, the conditions under which these writers struggled mitigated against pious abstractions, and my own reading occurred in a situation of overwhelming poverty, violence, and mental illness. The height of absurdity—or perhaps the truest means test—was reading Dorothy's meditation on community in my kitchen-cum-bedroom, my library tucked in the stove above my head, as my roommate ruminated in a somewhat drunken manner about a political report in the *New York Post*.

To be sure, new saintliness had a political aspect and as I served the soup to homeless men and refilled the baskets of day-old bread from exclusive upper West Side bakeries, the poster images of Mahatma Gandhi and Martin Luther King, Jr. hanging on the kitchen walls were present. Both were quoted on the posters and in the Catholic Worker newspaper—their words side-by-side with the poems of Peter Maurin and encyclical statements of John XXIII and Paul VI as if they belonged together. The poster quotes were noticeable while hardly dominating the first floor, as they seemed to appear, disappear, and reappear again without plan or notice. There was, perhaps, an appropriate Catholic Worker anarchism about the messages against hunger and for justice; an eclectic hope that a concern for the poor, non-violence, a decentralized, agrarian-village economy, and a personal response to life would somehow help right the wrong these man and women of the soup line represented. Books about Gandhi and King, as well as E. F. Schumacher's *Small is Beautiful,* soon found their way into my oven collection, as did George Bernanos's *Diary of a Country Priest,* who was quoted to me once by a Worker volunteer as I stood stirring the large cauldron of soup, preparing for the early morning soup line.

I also recall my last encounter with Dorothy, in the patio behind the first floor eating area. The patio was a relatively quiet place, except for Paul, who organized the pots and pans and also boxed pound after pound of day-old bread to feed his pigeons in Union Square Park. Paul yelled at everyone, and was quick to point out the hypocrisy of volunteers like me who "visited" the poor and then continued our affluent lives. He was quite sarcastic and perceptive and this day, as usual, he kept up his banter with me, a banter I had come to understand as a peculiar sign of affection.

Dorothy was sitting outside waiting for someone to take her to a doctor's appointment when she suddenly called me over to talk. This was somewhat unusual and I was a bit nervous as I sat down next to her. Then she simply told me that my time at the Worker was coming to an end and that it had been good that I had joined them for a year. It was appropriate that I move on now, she continued, for I had learned what I could here and I should feel no hesitation or guilt in moving to my next place in life. The Worker, she said, was like a school, sending its students on toward life's work. I wanted to ask her then what that work might be, to probe her wisdom as to my own life's journey, but at that moment such a question seemed to me to violate a special space into which I had been invited. I experienced this moment as a benediction, a sealing of a bond that in all its contradictions and even betrayals remains inviolate and a source of light.

4

Among the Jesuits

IT WAS DIFFICULT CONTEMPLATING leaving the Catholic Worker, even as I realized that Dorothy was intuitively correct. My time at the Worker was over, but where was I to go from there? I had few illusions about my ability to reach out to those who were suffering; any hope of a special, healing bond were dashed in the reality of this hard life. The men and women of the soup line remain now, decades since I departed; my presence in their lives was recognized by them, if at all, as a fleeting moment of no consequence. Though I grew used to some of the smells, the lice, the possibility of anger, chaos and violence that underlay each day, I often wanted to distance myself from any person who approached me in need. In my own mind, and this is still true today, I was a failure as a Catholic Worker.

Still, within this failure the ground had given way, or rather a foundation had been laid within which my questions about politics, the social order, humanity, and God could be understood. It was almost as if a new space had been created in my life through which I now viewed my place in the world. Indeed, I had entered a world that was not my own—a strange world of poverty and grace, chaos and liturgy—and it had become central to my own existence. When I arrived at the Worker, lonely and searching, I wrote in my diaries of a sense of exile. When I left the Worker, that sense remained.

I wondered, then, whether an exilic existence was fated for me especially, or was some part, however nascent or buried, of each person's condition. Is the challenge of life to deepen our relation to exile or work to overcome it? The last day of my stay at the Worker, I wrote in my diary Dostoevsky's words that Dorothy loved to quote: "Where there is no love, put love, and you shall find love." The answer for Dorothy had been love, a harsh and dreadful love, which was also a sign of exile. Perhaps for Dorothy, love was a sign of God within exile. Perhaps God's love called her to those who in their poverty were in an exile without reprieve. Was God's love a calling within or to exile? Or an end to that condition? This is how my diaries ended, with this question, and the most difficult question of all: How could one assert God's presence, whatever God's relation to exile, in the face of the suffering of the innocent?

Over the next years I continued this search: for a year, work on a master's degree under the biographer of the Worker movement, William Miller; for another year, at Hope House, a Catholic outreach among poor African Americans in the housing projects of New Orleans; then for three years (1977-1980), at a Jesuit university pursuing my doctorate with Miller, who had left Tallahassee for Marquette University in Milwaukee during my stay at the Worker.

It was at this time I saw other faces of the Catholic church, or rather the diversity within it. Miller himself personified part of this experience. A convert from Protestantism, then in his sixties, Miller was originally an historian of the South and had, in the middle of his academic career, embarked on a study of a little-known yet respected Catholic movement that had as its mission—and a failed one at that—the reorientation of social and spiritual life. With most academics benefiting from the "progress" of modern life, declaring their independence from religion, this book was hardly geared toward securing accolades and career advancement for its author. Yet Miller persevered and, more importantly, lived out the life about which he was writing.

Miller's hospitality was such that I was invited into his home and we spent long hours talking with one another about the aim of history, of community, and the possibility of God. In Tallahassee, and later in Milwaukee, Miller would phone me and ask if I would like to take a walk or a drive. The walks, during daylight hours, were several miles long and more often than not ended with dinner at his home. The drives were invariably at night and with no particular destination in mind. Miller would pick me up at my apartment and we would simply drive for an hour or so, returning me to continue my studies for the evening. Miller could be in turn loquacious or silent; he was in many ways a driven man, though in an unusual direction: driven out of sync with the academy, and hence with the evolution of Catholic universities. Miller was determined to reverse the course of his own institution, re-centering the human in community and God by exploring thought and practice that contributed to both.

For Miller the human was in danger of being displaced by the frantic and elusive search for progress. The power of technology had increased exponentially in his lifetime and so had the human carnage that was its cost. Catholic universities had joined the march of progress in the realm of knowledge, so that instead of discussing formative ideas, ideas that might reorient the direction of humanity, his younger colleagues were fellow-travelers of progress, lamenting only their placement at a second-rate

Jesuit school rather than their hoped-for Harvard appointment. Why have a Catholic university at all if it did not explore radical alternatives to the present human condition? Why accompany as subservient seconds those who were leading the way in a march of "progress" that was in fact engulfing, at times, degrading humanity?

My course of study with Miller reflected this focus without reservation. Rather than taking class after class in the traditional academic mode, Miller directed me to ensconce myself in the library, reading books and writing down my thoughts. My diaries over these years reflect these readings and serve as a road map to Miller's view of the world. The turn-of-the-century Russian philosopher Nicholas Berdayev, the iconoclast American historian Henry Adams, the French medievalist Etienne Gilson were the foundational works I read. Yet there was also a distaff side of Miller as intellect, nonetheless integrated into his philosophy as a whole, reflected in authors such as the Jewish feminist anarchist Emma Goldman and her companion, Alexander Berkman, and the editor of the radical socialist journal of the 1920s, *The Masses*, Max Eastman. Of course, the latter authors were uniformly atheistic, adding an intriguing element to the puzzle that was William Miller: a Catholic *and* an anarchist; conservative *and* a radical. Yet in reality these were merely contradictions imposed by liberal categories lacking in dimension and depth.

There was at this time of my doctoral studies a Catholic element within Marquette, drawn from older academics, both lay people and former priests, and some of the dwindling number of Jesuits, who were assuming an increasingly symbolic role in the administration of the school. Neo-Thomist in training and outlook, they had come of age in pre-Vatican II times, indeed, some had in various ways prepared the groundwork for the council. To these professors, Jacques Maritain, Thomas Merton, and Dorothy Day were part of an ethos they sought to communicate to their students. Many years earlier Maritain had delivered a lecture at Marquette that the university had published, and there were still on the faculty philosophy professors who had studied with Etienne Gilson in Toronto. The university archives held the papers of the Catholic Worker movement and included in this collection the papers of Dorothy Day and Peter Maurin. Around campus, one encountered Marquette alumni who had met both Maurin and Day in their travels to Milwaukee. A Catholic Worker house began in Milwaukee in the 1930s and a later incarnation existed in the 1970s.

There was also at Marquette a younger generation of Catholic intellectuals, in particular a small number of priests in their forties and fifties who had been schooled intimately in the Thomistic world and had advanced to a somewhat more contemporary theology centered around the Canadian Jesuit Bernard Lonergan and the German political theologian Johannes Baptist Metz. Among these were Matthew Lamb of the theology department, a former monk and then a priest who had studied with

Metz, and Sebastian Moore, a Benedictine monk from England's Downside Abbey.

Lamb had an encyclopedic knowledge not only of theology, but of history and science as well; his writings were almost impossibly dense and beyond my ability to understand fully. He further had the quite curious and completely unconscious habit of slipping into a variety of languages during class lectures and even during a single conversation. Those who had access to him often referred to their conversations as airplane journeys: with Matthew at take-off; nodding in apparent understanding during the flight; landing with him on return as the discussion came to an end.

Moore was eccentric in a classical English way, cobbling together books on spirituality and love from handouts he would prepare each morning for his classes. As one passed him walking or met him for a specific occasion, dinner, for instance, it was obligatory to ask him for his latest handout. That became the starting point for discussion, and invariably the next morning's handout constituted a response to the previous day's discussion.

I soon became part of this intriguing circle of Catholic intellectuals and was accepted without reservation. I often ate dinner with Matthew, who had the ingratiating habit of accepting only five dollars from graduate students toward our restaurant bill, insisting at the same time that we buy the more expensive items we generally could not purchase on our modest stipends. I ate meals with Sebastian, too, and drank as well. Of course, the success of these evenings depended upon whether, once called for at his apartment, Sebastian remembered his waiting dinner companions. If by chance he had to go upstairs to his room to retrieve something he sometimes disappeared, to be found later, right there in his room. Often he became absorbed in some reading or thought, oblivious to his waiting—and very hungry—friends.

Later, after the dinner, Sebastian often read from the poetry of T. S. Eliot. He would regale us with his encounters with Eliot's poetry, as a young monk waiting eagerly for Eliot's latest published poem or sending Eliot a copy of "The Waste Land," annotated with Moore's own comments and queries, hopeful for a response. And Eliot did in fact respond in his own handwriting, a document now of inestimable archival and certainly monetary value. It was typical of Sebastian that he had absolutely no idea where Eliot's response was, even among the meager material accumulation of a monk's life. This became part of the folklore surrounding Sebastian and part of the reasons that made him so easy to embrace.

The Jesuits were another story. On the whole they were less easy to approach and less interesting as thinkers. More often than not attired in clerical clothes, they were seen for the most part as symbolic guardians of the Jesuit and Marquette tradition. They were part of the school's identity, which of course, due to their dwindling numbers and the inherent limitations of such symbolic posturing, was dangerously eroding. This was occurring partly because of the crisis in vocations; still another reason was the infighting within the Jesuit community.

In the 1960s Marquette had an evolving and up-and-coming theology department that included such luminaries as the Jesuit pastoral theologian Bernard Cooke. When he and a few others decided to leave the Jesuits and the priesthood, the Jesuit community forced them to leave Marquette. An academic retrenchment then became necessary, and people of lesser caliber were hired for the department. The newer hires, some of them ex-priests themselves though none were ex-Jesuits, whatever their individual talents, knew and adhered to the parameters of thought and intellectual exploration. A dynamic department became one that prized security and stability.

By the late seventies the challenge from the more progressive elements of the Jesuit community had ended, only to be replaced by a challenge from those Jesuits who believed that even some of the moderate members of the department had abandoned the Catholic faith. At times the infighting assumed the character of a spectacle, but for most students it was already irrelevant, for the Jesuit character of Marquette was subsumed under the rubric of "excellence in education." Beyond that Catholicity was form without substance, a designation to be accepted or rebelled against, but rarely redefined or disputed in fact. There were students who wanted to pursue a religious and committed life, and they spent most of their time at the Newman Center on campus, with the requisite guitar masses and social outreach programs. It was a place of warmth for students away from home, where the language of faith was simple and inclusive, rather than academic. The center sponsored retreats and a weekly program dubbed "soup with substance," where students and faculty gathered to discuss the issues of the day.

In my second year of study, I helped form a monthly Catholic Worker discussion group in which issues of concern could be addressed. Sometimes we would invite a speaker to address us. Each meeting featured a pot-luck supper. In the cold Milwaukee winters these meetings were welcomed for the warmth of both food and company. I was surprised that this endeavor, formed outside the academic structure, also became entwined in Jesuit politics, as two of the more conservative Jesuits on campus attempted to control the content and direction of our discussions. Initially, their issue was framed as one of creedal affirmation: each member of the group should affirm the creed of the Catholic church. I, of course, being the only Jew involved, assumed this was directed at me; but there were others, Catholic in background, who were searching, unsure whether in all honesty they could assume that creed as their own. Still others recited the creed daily, yet were equally offended at the proposed admission ticket to the discussion group of strict orthodoxy. Such an affirmation had never been demanded, or even suggested, in the entire history of the Catholic Worker movement. To what purpose was it now being suggested?

This was the very first time in my journey among Catholics that my Jewishness became an issue, or rather a barrier, to my participation or acceptance into Catholic intellectual life. In the end the group vehemently rejected the creedal affirmation and spoke directly of their welcoming of diversity. In fact this was my general experience at the Worker and at Marquette; more than simple acceptance and welcome, my Jewishness was seen as special and central to fidelity and the ongoing love of God.

My Marquette experience was part of the post-Vatican II emphasis on the relation of the Hebrew bible and the New Testament—the unbroken covenant—and an understanding of Jesus as a Jew. The Catholic Worker relation to Jews predated Vatican II and I recalled, especially in light of this creedal challenge, Catholic Worker newspapers of the 1930s and '40s that emphasized the danger to Jews in Europe and argued for the immediate acceptance of all Jewish refugees into the United States. The argument was advanced at one level as simple humanitarianism, a people in need being accorded hospitality. Deeper still was the Worker's theological argument, which often provided headlines for the Worker paper during this time. The people who had given birth to Jesus were now being crucified as he had been; to reject the Jews was to reject Jesus, himself a Jew who cried over the agony of his people. Peter Maurin's easy essay, "To Save the Jews for Christ's Sake" was daring in this regard, as was the woodcut that accompanied it: Mary and the Christ child centered in a Star of David.

As this difficult experience ended, it brought home to me the peculiar nature of my evolving journey as a Jew among Catholics. Unintentionally, mostly through the chance of circumstance, I entered a world different from mine, one that historically had been actively hostile to my own people. Since my experience with Catholics on the whole had seen them emphasize my Jewishness, I in turn made little point of this negative history. Yet lurking in the background, even with my decision to live at the Catholic Worker, was the question of Christian complicity against and hatred of Jews.

Often I wondered whether these same Catholics would come to my aid as a Jew if the situation for Jews in America were to deteriorate. Had the Catholic tradition, even in the post- Vatican II era, really changed, or was the essence of Catholicism, indeed Christianity, immutably evil as regards the Jews? I wanted to see and judge for myself this tradition that loomed so large and dangerous in the Jewish imagination.

I also had to confront the question of whether I also wanted, as a Jew in search of security, to disappear, both literally and intellectually, in the larger Christian ethos. This presented itself as the quintessential question for every Jew: Did I seek to divorce myself from my own people out of shame or self-hate? At times the drama of the Mass captivated me; at other times, overwhelmed by an understanding of the history behind Christianity's ceaseless re-enactment of its own bloody redemptive sacrifice, I was repulsed by the ritual. Most often, as at the Catholic Worker, I saw myself merely as an observer, one seeking to understand yet remain uncommitted.

There exists a freedom in being somewhere, yet nowhere; it finds its mirror image in the price of loneliness and exile. From a distance one can romanticize the community feeling emanating from a Catholic mass, especially the rooted liturgies at the Catholic Worker and the progressive liturgies on a Catholic campus. But the Jesuit residence, which I entered only on the most rare of occasions, held the feeling of death to me. The kiss of peace was a place of warmth; the Jesuit residence a cold prison.

Hypocrisy, too, was present at Marquette, and was more readily apparent than at the Catholic Worker. The Jesuits controlled the university, were the outright owners of it, in fact, and asserted this control out of proportion to their numbers or, indeed, their talents. As time passed, the tension inherent in this disparity grew more difficult, especially as the actual number of Jesuits was rapidly declining. Since a Jesuit presence was of utmost importance at Marquette, any opening in the theology department or in university administration engendered a nation-wide search for Jesuit candidates. Though their performance was supposed to be judged like any other university faculty or administrator, in reality the standard of review was quite different. Everyone was aware of this disparity, especially the students, and some addressed it openly.

A cycle came into being: Jesuits were hired, welcomed, promoted, and treated as decorative pieces for display to donors and parents anxious to see their sons and daughters on a campus with assured values. This in turn made Jesuits who were interested in matters of substance search out other communities on campus with which to affiliate, or simply leave Marquette for other universities in hope of escaping their fate.

This was the first period in my life in which I was within an institutional religious setting and around individuals who were in an official sense religious. The expectations I had were no doubt too high. I would, over the years, constantly adjust them downward. At Marquette I began to realize more clearly what perhaps I intuitively understood at an early age, namely, that religious life was found in the main outside those who claimed to be religious or who were, because of their overt lifestyle, deemed to be so. I had witnessed this at the Catholic Worker; the dining room where the poor ate carried a religious sensibility well beyond the corridors of the Jesuit residence of Marquette. Indeed it was at the Worker that the officially religious deliberately lost their patent designation or had it humbled to the point of collapse. The brokenness I witnessed in the face of the hungry was an opening that some of the priests and sisters at Marquette sought in the summers, or even during the academic year, but outside the academic institution. They lived in apartments or satellite communities in the shadow of, but as far removed from the "official" religious center as possible.

Those who were searching were thus thrown together and the Catholic Worker clarification meetings, or even small groups in the cafeteria, became places of refuge. As a Jew I was fleeing a hypocrisy that I had felt as a youngster in the Jewish world: synagogue membership as a social expectation; reading of the prophets while in pursuit of profit; the difficulties of translating an ancient faith and culture in the modern world. As a child I preferred baseball over synagogue and as an adult, the freedom of the world over the constraints of religious ideology.

Gradually I realized at Marquette that my journey among Catholics was a grasping for a necessary independence from my own community, a space where I could be free to think through my own Jewish religiosity and spirituality. Free of the Jewish world, I could wander, at least for a time, among those who were also seeking their freedom. Of course, there were many differences between myself and the others, not the least of which was the community within which they labored and the distance I had established from my own community. I also witnessed a struggle to be free from authority within my Catholic friends that was foreign to my own religious background. In being liberated from the church, they engaged in a battle whose intensity was difficult for me to fathom; liberty and guilt, free thought and obedience were locked in a struggle impossible to disengage. Whatever their proclivities at the moment, it seemed to me that what my friends rebelled against was so deeply lodged within them that the rebellion itself affirmed their catholicity. As I watched their struggle I wondered whether in another way this was in fact my own struggle. Could my journey away be a preparation to return?

The two years of course study at Marquette went by quickly and now in my third year I was writing my dissertation. Marquette was generous in its support and my first year as a teaching assistant was followed by two years of fellowships that allowed me to forego any work outside my dissertation. Even my summers were free, and one year I traveled to different parts of the country to interview people and collect material related to Catholic Worker history. The interviews and material were deposited in the archives and the information provided background for my proposed dissertation, a biography of Peter Maurin.

The biography had, as it were, fallen into my lap. Or rather it had been planted there by William Miller as far back as my graduate studies in Tallahassee. It happened like this. Miller had written a biography of the Catholic Worker movement, which included some details about Dorothy Day's life. He embarked on a full biography of Dorothy, but she wanted that published only after her death. Instead, Dorothy encouraged Miller to first write a biography of Peter Maurin, which he dutifully began and then at some point just simply stopped.

I knew Miller was working on this biography and one day asked him how the work was proceeding. He replied that he could not work through Maurin's ideas and that he had ceased work on the book. To my query as to who, then, would write the biography, he replied simply that I would. I was stunned by his suggestion, for as a young master's degree student I had not begun to contemplate writing a book, and wondered how he thought I might be able to carry off such a daunting task. By the time I gathered myself together enough to protest his decision and laugh at his suggestion, Miller turned and entered his office building.

My final year at Marquette began and Miller's promise—that I would write Maurin's biography—was coming to fruition. I spent the fall completing my research, proceeding through Maurin's papers, comprised mostly of his handwritten "easy essays," working through Dorothy's early correspondence written on behalf of Maurin (usually in defense of his critique of the church's failure to live up to its own vision), and carefully perusing the Catholic Worker newspaper for hints of Maurin's travels and commentary from his later years.

It was a strange and seductive history that I meticulously studied, full of open letters to the bishops to commit themselves and the church to the unemployed and the poor, pleas to save the world from World War II and the spiral into destruction and death. It included the boldness and naivete of a street-corner preacher who stood in the center of Union Square in New York City, claiming as a Christian to be a true communist, and exhorting his listeners (who as often taunted him) to create a society where it was "easier to be good to one another." This from a man who hardly bathed, and yet always wore a suit; who read the latest books on capitalism and modern warfare and carried with him in a pocket edition the collected Papal encyclicals on St. Francis of Assisi. When one graduate student offered his opinion that such a study was irrelevant to contemporary reality, I told him simply that it was too late. The world I entered each morning in the archives was indeed past, but I felt somehow that it was also part of a future. At least, for better or worse, it was part of me and my future.

As I finished the Maurin biography, I read again Simone Weil's understanding of a new saintliness and realized that Dorothy and Maurin, in their Catholic particularity, were part of a larger community across religious and geographical boundaries that spanned the twentieth century. My introduction carried the heading "The Prophetic Voice in the Twentieth Century" and brought together such diverse figures as Mahatma Gandhi, Martin Buber, Martin Luther King, Jr., and Albert Camus. Nontheist, theist, and agnostic—Hindu, Jew, Christian, humanist—all were gathered in the furtherance of humanity and justice and in a kinship closer to one another than to many of their blood or religious communities. Their commitment grew out of their particularity and transcended it. A vision within and beyond their grasp was forming.

It was instructive to me that each grew in fidelity as they became more deeply who they were, and that the message that transcended their life and place grew from that particularity as well. The particularity—the depth of their witness—grew in relation to the others they encountered. For the Hindu Gandhi it was the British, Christianity, and Islam; for the agnostic Camus it was the world of Christian belief; Dorothy found it in the poor. The easy mistake, and one I saw made often at Marquette, was to model the content of the prophet's journey as if it were available for the taking. Rather, it seemed to me that you entered another's journey to come back to your own; admiring their deep entry into the history they lived through in order to enter more deeply into your own. Each had taken tremendous risks that only later were seen fully as logical choices that added up to a life worth living.

And that was the calling that I heard in Sebastian's voice as he read so beautifully the words of T. S. Eliot. As Krishna said to Arjuna, "on the field of battle/not fare well but fare forward/voyager."

5

An Invitation from the Maryknoll Missionaries

As I FINISHED THE SECOND CHAPTER of the Maurin biography during the winter of 1980, I received a letter from Saudi Arabia, its postmark, to put it mildly, surprising me. Actually the letter had been sent to me in care of Paulist Press, publisher of my diaries and poetry from my Worker days and, coincidentally, publisher of the first Catholic Worker newspaper in 1933. Paulist forwarded the letter to me and I retrieved it one snowy Wisconsin day from my graduate student mailbox. I had no idea who might write me from such a far-away place, and I opened the letter with anticipation.

The letter was from Gene Toland, a Maryknoll priest then serving on that society's General Council. He had bought my book in a New York bookstore on his way to the Middle East for society business. That business, it turned out, was to establish a Maryknoll mission somewhere in the Islamic world to facilitate a dialogue between Islam and Christianity. The missionaries would forego the more traditional role of converting others and would instead listen and learn from Islamic culture and religion. Toland was to search out the site for such a presence; included on his itinerary were Egypt, Yemen, and Jordan. He wrote the letter in an airport in Saudi Arabia, awaiting a flight to Yemen.

I had never met a missionary, nor heard of Maryknoll, but the letter was intriguing. Before his election to the council, Toland had been a missionary to Bolivia, a country which, as he described it, combined extraordinary beauty and indescribable poverty. He had been in the countryside and often in the mountains, working with the native peoples who retained, in what seemed to me the most difficult of situations, their own culture and religion. What he found in my book, and what prompted him to write, was a description of the poor in New York City that reconnected him to his experience in Bolivia.

As it was snowing outside and I was enjoying the warmth of the graduate lounge, I read the letter over several times, continuing to marvel at the postmark and the contents of the letter. Walking through the halls, I asked a few of my friends to read the letter and inquired whether they had ever heard of this group, "Maryknoll." Their reactions were uniformly immediate and animated, telling me that Maryknoll was literally a household name in the American Catholic world, largely through their magazine, which chronicled their mission work and was widely distributed and widely acclaimed. Their formal name was the Catholic Foreign Mission Society of America, but it was known popularly as Maryknoll for its devotion to Mary and the location of its headquarters on a knoll in New York with a panoramic view of the Hudson River. One friend excitedly commented that the Maryknollers were an incredible community devoted to the question of justice around the world; still another seconded the connection that Toland had made with my own writing and life. Why not write him a letter, someone suggested, and see if a further connection with a newly minted doctorate could be formed?

My initial reading of the letter never prompted such a thought, for though my knowledge of missionaries was slight and only in an historical context, the image was hardly enticing to a Jew. And yet the suggestion remained with me in an undefined way. The week prior to this I had been scanning the job opportunities bulletin, as the time had arrived for me to begin a search for a job. Nothing posted there was of interest to me, just ordinary entry-level positions in religion or history at various universities, none of which seemed particularly interesting or exciting. Since my own journey had been, academically speaking, "irregular," and at other than what were considered "first- rate" schools, I was not sure any department would be interested to employ me. Some time later, alternating between a sense of satisfaction that the Maurin biography was proceeding, and despair that no job future awaited me after Marquette, I took up the advice of my friends and wrote to Toland at the Maryknoll center in New York.

The letter was short, thanking Toland for writing me and, in explaining my immediate circumstances, telling him my desire to teach in a school where people come from a faith perspective and are committed to the issues of justice. Toland's letter in fact sparked an interest in me, and my reply inquired further as to whether Maryknoll might have a school or a program where such students were found, and where I perhaps might be of some use. I mentioned again, as I had in my Worker diaries, that I was Jewish and hoped this would not be an impediment to considering me, if indeed such a school or program did exist at Maryknoll.

It was a shot in the dark, to be sure, and when I received a return letter, this time postmarked "Maryknoll, New York" I was taken off guard. The Maurin biography was consuming me and I had buried the initial letter in my mind. This letter also was from Gene, as he wanted me to call him, and he had received my letter upon his return from the Middle East, several weeks after it had arrived at Maryknoll. There was very little specific information in the letter as to my queries; it simply advised me that the General Council was inviting me to visit Maryknoll later in the spring.

The weeks passed quickly and the day soon came when I arrived at Maryknoll, baggage in hand, sporting a new coat and tie. As the taxi pulled into the compound I was struck by the beauty of both the grounds and the main building itself: a large Chinese-roofed building constructed of grey granite stones. As I stepped out of the taxi, I became aware of a number of other buildings, all of the same stone, and immaculate, manicured grounds interspersed with gardens just hinting at the spring blooms to come, all stretching over hundreds of acres. The next day, touring the grounds, the buildings revealed their diverse operations, reflecting the wide-reaching actualization of the Maryknoll mission: administration and development; magazine and book publishing; radio and film programming; a relatively large nursing home. The parking area was full during the day—I was told Maryknoll employed almost 500 workers—and below the parking area, nestled between dense trees and a grey stone terrace, was a graveyard for Maryknoll priests.

The interior of the largest Maryknoll building, which I learned housed the administration and the seminary, was serene and beautiful. The architecture was majestic in what I came to know to be the church style of vaulted ceilings and large framed windows. A large terrace outlined the perimeter of some of the first floor offices, and from that terrace I looked out onto a quadrangle, in the center of which stood a large statue of Mary. Behind her was a Buddhist bell hung on a wooden frame. The bell was brass and the wood was painted red, as was the structure framing Mary. In pleasant weather meals could be eaten outside the refectory on the ground floor, overlooking this placid scene. It was exactly there, on the first morning after my arrival, that I ate breakfast.

On the evening of my arrival the receptionist dutifully rang for Gene, and we met for the first time and we embraced. What struck me initially about Gene was his youth—he appeared to be in his late thirties—and especially his vitality. He was handsome in a strong Irish way and clearly a warm man, and when he took me out for dinner that night, our conversation was welcoming and low- key. Little was said about any schedule for the next day. In response to my faint questions Gene assured me that I did not need any type of preparation, for I would simply be meeting Maryknollers and visiting a variety of departments.

When he deposited me back at my room, I was drowsy from jet-lag and drained by the anticipation of this visit. Our dinner discussion about missionaries and the changes in mission work—even the distinction between missionary and missioner, the latter being the preferred term—blurred in my head as I readied for sleep. My guest room, which included a private bath, would become familiar to me as I re-visited it over the years, including the evening, some five years later, when I greeted Rosemary Ruether.

The morning schedule was full and by breakfast the riddle of the Chinese architecture and Buddhist bell were explained. Maryknoll's first missions in the 1930s were in China, and the closing of China to missionaries after the Communist revolution in 1948 occasioned the imprisonment of some Maryknollers who subsequently became famous, at least in Catholic circles, for their faith and perseverance. One such Maryknoller, Bishop Walsh, had just been released from prison the previous year; pale and thin, he sat at the table next to ours.

China was deeply embedded in the Maryknoll psyche, hence the architectural theme. The dean of the seminary, John Kaserow, a Maryknoll priest, ate breakfast with us. He was a man of Gene's age and had spent some years in Hong Kong; his expertise was the history of missionary activity in China. When I asked him about contemporary missionary work, he spoke of cross-cultural approaches, dialogue, and activities for justice and peace. Like the terms missionary-missioner, "cross-cultural" seemed an important and elusive concept. My questions to Kaserow no doubt revealed my ignorance of the global reality Maryknoll took for granted. They spoke of travel to Africa and Latin America the way I thought of weekend excursions from Milwaukee to Chicago. Kaserow, like Gene, was also informal, insisting as we ate our breakfast, on my calling him by his first name.

My first appointment of the day turned out to be with my breakfast companion, John Kaserow. The seminary, he explained, traced its history back almost seventy years, and now was in the process of being accredited as a school of theology. The seminary had several constituencies, the most obvious of which was the Maryknoll seminary students themselves. The Maryknoll Sisters, located in their own compound across the street, sent their sister candidates to the seminary, as did the Maryknoll Brothers. But the largest number of students came from a local Capuchin community that used Maryknoll as their seminary. There were also a few laymen and priests unaffiliated with any of these groups; they had arrived in January or in the subsequent fall in anticipation of the beginning of a new program to train lay missioners to work alongside Maryknollers. In total, there were probably 120 full-time students; a small school, yet one located in an immeasurably large global context.

As I was sifting through this information, having now categorized to some degree the women and the young men in cassocks I had seen in the hallways, John spoke about new initiatives of the society which would take the shape of two new institutes at the school, one a program in myth and ritual, the other in justice and peace. John had read my resume and knew of my interest in justice work, my time at the Catholic Worker, and asked if I would be interested in teaching in the justice and peace institute. Though apparently a logical question to John, it came as a surprise to me, since we had been speaking for only some fifteen minutes. I had yet to have even one formal job interview and knew next-to-nothing about formal academic job searches. Still, I hardly expected this immediate offer, so I queried further as to whether John was indeed offering me a teaching position, to commence that fall.

In the moment between my question and John's response, I experienced an intense anxiety related to my own Jewishness. Maryknoll seemed fascinating, to be sure, and while the specifics of this engaging and incredibly complex reality eluded me, my instinctive response to the offer was an immediate "yes!" tempered by a feeling that because of my time at the Worker and graduate study at Marquette, John perhaps did not remember I was Jewish. So I broached this possible barrier to him; John assured me it was known to all and welcome at the school. Half an hour after walking into the dean's office, we shook hands and drank a cup of tea. A life's decision had been made that would carry me to areas of the world I was only dimly aware existed.

As the day unfolded I met many people working in different departments at Maryknoll—Mission Research; China Project; Development; Vocational Outreach. I also visited Orbis books, the Maryknoll publishing concern, and Maryknoll Magazine, which, to my astonishment, had a monthly circulation of almost one million. The books and magazines were all shipped from Maryknoll itself; hence Maryknoll had its own fully staffed post office. While walking the grounds I was introduced to three Kenyan bishops and their host, a newly arrived student from Tanzania, Fr. Leo Kazeri. These were the first Africans I had ever met, and the bishops' skin tones were as beautiful to me as their soft British accents.

Dinner came, and the day faded into a blur. This, I found, was typical, for at Maryknoll much can happen by the end of a single day. I had dinner with John and with the faculty of the school—eleven in all—who were quite surprised when I was introduced as a new hire. The seminary faculty was mostly comprised of Maryknollers, ranging in age from late thirties to early fifties. There were also Capuchins on the faculty, easily distinguished by their brown cassocks. Completing the group were a diocesan priest from Brooklyn and a Jesuit who had recently returned from mission work in the Philippines.

It was this Jesuit who later that evening complained to John of a Jewish presence at a Catholic school. He assured me that it was nothing personal, just a query as to the direction of Catholic education. John engaged him in a discussion about the relevance of dialogue in the new cross-cultural church. The Jesuit remained unconvinced. The exchange prompted a recollection of the discussion at dinner, which evidenced quite a bit of dissension about the direction of Maryknoll and the school, and though people were invariably polite, I seemed to symbolize for some exactly this tension. It was an awkward situation to be in, especially being unaware of the debate in which I was now an apparent catalyst. I was relieved when the evening ended and I returned alone to my room.

The following morning brought new people to meet, seminarians and priests working in justice and peace activities. One spoke of his time in Korea among workers and the amount of exploitation behind Korea's "economic miracle". Another related his experience among peasants in the rural areas of Peru. I tried to absorb as much of their discussion as possible, even as I wondered at my naivete. Among my peers, my junior year abroad to Europe, the Soviet Union, and Israel seemed expansive. In the midst of Maryknoll, I struggled simply to locate in my mind the countries being discussed, let alone imagine that I might one day live this geography lesson.

After breakfast I had only one more meeting before departing back to Milwaukee, and this was with the Superior General of Maryknoll, Jim Noonan. As John escorted me to Noonan's office, I was somewhat anxious again. While all my meetings thus far had been informal, I anticipated a certain level of formality in this one. The corridor we entered housed a secretarial pool and offices for the five other council members. At the end of the corridor were the offices of the Vicar General, and of the Superior General. They were by far the largest offices, and each had its own secretary seated in an anteroom.

The Vicar General, John Halbert, came out into the corridor to greet me. He seemed quite friendly, with a shock of gray hair and an Irish sensibility. Two years later he became president of the school. Then I was ushered in to meet Noonan, who quickly emerged from behind his desk, seating us across from each other in stuffed easy chairs. As did most of the Maryknollers that I had met, Noonan wore regular clothes rather than clerical garb. Soon we were on a first-name basis, and as tea was served the discussion turned to our mutual experiences among the poor, Jim's having been in the Philippines.

After a few minutes it became clear to me that Jim had read my book on the Catholic Worker. Given his position and his travel schedule, it took me somewhat by surprise that he had taken time to read my work. My academic credentials were fine to him, the first mention of them in my entire visit. To Jim, as to John, Gene, and others, it was the commitment—or more precisely the struggle to be committed—that they found so intriguing and so compatible to the Maryknoll sensibility. It was something we shared across generational and religious backgrounds, and soon, quite to my surprise, Jim was probing me for more insight into this struggle.

As he spoke of the difficulties in his own life of remaining faithful to the priesthood and to the poor, I marveled at the unexpected turn our discussion had taken, and the humility of this man who was elected to lead Maryknoll. It was an appropriate end to my first visit to Maryknoll, and on the flight home, as I recalled my time there, it occurred to me that among other things, I had also secured a teaching position.

Maryknoll, of course, was hardly considered an academic power-house, nor even in any way academically inclined, so the news of my success was greeted guardedly back at Marquette. Miller thought it a logical progression and was quite pleased. A Jesuit in the history department with a wry sense of humor thought I was falling off the academic globe and inquired whether I would be paid in kind with baptismal fonts. Since the question of salary had never come up during my time there, I confessed that I did not know the answer to his question. As I well knew, his sarcasm had less to do with money than with his sense that my abilities could be better directed elsewhere.

Several months later I finished the Maurin biography, defended it as my dissertation, and was awarded my doctorate. I spent the following months closing down my apartment and saying goodbye to people at Marquette. Milwaukee's beautiful and mild spring was a welcome respite from its difficult winter. During this transition time I often strolled from my downtown apartment to a park area on the tip of Lake Michigan. I felt as if a time awaited me that would be full, diverse, and challenging. The present, then, was a time of quiet and reflection; as I scanned the expanse of the lake, I felt a peace that drew close and enveloped me.

6

Encountering Liberation Theology and Martyrdom

MY ARRIVAL AT MARYKNOLL IN AUGUST was uneventful, and my meetings with the dean yielded little substantive information about my specific role in the school. I was hired to be a full-time faculty member, but the school still revolved around a seminary curriculum. I was asked to create and teach elective courses in the first semester, and sit on a committee that would give birth to the Institute for Justice and Peace.

As I had experienced in the spring, Maryknoll education was hardly traditional, and the course I suggested, "The Search for Commitment and Community in the Twentieth Century," was approved immediately. I also proposed a sequel to this course to be taught the following spring semester which would allow me to cover this search in more detail. Like most new teachers, I chose materials I had studied during graduate school, and I also tried to expand my own scope of study to include what I thought might be relevant to the Maryknoll world. Thus I chose readings by Jacques Maritain, Simone Weil, Mahatma Gandhi, and Dorothy Day, as well as the Latin American revolutionary figures of Che Guevara and Camilo Torres.

My class centered around the themes of suffering and commitment in the twentieth century—the reality of mass death and Simone Weil's notion of a new saintliness. My class was small in size, and among the ten students were two sister candidates, a Maryknoll seminarian, a Maryknoll brother, two Capuchin seminarians, the Tanzanian priest, Leo Kazeri, whom I had met in the spring, and a Protestant minister, Don Steele, who hailed from the South and had recently been working in the Appalachian Mountains.

At twenty-seven years old, I was easily the youngest member of my class, and my youth, coupled with the informality of Maryknoll, made it difficult for me to see myself as the professor and those who sat in front of me as my students. Years later, when I traveled to Tanzania to visit with Leo, we laughed about my initial presentations in class, for Leo had been struck by my youth and my serious demeanor and, as he remembers it, my poise. I recall only a deep anxiety, hoping that my lectures would be found to be intelligible and relevant to these students.

While my teaching duties represented one aspect of my anxiety, the faculty represented the other. I had been hired without their consideration or approval, and the tension I observed on my initial visit was but the tip of a deep and contentious situation. The seminary had begun to shift its focus to being a school, thus needing to draw in students from outside the Maryknoll orbit, that is, people unaffiliated with Maryknoll and not in training for religious life. This new constituency would be integrated into the student body to create a broader educational setting. The idea was to create an integrated educational atmosphere in which students from different parts of the world would gather, one that had a global and committed perspective addressing the social, political, and religious issues of our day.

It was this vision, or rather the changes needed to flesh out this vision, that created the tension among the faculty. The General Council of Maryknoll endorsed this new vision of the school of theology, while the seminary faculty sought to enlarge the student body without changing the essential seminary-oriented curriculum, thus attempting to preserve their own status and centrality in the educational process. The movement of the seminary changing into a school became, in their view, a fight to ensure that the school would in its essence remain a seminary.

I discerned this looming conflict almost immediately. The Maryknollers on the faculty were chosen by the community to leave their missionary work and pursue further studies. Yet to me they seemed to be priests rather than theologians. A number of the Maryknoll faculty members had never even worked overseas, and in lunchtime conversations I heard rumblings of discontent over teachers who had little experience of life in the missions. Maryknoll, it seemed—and this became clear in my first faculty meetings—was being pulled in many directions by forces both within and outside the Society.

This tension found its focus in the seminary/school dilemma. Some Maryknollers, for instance, believed that the seminary should remain steadfast in its function, and in the face of declining numbers should simply redouble its search for new vocations. Other Maryknollers thought the very seminary idea to be outmoded and even self-defeating; vocation to mission went beyond clerical or even religious status and included all those who sought justice and peace in the world. The faculty had its own dynamic on these issues. As often, though, we were simply the target of either camp. In retrospect, either option was impossible to achieve fully within the school, even with the most creative faculty and administration. And though the dimensions of the argument were still beyond me, I realized after the first month of the academic year that the faculty in general was incapable of negotiating these tensions or even engineering a reality that could embrace these tensions in a creative way.

The school was, of course, to be viewed within a much broader context, and though faculty matters were consuming, particularly in this time of transition, I was drawn to the other aspects of Maryknoll which to me could make the school interesting, even distinctive. Clearly the lunchroom, hosting visitors from all over the world, complemented or even itself became a classroom. The mission stories fascinated me, and visitors from various cultures brought new perspectives from which I could learn. The missionaries and visitors brought back stories of activities and new initiatives that expanded my horizons and interests. In this sense they were true teachers without the formal credentials, and when in later years some of these people enrolled as my students, the interchange and growth we shared was beyond anything in formal academic life. To this aspect of Maryknoll I brought a hunger that even the lunchroom could not satisfy.

I soon began reading essays on liberation theology and, with a group of students, Gustavo Gutierrez's *A Theology of Liberation*. Gutierrez's book was recommended by many, and when students approached me to read the book with them and be their guide, I was surprised. How could I serve such a function if I had never read the book and knew nothing about the subject? And wasn't there in fact a course offered on liberation theology, one that perhaps I should attend as a student? This, of course, turned out to be part of the problem, as indeed the subject of liberation theology was not even taught. Thus I agreed to read the book with the students and hoped that I would understand this theology. As so much of the Maryknoll experience was foreign to me, I was anxious about my ability to understand and help articulate a theology emanating from a Latin American world about which I knew so little.

It was an adventure, and soon my anxiety was assuaged. The major themes of liberation theology were, at least to my mind, traditional: the Exodus and Jesus were central, and what was fascinating to me was the motion these events assumed in Gutierrez's writing. The key seemed to be in liberating the Exodus and Jesus from a certain captivity, an imprisonment by the church tradition and hierarchy. Gutierrez called for in his context what Peter Maurin had called for in the United States, exploding the dynamite of the gospel. What interested me particularly was the insistence that only by recapturing the dynamite of the Jewish Exodus tradition would Jesus himself be freed to operate in a prophetic way.

If Jesus was perceived to be a prophet, then the church was called to be prophetic. To be prophetic one had to call to account the powers and the structures of injustice. Instead of reinforcing domination, as the church often did, Gutierrez called for the opposite. Christians, in fidelity to Jesus, were called to oppose injustice, even to suffer persecution in that opposition. To oppose injustice was to propose a world beyond injustice, and as I read Gutierrez's book, it reminded me that a vision of the future was as central to religious belief as a critique of the present. This is how Marxism and other forms of social analysis were used in liberation theology: to analyze the present, which had to be overcome, even at the cost of revolution.

Revolution was in the air at Maryknoll. The Nicaraguan revolution had just taken place, and some Maryknoll priests and sisters, along with Maryknoll lay missioners, were active in that ongoing event. In fact, the Sandinista leadership included a Maryknoll priest, a native Nicaraguan, Miguel D'Escoto, who was now serving as that nation's secretary of state. About thirty Maryknollers were in Nicaragua at the time of the revolution and periodically they returned to New York. Some others, including two in our reading group, were preparing to work in Nicaragua.

Returning missioners often spoke of the involvement of Christians in what was perceived by the outside world to be a Marxian revolution, and how small Christian communities of poor peasants and workers decided to join in the revolution. Though the American press and later the American government would enlarge the revolution of this small, impoverished nation to the level of an international symbol, the missioners, including D'Escoto, spoke of the Christian imperative to protect and enhance life. Of course, D'Escoto himself was quite controversial with both the Vatican and the Maryknoll community; he had chosen an overt political option and now served in a controversial revolutionary government. On this choice the Catholic hierarchy, outside and inside Nicaragua, was split, as it was on liberation theology in general.

Does the political option—the banner of liberation theology—simply affirm the divisive nature of politics and theology, and thus demand a decision on where the person and the church stood vis-à-vis the social and political order? Or does such a political and theological choice actually divide Christians from one another and create a conflict that the Jesus of traditional theology sought to overcome? As Gutierrez wrote in his book, and D'Escoto chose in his life, God has a special preference for the poor and the oppressed. The Bishops of Latin America spoke of this as the "preferential option for the poor." As God's preference, it was also incumbent on the church to choose likewise.

While divided within itself on these issues, Maryknoll was clearly making a contribution to a revolutionary Christianity surfacing in Latin America. Orbis Books was the main translator and publisher of Latin American liberation theology, creating a market in the English-speaking world and beyond, for now people in Africa and Asia who knew English could read of this theology and follow these ideas in their own unique context.

Our reading group thus also read theologies from these areas, often denoted as "emerging theologies." The African and Asian theologians seemed more immersed in understanding Christianity and cultural transformation, while the Latin American theologians were interested in the relation between Christianity and political revolution.

The Latin American reality was closer geographically and more immediately accessible to me. Indeed, because of the political situation at this time, it dominated discussions and even became the focus of substantive debate. After all, the early Maryknoll missions in China had been closed by communists and the church had fought communism and atheism for over a century, declaring Marxism to be anathema to Christianity.

Are those who raise the banner of a revolutionary Christianity in league with Marxist analysis and political action authentic Christians, or duped followers of a revolutionary ideology that seeks to destroy the church? Can one be a Christian and agree with Marx's understanding that often religion serves as the opiate of the people? Can one be a Christian and allow injustice to continue, refusing to join forces with others who hold different faiths, or no faith at all? In the background was the fundamental question of what it means to be a Christian. Is a Christian defined by belief—say, the acceptance of Jesus Christ as savior—or by action on behalf of justice and peace? One member of our study group proposed that it was through action that people demonstrated their beliefs.

The discussions were heady, at least for me, yet the consequences of commitment were all too real for some Maryknollers. The Nicaraguan revolution had been won and the casualties were seen in the larger context of victory and hope. The civil wars in Guatemala and El Salvador were worsening daily. Missioners returned from these countries without optimism and with horror stories of torture and murder. Death squads roamed freely in both countries. Morning time, priests and sisters would find friends, even those they had trained, dead by the side of the road, their bodies left as a lesson—and warning—to those who would oppose the army. The complicated issues within the church were thus heightened by the American support, training, and arming of these governments and death squads. Another confrontation brewed that in the immediate sense was more complex and demanding than the inner church debates—the debate with the United States government and its foreign policy.

Several months after I arrived at Maryknoll, the tragedy hit home with the deaths of three sisters, two of them Maryknollers, and a lay missioner who had been trained by Maryknoll. As the news filtered in—slowly, a bit confused at first—the discussions ended and a period of mourning began. The church bell rang and people gathered for liturgy and reflection. Most of the Maryknollers on both sides of the street knew one or all of the women, and so the news of their deaths was in the first instance personal, for cherished friends had been brutally murdered.

As time went on, however, the emphasis moved to the larger context of the thousands of people who, without religious affiliation, protection, or status had been and were being systematically murdered. These were the people "without names"—the anonymous poor, the human rights workers, the catechists who were known only to their family and friends who had died in the same way and for the same reasons. The Maryknoll sisters, Maura Clark and Ita Ford were, as one Maryknoll priest described them, martyrs, but then so, too, were the thousands who had disappeared before their time. The church was living through a new martyrdom that necessitated a different kind of conversion: to humanity and God in the form of justice and community. One priest ended his sermon by quoting the recently martyred Archbishop of San Salvador, Oscar Romero: "May my death be like a seed of liberty and may I rise in the struggle of the Salvadoran people."

The deaths of the sisters were of local interest, certainly, as they affected the lives and psyches of each Maryknoller. They also quickly became a national and international story, juxtaposing the innocence of the murdered with the gratuitous violence of the government in El Salvador. The women had been doing nothing more than caring for orphans and performing what the church denoted as "works of mercy." They were raped and murdered to intimidate the people in El Salvador who were increasingly mobilized to work for justice, promising to them the same fate as these women. It was a lesson well taken, and I remember the fear that gripped the two women in the reading group who in the following months would leave for Central America. They were both in their early forties, one a mother of three, and they wept at the news of the deaths. They wept, too, about their own pending journey, and often when I saw the almost daily news reports on Central America and the murdered women, I also had troubled thoughts about their possible fates.

Perhaps it was a strange coincidence that I learned of the death of the women just as I was returning from the funeral of Dorothy Day. Dorothy had died a few days earlier at the age of 83 and a friend from the Catholic Worker called to invite me to her funeral. I drove down to New York City with Gene Toland to the Church of the Nativity, the local church around the corner from the Worker where Dorothy had often attended Mass.

The day was solemn. Cardinal Cooke greeted people at the door to the church, and a diverse group of longtime friends as well as many influenced by Dorothy gathered to celebrate her life. As I walked into the church I spotted William Miller outside, behind a police barricade. He had driven to New York from Milwaukee. As I motioned him to come inside with us, he signaled that he would stay and listen to the liturgy through the loudspeakers that had been set up outside to accommodate the overflow crowd.

Inside, the liturgy began, and a young priest currently associated with the Worker presided. Clearly Dorothy had chosen to have her funeral celebrated in the neighborhood in which she lived, worked, and died over St. Patrick's Cathedral, where the Cardinal had offered to preside. It was

Dorothy's last statement of the call of the church to be among the poor. She had lived among them and would be eulogized there as well. The liturgy was beautiful, though the celebrant's sermon focused on the evil of nuclear weapons and seemed oddly impersonal, as if the funeral mass were to be made into a platform for a contemporary political speech.

After the liturgy I walked back to the Worker house where tea was served. I had a chance then to speak with Miller, who was returning to Milwaukee later in the evening. His biography of Dorothy was proceeding on schedule, and he had received my Maurin biography just published by Paulist Press. Miller asked me how things were going at Maryknoll, and I told him of my classes and the broader world to which I was being introduced. He cautioned me in a humorous way about my Catholic proclivities, then I walked him to his car for the drive home.

An hour later I left with Gene to drive back to Maryknoll. As we left the city, the countryside appeared in its autumn beauty. We were both quiet, knowing that with Dorothy's death a Catholic era had come to a close. Gene spoke of the historic ties between Maryknoll and the Catholic Worker. In the 1950s seminarians would volunteer on their only days off to work the soup lines, and a number of Maryknoll priests had actually lived at the Worker before finding their vocation. In the early 1960s a Maryknoll priest had hosted Dorothy in Mexico City after her travel to revolutionary Cuba, a controversial visit in which she had suggested that if Christians had pursued justice, a Christian rather than Communist revolution might have taken place there. In a small and very poor village outside Mexico City, the Maryknoller told the villagers of Dorothy's visit to Cuba. They gathered around her, hungry for news of the revolution. She never forgot their faces, and when she wrote of the priest-guerrilla, Camilo Torres, she invoked the experience of these poor and the oppressed.

I had read Dorothy's essay on Torres years earlier, but without a context in which to understand it. As Gene recalled the Maryknoll-Worker connection, the words took on a new significance and, coupled with the recent deaths, became a haunting elegy to a hope of liberation which many around me clung to even in the face of tragedy. The next morning I went to the library and before I canceled class in memory of the women, I read Dorothy's words again:

> Camilo Torres joined the guerrillas, their life in the mountain and jungle, joined their pilgrimage to the people, the *campesinos*. He broke bread with them, and so truly became the *companero*, the one who breaks bread, the companion. What would Mass be like in a jungle, in one of the encampments of the republics in Colombia where no priest had been sent as missionary, where the idea of the church was linked up in the minds of the destitute with the rich, the exploiter? Suppose a priest like Father Torres looked at his companions sitting around a fire by night, hunted men, but men bringing a gospel of hope to the poor, men who were bro-

ken themselves, unlearned men like the twelve apostles. Suppose he picked up bread—in this case tortillas—and after speaking to them of the first communion at the Last Supper, and using the gospel words, broke and gave it to them. Suppose he had wine, as the fugitive priest did in Graham Greene's book *The Power and the Glory*. And suppose he blessed the cup, broke and gave it to them all for the forgiveness of sins. Would not this be a church in the wilderness? Would not this be a Mass? Would not this community of men have communion together just as the two men walking with Christ on the way to Emmaus did, as they sat at the inn and knew Him in the breaking of bread? And could it not be just as casual and as quiet, and yet just as earthshaking?

7

In the Mission Fields of Latin America

IN FEBRUARY 1981 I WAS APPOINTED to direct the Institute for Justice and Peace and to develop a Master's degree program in that field. Though this program had been in the planning stages for some time and I had been hired to be part of it, the deaths in El Salvador and the increasing visibility of Maryknoll became the final impetus for its formation. The General Council, as before, made this appointment over the objections of some of the faculty.

News of this new educational initiative spread through the compound. The objections were multiple and communicated to me only indirectly: the General Council's usurpation of faculty prerogative; the creation of a program intended, as some saw it, to transform education at Maryknoll, diminishing theological orthodoxy; the appointment of a Jew to spearhead it. From the council's perspective the school had little intention of transforming itself and only an outsider such as myself could see and move toward a future beyond the seminary curriculum and student body. In fact, several Maryknollers on the faculty were in the process of being reassigned as I arrived in the fall, the transformation already in its nascent stages. These individuals had refused to leave their faculty appointments and go overseas; the council in turn established the Justice and Peace Institute, anticipating that it would prevail in academic battle with the traditional seminary curriculum.

I was delighted and energized by the appointment and began to piece together elements of a program which would bring together faith and justice in the context of Maryknoll's global sensibility. Liberation theology was an obvious component, perhaps even the underlying foundation of such a program. Analysis of social and political structures was also crucial. I had no education or experience in administration or program formation, and simply tried the best I could in exploring elements of the

Maryknoll world and combining them with my own background and abilities. I saw that justice perspectives in the bible were important to missioners and to Orbis authors. Courses on basic Christian communities, feminism, and black theology were also needed. Focusing courses on Latin America, Africa, and Asia would be crucial to place biblical and theological questions in their context, for as I was beginning to understand, liberation theology arose from particular contexts rather than an assumed universal message. Of course, all of this needed to be framed in a Christian and specifically Catholic framework.

If I had understood the complexity of the task handed to me or the difficulties of navigating the diverse constituencies of Maryknoll, or had even worked previously in an institutional setting where turf was protected and personal security and status took precedence over the larger vision, I would have thanked the council for their confidence in me and turned down the appointment. But I was young and naive and so plunged into the work without a second thought. A Maryknoller not part of the school mentioned that a summer offering might be an option to complement the two-year degree program; sisters who were teachers often had the summers free to pursue educational opportunities, and perhaps others who could not pursue the degree in the regular academic year would be able to afford the time for short summer courses.

Thus the idea for the summer program was born, and since the advertising deadline in Catholic journals and weeklies for summer programs was early March, I had only a month to plan, invite faculty members, and advertise our program. People were already making their plans for the fall so that the broad outlines of the degree program had to be determined and advertised the next month. Time, certainly, was of the essence.

The response to our ads was tremendous, beyond anything that I had expected. Just weeks after the initial advertisements had run, hundreds of letters of inquiry poured in. Then applications followed by the dozens. There was little in the way of secretarial help for this new and unexpected deluge, nor was there assistance in combing through the applications. I answered most letters by hand, and the few that were typed were produced by a shared secretary who, though sympathetic, resented the added work.

Most letters I received were short, asking only for the details of the summer and degree programs, and the *pro forma* response soon evolved into a brochure. Some letters were longer and more personal, very nearly pleas for guidance in the search to remain within the Catholic community. Most of these letters recalled with bitterness aspects of the writer's Catholic upbringing and adult interaction with the church. Maryknoll seemed to be different to them, being more progressive and open to the world. It was almost as if Maryknoll might mend their Catholic identity or even save it. Many others wrote of their love for and devotion to Maryknoll and recognized that Maryknoll was significantly different from other Catholic institutions.

I also received more than a dozen threatening letters, with messages of doom and death, often laced with anti-Semitic diatribes. I wondered just where these letters had come from, since few people in the larger public had heard of me, and even fewer would know I was Jewish. I gave these letters little thought until some months later when a prospective applicant telephoned me at home on a holiday, demanding to see me at once. I hurried over to Maryknoll; as he paced to and fro in my office, it was obvious that he was simply disturbed. I wondered, as he passed back and forth in front of me, whether he might simply pull out a gun or knife and kill me. Instead, after a half-hour of ranting and raving, he turned away from me and left.

The overwhelming response to our ads encouraged me. I wanted to share the success of this venture with others, but the faculty were ambivalent toward an influx of new—and non-seminarian—people, and many Maryknollers were resistant to new faces, especially women, in their buildings. For the first time in the society's history women were to live in the seminary building.

As the first summer session approached, signs appeared in the seminary directing which stairwells were to be used by women students and which were reserved for priests and seminarians. Intense debate arose over whether women should be allowed access to the pool with priests. The issue was resolved, at least initially, by allowing female students to swim at the restricted early morning hours reserved for the Maryknoll sisters. The dining room, usually a focal point for conversation, in fact became the topic of conversation, for the quiet rectitude of meals now was disturbed by a flow of people who would not only appear at lunchtime, for to some extent this had already been happening, but at breakfast and dinner as well.

I myself experienced a juxtaposition of feelings, fearing that the students would find it difficult, restrictive, and altogether unacceptable to live in a building so externally beautiful, yet internally drab and depressing, with its long, dark halls, small seminary rooms with shared bathroom facilities, and the basement dining area that allowed only a minimum of sunlight. The drabness even extended in some cases to the priests themselves, some without an affective life, others broken by their years in mission. Within days of arrival students were able to discern which Maryknollers were receptive to the changing church and which were embittered by it. Areas of Maryknoll were depressing, and people who had lived in that environment for years simply took it for normal and appropriate life. But what was normal for them clearly was not normal for people from outside the society.

Perhaps that is why I took so eagerly to the creation of this program. Maryknoll was intriguing and the possibility of life and exploration was, I though, almost endless. The other side of Maryknoll was dying and dead and the struggle was whether life or death would win out. When I entered the daily life at Maryknoll I embraced this struggle as my own, at times for the corporate aspect of Maryknoll, at times for my personal survival. Whether Maryknoll lived or died quickly became an existential issue for me. The dining room would become as important to me, an agent of change, as it was to those resistant Maryknollers I passed in the hallways and whose tables, I quickly realized, were closed to me.

Those Maryknollers who were supportive encouraged me to travel to the missions where "real" Maryknoll life was lived. The center, after all, was artificial, where Maryknollers came back to raise money, serve in administrative capacities, recover from illness and retire. Many Maryknollers saw the center as both necessary and a place to be avoided; when called back to Maryknoll to serve the overall needs of the society, they resisted the call and served reluctantly. To admit pleasure in being in the United States was tantamount to a confession of inadequacy, a broken vocation or, worst of all, irretrievable failure. In the macho world of missionary work, independence and self-reliance in service of a higher truth (the spreading of the gospel) were essential elements of identity and self-esteem. Pleasure, or even the need to be home, was a sign of emasculation. Since women were in theory unavailable to priests, how else could one prove one's manhood in a missionary order except in the unrelenting and isolated mission field? A missioner home for an extended period of time became in this sense feminized—he had become a woman.

Hence the discussions about women and sexuality took turns that were unfamiliar to me. The Maryknoll priests on mission were men, even if their behavior suggested the need for psychological assistance. Maryknoll priests at home in the United States, even if they were fairly well-adjusted, were "women" in need of help. Maryknoll sisters, at least in the priests' imagination, were not really fit for men's work—that is mission work—or became honorary men if their behavior mimicked male sensibilities. The interaction between priests and sisters therefore took on a charged and often unhealthy dimension: the men had to assert their masculinity, again without overt sexual advances; the sisters had to be women without exuding overt sexual attraction to the priests. For some priests, the "good" sisters were masculine in their appearance and style; other priests preferred their masculinity to be protected by "cute" sisters. Sisters could be cute well into their forties when they passed definitively into "motherhood." The priests projected their own biological mother onto these women, who thereby became another category of untouchable.

In this atmosphere the issue of homosexuality became highly charged. During my first year at Maryknoll I became aware that a gay subculture existed at Maryknoll among the priests and the sisters, and that this, like the heterosexual dynamics, was hidden and so remained, for the most part, unanalyzed. At Maryknoll the most obvious homosexual population was among the Capuchin presence in the seminary; the two Capuchin students in my class were gay and perhaps as high as eighty percent of the Capuchin seminarians were similarly oriented. The percentage was much lower among Maryknollers and less obvious. For the most part, Capuchins were attracted to a sensitive Franciscan spirituality embraced by portions of the gay community, and when at the end of my first semester a graduation party was held at the Capuchin house, same-sex dancing was tolerated.

The Maryknoll tradition, however, was one of the hardened, imprisoned, even martyred priest. Gay life could be viewed only with revulsion as the epitome of the soft woman who loved and diverted men. That men would be so intimate with other men was unthinkable. Of course, even the Capuchin community sought to channel and limit gay tendencies and expression among its members, and they could not escape a sense of Catholic guilt for their orientation. I learned this much later when one of my original Capuchin students bravely came out of the closet but was so riddled with guilt that periodically suicide watches would be established to guard against any such act of self-hatred.

The missions were different and yet surprisingly the same. This I discovered when I traveled to Latin America at the end of the academic year, travel that the General Council and I felt was important. As director of the justice and peace program, I needed a more global sensibility and knowledge of Maryknoll's work in the field. It would also allow Maryknollers to meet me, thus encouraging their support for the new program. In short, it was a personal and political journey.

After hearing so many mission stories, I was excited to be on my way. Each part of the journey had been meticulously planned, and the countries I visited had significant Maryknoll communities except for the first one, Colombia. The others—Venezuela, Chile, Peru, and Nicaragua—promised a further introduction to the Maryknoll world.

I traveled to Colombia to meet with prospective students, and with Joseph Callens, a Josephite priest who, when he found that I was coming to Latin America, invited me to visit. I had also heard of an immersion program in Bogota, run by Mennonite missionaries, which in a six-week time period familiarized students with aspects of Colombian and Latin American reality. I wondered if this program would help our students bridge the gap between theology and reality.

Once I overcame my jet lag, the week I spent in Bogota was fascinating. I met with Joseph and later with the Mennonites to discuss the various elements of what we later called the Bogota internship. The Mennonite community lived among the poor in Bogota and the students in the internship would as well. There was plenty of poverty in Bogota side-by-side with a small middle-class element and, of course, the few very wealthy. Much of the discussion and the spirituality I had been absorbing in Maryknoll was about the poor, and what caught my eye immediately was the consumerism and displays of wealth in Bogota. I walked in wealthy residential districts and shopping areas and saw all the luxuries available in the United States.

The contrast with the poor was thus all-the-more devastating. The street children especially struck me—seemingly thousands of homeless children begged on street corners while the supermarkets were full of food. Joseph worked with these children and he introduced me to the communities they developed, which featured the primary necessities of their street life: group shelter and protection from gangs and drugs. The children had of necessity developed this strategy for survival and at times assumed an adult guardianship of each other. As in adult society, however, they also could exploit one another, and roving gangs sometimes invaded and conquered other gangs. Coupled with their exploitation by adults, these children led organized yet miserable lives. Come morning, dead children were found on the street. They were buried in anonymous graves outside the city.

Venezuela was somewhat different, at least to my eyes. Caracas could also combine poverty and wealth, but homeless children were not in such evidence. The Maryknoll house was actually a series of floors in a modern apartment highrise. Like most Maryknoll center houses in Latin America, the Caracas center was in an upper-middle-class neighborhood. Satellite houses and apartments were located in varying areas of the city and countryside, some in very poor areas. The center houses were themselves almost always controversial, as many had been purchased years ago and were situated in wealthy areas while being staffed by native domestic help.

The net effect was to create an atmosphere imbued with the comforts and standards of life in the United States. This lifestyle comported with the pervasive traditional sense that the missioner came from a superior culture and was there to baptize the uncivilized into a higher faith. Interaction with the native culture was limited among most missionaries, and even the language was learned to pronounce the mass, hear confessions, and in general advance the number of baptisms.

The Caracas center house had just been sold, as the new idea of mission now taking precedence called the missioner to be among and accompany the people, especially the poor, as a presence and a witness. Language training and immersion in the daily life of the people was thus crucial, and any separation between the missionaries and those they served through wealth or culture had to be overcome. The Maryknollers in Caracas had debated the issue to a draw. The new center house was less ostentatious and affluent by North American standards, even though to the poor Venezuelans it represented wealth beyond their imagination.

I found that what was true of the Caracas center house was also true of most Maryknoll center houses throughout Latin America; they were fully staffed and, except for times of regional meetings, largely empty. As the younger missionaries sought to disassociate themselves from the old way of mission, only the administrative staff of the region and the older missionaries generally lived in them.

The Maryknoll missionary work had often been made possible by United States military and foreign policy, and with the help of the wealthy and corrupt segments of Latin American societies. The debate that focussed on the center houses was a debate about breaking with the powerful and creating a new alliance with the poor and marginalized. From my center house room in Caracas, I could see the stark dimensions of this conflict. From my window, on the side of the rolling hills, I saw dozens of shanty towns dotting the landscape.

When I entered the towns and cities of Latin America I saw poverty, but I also observed an organized presence that instilled a sense of dignity and purpose to a struggle in which each person shared a common interest. The church, represented by Maryknoll and other, mostly European missionary groups, had been a part of the oppression of the poor and disenfranchised here. Now, however, a different kind of church was represented here, as local and foreign clergy, along with many lay workers, provided medical care, education and organizing workshops.

On the second day of my visit I went to a base Christian community meeting where practical issues like open sewers and garbage disposal were discussed. Prayer and gospel readings opened the meeting, but soon details of life became the focus. The priest, in this case a Maryknoller, facilitated the meeting, but as it progressed simply became one of the participants. Each person brought food or drink to share, creating an informal and close atmosphere. When I was invited back to a lay missioner's house in the same poor area after the meeting, the contrast between the old Maryknoll based in the center houses and the new Maryknoll based close to the life of the poor was clear.

But this line between old and new was at times blurred. In small towns outside of Caracas, I found groups of Maryknollers living together, priests and sisters and married lay people, as well as the children of the couple. Daily life was sometimes shared, but the power relations between priests and laity were far from equal.

The regional superior who directed the missionaries in Venezuela could only be a priest, and only priests could vote for the regional superior. Though there was often a sense of shared responsibility, in the end priests held sway over all. The lay missionaries tended to be much younger than most of the clerics, usually in their late twenties or early thirties. They could be assertive, and most often had professional training for the jobs they held, whether engineer, nurse, doctor, or community organizer. Priests, on the other hand, usually had as their credential exactly that, their priesthood. They were most often promoted to positions of responsibility beyond their training or ability, and thus could feel threatened by what seemed an influx of those with obvious talent and training prepared to displace them. Nor were priests generally held accountable in their positions for how they performed. Like the Jesuits at Marquette, often the priests I met in Venezuela were decorative pieces, albeit with power.

One of the highlights of my stay was my meeting with Otto Maduro, a Venezuelan sociologist of religion. He had been a university professor, then resigned his position and worked different jobs, including as a part-time consultant for Maryknoll. In general he served as a local contact person who knew the social, political, and religious aspects of his own country. He conducted workshops for the Maryknollers, and often opened doors for them into the academic and political world of Venezuela.

Otto was in his mid-forties, with a large beard that was often teasingly compared with that of Karl Marx. Indeed, Otto is a Marxist with an open mind; for example, he views religion as sometimes a force of oppression yet other times a force for liberation. He defined himself to me as a Catholic with reservations, reservations about some of the doctrines and dogmas of the church. What struck me about Otto was his free and questioning spirit, one that was open to possibilities beyond his knowledge and experience. I asked Otto if he would be interested in coming to Maryknoll to teach in the justice and peace program. Even as my time as director was just beginning, I realized the need for a faculty oriented beyond the United States mission culture, and this is what Otto represented to me.

From Venezuela I flew to Chile, a long plane ride and a telling lesson in geography and distance in Latin America. A lesson I did not want at the time on the dangers of flying was also part of the package, for our plane had to make three passes at the Santiago airport through blinding fog before landing. Peering out the window, the runway appeared beneath the plane only seconds before touchdown and each of the three times saw our plane land perpendicular to the runway before it pulled up and circled the airport. My anxiety over flying turned to admiration for how easily a jumbo jet could be pulled back safely at the last moment. After I landed, however, the priest who met me at the airport told me how often and dangerous the fog could be. Sometime later a plane crashed at the same airport with three Maryknoll sisters on board. All were killed.

Chile seemed in some respects different from Venezuela. On the whole it was more developed, with a long political and democratic tradition, though it was now suffering under the Pinochet dictatorship. I was received at very high church circles, which surprised me. When I inquired as to why these officials met with me, the response involved church and state politics. One of the few protected zones opposed to the Pinochet dictatorship, indeed one of the few surviving opposition institutions with international connections, was the church. In this situation the church created an umbrella under which some Catholic and non-Catholic dissenters could find shelter. Meeting with foreign visitors without clearance from the government usurped civil power and heightened the appearance of church power. Thus I was elevated well beyond my stature, though the discussions in these meetings revolved around generalities hardly threatening to the dictatorship.

Political repression in Chile was terrible, and everywhere I went I was introduced to people who had lost friends and relatives in the maelstrom of the overthrow of the Allende government. Allende had an almost mythic status among the underground that was quietly and deliberately working to bring democracy back to Chile. Clearly some of the Maryknollers were, like the church in general, providing a zone of protection on the local level. Their work, ostensibly in education and leadership, was also a politics of the long run, rebuilding a base to promote a transition to a socialist democracy. Here again, the foreign policy of the United States, which had promoted the Pinochet government, was opposed. These Maryknollers had seen the possibility of the Allende government and the terror of the Pinochet dictatorship, so the abstract ideological battle of socialism vs. capitalism often written about in the American press was tempered.

The Maryknoll center house, located in one of the wealthy areas of Santiago, seemed remote from this political battle. The streets were patrolled by the military to protect the homeowners, and when meals were served, priests of the house rang little bells to summon the servants to appear. It was shocking the first time, and thereafter simply embarrassing. Each day the rooms were cleaned and the laundry done by the house staff. As a traveler it was convenient, but far removed from the liberation theology promoted by segments of Maryknoll.

The countryside was different, and the Maryknollers living in small towns outside of Santiago lived mostly among the poor. I met a young Maryknoller living in a simple hut who, though born into a wealthy family, had signed away his multi- million-dollar inheritance. Having heard this story, I laughed to myself upon meeting him, for even in this most poor of areas he exuded, despite his best intentions, the earmarks of a wealth that no signature could erase.

Later I was brought to a Chilean home where a woman offered me tea and cookies. The house was wood frame, with a dirt floor. It was immaculate, and the woman herself possessed a quiet and unassuming dignity. When my escort alluded to the fact that I was Jewish, I wondered how she would respond. It was an awkward moment for me as I awaited her response, not knowing whether she had ever heard of Jews. In her catechism class, she said, she had learned of the Jewishness of Jesus and then said simply and respectfully, "Ah, another way to God."

I arrived in Peru somewhat tired. I had been gone almost three weeks and the travel was wearying. The tiredness was balanced by the excitement of arriving in a country whose native theologian, Gustavo Gutierrez, had given birth to liberation theology. Gustavo, as he invariably was known, was out of the country at the time. Seven years later, in 1988, I would meet him at Maryknoll when he came to teach in our summer institute and be honored on the fifteenth anniversary publication of *A Theology of Liberation*. The background out of which this theology was formed took on a deeper sense for me here, especially when I went to the outskirts of Lima where hundreds of thousands of poor people lived almost as society's cast-offs. Like Caracas and Santiago, Lima had its wealthy and poor sections, but this encampment outside the city evoked a vast human garbage dump, in the biblical imagery of Job, a dung heap. When I read Gustavo's book about Job some years later, my visit to Lima came to mind. The imagery was biblical, the reality quite contemporary and immediate.

In this area of poverty and despair lived two Maryknollers, a middle-aged priest whom I had never met, and a brother candidate I met briefly in New York. The priest was known as a radical, combining Christianity and Marxism in a way similar to Otto Maduro; the brother candidate, Michael, was in a sense the student of the priest, experiencing a year in the missions before returning to join the Brothers on a permanent basis. It was Michael who took me around, explained the situation of the people and over tea told me of some of his own more formative encounters with the people of Peru.

Michael was intrigued by the religiosity of the people, a combination of native religions brought from the countryside and the Christianity encountered in the cities. The move from countryside to city had uprooted people geographically and thus in their native religiosity as well, which was centered in the locales of their people. Christianity, while foreign, carried a power in their new geographic location. The people wondered whether in entering this new physical territory they should now adopt the religion that was tied to the terrain. The priests, of course, advanced that Christianity was a universal rather than a local religion, transcending geography and culture. Indigenous religions, offered the priests, were based on superstition. By adopting Christianity, the people entered into a universal religion of salvation that placed truth above superstition.

What Michael noticed in this experience, though, was that the people listened to the priests and then simply went their own ways, using Christianity when it seemed to work and what remained of their native religiosity where that seemed effective. The people had little problem integrating both into their world view, giving alternating values to each view. They held the uniqueness of Christianity and the choice of either/or in abeyance, even while nodding in assent to creedal formulae. Abstract universalism was rejected. The assent of these people lay in the power, or lack thereof, to cure a dying infant.

The questions that the missionaries were working out for themselves were also relativized. In most cases they were rarely understood and after a few months most missionaries ceased to explain the questions to the people or realized that the questions were in fact irrelevant. To some I met in Peru, this transformation had already happened and the stories they told of their "conversion" were startling.

Michael's conversion story had to do with a mother who brought her dying child to him for baptism. Michael began to explain to her in his faulty Spanish that since he was not a priest, he could not baptize her child and, because of the elite power of the priesthood, he had chosen to become a brother. He wanted a lay church where perhaps one day people could baptize each other. Michael faced a woman with a dying child who had approached him because his white skin and church affiliation spoke to her of a power, the power to heal. After speaking his piece, the mother then lifted up her son to him for baptism. Michael, in awe of his own inadequacy in the face of the woman's resolve on behalf of her dying child, blessed the boy.

Nicaragua was different from any of the countries I had yet visited. To begin with, Managua, the capital city, existed without an urban center, since the devastating earthquake a few years later had leveled the city center and it had never been rebuilt. Much of the international funding for the rebuilding had been siphoned off by the Somoza dictatorship. The immediate anger of the people toward this blatant theft fueled the simmering anger accumulating over the years of the Somoza reign, resulting in the Nicaraguan revolution.

The disorienting feeling of a city without a center was remedied by the reorientation orchestrated by the Sandinista revolution. The countries I had visited thus far were all organizing to ameliorate or resist oppression. In Nicaragua, people were building an entirely new society from the ground up. The initial aspect of the revolution—the deposing of Somoza and the ascendancy of the Sandinistas—was part of an ongoing process. The revolution continued.

The people were poor and the society as a whole lacked the resources or the political traditions that I experienced in Venezuela, Chile, and Peru. The scale was wholly different and the idea, then being circulated in the press in the United States, that Nicaragua somehow posed a strategic threat to the United States, struck me as incredible. As I drove from the airport into the humid night, reflecting on a capital city that was almost totally suburban, I almost laughed out loud.

The Maryknollers in Nicaragua proved to be different as well. Those who had been there for years, before and through the revolution, had made a conscious choice in support of the revolution. Sometimes the choice had been forced upon them. Other times it had been freely embraced. Some Maryknollers had participated clandestinely in the revolution, at times providing safe zones for guerillas and church workers, other times offering medical assistance, food, even child care.

Educating people to their rights and providing a biblical and Christian basis for these rights convinced many suffering Nicaraguans that it was Christian to join the revolution. Because of this aspect of the revolution, symbolized by Miguel D'Escoto's high position in the government, Maryknollers were held in high esteem by the people and felt themselves to be participants in a common cause rather than mere guests. Rather than missionizing the country, Maryknollers were part of a people creating their own future.

Those Maryknollers who came to Nicaragua after the revolution, including the two lay missioners in my liberation theology reading group, Pat and Ilene, were likewise energized. In a sense they came with even a more idealistic vision, as they had avoided the suffering of war and Nicaragua had become a symbol among progressive Catholics of a revolutionary future that Christians could help build. Already at Maryknoll I wondered if this enthusiasm was as much a displacement of their own frustrated hope in America, as the complexity and contradictions of American idealism and reality could be displaced by a situation that offered an analysis in black and white. A society based on justice, peace, and faith could come into being, if not in the United States, then in Nicaragua.

The legacy of the women killed in El Salvador was still present in Nicaragua. On the one hand, Christians, and Maryknollers in particular, took the deaths of those women as a sign that the struggle continued and that threats to the revolution remained. Nicaragua indeed was a symbol to many sides. Would the neighboring countries of El Salvador and Guatemala continue the massacres of the innocent and civil war or would there be successful revolutions in these countries? Would Nicaragua be the beginning of the end of oppressive dictatorships in Central America or would the revolution in Nicaragua be overcome by a new dictatorship imposed from outside?

Because of the situation, discussions about the church were different in Nicaragua. In fact in my tour of Managua, which included visits with base Christian communities, internal church matters were rarely mentioned. Rather, the participation of Christians in society was the issue, and what values they might bring to this broader arena. Do Christians have a unique and specific set of values to bring to the revolution? Or are these values already present in the revolution, and did Christians need to name these for themselves? The Sandinistas were Marxist in their ideology and atheistic in outlook, though both beliefs seemed tempered by the poverty and religiosity inherent in Nicaraguan society. Was there to be, at least in Central America, a grassroots blending of Marxism and Christianity that defied both Marxist theorists and Catholic theologians?

On the ground, the discussions were often more mundane, or in real terms, more important. Pat was working in a press office in Managua, trying to articulate to the outside world what was happening. Her second role was to search for the physical resources to facilitate that work. Everything was in short supply, including petrol and food, as the years of plunder and civil war depleted resources. The attempt to undermine the revolution through covert operations and an economic embargo had already begun under the Reagan administration, and it was clear to Pat that a second war designed to destroy the revolution and financed by the United States was in the air. What later became known in the United States as the Contras, armed groups dedicated to the overthrow of the Sandinistas, were already known in Nicaragua, mostly from stories of looted villages and terrorist killings.

But the cost of this subversion was still ahead, and Pat and I spent many hours visiting communities and talking about her commitment, which involved leaving her young adult children to fend for themselves in California. Her life had seen its own tragedy, as her alcoholic husband had been recently killed in an automobile accident. The death of her husband and the maturing of her children prompted the issue of what her life's journey would now be. She had always been drawn to Latin America and now was the time to pursue her dream of living and working with the people to whom she was drawn. We talked about the political revolution and her own personal one, and when she drove me to the airport to return to New York, she hoped that my travel had brought me a knowledge that I could in turn transmit to others. It was a task to which I was committed and one whose foundation had been laid in this few weeks' journey.

8

Travels to Africa and Asia

I ALWAYS FOUND IT DIFFICULT to return to Maryknoll after travel abroad. Part of the difficulty was simply in returning to the routine of everyday life after weeks of intense and sometimes exotic travel. Another difficulty was sharing the experience of travel. So much happened in a day or two, let alone in six weeks, and for those who had not traveled to these countries, it became impossible in my mind to communicate the experience. While gone, the lives of others who remained at home continued, and the momentum of everyday life and its concerns overwhelmed the "foreign" experience the traveler had. In short, there was too little time and a lack of context for such sharing. The Maryknoller who had similar travel experiences related to this problem and simply took it for granted. But for me, a newcomer, the experience was wrenching.

Even more difficult to me was to see returning Maryknollers who, despite their travels, had seemed never to have left home. As I returned from Latin America both the same and yet a changed person, I wanted to integrate my new knowledge into the everyday life of the school, especially in our vision and curriculum. Noting our Maryknoll context and our global perspective, this seemed only logical.

The experience of seeing abandoned children on the streets of Bogota, the revolutionary energy of a poor and proud Nicaraguan people, needed to be integrated into our concerns, or even more to the point, should be central to our life in the school. This is what I often heard in discussions with Maryknollers in Latin America, that the seminary and school continued in a pattern where theological assertions of truth and salvation relegated to the periphery or even buried the realities of poor children and revolution. In doing so, theology missed its mark and its challenge, and the life which came within struggle was denied.

This remained over the years. Much of the faculty—Maryknoll, Capuchin and lay—experienced realities in encounters and travel which they could not or thought they could not integrate into their received faith tradition, or even into the expansion of that tradition under Vatican II. The poor were talked about, the need for political, social, and religious transformation was affirmed but the questions posed here were seen as too threatening. Could the continuing and growing presence of the poor become a call to move out of the patterns of priesthood and institutional church life into a more committed and grounded way of living? Were the poor to be talked about in class, sung about in liturgy, in short to be used for the spiritual renewal of the affluent and then left to be on their own? What did Maryknoll's almost constant refrain of a desire to accompany the poor really mean for the poor themselves?

Here the question of God was also posed. What could one say about God in the face of the abandoned children I had seen in Bogota or the children on the hillsides of Caracas who suffered from dysentery and malnutrition? What could one say about God when the reluctant baptism in Peru was performed and the mother brought the child back to Michael for burial the next day? I had faced these questions at the Catholic Worker each morning as I saw the soup lines forming and now again in Latin America. Surely I had no answer, but the question haunted me and I thought, perhaps naively, that it should haunt us as well.

What role did the missionary tradition and Maryknoll itself play in the problems facing the people of Latin America and their difficulty in addressing these questions in their contemporary religious life? I became more aware of this as I traveled through Latin America and discussed concerns with Marxists, catechists, and even some Maryknollers. The missionaries to Latin America originally accompanied the wealthy and the powerful rather than the poor. The poor were subjects of conversion to Catholicism and European "civilization." Often the enforced Christianity of the indigenous population was a sign of slavery. Perhaps the last element of native resistance to the European invasion of Latin America was the people's own religiosity, a symbolic universe that ordered their lives and identity. Christianity helped destroy this universe and thus contributed to the disorientation of the native peoples. In the face of this could we assume, therefore, the general beneficence and validity of the Catholic tradition? Did the "new" missionary effort reverse, nullify, or overcome this tradition or could it be seen as a similar effort dressed in new clothes and language?

I shared these questions with my students in the summer program and then again during the fall of my second year at Maryknoll. In the main they were receptive, especially the young students from the United States and the few students we had from Africa. These included lay people, sisters and priests, though the latter two groups were decidedly mixed in their response. I found that the more their status and identity were invested in the hierarchical church, the less open students were to these questions.

I was intrigued when I realized that theology had so little to do with one's view of these matters. Theology, it seemed to me, was secondary to position and comfort level. This, of course, led to confusion among Maryknollers and students, A discussion about the poor, for example, might be interpreted as an attack on the priesthood. To embrace liberation theology might be seen as an attack on the church.

The consequences of this confusion were illustrated one day by a Maryknoll priest. He had lived abroad on mission for ten years, then left the Maryknoll community to live by himself. Now he was returning to try to live as a Maryknoller again. Maryknoll accepted him back and enrolled him in the school. One day in the middle of class he threw his books down on the table and stormed out of my class. As he approached the door, he turned and screamed that I had no right to talk about suffering and then slammed the door behind him. The next day I was called into the dean's office and questioned as to what had happened in class. The priest's story was that I was haranguing the class and attacking the priesthood until it drove him to his extreme behavior.

I was baffled by this accusation, as priesthood had not even entered the conversation at all. Two years later, I was told by another student that the priest confessed that the discussion of suffering was too close to his own life. He had been unable to remain in class because of the sheer immediacy of the subject to him. The priest, as it turned out, was also gay, and some of his close friends had recently died of a mysterious illness we now know as AIDS.

The following year an Australian priest, also a student, sent me a long letter—six single-spaced typed pages—accusing me of, among other things, attempting to destroy the Catholic faith and especially the faith of my lay students. According to him, several students were no longer attending Mass, and others in hallway discussions were troubled by the questions raised by the lives of the poor.

In the letter he asked if we could speak personally, and when we met in my office he pulled his chair across the room, so close to mine that our knees were nearly touching. At that point he produced a small case and asked if I knew what was inside. I recognized it as a case to hold rosary beads, and he proceeded to tell me how the particular rosary it held had been inherited from his grandmother and was precious to him. To him my teaching was jeopardizing this inheritance and the faith that it stood for. As a priest he was a protector of the Catholic faith and thus he had to speak out, especially for those whose faith was less secure and developed. Women especially, he insisted, were vulnerable to the destructive aspects of questions that had no immediate answers, for they lacked the theological training and discipline necessary to maintain the strength of their faith.

When this remarkable discussion came to an end, we could only agree to disagree. Because I was his academic adviser, I spoke to the dean about pairing him with someone better suited to guide his schooling. The dean was aware of the acutely conservative background of this student and simply laughed. No, he thought, better that I should continue as his adviser, as it would be good for him.

Other students were more open to these questions, and in being so, our roles were at times reversed: at least in my mind, I became their students. In this same class was a Redemptorist priest from Canada, Paul Hansen, who had worked in justice concerns in Toronto and Germany and now was at Maryknoll. In recent years he had focused on the area of corporate responsibility, attempting through stockholder action to compel corporations to act ethically toward the environment, labor, and their third-world operations. In his own community he had recently completed a term as superior.

Paul came to Maryknoll on a sabbatical year of rest and discernment, attempting to focus his energy on the future. Increasingly his work and personal fulfillment were found outside his own religious community. Many of his peer group had left the priesthood and those remaining were older and more conservative politically and theologically. Paul traveled often to the third world and his corporate responsibility work alerted him to many of the issues I was just coming to understand. Moreover, it was clear that the old theological answers that Paul had studied, even the progressive political theology of the German Catholic theologian Johannes Baptist Metz, were wanting. In our first classes together, his responses made me wonder even if he was questioning his very vocation as a priest. I already knew not to broach such a question directly, as it was the most complex and delicate of all for priests to respond to. It was in a sense a taboo subject which was assumed and kept quiet, the secret that everybody knew.

In the end, though, the discussion was about commitment and how each of us within our own particularity live out that commitment. Was he being faithful to those he served by remaining a priest? Could he be more faithful by leaving the priesthood? Did the priesthood, as an institution without the need to support a family, actually give him a freedom to pursue activities that others so obligated were not free to do? With Paul, though, the mutual search for commitment was dominant, and in this I could learn from him. All of our lives contain fulfillment and disappointment, possibility and limitations. For Paul the challenge is to do with them what we can. To continue on we need one another, and his critique of the church rested with whether or not it nurtured our commitment and our ability to be for one another. The continuing failure of the church cautioned him against absolutizing its claims on truth and on himself.

Leo Kazeri was another student from whom I could learn as well. I met him when I first came to Maryknoll for my interview, and during my first year, when I had him as a student, my initial impression of Leo was confirmed. As a priest from Tanzania, Leo came from one of the poorest countries on earth, even poorer than Nicaragua. Still, he exhibited what I later found to be common among my Tanzanian students: a certain sensibility that combined dignity and honesty, along with a wry sense of humor.

The theology taught at Maryknoll was often about the poor, but Leo was *from* the poor, thus offering an entirely different perspective. His mother earned forty dollars a year as a tenant farmer. When missionaries spoke about traveling to Tanzania to be with the poor, he chuckled, as the cost of flying someone to do mission work in Tanzania was more than his mother would earn in her lifetime. Interreligious dialogue in a Western context also struck Leo oddly, for his father was from a traditional African religion, his mother was Muslim, and he himself was Catholic. When I asked him why he had become a Catholic, he told me of the schooling offered by the church and of the priesthood as a further avenue of education and status.

Leo had a Christian faith but, as we talked both between ourselves and among other international students, it became clearer to me that their faith perspectives were a complex mixture of assent and advancement, a desire for a certain way of life and the promise of financial security and personal betterment. There was a cost to their acquiescence to Christianity that became obvious in the stories that Leo told. When we discussed in class the advance of modernity and the ambivalent nature of modern life, Leo related this to his own life, particularly in his sojourn into Catholicism. It was as a youth in the minor seminary that Leo was separated from his family and his village, to be remade, as it were, into a Christian. At home he slept in a common bed with his brothers. The seminary provided him with his own room and bed, practically and symbolically forming him in the way of Western individualism. Celibacy was another aspect of this individualism and isolation, as family is central to his African culture.

I felt in speaking with Leo that his whole life would be spent in trying to return to the village he left as a child. But how could he return to a place within himself that had forever been altered? If he returned to the common bed, it would be in altered form, since now he had been indoctrinated that the common bed that had been his since childhood was part of the backwardness of Tanzania and African culture in general. How could he now view his parents, his family, his village life, indeed even himself, without this ambivalence? Yet at the same time and for the same reason, Christianity had to be ambivalent as well. How could one wholly embrace a religion that effectively denigrated one's own culture, family, and self?

It was these questions that drew me to Leo. On the surface there was little or no connection between us. I knew nothing about Tanzania and little about Africa. Leo had never met a Jew or heard of Judaism, except in reference to the Biblical period before Jesus. In fact, he had learned from the missionaries that the Jews had betrayed Jesus and that Jewish history had ended with that betrayal. As a child he had been cautioned by the missionaries not to betray Jesus in the way Jews had, and he confessed to me one evening over dinner that he had appealed to his own countrymen, in the same language, to make a similar choice. Thus he was quite surprised to find, and at Maryknoll no less, a "living Jew," as he phrased it.

What ultimately drew us together was a sense of peoplehood, African and Jewish, a sense of shared suffering, slavery and the Holocaust, and a shared experience of Christianity as invasive and oftentimes oppressive. It would take years for me to articulate intellectually this bond I first experienced intuitively. It was a sharing across cultures and religions that deepened my own search and sensitivity.

I was also drawn to a Kenyan student, Sister Eugene Jon Guerre, who came to Maryknoll in 1987. Like Leo, Jon Guerre was special; there was a luminous quality to her face which radiated outward. She first appeared in her habit, and only after months had passed did she begin to wear ordinary clothes. It was a sign that she was becoming more comfortable at Maryknoll and more distant from the authority structure back home.

Jon Guerre, too, was a convert to Catholicism and she was quite embarrassed when I found out her father had several wives. I asked her whether she was ashamed of this, and after some hesitation, she told me that she was not, but feared the judgment of others. When I then asked who was to judge such a thing, especially missionaries who had all sorts of arrangements with both women and men, she laughed. The tension had been broken. A fear of her own thought and speech had been dissipated.

I found this in most of my African students, a stream of repressed thoughts and culture waiting to be unleashed. They had been trained as small children and confined as adults within a religious system that disciplined and isolated them. Coming to Maryknoll was often their first experience outside of Africa, and though they were at a religious institution, the diversity of students and the lack of immediate authority allowed them a first glance at their lives from a distance. Instead of observing missionaries from a distance and as subservient, for example, they were now living with and observing them in an intimate setting. The critical theology they were learning, including a critical view of mission, allowed a new perspective. After this experience, many of the African students felt an aversion to the Western church and even to Christianity, sometimes even to the God of Christianity. For what kind of God had allowed slavery, or even the contemporary form of colonialism Africa experienced today? Were they now to join as part of this system of exploitation?

Jon Guerre was soft spoken, yet determined. After her first year at Maryknoll, she expressed interest in pursuing her studies beyond her master's degree. I encouraged her in this, as she clearly had an intellectual vocation. It was then in my office that she cried and confided to me that her community would not allow it. She had come to a juncture in her life, because her superiors feared what she in fact was already discovering in her history and in herself: a desire to explore, to be free, to return, like Leo, to her village. I offered to write her community on her behalf, which she accepted, knowing nonetheless that it was futile. She was caught between a loyalty to a community that had uprooted her and provided her opportunities—that had loved her in its own way—and her desire to take the next step on the journey.

In my discussions with Leo and Jon Guerre I found the African situation to be very different from the one in Latin America. Christianity was brought to Latin America almost five hundred years ago, and the struggle I saw in Latin America and liberation theology was related to the history and direction of that Christianity. The liberating power of Christianity was emphasized as a triumph of a history that had begun in bloodshed. The issue was not whether Christianity was involved in politics, because the church had been powerful in Latin America for centuries. Liberation theologians asked only which side the church was going to be on today, the side of the wealthy or the poor.

Leo, in his thirties, and Jon Guerre, in her twenties, were converts in their own lifetimes. There was an ancient history of Christianity in Africa, but most of the continent was experiencing a westernized Christianity that had gained force in the 19th and 20th centuries. Christianity was less a part of the African fabric than a late, albeit powerful addition heaped upon cultures and social systems that were in disarray. In fact, I heard this openly discussed when some missionaries referred to Africa as "open for our taking," and said that the future religious battle for Africa would be between the missionaries of Christianity and Islam. It was simply assumed that African culture and religion had ceased to be effective agents of symbolic and cultural ordering. Could Leo and Jon Guerre really choose to return to their culture or was their only option to remain and do what they could in orienting the church to justice and respect for the African life that remained? It was a life choice which they often presented to me for comment and even decision. But I could only listen and witness the pain of a history and a religion which was personalized in people I had come to know and care about deeply.

The Asian students were, at least initially, more difficult for me to communicate with and understand. I worked to overcome this barrier by talking to them. In the beginning of the program, most were from Indonesia, and their English language skills were deficient. The language barrier was significant, yet I still saw a strength that intrigued me. Nanuk, a lay woman from Jakarta, listened intently in class and through sheer force of personality communicated her views. Fr. Gregorius Utomo did as well, and when we discussed nonviolence and Christianity, which most American students felt were synonymous, he spoke of his bishop, who had joined the rebel forces fighting for independence from Dutch rule in the 1940s. By joining the movement for independence, Christians, who in a largely Muslim country were seen as Western implants, demonstrated their rootedness and commitment to their own country. Both Nanuk and Gregorius worked in justice efforts across Indonesia with farmers and cooperatives and workers' unions. I noticed in them a certain pride of country and care in their speech. Unlike most of my other students, they lived in a dictatorship where the church was carefully monitored and no doubt their presence at Maryknoll was as well.

The Korean students were highly politicized. Many of them had been involved in student movements and were now part of a church structure that provided strength to opposition stances in a highly polarized situation. Their language skills, though better than the Indonesians, were also lacking. I could listen to their stories and ideas but still had difficulty penetrating the exterior. Still, I could see the excitement when ideas were discussed in class, and they rarely commented on criticism of the church, though it was clear that they, too, had criticism. Often, after weeks of silence, a student would venture a comment that would stun the rest of the class and myself as well. It was as if the correct formulation of the ideas was so important that it had to wait, but once formulated, had to be spoken.

Father Paul Mun was like that. Though he never took a course with me, he often joined me at lunch. He rarely spoke. One day he came to my office and asked if he could write his thesis with me. I inquired why he chose me, and he said simply that it was the right choice to make. His topic was a theological vision of the reunification of the two Koreas, a topic about which I knew little, but which intrigued me. Over the next months we worked together on his ideas, and when he was finished, he asked to see me. He put before me the idea that now, since his theological work was done, his practical work must begin. He proposed traveling to North Korea and then crossing over into South Korea as a symbolic gesture of the unity of the two Koreas.

When I asked what would happen to him if he followed this plan, he responded that he would be arrested and jailed. As his teacher, he requested my advice. I knew it was thus a sign of respect which was to be taken seriously. I told him to follow his path, which, in the end, I knew he would do anyway. Two weeks after leaving my office, he was indeed in North Korea, crossing into the south. Arrested, tried, and convicted, Paul spent the next years in jail and became in the process a heroic figure for many Koreans.

I was determined to understand more about my Asian students and I knew that I could do this only through travel to where they came from, to see and touch the places they lived and worked in. My journey began in 1986 and continued over the years: first India and Pakistan, then Japan, China, Hong Kong, Korea, and finally Indonesia.

The diversity of Asia amazed me and the lessons I learned are many. I was, to be honest, afraid of India—I thought the immense poverty would overwhelm me—but I left India with a sense of the dignity of the people, especially the poor. Thousands of homeless people made the train stations their home, and I remember arriving early one morning by train in Bombay watching the people wash themselves and prepare themselves and their families for the day ahead. One day, standing outside a hotel in Bombay, a young man approached me to sell some postcards of India. His appearance left much to be desired: he looked like a beggar in need of food and clothing. He spoke to me in perfect English, then to other tourists in German and French. It turned out that he had siblings in the United States and Germany, as well as friends in France. He had visited them on occasion, but had remained in India to take care of his ailing mother.

The colors of India were amazing and for me almost overwhelming. When I went to India, Maryknoll had but a few Indian students, though the numbers increased later. I had met Indian theologians who were trying to contextualize Christianity in an overwhelming Hindu culture. One way of doing this was to see the old testament of Indian Christians as the Hindu scriptures, for example, the Bhagavad Gita, rather than the Jewish scriptures. The Indian Christians were such a tiny minority in India that they really had no choice but to Indianize their religion. Because there was little chance of India becoming Christian, Christians could concentrate on contributing certain values and perspectives in their culture. It was the first time I had traveled to a country where Christianity was a minority religion, and it seemed to me healthy. It allowed a certain freedom to Christians, to be who they were without an agenda of conversion and to search out what their contribution might be to another religion, Hinduism. Could Christianity exist and flourish as a tiny minority in India simply in the context of contributing to and gaining insight from Hinduism?

Christianity in Muslim Pakistan seemed in quite a different situation. I saw this through two Dominican students of mine, both missionaries who specialized in the work of strengthening the Christian community in good relation with the surrounding Muslim culture. I had heard them in class, but now saw with my own eyes that the Christians in Pakistan were a ghettoized minority almost under siege. In Karachi, I stayed with the Dominicans and gave talks at the seminary. In Multan I gave a three-day seminar, and among the participants was a Sri Lankan priest who traveled twenty-four hours by bus to hear me, and the local bishop. The priest humbled me, as I wondered what I could possibly say that would justify his sacrifice. The presence of the bishop initially made me anxious, as I wondered if I would offend him with criticism of the church or my evolving understanding of God.

I was nervous the first evening of my seminar, and when I spoke of the European experience of the Jewish people—including the Holocaust—I wondered if the group could at all relate to this particular and foreign experience. What did they think of Jews? The next morning I began again with Europe, this time emphasizing the Christian relationship with the Jews. I wondered now what they would think of the obvious negative light this shed on the Christianity which they embraced. I left time for questions and comments and both revolved around the previous evening's discussion of Jewish life in Europe.

I was lost as to the reason for their interest in this, until the bishop clarified it for me. As Christians in Pakistan, they identified with the Jews of Europe. They wanted and needed to know that which strengthened the Jews to survive the European Christians and at the same time to contribute so much to European culture. In their context these Christians saw themselves as Jews and the Muslims as the European Christians. That is why I abandoned my seminar notes and spent hours on the culture and ghetto life of European Jews before the Holocaust. At the close of the seminar, I was the guest of honor at the bishop's house when he recalled this strange inversion and thanked me for contributing my own history to their struggle.

Hong Kong was a world unto itself, highly developed and increasingly poor. The Maryknollers had a history in this tiny series of islands, for it was here that they had landed after their expulsion from China. In the 1980s, everything seemed to revolve around 1997, when Hong Kong would be reabsorbed by China. Under British governance, Hong Kong had evolved differently from China, especially in the areas of political and religious freedom. What was the task of social activists and Christians in Hong Kong in light of 1997?

This was the more pressing issue to be sure, but the larger context was Christianity in a Buddhist, animist, and atheistic culture. Christians were a significant minority in Hong Kong, but the percentage of Christians when Hong Kong rejoined China would be so small as to go unnoticed. The dream of a Christian China was the fuel of nineteenth and early twentieth century missionary work, and provided the impetus for the founding of Maryknoll. Was this to be the attitude of contemporary Hong Kong Christians? Was the task of Christians to evangelize the largest country on earth? And with the interest of the Western missionary communities, Catholic and Protestant, would the Christianization of China be Chinese in content, or would the Chinese Christians be submerged and become subservient to a more sophisticated, Western colonialism?

My students from Hong Kong worried about these issues. Though they affirmed their Chinese culture, they were fearful of the Chinese government.They were Christians but feared both for their freedom to worship and act out of Christian conviction and for the re-opening of China to Western missionary activity. Some, especially the social and political activists, feared that their institutions and centers would be closed down.

Others feared that they or the people they knew might be jailed or even killed. Few had faith in the guarantees worked out by Britain and China and there was the sense that their fate was being decided by others rather than by the people of Hong Kong themselves.

The Maryknoll presence was interesting. The center house, like the ones I had visited in Latin America, was large and in a wealthy area. There was little hint in either the decor or food that it was in Asia. Outside of the center house Maryknollers were involved in education, hospitals and justice work. Some lived in poorer areas in individual apartments, while others lived in small group homes. I visited the Center for the Progress of Peoples, which had been founded by Maryknoll but was now almost completely independent of it. The center concentrated on linking the peoples of Asia in cultural exchange and human rights work. The staff was diverse, with people from Hong Kong, Philippines, Korea, and Sri Lanka. There was also a former Maryknoller, Jack Clancy, who had left the priesthood many years ago and yet continued his commitment to the people of Asia by living and working there. In a sense the center was a clearing house for these issues. By publishing a newsletter in English it alerted people across borders of what was happening in Asia.

I spent much of my time visiting Buddhist temples and often my students accompanied me. Though my Asian students were all Christian, and with rare exception Catholic, and most were raised within relatively wealthy, Western circumstances, their presence reminded me of my early and persistent interest in Asia. It had started in junior high when I wrote a report on India, and had continued in my university years when I studied Eastern religions. Zen Buddhism was of particular interest to me, and later at the Catholic Worker I read Merton's Asian journal slowly and carefully.

All of this study was heavily filtered through Western eyes, of course, and in my travels I discovered elements that were quite surprising to me. In India I visited many Hindu temples and their beauty appealed to me at a very deep level. I re-read the Bhagavad Gita with new eyes. In Hong Kong the Buddhist temples were often placed outside the business of everyday life, and I watched as people burned incense and offered food with reverence. But there were also temples situated in the heart of everyday life, including one I visited in the middle of a massive housing project. As the Buddha sat serenely, the worshippers gathered in great numbers, burning incense and chanting as they passed the Buddha's statue. Because I was taller than anyone there, and because they held the flaming incense with their hands raised above their heads, I had to be careful of my hair catching fire.

The temples were beautiful but there was also a sadness attached to my visits. At one temple in Hong Kong, the figures of Lao Tsu, the founder of Taoism, Confucius, the great Chinese philosopher, and the Buddha were all seated together in traditional Chinese dress. I asked a student of mine and other students from a nearby seminary if they one day would like to see Jesus placed there alongside the others in similar dress. They appeared quite nervous at the suggestion, and admitted that they had never thought of the possibility and were, if they were to be honest, unsure of their desire. When I suggested that perhaps if this were to happen, it would symbolize the acceptance of an indigenous Christianity in Asia, rather than a Western colonial religion, they were confused. Most of the students had never been inside a Buddhist temple, and had been taught that Christianity was a superior religion. Why place Jesus with the others, when he should be placed above them?

Among Maryknollers in Korea, that issue had already been settled. Christianity was indeed triumphant, which posed a corollary question. Because of the success of missionary work and the growth of a Korean Catholic clergy and institutional infrastructure, should they, as missionaries, move on to other countries longing for the message of Jesus Christ? I arrived in Seoul during Easter week, a time when Maryknollers in Korea gathered for meetings and to celebrate the holiday. Discussions about mission predominated, and it seemed to me that the region was split on the issue of remaining in Korea or moving on, leaving the future of Korean Christianity to the Koreans. Conversion statistics were not an issue, but rather the maturity of the Korean Catholics. Could the Korean clergy be trusted to develop a mature Catholicism in the masses? Were they ready and able to lead in this ongoing process? Or were many of the conversions superficial, with backsliding into animism and Buddhism (or more often, a combination of both) the more likely outcome?

I attended several liturgies in Maryknoll parishes and felt another reality at play. The liturgies and the congregations seemed quite conservative and the atmosphere of respect for the clergy, the centrality of regular attendance at liturgy and confession, seemed almost a throwback to the American Catholicism of the 1950s Everything was intact, under control, with dissent, at least on the parish level, almost unheard of. I wondered if the missionaries stayed to nurture the peoples' faith, or if the peoples' faith and attitude nurtured the missionary vocation. In the United States, the status, not to mention numbers, of the priesthood had declined, even within the Catholic population. In Korea, it was elevated as it once had been back home in the era when most of these priests had come of age and followed their vocation. Was Korea a form of security, a protection from a Western church in decline?

The Maryknollers who were outside the parish structure often had a different perspective. Some worked with labor and told of the other side of the Korean economic miracle—low wages and unsafe conditions. The injury rate for workers was unbelievably high, and when a worker was injured, more often than not he was simply fired. Maryknollers who were politically aware often provided a safe space for Korean Christians to hold meetings and organize, and several Maryknollers had been deported from Korea for such activities.

Even with these Maryknollers, the gap between them and the Koreans they worked with was obvious, at least to the outsider. Susanah Cho, a political activist who planned most of my itinerary and accompanied me throughout my travel, spoke very little English, and though respectful of the missionaries, also kept her distance from them. I felt this same attitude from Paul Mun as well, a sense of pride and dignity, a resolute character which could only see the missionaries as foreign and as invaders. For those who worked toward a reunified Korea and an end to United States military presence in the south, the missionaries were seen as apart of the process of division and occupation. They were the religious arm of the foreign establishment that had participated in the division of Korea and the repression of democratic dissent. Even the most liberal of Maryknollers could not escape their approbation.

By Easter Sunday most of the Maryknollers had gone back to their parishes and only a few remained in the center house. I was invited to the liturgy and accepted, though in the end I wished I had gone elsewhere. A young Maryknoller presided over the Mass, but seemed unprepared, stumbling from one part to the next. The Maryknoller next to me, a priest in his early fifties, was intoxicated. He sang the hymns too loudly and slurred the words of the creed. Though I had lost much of my naivete about religious life, this Easter liturgy shocked me. When I went up to my room for bed, I wondered where my life would have led me if I, too, had become a religious. There were religious who lived a life of commitment, but inside these communities, one saw lives destroyed by the very vocation that had promised life.

China and Japan were worlds unto themselves. In China I stayed with a family of one of my students, Mae Bai. His father was a middle level functionary in the communist party, and when I arrived in Beijing, his car, with driver, was waiting to pick me up. The apartment I stayed in was small by our standards, but privileged in Chinese society. With typical Asian hospitality, and despite my protests, the master bedroom was given over to me. Each evening a large thermos filled with hot water was provided for me to bathe.

I spent my days touring the Great Wall and riding bicycles for the first time since my teens. Since Western tourists were rarely seen outside the hotels, people stared at me from a distance, sometimes following me, and once in a while practicing their English. At parties, I became for the Chinese a representative of my country, and was expected to possess the talent to present the most coveted American export. Rock and roll music. I was asked to sing the current hit songs, and when I tried to explain my interest in these songs and my own inability to sing them, especially in public, my protests were politely denied. It was something that simply had to be done.

Maryknoll was as remote a presence for me in China as was religion in general. Only a few Maryknollers were in China teaching English.

Missionary work, or even work with Chinese Catholics, was prohibited. The people I traveled with had no religion at all, and the last vestiges of commitment even to the revolution seemed to have ended with Mao's cultural revolution. Mao was already a distant figure, and when I searched for a souvenir poster of him, we went from store to store without success. This search became a running joke with the clerks and with my host, until at long last, we found one.

In Japan, Maryknoll had a strong presence and typically the center house was in an exclusive area, bearing little relation to Japanese culture. Here the Maryknollers were known to be conservative and careful, as the idea was to learn as much about this ancient and complex culture in order to at some later date evangelize it. As in China, centuries of missionaries had been largely unsuccessful here. But unlike China, Japan was a modern society and, over the last century, comparatively open. Still, the percentage of Christians in Japan was small.

When I visited Japan, I had yet to have Japanese students. So I latched on to small groups of visitors affiliated with Maryknoll people. This is how I visited the various Buddhist temples around Tokyo. In the afternoons I would often spend time sitting in the gardens of the temples looking at the Buddhas and watching the people come and go.

Tokyo was busy with little attention paid to beauty or serenity. The temples were different. It was almost as if one was hurled from the craziness of the city into the Buddha's quiet arms. In the gardens I felt the quiet calling me, and I was reminded, though in a somewhat different way, of the Hindu temples in India and the crowded Buddhist temples in Hong Kong. The contrast between the Maryknoll house, and indeed the Maryknoll Catholic reality, and the Asian world of Buddhism was impressive and for me instructive. I was neither Catholic nor Buddhist. Primary affiliation and ultimate truth were not the issue. Perhaps it was the wordiness of the West in explaining the theologies of truth and justice, a project I was deeply involved in, which was growing tired within me. Perhaps it was my own wordiness that I had ceased to trust. Even the label of "justice and peace" seemed trite in Japan.

9

Honoring Gustavo Gutierrez

WHEN I RETURNED FROM MY ASIAN TRAVELS in 1987, I realized that my time at and commitment to Maryknoll was drawing to a close. My own sense was that Maryknoll was coming to an end—symbolically for me, and literally for them. I saw the signs everywhere at Maryknoll, from the Vatican investigation of the seminary to the increasing number of priests wearing their clerical outfits for official events. The transition from my travels to the internal world of Maryknoll was becoming more and more difficult.

The initial energy that I had drawn from my Latin American journey was unmatched by my Asian travels, or perhaps I was simply unable to translate the images of Buddhist Asia into my life at Catholic Maryknoll. I was also losing hope that Maryknoll would commit itself more vigorously to the program I directed and the school it sponsored. I felt despair that Maryknoll would ultimately be unable to make the vision it projected its own.

By 1987, Maryknoll had lost almost one third of its members to death, retirement and voluntary exit. The actuarial figures showed a similar decrease in the decade ahead. Many of the most interesting Maryknollers had left before I had arrived, and the eighties saw a further diminution of the most progressive and energetic members. Those who remained either engaged in the ever-widening debate between the liberal and conservative camps, or drifted off into isolated mission outposts far from the arguments and the complacency that was settling in.

People left or stayed in the community for different reasons. Many who left married. But since some who stayed were active sexually, the issue of celibacy seemed to really be an issue of intimacy, the desire to love and be loved. Of course, some who stayed were gay, and therefore the setting of men living together was more conducive to intimacy. Still, since most of the Maryknollers who were gay remained closeted in the larger

world, and since the status afforded priests was largely unavailable outside the priesthood, relationships tended to be clandestine.

People also stayed for reasons of security. Many had little or no mar-
ketable skills, and in our economy their prospects were dim. Some stayed
out of guilt, as if by leaving they were betraying a promise they had made
years before. Finally, there were those who had, with all of the questions
before them, simply chosen to recommit themselves to life with people
whom they had grown to love. Life is complex. I respected those who left
and those who remained.

The fact that Maryknoll was dying was undeniable. A corollary also
became clear: living within or too close to this dying society was simply
unhealthy. Over the years I had become a fellow traveler with Maryknoll,
through necessity and through choice, and so its hopes and despair had
become my own. Yet I was neither a Maryknoller nor a Catholic. I was a
participant in a drama which touched me, but which was not my own.
The decisions made and the tradition itself, the future of Maryknoll and
Catholicism, were out of my hands.

The death was also a long, drawn-out affair where the players and the
rules of engagement constantly shifted. Since the building and the
finances remained, death took on an abstract character. It was almost as
if with life ebbing, an elaborate make-up was applied to signify a renewed
vitality. The chapel was made over at a cost of hundreds of thousands of
dollars. Expensive drapes were hand made for the irregular and beautiful
windows that Maryknoll had in abundance. The entire building was
rewired for the most advanced computer network.

Life now came from outside Maryknoll. Each summer we brought people from around the world to live together and think through the issues
of our time. Rosemary Ruether's visit in 1985 was a turning point, as feminism and liberation theology became central to our summers. The following year James Cone, the enigmatic and forceful founder of Black liberation theology, taught a course for us. In 1988 we held a month-long
celebration of liberation theology, which had as its center a celebration of
the twentieth anniversary of the Latin American Bishops' conference in
Medellin, Colombia, which first addressed the need of the church to
accompany and speak for the poor, and the fifteenth anniversary of the
English-language edition of *A Theology of Liberation*, as well as the sixti-
eth birthday of its author, Gustavo Gutierrez.

In many ways this celebration was the culmination of my stay at
Maryknoll. The ideas were mine and, at least initially, very simple: honor
liberation theology and the man who helped found it. The reality turned
out to be much more complex, a labyrinth of church politics which I hardly knew existed, let along anticipated or knew how to navigate. Because
of liberation theology's link to politics, the story was much broader than
Maryknoll, and as the event proceeded, articles appeared in *The New York
Times*, *Philadelphia Enquirer*, *Boston Globe*, and in newspapers and peri-

odicals as far away as Hong Kong and Peru. The Vatican was also interested, as many of our advertised speakers and contributors to Gutierrez's
Festschrift were unwelcome, or even censored by Rome.

It was in preparation for this summer that I met and came to know
Gustavo. When I had first read his book on my arrival at Maryknoll, I
knew only his words, which were intriguing and important. Later I realized his stature was almost legendary, and more so as the Vatican sought
to discipline the main voices of liberation theology. But Gustavo was
interesting apart from this controversy and evoked a presence that
reminded me of Dorothy Day. Like Dorothy, Gustavo lived among the poor
and tried to enter their lives; like her, he was a deeply spiritual man and
at the same time a fighter. They both believed that their sensibility was at
the center of Christian and Catholic life and the church was often,
because of its policies and connections, at the periphery of that life. What
made the argument between the Vatican and Gustavo so interesting, and
this was true in the case of Dorothy as well, was that they were fighting
over the definition of the center, both claiming the center as their own. Or
rather, they claimed the center for others, the poor, who had no voice, the
people who were considered, in Gustavo's words, "nonpersons," and who
often "died before their time."

Over the year of preparation, I met with Gustavo many times. He was
intensely political in the church sense and realized at a much deeper level
the importance and the possible pitfalls of the celebration I was fashion-
ing. He often arrived at my office door unannounced. We sat and chatted
and before long we were talking about the list of invitations for speakers,
what bishops had been contacted, how Maryknollers were responding—
in short, he was, in a respectful and casual way, though with intensity
and purpose as well, checking that all was proceeding in the proper manner. He affirmed me as the director of the program and at the same time
he was also the director. It was something I noticed only once he took his
leave.

Yet with all of the politics, what impressed me most was Gustavo's
sensibility and spirituality. He was Catholic, deeply so, yet respectful of
other religions and ways of life, and I recall his delight when he told me
that a Hebrew publisher had taken an option to translate his book *On
Job*. Like other liberation theologians I had met, he was deeply respectful
of Jewish history and the Jewish people, and he often inquired about my
Jewishness. Gustavo had written his master's thesis on Sigmund Freud,
and he was aware of the great German Jewish thinkers Ernst Bloch, Max
Horkheimer, and Hannah Arendt. He was deeply affected, pained, and in
sorrow over the Holocaust. When Elie Wiesel, a survivor of Auschwitz and
Nobel Laureate, contributed a short welcome to Gustavo's *Festschrift*, he
was deeply moved.

Gustavo was a force of vitality but he was also on the defensive. He
understood the Maryknoll situation as part of the larger church context,

becoming more defensive and conservative even as its image of dedication and innovation was trumpeted. In fact, Gustavo was deeply grateful to Maryknoll for raising the banner of liberation theology at a time of retrenchment in both the society and the church at large. The cardinals and bishops from whom I solicited statements on behalf of Gustavo were illustrative of these difficulties. Cardinal Kim of Korea wrote a beautiful statement, as did Cardinal Arnes of Brazil, while others either wrote negative replies or were "too busy." Even progressive bishops in the United States demurred, Archbishop Rembrandt Weakland among them.

The celebration was nonetheless a success. The number of applicants overwhelmed us, and we stopped opening letters requesting information months before the deadline for applications arrived. Ultimately, we were able to take seventy-five people for the summer, expanding to one hundred twenty-five for the final week. Hundreds of people came to the liturgy celebrating Gustavo's life and work, and when we presented him the bound essays, which had been written to honor and celebrate him, we embraced. Then he turned and bowed his head to the ovation that greeted him.

Part II

ON THE THRESHOLD OF THE TWENTY-FIRST CENTURY

10

On the Future of Judaism and Zionism:
A Meditation for Those Who Come
After the Holocaust and Israel

OFTEN JEWS, IN THEIR DESIRE TO SUPPORT the state of Israel, conflate Judaism and Zionism into one entity, as if they could not be understood apart. Palestinians often do just the opposite: in their desire to be generous and respectable in the West, they separate Judaism and Zionism as if they are two distinct entities, able to exist without one another. Both Jews and Palestinians are wrong in their respective delineations.

Though there is much to be analyzed in the Hebrew bible and in the history of the Jewish people regarding the interconnection of Judaism and Zionism, including themes in the tradition that join them and those that separate the two, the reality today tells us of their alliance, uneasy as it may be. Without Judaism and the history of the Jewish people there is no Zionism, and without Zionism a central aspect of contemporary Jewish identity is void. Without Judaism and the history of the Jews, Zionism is unthinkable, lacking any foundational symbolic and moral thrust. Without Zionism, Israel becomes a state like any other state and, because of its peculiar and contemporary history, a colonial imperial state still occupying and conquering at the beginning of the twenty-first century while appealing to the Western tradition of democracy and citizenship.

No matter where one places oneself in the support of Israel and its policies or how one defines oneself on the Jewish continuum of belief and practice, another unavoidable connection appears at the dawn of the twenty-first century: that the end of Judaism and Zionism *as we have known and inherited them* is at hand. If it is true that Judaism and Zionism in their ancient and contemporary forms have existed in an uneasy relationship, the last decades have brought both to a fulfillment and to an unexpected dissipation.

It is in the triumph of Judaism and Zionism that the end has come, which, of course, as with other dying symbolic and institutional forms,

does not mean their physical end. Failed entities live on, may even pros-
per, sometimes increase their power, and often trumpet their history as
they come to their end. At this end all is squandered, at least in the ethical and moral realm, precisely as power increases and millennial dreams
are translated into reality.

Judaism and the State

An Israeli sociologist of religion has written that most Jewish Israelis
are hardly Jewish at all; secular to the extreme and culturally Israeli in a
modern sense, they are, in his terminology, Hebrew-speaking gentiles.
The rising percentage of Israelis who identify themselves as religious are
Jewish but in a way that is less and less identifiable in the sense of the
Judaism developed in the Common Era, that is in the last two thousand
years.

Or perhaps it would be more accurate to write that both secular and
religious Israelis combine aspects of tradition and modernity in the context of power and the state in a way that stretches Judaism and
Jewishness to the limit. Without power and the state neither of these
communities could exist for long physically or in the realm of culture and
religion. For the first time since the founding of Judaism, that is for the
first time in 1500 years, secular and religious Israelis are defined as
much by their relation to the state as to their inheritance.

A Jewish-state culture has evolved from the ideology of Zionism and
from the narrative of the European Holocaust. That evolution, however,
distances that same culture from these very sources. How long can
Israelis call upon the Holocaust when time, geography, and continuous
expansion of territory trumpet a reality far distant from the furnaces of
the Nazi era? How long can secular and religious Jews call on Zionism
when the ideology of return and statehood has been achieved beyond
question? How long can the connection between Jewishness and Judaism
be invoked when it becomes more and more obvious that the particularity of Israeli culture has formed another entity in many ways separate
from the culture and history it came from?

In the United States, challenging questions also abound. Since Jews
have developed their post-Holocaust identity through the Holocaust and
Israel, and since these events and culture are becoming more distant and
distinct, what is the future of Jewish life here? The Jewish community in
America is also deeply involved in power and the state, hence its affluence
and ever-increasing status.

The recent emphasis on developing Jewish life in the United States,
rather than relying on the past and Israel for identity, simply highlights
the problem facing American Jewry. To what sources do contemporary
American Jews turn for their identity? Does recognition by the American
state, signaled by the United States Holocaust Memorial Museum in
Washington, D.C., or the placement of prominent Jews in the govern-

ment, provide Jews with a source for Jewish life outside the framework of respect and success?

The forces of Jewish renewal, interesting and provocative, are small, and most Jewish progressives are now employed by or serve the Israeli and American states, at least in their thought and theology. Orthodox Jewry continues to link itself with Israel and with the question of assimilation as if, as servants of the state, the refusal of assimilation can be defined by the study of ancient texts, distinctive dress, and refusing intermarriage.

What American Jewish progressives, centrists, and Orthodox religious fail to grasp is that the same trends that affect the Israeli secular and religious communities help define us as well, that the assimilation of Jewish life to power and the state is occurring so rapidly that it proceeds almost without comment. In the space of little more than fifty years, with the Nazi period coming to a close and the founding of the state of Israel, and, as importantly, the empowerment of the Jewish community in the United States, the entire position of world Jewry has changed dramatically. In 1943 who would have thought contemporary Jewish life possible? In 1943 who would have dared dream that Jews would have a state that dominates the Middle East and would be so closely and prominently linked with the United States, the global superpower of our age?

A Constantinian Judaism has emerged in Israel and America and that form of Judaism follows the same pattern of Constantinian Christianity, or any religion in service to the state. The benefits of such a relationship are obvious, especially to a religion and a community that has been outside and pursued by the state for so long. Who could deny the advantages of being among the powerful rather than being hounded by them? And who as a Jewish community leader after the Holocaust could argue that the connection with power would elevate *and* demean us at the same time, thus arguing to choose moral elevation at the expense of physical security?

As a government official or military officer in Israel, the argument of solidarity for justice over power or security is impossible to make. There is a logic to statehood and power as there is to a Constantinian religiosity: support the state, quiet dissent, look the other way, assert innocence, portray power as promised by God and as a way toward redemption, depict those who dispute your power as political and cosmic enemies, make alliances wherever and with whomever to further your goals. Did we really think that placing Jewish before state would somehow defy the logic of the state and its intellectual and theological servants, including those in America?

The situation cannot be worse, as the state of Israel, which claims to act in the name of the Jewish people, settles its borders and consolidates its power, and the Palestinians even with their state, survive as remnants of a population and a territory formerly known as Palestine. Jewish dissent is limited to questions of percentages: percentage of land taken or given; percentage of Jerusalem held or shared; percentage of the population as Jewish or Palestinian. What is really at stake is the percentage of the Jewish ethical and moral tradition to be jettisoned or retained. But can an ethical and moral tradition be portioned out, keeping this, throwing away that, as if justice is relative to the needs of the powerful?

On the other side of Jewish power a Palestinian diaspora has been created and the remnants of that diaspora within historic Palestine are segmented and ghettoized. The argument today within the Jewish world is about the relative nature of this situation, how much is to be alleviated or extended. There has been almost no discussion of justice in any meaningful sense of the term, for that would mean the end of the Jewish state *as it has been defined by those in power and by the intellectuals and theologians in their service.*

A Judaism Passing from History

What then is to be done? The parameters are small. To oppose Israel on the grounds of justice is to commit a sin defined theologically by the powerful as a betrayal of a people and a history. To be silent on Israel is to participate in gutting the tradition of any real sense of justice and compassion. Regardless of one's perspective, Israel continues more or less on the same path. States do not reverse their gains out of ethical considerations and there are always those intellectuals and theologians who will legitimate policies which in any other situation they would condemn outright.

The dilemma is significant for the generation that has struggled with and through the sea-change in Jewish life even as it becomes more problematic at its conclusion. Those who thought it was impossible for Israel to carry its territorial ambition to its logical conclusion were wrong, as were those who felt the traditions of justice within Jewish life would mitigate the tragedy that has befallen the Palestinian people.

The emergency years of post-Holocaust Jewish life ended with no just reconciliation and the destruction of Palestine accelerated after the Palestinian surrender at Oslo. Still, in the struggle and in defeat, a battle has been waged and some Jews remain rooted in the pursuit of justice. *In a solidarity with the Palestinian people, even in the exile that comes with this solidarity, these Jews carry the tradition of Jewish justice and compassion with them. They are witnesses to a face of Judaism and Jewish life that is now passing from history.*

What of the next generation? Jews of the next generation can only dimly feel the pulse of Jewish life that existed before the Holocaust *and* before Israel. They inherit a Judaism and Jewish life, even a Zionism, imbued with state-culture and all its attributes. The *before* of Jewish life, including its rich and diverse tapestry of testimony and argumentation, is mostly rhetoric, and transparently so.

What are the young to do with this transparency and the identity they are encouraged to embrace that cannot stand the light of intellectual and religious probing? The *after* of Jewish life is often without substance and foundation, and the twin formative events of our time, Holocaust and Israel, with the obvious bridge to Palestinian suffering and freedom, cannot be discussed openly and pursued to their logical conclusion because that conclusion leads to charges of betrayal and complicity in the destruction of the Jewish people.

Lamenting this situation is necessary and yet limited. The question before us is the future. There is no future in the past, and the present is so radically different from the past that it provides little in the way of instruction. As the expansion of Israel comes to its conclusion, the past recedes, and even the traces still present, recognizable to those who struggled within the coming hegemony of the state, are too weak to resurrect.

What is left is the intuitive sense of justice and compassion that young Jews may feel, whatever its source, and the struggle for identity common to those of their age. One wonders if there is a way to guide this intuition and identity against the community leadership and general societal indifference to thought and action in pursuit of justice.

When limited to the framework of Jewish life, this task is nearly impossible. The framework itself mitigates against this formation both because of its overall direction and dwindling ethical resources. The tradition of ethics and morality has been gutted to such an extent that even those within the community leadership who see the need for a way forward are stymied, unable to turn toward their own sensibilities for lack of direction. If they move forward where will they be and with whom will they affiliate? If they are committed to Jewish life, in what institutions will they work?

The way forward within is paradoxically outside, with others who are also struggling to name the intuitive sense of justice and compassion in an identity that is linked to the past yet open to the future. One searches in vain to find any Jewish institutional framework that combines this internal search within the larger non-Jewish community of seekers and activists.

Though there are pockets of hope, small groups that spring up in response to justice concerns and the Jewish renewal movement, captured intelligently by *Tikkun* magazine, these are mostly within the present generation raised in the tradition and forced to define themselves in the post-Holocaust and Israel era. Their influences are predictably dated. They include the theology and activism of Abraham Joshua Heschel, the civil rights, anti-Vietnam war, feminist movements of the 1960s and 1970s, the Holocaust theology of Elie Wiesel and Emil Fackenheim, as well as the later mysticism/activism of Arthur Waskow and Michael Lerner.

The latter returnees to Judaism and Jewish life, now adorned by the honorific and self- appropriated title "rabbi," are generationally formed and now in their 50s and 60s. What is as important is their battle with the Jewish establishment and their desire to form the nucleus of the next Jewish establishment. Though the crisis in the present Jewish establishment is real and abiding, with little future beside that which institutional and financial power provides, there should be little illusion as to the success of the insurgent forces.

To battle for the center of the tradition, renewal forces have given over much of their own critique, if you will, narrowed it so as to be seen as responsible. To be seen as responsible, Jewish renewal has been willing to jettison ideas to their left and argue only within a Jewish-identified concern. The result is an inbred argument, almost a civil war, with a Jewish establishment that is irrelevant and unknown to the next generation. Couched in a Jewish framework that they know and seek to perpetuate, Jewish renewal forces argue for a return to innocence and commitment, and this within a rabbinic framework that no longer exists and for most Jews cannot be accessed. Fighting the battles of their generation, they cannot speak to the next generation of Jews for whom the struggle has already been lost.

Of course the struggle of each generation, forward though it be in its intent, is, by the end, retrospective as well. The struggle is about events and actions occurring and soon enough, or even at the same time, past. Each generation passes on its struggles as if they are ongoing. The next generation declare those struggles resolved or irrelevant.

In Jewish life this is occurring already with the refocusing of identity most often demonstrated in the wearing of religious jewelry, such as a star of David and clothing accessories, such as a kippa. But beyond these religious articles and an often strident assertion of Jewishness in the public, most often university, arena, the emptiness is clear. Who among the young wanted to celebrate Israel on its fiftieth anniversary and, at the same time, how many times can Jews continue to read out the names of the Jewish dead from the Holocaust *as if nothing has happened in Jewish life since the liberation of the death camps.*

The contradictions, though for the most part inarticulate, are too many and ongoing. The young inherit the calamities that have befallen the Jews of Europe and Israel, one imposed externally, the other promulgated internally. They also inherit the disaster that has befallen the Palestinian people, especially in the faces of the diaspora Palestinians they meet more and more frequently today. What do they do with the tragedies they confront, which they had no hand in creating? They have little knowledge from which to discern a direction, and few leaders that will confess and take the bold steps that might at least witness to them the possibility of a future.

They leave, wander, find other communities to associate with. They disappear in universities and later in the professions. At some point they travel to Israel only to find Palestine, or what it once was *before.* They marvel at the identity that other groups assert—African Americans, women, gays and lesbians, and sometimes Palestinians. Much of this identity is romanticized to be sure, an identity before empowerment or covering over aspects of empowerment that have yet to be acknowledged.

Sometimes Jews meet members of these groups who recognize their own identity beyond a romanticization of the innocent and here the meeting of the disappointed may yield a different kind of dialogue. Is it here among the chastened and humbled, those in exile from the institutionalized propaganda of the leaders who rarely live what they speak, far away from the struggle to be the new establishments, that Jews may find a way forward? If so, what will provide the anchor for this search, the identifiable mark of Jewishness that is distinctive and a bridge to others?

Embracing the Covenant in Exile

There can be only one answer to the question of Jewish distinctiveness, though the elements and expression of that distinctiveness may vary: that is the covenant. The covenant has been and continues to be the collective binding and calling of the Jewish people, and those elements that surround the covenant—language, sacred texts, ethnic and cultural expressions, politics, and now statehood—are contextual, add-ons that form a history but cannot project a future. This covenant cannot be rescued from the past and reformulated, though the echoes of the past covenant may be instructive. Nor can the covenant be constructed anew, as if the deepest part of the person and his or her commitment can be assembled from indiscriminate materials.

Rather, the Jewish covenant, as it has been throughout history despite the claims upon it and against it, is freely chosen *as a grounding from which a future can be envisioned, a rootedness that allows trust and exploration, a commitment that demands a justice with compassion, a fidelity that is engaged without finality and in hope, a witness to the possibility of more truth and life.* Ultimately, the Jewish covenant is embraced as a testimony to the above—grounding, rootedness, commitment, fidelity and witness—and it is this testimony that establishes or, if you will, continually reestablishes the covenant.

Though many understand the covenant as coming from God and to which we either assent or deny, this understanding of covenant is different: *that our grounding and fidelity—our very witness—establishes the possibility of God or, if not God, the possibility of trust as a vehicle for human flourishing.* Could this perspective on covenant be a place where intuition and fidelity come together in a configuration of justice and compassion, healing and forgiveness, so that the possibility of radical newness, of beginning again, of reconciling what was once thought irreconcilable, of embracing the "other" who is no longer other, can come into being?

Traditionally, the covenant cannot be embraced alone. Community is primary to that embrace because the covenant is a public embrace of a

God and a world with inherent questions and difficulties, rather than a privatized, ecstatic experience. Above all, the covenant is a series of ancient and contemporary conversations, about meaning and justice in the world, that in our embrace we agree to be attentive to, participate in, and carry forth into the future. This very conversation presupposes a dynamic of changing partners, various contexts, and explosive possibilities.

Those who claim the covenant through the ages, and here we can include Christians and Muslims as well, often seek ownership and use of it to excuse injustice and atrocity. Institutionalized claims are often the weakest and the community closest to the covenant is more likely to be one in exile from the religion it claims. If Christianity, because of the atrocities it justified, forfeited what it claimed so boldly, thus leaving those who seek the Christian covenant wandering in exile, is it any less true of Judaism today? Why else the false claims and the increasing exilic community of Jews that swells as the twenty-first century dawns?

It is also true that the shared exile of Jews and Christians may mean a shared covenant as well. Thus the division of Judaism and Christianity, a peculiar and fascinating tragedy emanating from the first centuries of the Common Era, may now be in the process of being healed because of the failure of Judaism and Christianity individually and together. Attentive to but not dependent on the particularity of the traditions as they represent themselves to the world, exilic Jews and Christians may be finding a commonality that will emerge one day as a particularity.

There is reason to assume that many Muslims, including Palestinians, are in exile as well, and will join this journey of covenantal embrace. For Jews it is worth noting that the way forward is less to anticipate a joint embrace of the covenant than to continually move toward such an embrace with those Jews and non-Jews who are moving in a similar direction.

The failure of Judaism, a failure shared with other world religions, and the triumph of Israel, a triumph over another people shared by other states, means there is no way back to the Judaism and Jewish life *before*. There is only an *after* that remains undefined. If there is a Jewish particularity to be found *after* it is difficult to recognize from here.

For some Jews, these perspectives on the future of Judaism and Zionism, as the *before* for which there is no *after*, signal an end too difficult to contemplate. For others, such a scenario allows a victory to those who seek a Judaism and a Zionism turned into an expanded Israeli state, as they have become in our time. For Palestinians the loss of the struggle within the Jewish community over both Judaism and Israel and the inability of the next generation to take up that struggle represents a political and moral loss.

Politically, Jewish dissenters have at least helped to minimize what would have been even greater losses of land and life on the Palestinian side.

Morally, those who have stood with the Palestinians have at least demonstrated the possibility of a reconciliation between Jew and Palestinian. Still, loss is almost always contextual and limited. It also is generational.

Perhaps the covenantal center shorn of its particularity will suggest to the next generation of Jews and those with whom they journey that the division of Jews and Palestinians is itself a division and an injustice that rests on a particularity that is untenable. The loss of history here may serve as a place from which a different perspective, unavailable to those who fought for the center of a tradition that has come to an end, can emerge.

In the expanded Israel they inherit, a successful Zionism reaches from Tel Aviv to the Jordan River and contains within it the remnants of Palestinian life, almost four million Palestinians, those with citizenship in the pre-1967 borders of Israel and those in Palestinian areas of the West Bank and Gaza. Though Palestinian citizenship is offered, it will nonetheless be enveloped and surrounded by Israel, becoming clearly visible as an apartheid, unjustifiable, division between Jews and Palestinians.

The next generation of Jews may simply see this division as a historical compromise that needs to be overcome because other divisions in this generation's life have become irrelevant. Even the growing Palestinian diaspora will influence this next generation of Jews, for their meeting inside and outside the Middle East will encompass more closely shared aspirations and questions. To the next generation of Jews this injustice and division in Israel/Palestine might look like other borders and boundaries that are crossed so regularly they cease to exist, at least in the imagination of those who cross them.

The other option for the next generation, one likely to be taken by most, is an apathy toward Judaism and Israel and the religious quest in general. They will observe others in their quest for identity and continue to struggle for affluence and status in the lands in which they live. The great crime of those who squander traditions, who identify so proudly with a stream of history that they systematically empty of content, is that the following generations are characterized by alienation and indifference. The assimilation of the previous generation to power and the state leads in the next generation to an assimilation into the general culture where the struggle for meaning and purpose is buried.

Hence in America the Jew disappears into the professions and in Israel Hebrew-speaking gentiles appear. At some point, the distance that the assimilated travel from their place of departure, or rather the accumulated distance traveled by both forms of assimilation, becomes a place of no return. In the truest sense of the term, the assimilated are out of touch, lost, unrecoverable, gone.

Still, the search for meaning continues as a constitutive aspect of life and with that the search for justice and compassion. Though articulated differently in every generation, the question of God is present in this search and thus the covenant as well.

In the end, and at the end, after a long struggle in which much has been suffered and now much has been abused, the next generation is left the task of reconstruction. That reconstruction is open, like the covenant, and is grounded in a fidelity that has a direction that sometimes surprises even the analysts lamenting the loss of what has been inherited.

There will always be those who embrace a covenant that is as elusive as it is demanding. No doubt some will call themselves Jews in the future, as they have in the past.

However, the exile today poses questions and possibilities for that embrace that are peculiar and unremitting. The guidance that we, the generation of the *before*, has offered has been, for the most part, unhelpful, and, too often, a scandal. Those who come *after* Judaism and Israel are on their own.

11

On the Future of Christianity:
Reflections on the Burden of Victory
and the Dissolution of Empire

TO BE A CHRISTIAN TODAY is also to come *after*: after the globalization of Christianity. This globalization was accomplished sometimes through witness but more often by linking with expanding and conquering empires. There is little doubt that most of the world's Christians received Christianity through acts of military conquest than through willful consent. As was true here in the Americas, parts of Africa and Asia have also seen Christianization through conquest.

What is done with that Christianity over time is often at odds with the will of the dominant. Hence, a colonial Christianity is a contract which often explodes in the face of those who control power in the name of Christianity. If colonial Christianity is the heir and engine of the expansion of Constantinian Christianity, it is also part of the demise of Christianity *as it has been known and inherited.*

When we add to Christianity and its canonical gospels the history which it has created over the last two thousand years—what we might call the historical gospels—then the narrative of Christianity becomes complex and difficult. The Hebrew scriptures can act as a model here: they are a sacred book, canonical in status, but also a history, at least a history in the more traditional way of exploring the meaning of formative events in a people's experience. Thus the beautiful stories of early Israelite life are read in the synagogue along with the most vindictive and violent ones.

Prophetic condemnations are also preserved and read, so the covenant is revealed and challenged, as is God's love and anger. The Hebrew scriptures, as the story of the origins of the Jewish people, is extended in different form through Talmudic discussion and ought to be extended beyond those first centuries of the common era. Should not the reading of Jewish history, including in our own time the formative events of the Holocaust and Israel—with, of course, the displacement of the Palestinians—also be read in the synagogue? The history of the Jewish people would then be seen in a continuity of its drama, questions, culpability, and hope.

For Christianity the canonical gospels would be supplemented by the historical gospels, the gospels of Columbus and Colonialism, of Treblinka, Apartheid, and Christo-Slavism. These more violent gospels would also give birth to gospels reflecting those who opposed this violence, gospels of resistance of native peoples and Christians who argued for a different path. One thinks here of such figures as Bartolome de Las Casas, Dietrich Bonhoeffer, Dorothy Day, and Martin Luther King, Jr.

What would it mean for Christian liturgy if the canonical gospels were supplemented by both the gospels of violence and resistance? Surely, acknowledgment that the *before* of Christianity—the stories of Jesus for example—has a history of two thousand years that is part of Christianity itself. At the turn of the millennium, the *after* of Christianity would meet a deeper challenge.

The Challenge of the Historical Gospels

What is that deeper challenge? Could it be the recognition that Christianity, birthed from Judaism and influenced by the various cultures it conquered and became part of, is a particular faith and something more? This "more" is, at one level, a continuation of Judaism and the development of its specific path. Yet it continues to evolve into patterns that diverge from both Judaism and what has been known as Christianity.

In fact, Christianity is itself a term for a variety of communities in the West and elsewhere that carry the same name but diverge in belief and creedal structures. Contemporary ecumenism and its hope for unity aside for a moment, Christianity is as diverse today as at any time in its history. This is part of the burden of victory—more than a billion people carry the label of Christian as the definition of what Christian means becomes more elusive.

The creedal structure is the easy part, as councils can begin to hammer out more conventional definitions of the unity of Christians, at least in terms of belief. However, this unity in belief has often obscured the differences in culture and activity that Christians engage in on a daily and communal basis.

Are the affluent Christians of America in community *because of a common faith* with the poor of Latin America? More bluntly stated: Are those wealthy white teenage American Christians who wear the apparel produced by the poor indigenous teenagers of Peru in the same Christian community? James Cone, the African-American liberation theologian, wrote of this dichotomy in terms of African American and white within the United States many years ago, as did the Latin American liberation theologian, Gustavo Gutierrez, with reference to the division between first and third world Christianity.

Still, both Cone and Gutierrez, while writing of the more obvious divisions within Christianity, also write of the divisions within communities. Thus churches standing right next to one another may be divided into rich and poor, and some churches have both the poor and the wealthy within the same church. Are the wealthy and the poor connected by belief or divided by socioeconomic status? Is the division of socioeconomic status itself a question of faith? Here faith is seen less in terms of belief than in patterns of societal interaction that influence understandings of Christianity. Or rather, the divisions within society call forth a response that challenges the faith of those who help create or benefit from societal injustice.

Few Christian theologians would argue with the statement that the expansion of Christianity has been accompanied by great crimes and that the globalization of Christianity has led to new and pressing questions about the efficacy of Christian belief and practice. While the *before* of Christianity is diverse, holding forth commitment *and* violence, the most difficult understanding is that often committed Christians were and sometimes today are violent. The attempt *after* to separate commitment and violence, as if authentic Christianity would never countenance such abuse, cannot be historically verified.

As historians of the conquest of the Americas point out, for the most part the conquistadors were Christian in their outlook and mission. It is a Christianity that most Christians *after* the conquest would prefer to deny as real Christianity. For when a history is carried for more than a thousand years within a tradition, and when this part of the tradition erupts in the contemporary world in Nazism, apartheid, and Christo-Slavism, to cite just the most known examples of Christian-influenced violence of our time, then the separation of authentic and unauthentic Christianity seems difficult, if not spurious.

As is now evident in Judaism, Christianity contains within it a cycle of violence *and* resistance, militarism *and* reform, that seems to have no end. So often those Christians who seek another way are disciplined by Christians themselves and by the hierarchies that speak in the name of Christianity. And as often the Christian prophets, once disciplined by the church, are then posthumously resurrected into official or non-official sainthood. In this resurrection, however, the dominant tradition reasserts itself and defines and restricts the message of the prophet. The cycle continues, chastened to be sure for a time, yet always threatening to erupt. Even *after,* the *before* is present, waiting.

Within Colonization and Evangelization

Clearly, Jesus is caught up in the very cycle he sought to end. A militarized Jesus, especially against his own people, is a main theme of Christian history, though it hardly ends there. A militarized Jesus has been presented to the peoples of the globe, arriving with the conquerors and used to decimate local cultures and religions. At the same time he has been both comforter and liberator, often being turned against the very power that subjugates the people.

In conquering and resistance, the language and symbolism of Jesus has become Christianized and the figure of Jesus has replaced indigenous symbols and language. But was this the message of Jesus himself, writ large in a cycle of domination and uprising? As importantly, is this Jesus himself being fought over and argued about or are the powerful conveniently using the symbols of Christianity in their empowerment?

Without judging all Christian denominations or Christian history itself, it is clear something essential has been missed. Instead of asking about the mission of Jesus as objectively understood, as if with the historical information known about Jesus this could be ascertained, perhaps it is more important to understand the contextual impulse of Jesus, an impulse that can be seen in other situations before and after Jesus.

When writing of the Mexican adoration of Our Lady of Guadalupe, an adoration that combines Christian and indigenous elements of Mexican culture, the anthropologist Clodomiro Siller suggests that this combination is an attempt by the indigenous people to comprehend their "own living religious tradition in the new circumstances of colonization and evangelization." That is, confronted by this new and overwhelming force, in this case Christianity, the indigenous people struggle to maintain their religious voice even if combined and sometimes disguised in the symbols of the conqueror.

The situation in Palestine in the first century was quite like this more recent event of conquest, though the end result was somewhat different. Jesus' life and ministry is lived within first century Palestine under occupation by the Romans and with the independence of Jewish life and worship under assault. Jewish religious authorities are the mediators between Roman authority and the Jewish people: for all their failings they are trying to keep together a social and religious fabric under political and religious attack.

Jesus operates within this situation, aware of the predicament of both Roman and Jewish authorities, and despite the inherent danger, through parables and appeals to the prophetic tradition, attempts to subvert both. His language is coded, almost secretive, though it is ultimately understood by many who hear him. Over time the Roman and Jewish authorities become aware of the challenge presented by Jesus *because other Jews throughout Palestine are also challenging these authorities*. Could it be that the challenge of Jesus and those who followed him, as well as other Jews who were likewise apprehended and crucified, is what many continue to do in the contemporary world, that is, seek within colonization and evangelization their own living religious tradition?

Surely both the elite leaders of Judaism and the emerging Christian religious authorities missed this understanding and in so doing, at least to some extent, misunderstood the meaning of Jesus. As the Jewish tradition continued, Jesus was defined as violating the very essence of Judaism by living outside and beyond the law and introducing a messianic vision in his name that violated Jewish sensibility.

Emerging Christianity saw Jesus in an opposite way, as fulfilling and nullifying a Judaism chained to a law that blinded Jews to their own salvation. Jesus as the messiah became the defining message of Christianity, though how the messiah did not accomplish his task of redeeming the world, at least in its most obvious sense, continues to fuel theological speculation and debate. Historically speaking, wars have been fought over these interpretations and Christians remain divided over them.

It could be that both the Jewish and Christian traditions, caught up in the theological debates of law and love, awaiting the messiah and embracing the messiah who has come, have both turned their backs on the essential message of Jesus himself. Or perhaps the message of Jesus is less the issue or even the particular vision that Jesus had, if in fact either can be ascertained with any certainty.

Perhaps the importance of Jesus is found less in the division introduced after his death than in the continuity he represents in Judaism and in the religious quest itself. Jesus knew himself in only one way, as a Jew, though his Judaism was diverse and influenced not only by different currents within the Judaism of his time and the peasant culture he was raised in, but by Greco-Roman culture in its imperial and military power.

The Judaism and the Palestine Jesus was born within—his context of colonization and evangelization—helped shaped Jesus' life and view of the world. Jesus' religious vision, a combination of his inheritance and context infused with his particular synthesis of the past and present, is what he presented to the world. For Jesus at least, the prophetic call he experienced was what was needed at that particular time in the land and religion of his birth. Those in authority were, at least to his mind, unable to present a vision requisite to the needs of the people and respond to the commanding voice of God.

Though Jesus is now at the center of the narrative, the canonical gospels, writers some years later, describe their religiosity, Jewish and Christian, within the new situation of struggle. Read in this way, the gospels record an ongoing dialogue of what it means for particular communities to maintain their living faith in new circumstances of colonization and evangelization. Jesus is, in his life and in the interpretation of his life, within a continuity of Jewish history. These new communities are defining themselves over against the contemporary Jewish communities of the latter half of the first century and the second century in their struggle to realize the living tradition as they interpret it.

What were Jesus and the early Christian communities about in the larger horizon? If for the moment we set aside the polemical aspects of Jesus' life and the life of the early Christian communities as recorded in the canonical gospels, and if we see the particular call of Jesus and the early Christians as the contextual expression of Judaism and Jewish life within colonization and evangelization, then the horizon becomes clear. Jesus and his followers were trying to introduce a practice of religion that combined spirituality and social reconstruction, a radical response to the alienation and disarray of their day.

Jesus especially saw the Judaism of his day as inadequately responding to the militarism, urbanization and Romanization of Palestine, at the same time enforcing a Jewish way of life that suffered or even acquiesced to this oppression. The Judaism of the prophets which Jesus identified with and the subversion of injustice through an inclusive social program of common life was, at least from his perspective, in abeyance, if not actively persecuted. In the end, Jesus realized that both the colonial authorities and the internal Jewish authorities were in collaboration, albeit with different means and ends in mind. What the Roman *and* Jewish authorities demanded was a partial practice of Judaism, one that Jesus and those who followed him could not accept.

Those Jews who followed Jesus, and those after him who raised up Jesus as an emissary from God, linked with prophetic Jews of earlier times in the desire to overcome the partial practice of their inheritance. Rather than being for or against Judaism, as if the prophets and Jesus were simply arguing for the renewal of a religion, the task was something different: to crystallize in each generation an approach that carried forth the question of God and justice over against those who sought an easy accommodation with the ethos and powers of that time.

The formative events of Judaism and Christianity are clear in this regard, as Sinai and Jesus are less about establishing religions than they are about re-embracing a call to a practice that overcomes injustice and establishes a social realm that enshrines a way of life that honors the creator and humanity. The attempt to respond to this call in each generation is itself an attempt to overcome partial practice and the need for each generation to engage in this struggle is precisely because the struggle is never complete.

Overcoming Partial Practice

As both the Jewish and Christian traditions record in their scriptures, the attempt to overcome partial practice is essential and itself incomplete. Practice is constantly in need of critique and expansion. The accretion to the next generation, sometimes in the name of a previous struggle, is no guarantee of a practice which attempts to overcome its partial nature. In fact, it is this very claim, enshrined now as *the* practice, that often has religions deflecting new attempts to overcome partial practice in the next generation or beyond.

In an ironic way, Judaism and Christianity carry forth formative events that sought historically and in dramatic fashion to overcome partial practice, but even as they celebrate and liturgize these events they too often seek to limit practice in the present. Those who claim to have overcome partial practice most often do so as if their practice represents an ontological truth which must be imitated by all those who come after these events. Religions in general, and Judaism and Christianity in particular, use the context of colonization and evangelization and the attempt to overcome partial practice in light of that situation, to illumine truths that are then decontextualized. Instead of seeing a common struggle over the generations and cross-culturally in light of practice, practice is seen in light of truths that rise above struggle and context.

But what if the attempt to overcome partial practice is the essence of the religious quest? What if formative events within particular peoples and communities provide the revelation and discipline—if you will, the foundation and symbol structure—that shape this attempt and also catalogue its failures? What if the founding of religions, always after the formative event itself, preserves this particular attempt at overcoming partial practice *and* at the same time sets up boundaries that practice cannot transgress in the future?

In this sense, tradition makes available to those who come *after* a particular overcoming of partial practice, at the same time also making it more difficult to overcome partial practice in the present. Religions seek to capture the formative event as its own and define it, yet the overcoming of partial practice is always a crossing of boundaries from the past to a future as yet undefined.

This is as true with Christianity as it is with Judaism. The event of Jesus, as it was with Sinai, is one of crossing boundaries within and outside of the religion's and people's inheritance. It is the charting of new ground *as a struggle to be faithful to the times in which one lives* that is then captured and canonized. That difficult and original fidelity, a fidelity that did not know the future and risked everything in the present, becomes in a short time and sometimes beautifully, a religious calendar where everything is known in advance.

Exodus is followed by Sinai every year and at an appointed time, as Christmas is followed by Easter. Unlike the Israelites and Jesus and his followers, our destination is known in advance. Our fidelity is lived within another fidelity, sometimes with depth and other times superficially. Real history becomes symbolic and the struggle within history often becomes an internal struggle that is hidden and pious.

In religion, truth is known and the object is to bring oneself and others to know and embody that truth. Has this been the Achilles' heal of Christianity, beginning in some of the canonical gospels and framing the historical gospels of 1492 and apartheid? Perhaps this is why force has been so important to the spreading of the gospels and why the good news has often been oppressive for those who have involuntarily received it.

The show of force with religious legitimation and as a religious act also accounts for the inability of many Christians to recognize the fidelity of others, their struggle to be faithful in the context of colonization and evangelization. For each culture and people has its own history, its own evolving struggle and need to cross boundaries, in short, its own context and journey. Possessing "truth" means definition over against the other who does not possess it. Thus the practice of Jesus and his Jewish compatriots, which should be seen in a continuity within Jewish history and as a crossing of boundaries to overcome partial practice in the first century, early on is seen as a defining point between the old and new Israel.

This defining point is a judgment on the previous practice of Jews and Judaism, as if there were only one practice, and because of this, Jesus' practice itself is defined as not truly Jewish. In the first centuries of the common era, Jesus' practice is used as a defining point within Christianity itself, as orthodoxy and heresy are explored and enforced by an emerging Constantinian Christianity. Using the state, Christianity then defined itself over against other religions, upholding the practice of Jesus as truth even as it violated that practice with such regularity that the offense was buried too deep to recognize.

After the rise and fall of Constantinian Christianity, what does it mean to be Christian? At one level, and this has been affirmed by many Christians in recent decades, to be Christian is to be Jewish. The Hebrew scriptures and the Jewishness of Jesus is crucial in this understanding of a renewed Christianity. Yet at the time of this belated affirmation, Judaism itself is embarking on its own Constantinian project.

Just as the Jewish community needs to be confronted in its claims of innocence and redemption in the United States and Israel, a renewed Christianity too often romanticizes the tradition it once demonized. Often this claimed inheritance takes the place of a critical analysis of Jewish and Christian history as it has been and is lived today. Instead of acknowledging its Jewish past as one aspect of a diverse history that continues to evolve, the Hebrew scriptures and the Jewishness of Jesus can become a shelter where other critical questions, questions posed to Christians, are placed off limits.

It seems that the question is less the *before* of Judaism and Christianity or even the *after* of Constantinian Judaism and Christianity, than it is the struggle to identify the religiosity requisite to the context of colonization and evangelization in our time. What are the resources needed to confront the cycle of atrocity, the affluence of the few and the poverty of the many, the lure of modernity as defining of life and possibility? If Christianity has spoken of the certainty of salvation, the question now shifts: for most of the developed world, at least, the question is whether there is any salvation outside modernity.

Overcoming partial practice thus is joined to the times in which we live. In the era of modernity, colonization and evangelization demand a response that neither asserts nor denies Judaism or Christianity, for in one sense they are weak and irrelevant. Since most Jews and Christians are either benefiting from colonization and evangelization or are on the underside of it, the values and vision of this system are defining. For the most part, Judaism and Christianity live within and at the pleasure of this more powerful socioeconomic and religious system.

To survive and benefit from this system, both Judaism and Christianity have assimilated to modernity and those who defy aspects of the modern project with jeremiads against it are themselves benefiting from the system. In America, Judaism and Christianity have combined Americanism and modernity in a peculiar way, to be sure, but the result is mostly the same. In the end it is difficult to disengage these values and visions, especially when protest actually reinforces the very system at issue.

But overcoming partial practice is never simply resisting a system of values and beliefs, as if there is a place to go that escapes the power of colonization and evangelization. The *before* of colonization and evange-lization is a myth, for these forces always coalesce in different configura-tions. There is no *after* either, for a new set of forces will come into play even as the old ones pass away.

Romanticization of the past and the prediction of a messianic future are, in the end, the same projection of a purity and unity that has never and will never exist. What can be gleaned from the past and projected into the future as a way of dialogue with the present is a discipline that seeks an ever deepening ground. This discipline has always been eclectic—one thinks of the discipline forged at Sinai and in the life of Jesus and his fol-lowers—and will always be so. Is it helpful, then, to see this discipline only within the framework of Judaism and Christianity?

Clearly the discipline so essential to overcoming partial practice has been forged within and defined by these religions, but the evolution and eclectic nature of the discipline tells us that the religion itself has been an overall framework, a superstructure if you will, for a variety of thoughts and actions that are defined as Jewish and Christian in retrospect. Still, by granting on ontological significance to the religions themselves, as if God ordained the survival of Judaism and Christianity as essential to redemption, the resources we need to draw upon today are limited or need to be revised in order to be incorporated.

Often this means rejecting certain resources as foreign or even demonic, as unJewish or unChristian. Is this why the Jewish exilic com-munity, formed in the movement from oppressed to oppressor, is joined by an increasing Christian exilic community, formed in the attempt to overcome a history of oppression and injustice? Though using different symbol structures or distancing themselves from any at all, these Jews and Christians are increasingly drawn together in hope and despair, in articulation and the inability to speak to the public. When they act and speak do the divisions of Jew and Christian or even the joining of the two traditions as Judeo-Christian make sense of them and to them? Will those in exile from Constantinian Judaism and Christianity form the next stage of Judaism and Christianity or are they involved in a movement within and beyond these traditions and history?

The contextual nature of partial practice provides a response to this question. Since the times in which we live change and since the practice we inherit is time-bound and eclectic—since there has never been a pure or static Judaism and Christianity—then surely our practice is also time-bound and eclectic. What is changing is the ability of Judaism and Christianity to orient, absorb, and redefine practice as its own.

At the same time disciplines outside Judaism and Christianity—we might call this Enlightenment or secular practice—have grown in power and importance. Since most of life in the West is lived within this latter practice, religion either legitimates and sometimes adds elements to it or is further marginalized. If there is no salvation outside of modernity, Judaism and Christianity have little choice but to confirm that salvation, albeit in their own language and symbol structure.

There are movements that seek to break with the Enlightenment and secular world, as if resistance through symbols and faith statements can transcend the world. The desire for another world is false when those who affirm it are in fact deeply enmeshed, often happily, in the fruits of the world they condemn. If the vast majority of Jews and Christians practice modernity, then the partiality of practice has to be found within that symbolic and physical system of belief and activity. Rather than accepting or rejecting modernity in thought and religion, the struggle is within, and the partial practice to be thought through and overcome is found within this reality rather than outside it.

Overcoming partial practice and the discipline requisite to it can only be understood within the context of our lives, our real practice of life, and the partial quality we find there. For us, at least, partial practice can only be seen on the threshold of the twenty-first century, within modernity, Constantinian Judaism, and Constantinian Christianity. Only then can a practice and a discipline *after* be envisioned.

A New Diaspora

If there is no going back to recapture the *before,* there is also no definition of *after* if the present is thought to be transcended. Yet if neither *before* nor *after* are available in the present, what resources are there to overcome partial practice? What will give substance and structure to a discipline crucial to contemporary life?

Here the covenant comes into view. Rather than a revealed truth which gives birth in the formative events of Judaism and Christianity to a way of life endlessly emulated, the covenant is a place of commitment where the deeper structures of life and mystery are available to be embraced. The covenant offered and embraced at Sinai and in the life of Jesus is available to all generations who search for a language and symbolism that is understandable and available.

Instead of seeing Sinai and Jesus as the revelation of God in a unique way, the challenge is to understand the embrace of the covenant as ongoing, within Sinai and Jesus and beyond as well. One might say that the covenant passed through Sinai and Jesus, became visible and explicit for that time and place, and was so powerful as to form peoples around that experience. For those who seek to embrace the covenant, Sinai and Jesus are relevant as reminders of that covenant and the call to search out the covenant in our time.

Thus the *after* of modernity, Constantinian Judaism, and Christianity, must be envisioned within contemporary life, and this does not mean jettisoning Judaism and Christianity or the events and figures within them. Rather the particularities of the embrace of the covenant *then* must be studied and relativized: they are part of our inheritance and point to obligation and possibility. The history of the covenant once embraced as the only way to authentic spirituality is also part of our inheritance, one that points to the limitations of covenantal embrace when sought in one particular way and thought valid for all time.

Though some may see this as a relativization of the covenant, it is a relativization that may free the covenant from an embrace that pretends an unchanging absoluteness. Instead of relativism or absolutism, perhaps we should see ourselves as journeying with the covenant and with each other. Then the embrace of the covenant is always before us as a challenge and the journey is less within a set religious calendar than into the unknown, as the future is anyway. Journeying with the covenant therefore frees the covenant and ourselves to continue on within our context.

Christians who embrace the covenant as a challenge and a journey find themselves with Jews and others who, in exile from their own communities, are coming together. Yet community in exile is a contradiction in terms, as that exile becomes more articulate and as the destination of exile becomes more apparent. Exile often begins with force, physical displacement through war and persecution. But exile can also be chosen in order to continue to be faithful to values and visions essential to life and dignity. Most exiles understand their physical and spiritual displacement as temporary, at least in the early years. Yet the reality of exile is less the return to geography or tradition than it is a journey without return.

In the beginning of exile, the recognition of other exiles is placed in the category of "other." It is interesting that there are other communities producing exiles, but this is viewed as irrelevant in the long run because of the anticipation of an imminent return to the mother community. Over time, the realization that the exile continues and for most is permanent allows another understanding: that one's community is where experience and values are shared and the exilic community is that place of sharing. For exiles share everything except a common symbol and belief structure, and it is only a matter of time before a shared experience leads to the development of such a structure.

The recognition on the part of exiles that there is no return, only a journey forward with others who share a common fate, creates a new diaspora. Here the difficulties of exile are complemented by the realization of common commitments, and dispersion, whether involuntary or voluntary, becomes a hope rather than simply a travail. Into exile the traditions are brought in articulate and inarticulate ways. Diaspora welcomes those diverse resources as elements of an emerging world view, neither disparaging nor affirming of any one tradition.

In effect, the abuse and brokenness of each tradition, the cause of exile, renders triumphalism mute and humility, born of necessity, the norm. Each tradition and rebellion against it, thus the Enlightenment and secular tradition as well, are part of the new diaspora. As the Enlightenment and the secular have produced an exile from the abuse of their own initial vision, a cycle of tradition and rebellion against it is found within this evolving diaspora in hope of taking this cycle beyond assertion, critique, and negation.

The hope is to build an affirmation within analysis, a vision that has within it a critical base of thought and action. By refusing to privilege any one tradition or perspective, the new diaspora cannot assert a truth that calls others to obedience, a truth for all time or one that transcends time. Rather, the building of a value structure from many historical, geographical, and cultural experiences allows a diaspora aware of the exile that created it and determined to build a world that at least minimizes a further creation of exiles.

Does Christianity survive and flourish within this new diaspora? Does this diaspora, as it does for Judaism, spell the end of Christianity *as it has been known and inherited*? The question can be understood within a prior affirmation. It is the end of Judaism and Christianity as we have known and inherited them that has produced exile and thus the beginnings of the new diaspora on the threshold of the twenty-first century.

Even more basic a question is the ontological need to concern oneself with the survival of either religion or religiosity. If both Judaism and Christianity are the sum total of those who in the past struggled to embrace the covenant in their time of colonization and evangelization and those who abused that covenant in violence and injustice, then the preservation of these frameworks is secondary.

Perhaps a later generation will label the new diaspora, or aspects of it, as a continuation of these traditions under a different name. Perhaps a later generation will call the new diaspora Jewish or Christian or Judeo-Christian in a substantive sense. The naming of this struggle in retrospect is hardly the issue. Rather, the struggle itself in our time is the task.

The victory of Christianity has become its own burden or, if you will, its possibility. There is no return to the *before* of Christianity *as if nothing has happened since the promulgation of Jesus as the messiah*: the *after* of Constantinian Christianity cannot be simply a renewal of old themes and imagery. As Jews in exile must deal with life after the Holocaust and Israel while both continue in memory and expansion, so too Christians live after a Christianity that continues on the public stage. Competing for the defining label of Jew and Christian is provocative to be sure. In the end, however, it falsifies the exilic experience and hinders the creation of the new diaspora.

12

Spirituality and Politics in the New Diaspora

FOR JEWS AND CHRISTIANS who come *after*, there remains a variety of religious realities that are important to the development of the new diaspora. The religious base from which Jews and Christians come continues on as if the *after* does not exist. Institutionalized Judaism and Christianity flourish and seek their own future; debates within the mainstreams of these traditions are cyclical, maintaining a dynamic that seeks to enlarge its audience and membership.

Those who come *after* also participate in this religious world, sometimes on the fringes of these institutions and often within acceptable limits of the debate. The lure to identify with these institutionalized forms of Judaism and Christianity is tremendous, as status and legitimacy of authentic religiosity is defined by them. There is also the strategic lure, refusing to cede the religious terrain to those who seek to define moral and political agendas.

Still there is more. For those who come *after*, the *before* of Judaism and Christianity has been internalized. The narratives within Judaism and Christianity are powerful forces for meaning and order and those who have been raised within these narratives are shaped by them. If those who carry these narratives forward in an official and recognized way are themselves unaware of the new diaspora or seek to repress its existence, are the narratives themselves to be abandoned? If the traditions that carry these narratives seek an ownership and exclusive right to them, depriving those who seek *after* their insights the possibility of developing a new and expanded configuration, are the traditions themselves to be seen as captive and incapable of movement?

The reality is more complex and diverse. It may be that tradition tends to conform to power, as the Jewish philosopher Walter Benjamin once commented, but it also has a revolutionary potential inside and outside the parameters that have been assigned to it. For is it true that the Jewish covenant is now only to be found within rabbinic interpretation or that the life of Jesus is to be constrained by those who preach his word from church pulpits?

Seen within the broader tradition of faith and struggle, the covenant and the life of Jesus are two, albeit powerful, expressions of the struggle to be faithful. This fidelity is found within the historical moment to questions and challenges that are contextual and common across geographical and generational boundaries. Hence they are able to speak to us when loosed from the carriers of these events and narratives that use them to protect the status quo.

The preservation of these explosive narratives can be applauded only if the continuation of this meaning in our lives is at the forefront. On occasion this occurs, as those who, in power and status, inherit the Constantinian synthesis of Judaism and Christianity reach beyond the borders of their claims and legitimation of the structures and the state to touch the power of the narratives they proclaim. In these cases, fuel is provided for corporate renewal, as in the Protestant Reformation, or individual commitment, as in the case of Dietrich Bonhoeffer.

Thus the struggle to be faithful reaches within the very institutions that originally cause the exile of so many. Narratives remain, and witnesses to the power of the narratives periodically arise. Still, the main force of religion is to limit renewal and witness, so as to limit the power of reform. The power of institutionalized religion is found exactly in its ability to carry these explosive narratives *and* limit their effects, that is, manage what is almost impossible to control. Those in exile experience and embody this irony, as the religion that introduced the narrative and language of protest is also the one that expels its embodied voice in the present. In short, the desire for a radical inclusion across boundaries of geography and faith is often formed within a Judaism and Christianity that seek to limit those same boundaries.

Those in the exile have their feet in both worlds, the world that brought the narrative to their attention and the world beyond the religion's grasp. This is often true for those who remain within the institutionalized form of religion. They have their feet in both worlds as well, except they are able to remain in the form that is outmoded for others. The possibility of an alliance is therefore suggested, as the exiles within and without share a common ground. Just as those outside explore areas forbidden by the institutionalized religion, so those inside attempt to take that institution to new ground. Could the broader tradition of faith and struggle be enhanced, is it, in fact, given birth by this dual reality that transmits and explodes the radical narratives of different religions and religiosities?

The third party, those who seek to diminish or harness the change involved in the solidarity of those exiles within and outside the gates of organized religion, also comes into play. The exile outside is one in danger of losing contact with religious language and ritual, in effect being spun out into a universe where the evolution of religious thought and perspectives becomes unavailable. The exile within faces the danger of being trapped in an unproductive and at times destructive debate about what it means to be Jewish or Christian.

The third party seeks to define as "outside" both groups and to delegitimize them or, if this is impossible, to coopt the language and the movement that both exilic groups bring to religious life. In large part, though there are exceptions, the conservative reaction and the liberal ecumenical groups have made up this third force. They seek to prolong what is coming to an end and therefore name their own broader tradition as preserving religiosity against secularism and religious radicalism.

Yet it is here that the strict dichotomy between secular and religious is also exposed, because religious change, indeed religious life itself, is always embedded in the world. Salvation history or a transcendent sphere that organizes and gives meaning to life on earth above or without humanity is a mythic understanding of the world that often seeks to domesticate the radical events that are formative to Judaism and Christianity. *It is as if the Exodus or the life of Jesus was pre- ordained, fixed before its occurrence, without the details or the sometime random quality of history. It is as if the covenant were only given but not received, accepted but not argued over, forced rather than embraced.* It is only within this understanding that the exclusive nature of Judaism and Christianity can be upheld.

The secular, that is the living and interpretation of life as if history has its own force, allows a critical understanding of these stories that are now in mythic form. Secular history and criticism can refocus the main elements of the events that became religious in retrospect and enhance those elements of the events that were religious at that time. Of course, secular history that accepts its own bias toward secularity uncritically can lose the religious dimension of the event as well, as if the actors within the event were modern secularists. Thus the mythic combined with the secular may be able to recapture the struggle within the formative events of Judaism and Christianity as a way of identifying the substance of ancient times.

With this alliance of mythic and secular, the religious sensibility takes on a different form, or rather allows a different entry point. Seen from a distance, respected but demystified, a critical religious and secular understanding of the formative events of Judaism and Christianity teaches those within and outside of these respective communities that the essence of these events cannot be captured or owned. Exclusivity and uniqueness is challenged as well, for the experiences at Sinai and with Jesus are seen as extraordinary and ordinary experiences within history: extraordinary in their effects, ordinary in the issues faced over the ages.

Justice and injustice, meaning and anomie, the formation and break-down of community, the struggle between liberation and domination, the choice of community or empire, the willingness to struggle and suffer for ideals, the claim of martyrdom as desire to wrestle meaning from death— these realities are specific to certain times and cultures *and* common in the history of humanity. They are therefore found in the past— and here the preservation of these events is crucial— and also in the contemporary world.

Are the lives and texts of Elie Wiesel or Etty Hillesum, both witnesses to the destruction of European Jewry, any less precious or revealing than the canonical texts revered in Judaism and Christianity? Surely they can be read side by side with Biblical texts; they in fact explore the meaning of Biblical texts within their own experience. In doing so they provide further commentary, and here many in institutionalized religion see their significance. At the same time they are witnesses that provide texts themselves with their own validity and they, whether affirmed or not, change the religiosity possible in our time.

Who today can relate the formative experiences of Sinai and Jesus without being shadowed by Auschwitz? Still, if the reference point is only how these witnesses and texts interact with the bible, then the force and the reality of their witness is narrowed. Why not see Wiesel and Hillesum as part of the long and continuing struggle in history to affirm humanity even in the darkest places? Wiesel and Hillesum therefore are equal contributors to this story in the new formative event of Holocaust, which, though unique, also shares a commonality with other suffering in history.

An evolution within religious life is found as the struggle to be faithful continues and is recognized in a more inclusive pattern. This evolution is neither progressive, in the sense that we are above the past, transcending its narrowness, nor liberating, if we mean by this a liberation from the formative events that have shaped Judaism and Christianity. Rather the movement toward inclusivity and the elevation of our own experience to the level of religious seriousness and responsibility simply affirms that the commitments that gave rise to religions are in evidence today.

The same sufferings, questions, daring, and hope that drove the Israelites into the desert and the early followers of Jesus to endure persecution is available to us and must be pursued in our context. Though for some the strength to venture forth will come from the Sinai and Jesus events and will be named in a traditional way, for many more these events will be in the background, and for still others, perhaps the majority in modern culture, these events will be too distant in language and force to even name as important.

To think that the majority of those born Jewish or Christian will journey through life centered on the formative events of these faiths is an illusion. As we know, even those who claim these events as formative too often live the illusion of owning these events for their own purposes, thereby diluting their power. Is this pretense to ownership any different from the distance from religious language and ritual experienced by so many? Are they not tied together?

The assimilation of those who name God and those who cannot speak the name of God are connected in so many ways. This is true of those who refuse assimilation or at least struggle against assimilation in its totality. In the modern era, the search for life and meaning, for justice and commitment, takes place within a colonization and evangelization that is Jewish, Christian, and modern. Could it be that these elements, configured in a different way, are the only way forward? The prospect is not perfection or a pretense of transcendence. Those on all sides of these issues, within religion and outside it, who struggle over religious terrain and who feel they have left it behind, are all together, here on the threshold of the twenty-first century.

The differences of opinion and the struggles that define our sensibilities and prospects do not separate us out of the world in which we live. Rather the struggle to be faithful should be seen as a series of insights, embodied in the world, that seek light in a world often shrouded in darkness and seek to speak for a humanity that is just and caring in a world of indifference and atrocity. Revealed truth as an appeal to separation and salvation falls away.

If spoken at all, revelation can only contribute to the larger public discussion as an insight to consider, and here too that insight will only take on force if revelation is seen as possible here and now. Revelation can only make sense as ongoing within and beyond the borders of ancient times and the religions we inherit. It must be possible within an overall assimilation to the modern world—in history, in the secular, informing it but not overwhelming it, moving us deeper into the world rather than overcoming it.

One is struck with the worldliness of Sinai and Jesus as well as those who have gone before and after in the traditions that grew around these events. Sinai and Jesus make sense in their worldliness and take on a power when their humanity and historicity are affirmed. The sheer struggle to leave Egypt and wander in the desert, and the courage of those who evangelized in Jesus' name, those who, like Paul, were imprisoned and executed, are highlighted in this history rather than diminished. At the same time, the limitations of these events are brought to the fore.

Who today affirms the decision to execute those who defied Moses' vision or the definitions of orthodoxy in the early history of the Christianity that separated Christians from one another and also excluded Jews? The violence in the desert is mirrored in the violence of later Christianity, and though the cycle of atrocity began long before either Judaism or Christianity and exists today when the power of both religions have waned, the contribution of these religions to atrocity is obvious.

Simply by shading the events with goodness and purpose—or as often being silent about the night side of these events or the history they gave birth to—does not address the questions raised by history. By cleaning up Judaism and Christianity the cycle of atrocity can continue and return almost without recognition, as the religious militarism of Jews in Israel/Palestine and Christians in Bosnia demonstrate. Even with the best of intentions, being silent on the violence of Judaism and Christianity in their historical journey allows new violence to erupt in their respective names thousands of years after their formation.

If the secular criticism of religious orthodoxy is important, a religious criticism of secular orthodoxy is also important. Fidelity is found within history, but history is neither mythic nor linear. Rather, history is the place through which we enter the struggle to come to grips with life in its personal and communal dimensions. Without a discipline, albeit constantly questioned and refined, only a surface reality can be encountered.

The meeting of insight and commitment in history can be found within an evolving discipline, a practice that is inherited and improvised in every generation. What is history if seen only in mythic or secular terms? In the former, life is lived within an event that is no longer historical: there is nothing left to do but to imitate patterns of life that because of the changed context cannot be imitated. In the latter, life is lived as if there is nothing else but the moment and that moment is always unique and fleeting. Thus connections are tenuous, as are commitments beyond those of self and pleasure. Even self is fragmented and ephemeral. Why develop a discipline when all is obvious and surface?

In the new diaspora, history is neither determined nor completely open. As actors in history, we are linked to the past and the future through a present that calls us to encounter life in a focused and open way. The focus is on the self and community in relation to a life that cannot be understood simply or completely, one that probes the questions of God and humanity without a predetermined beginning or ending. Those in the new diaspora are poised between affirmation and negation as traditionally seen by religious and secular leaders, refusing an easy solution of the complexities of the world.

Faith, as if there is no doubt or anxiety, or doubt, as if there is no possibility of affirmation and commitment, are two sides of the same conclusion. Both are resolutions of that which cannot be resolved without the loss of depth and struggle. Both are partial without the knowledge of their partiality and without a practice that seeks to overcome it. It is the discipline that seeks to overcome partial practice that can inform us that while a definitive resolution of questions of ultimate concern are impossible in history, a practice of discernment and action are essential to the probing of these questions.

To critique the religious and the secular is to employ both in a new dynamic. The exposure of the violence of Judaism and Christianity is neither to affirm nor deny the insights that these religions offer. Instead, Judaism and Christianity are relativized as imperfect carriers of events and narratives and as imperfect vessels of practices that have at different points in history offered the world death and life. Relativizing religion is not relativizing faith but understanding the connection between the two in a different way. Judaism and Christianity *as religions* are neither ordained by God nor ontologically essential to the faith journey. Faith itself is always seeking deeper ground and rests uneasily in simple formulas and assertions.

Perhaps faith is an entry point into the unknown and, when pursued, places us in a different place, one lacking definition or finality. The secular reminds us of the openness of reality as faith reminds us of being drawn to a place within *and* beyond history. Attempting to overcome partial practice comes from a discipline that relativizes the known and seeks the unknown through a committed way of life. It is commitment and the ongoing reflection that relativizes and pursues questions that cannot be answered.

Here the covenant returns in importance, though now freed from the confines of any one articulation. At Sinai the covenant was heard rather than revealed and embraced rather than owned. In Jesus, the covenant returns in dynamic fashion. His entry into the covenant is portrayed as tender and explosive.

Of course, there were many before Sinai and after, between Sinai and Jesus and after, in our day and in the future, who hear and embrace the covenant, as well as those through the ages who encounter the covenant in different languages, cultures, and religions. *At the same time, the covenant is neither formed nor static but exists in the tension of history and culture as the beyond that we are drawn to. The covenant baffles and enlightens, resists definition and calls for it. The covenant demands a practice that is always seeking to overcome its limitations.*

Worldliness and the Spirit

To embrace the covenant, to struggle to be faithful within the broader tradition of faith on the boundary of organized religious life, is to be in a difficult situation. The status and order provided by institutional religion is denied and at the same time the naming of the boundary is still in the future. The world continues, indeed the world is at the forefront of the calling, but the secular is uncomfortable as well. Between the known and the uncertain, those exiles who form the new diaspora are aware of the pain of the world and the power of religious and secular institutions. Forging a critical understanding of history and faith can be a lonely task, and more than a few of the exiles disappear into spaces that have as yet neither name nor place.

In the final analysis, of course, that which is named and empowered is real *and* illusory, created by human beings and always changing. Power exercised today is power lost tomorrow or changed beyond recognition while carried under the same nomenclature. Is the Judaism and Christianity of our day the same as yesterday? Would a first century Jew or Christian recognize contemporary Jews and Christians as linear inheritors of these respective faiths? Though the orienting symbols remain intact, the meaning of those symbols has changed tremendously. It is difficult to conceive of an immediate recognition in more than the symbols that decorate synagogues and churches. Interpretations and the clusters of meaning that are related to social, cultural, and political forces are more determinative of religious hope and meaning than is often understood or acknowledged.

The tension between inherited orienting symbols and their meaning is an opening for the continuation of Jewish and Christian tradition as well as its transformation. Orienting symbols have remained even as their interpretations have changed in evolutionary and sometimes radical ways. These symbols are always awaiting new meanings to be assigned to them. For Jews, covenant, Torah, and liberation are foundational; for Christians, covenant, messiah, and salvation are foundational.

Placed in history and in the broader tradition of faith and struggle, these foundational elements merge into a new configuration where covenant is central and where Torah and messiah, liberation and salvation search out new meanings and practices. Finality and static assertion, *as if what was known in the first centuries of the Common Era guides us today,* drop away, and the search itself suggests different meanings and the inclusion of different symbols. Even the guides that become available to us at the close of the twentieth century are provisional rather than ontological, created by us rather than transcending history.

What kind of politics can emerge from such a view of religion and religiosity? If all is in flux, if the conversation carried through the centuries in the Jewish and Christian community is affirmed and transformed into a community as yet unnamed, what politics can be generated and sustained from such a sensibility?

Clearly politics as institutional legitimation or confrontation is unavailable here, as is the future development of such a politics. Rather than abandonment of this form of politics, the relativization of religious orthodoxy demands the relativization of political orthodoxy. Constantinian Judaism and Constantinian Christianity demand certain kinds of political structures and interventions to continue their own power. As institutional forces with their own need for a distinct sphere and protection within the state, Constantinian Judaism and Christianity demand a Constantinian state, one that has a power to enforce order, that needs religion to legitimate its status as organizing authority and has the power to create the space for organized religion.

There is no end to this Constantinian cycle, though the cycle itself has had and will continue to have different manifestations. The relation between synagogue, church, and state is different in every society, and the attempt to eliminate the religious part of this cycle, for example in the former Soviet Union, only raises one part of the system to a higher and more powerful status. Legitimation shifts, to be sure, but the need for religious justification simply takes on a different symbolic form. All states need religion and all religions in their institutional form need states. This was the point of Walter Benjamin's insightful statement that tradition has a tendency to conform to power. In fact, all traditional and institutional formations, whether religious or political, need power to continue and expand. The relationship of synagogue, church, and state is symbiotic.

The new diaspora is weak in this regard. Lacking an institutional framework, those who find a home in neither religious nor secular life are powerless in the framework of politics as it is typically practiced. In this sense, the new diaspora is hidden, unnamed and unorganized, but because of this hiddenness it is also free of the constraints and culpability that institutions breed. As citizens within nation-states and as heirs of cultural and religious traditions, those in the new diaspora have responsibilities. No innocence with regard to power and its abuse can or should be asserted.

Rather, within responsibility is a freedom to continue on with the search without the responsibilities that institutions assign themselves, including the responsibilities for upholding the "truth" and for passing the tradition to the next generation that so often dominate institutionalized Judaism and Christianity. By maintaining a distance from religion and the secular, by being, as it were, in between the two, a freedom and insight is possible as well as a crossing of boundaries in and out of both spheres. Influencing both but being beholden to neither allows a journey to continue that is faithful to the world and free to seek out the unknown and the prohibited.

Hiddenness is a weakness and a strength as the paths explored become an opening to anyone who seeks to embark on the journey regardless of their status or affiliation. Those within the institutions of religion and state may find aspects discovered in the new diaspora to be intriguing and life giving, for they may help orient policies and values in a different direction. At the same time, the feeling that others within these institutions see merit within exploration of the new diaspora reinforces the sense that this difficult path is bearing fruit beyond the individual's journey. Though a sense of exile continues in the new diaspora, the sense of participation in the wider society is crucial to the sanity and responsibility of those who seek out an as yet unexplored terrain. Hiddenness cannot be a place of nonparticipation or self-congratulation. The stakes are too high.

Hiddenness within Jewish and Christian life is hardly novel, attested to by prophets and saints. Historically, these prophets and saints have helped call Judaism and Christianity back to certain core principles and it is their preservation that makes them available to us. But today the prophets and saints of ancient times call us to a community that crosses the boundaries of these religions, and those who have responded to the prophetic and saintly call in our time have done just that. We might say that a prophetic community has emerged in the twentieth century within a variety of traditions and contexts, but that its message can only be understood in a framework as yet unnamed. Will the framework for understanding this message emerge in the twenty-first century?

It is interesting too, perhaps foundational to the new diaspora, that these figures share a commonality of deep spirituality and criticism of the abuse of state and economic power. One thinks historically of Dorothy Day, the founder of the Catholic Worker movement, Mahatma Gandhi, the leader of Indian independence, and Martin Luther King, Jr., the great African-American civil rights leader. Today the theologians of liberation, Gustavo Gutierrez of Peru and Rosemary Radford Ruether of the United States for example, carry on this tradition. They argue within certain contexts and religions but also clear a path for a broader solidarity in the future.

The strength of this prophetic community is found in its response to a century of dislocation and death. Its power of insight and commitment remains strong as models who have crossed over into a broader reality, and then diminishes as those models are remembered within their own community or nation-state. In reality, the proclamation of prophet and sainthood within an institutional framework must diminish its power even when recognized and elevated, because the institution itself must harness power and claim it as its own. Martin Luther King, Jr. becomes an integrationist and an American hero in the national celebration of his birthday, but the other side of King, his increasingly critical sense of the limitations of integration and American domestic and foreign policy, are neglected or even unknown. Preserved in the national psyche but in the process domesticated and bound, King can only be rescued in his authenticity by those who live their lives in a similar pattern of affirmation and dissent.

Still a larger issue confronts the twenty-first century. Without a new diaspora, named and affirmed, who will remember the cutting-edge critiques and movements that have shaped resistance in the twentieth century? Who will remember those who are not elevated within synagogue, church, and state? Liberation theology in all its variety is in danger here as the forces of reaction disparage these theologies and the forces of renewal use much of their language for their own purposes. The driving force, the powerful invocation of the prophetic and saintly, are always in danger of disappearing.

Are those voices that reached prominence and thus an audience and who, against the current, spoke for so many on the periphery of religious and state power, destined for obscurity? Can the new diaspora in forming around these prophetic voices because they also speak to our experience remember them in the very dynamic of the forming community? Can we claim the voices of liberation in their authenticity through the very dynamic of living within a similar one? Can the voices of the prophetic community pass on this memory to the next generation in its force and starkness?

Martin Buber, one of the great Jewish religious figures of the twentieth century, wrote of the hidden circle of prophets who, as heirs to the original prophets, await the reemergence of prophetic speech and action in each generation. The challenge of this group is to reawaken the prophetic spirit in each generation, which is also a call to recover the original message of a particular community. In that original message is the community's destiny, and the role of the hidden prophets is to make that destiny articulate. Though each community has its own destiny, the recovery of that destiny allows the emergence of a community of communities, in effect unfolding a destiny larger than any particular community.

Buber's understanding comports with the view of the Jewish literary critic and philosopher George Steiner, who writes of the Jewish tradition of concentric reading. For Steiner, as for Buber, all that unfolds in history is contained in the original revelation. Events in history and texts that flow from them are always referring back to the origins in which Jewish destiny is contained. Even the challenges of history, including the overwhelming challenge of the Holocaust, is interpreted within the original framework, or at least the meaning of the event must be worked out within this framework.

In different generations but with similar viewpoints, Buber and Steiner faced as well the possibility that the original destiny of the community is losing force and the hiddenness of the prophets is deepening. Especially for Steiner, although Buber glimpsed this too, the Holocaust and Israel deepen the crisis in Jewish life. The borrowing from the past, the attempt to juxtapose the present with the original revelation, makes a destiny once agreed upon fragmented almost to the point of non-recognition.

Steiner laments the fact that the tradition of concentric reading may be coming to an end; for Buber the last chance of the hidden prophets may have been the return of the Jews to their ancient homeland. Both Buber and Steiner find that this tradition has been compromised in Israel by the emphasis on the state and the military, and so the tragedy of the Holocaust is followed by a missed opportunity to reassert a connection with God in solidarity with other Jews and their neighbors.

Here the question of memory looms. In the Jewish diaspora and homeland the memory of the prophets remains accessible. Though hidden for most of Jewish history, the texts and community allow for the survival of this circle and the message of Jewish destiny that it embodies. At any moment the community may hear this message as a call to every Jew. Once articulate, those who hear and understand will follow the call until the community rights itself. In concert with other communities who are also recovering their own particular destiny, the message of God and humanity once again becomes a force in the world.

And yet how long can the circle of hidden prophets remain alive, and is it true that a majority of any one community will hear this voice and adopt it as their own? Is it true that the destiny of each community has been established and that subsequent generations—in effect most of human history—is simply an attempt to recover this original revelation? Perhaps the memory of the original revelation is itself a memory for humanity at large and the prophets who arise at different times in history in different geographic, cultural, and religious locations. Perhaps the concentric tradition of reading is much wider than any one community so that the prophetic voice in one community is a prophetic voice for all communities.

Memory then is available to all who struggle to be faithful, and the understanding of exile and diaspora, while local and particular, is also beyond the parochial. The hidden circle of prophets is thus Jewish and non-Jewish, speaking to the Jewish community and others as well. When those who identify as Jews hear this voice it is important, and when others hear the same voice it is important as well.

In fact, the new diaspora, containing aspects of many communities and destinies but privileging none of them, allows the hidden circle of prophets to be alive somewhere and available to all when any one community is unable to respond. Arising in a particular history but available to all, the broader tradition of faith and struggle keeps alive the fidelity of any one community even as a new community is forming. This hidden circle of prophets, broadly conceived, may carry the memory of the struggle to be faithful into the future.

A new universality thus is formed, as the traditions themselves fade in relevance and commitment. Universality here is less the assertion of truth or salvation through a certain faith or discipline than a shared sense of commitment to a critical affirmation of faith and struggle in the world. A common destiny of struggle, limitation, and humility is affirmed, as is the shifting and sharing of voices that are reminders of depth and fidelity.

Religious calendars and particular disciplines are relativized in their claims and yet become important in certain moments well beyond their immediate circumstances. Memory becomes more inclusive as its boundaries, especially for the memory of suffering and struggle, broaden. The original revelation and destiny become plural and shared *as a path toward a future where both are inclusive and without boundary.*

Still the question remains whether the memory of suffering and struggle has an origin from which it unfolds. Steiner's understanding of the concentric tradition of reading, where the experiences of the individual and community in the present are interpreted within the framework of texts and narratives formed in the past, is difficult to jettison completely. Rather, the boundaries of the concentric tradition have shifted, as has its trajectory: reading contemporary experience backward and forward, within and without, allows a mobility and a subversive quality that defies conformity or ownership. Just at the moment when the explosive quality of formative events then and now seems captured and oriented toward conformism, the force of these events appears somewhere else and in a different form. Thus it becomes available, albeit in different form and dress.

The example of the Holocaust is illustrative here. On its own and with an interpretation strictly adhering to its own logic and community, the Holocaust closes in on itself. In a world of death, the options after the Holocaust are constrained. Certainty about God is foreclosed and the empowerment as a form of protection against another Holocaust is self-evident and consuming. Anger toward God and humanity within the Jewish community is understandable and continues well after the Holocaust itself; a deepening crisis forces the question of surviving Hitler as the motivation for continuing Judaism.

At the same time as the memory of the Holocaust constrains Jewish thought and action, theologies of liberation emerge among Christians of the third world to speak to their suffering. These theologies are partly indebted to the Holocaust event as Christians in Europe and America sought a different theological base to express their faith in a post-Holocaust world. Theologians of liberation, most of whom studied in Europe in the 1950s and 1960s, are keenly aware of the Holocaust and its aftermath as well as the complicity and silence of most Christians during the Nazi years. At the same time, they are aware of and studied those Christians who resisted the Nazi program, for example martyrs like Dietrich Bonhoeffer.

On their return home and in the context of a continent in upheaval, many liberation theologians in Latin America saw the widening gap between rich and poor, indeed the systemic relations of injustice that institutionalized violence, as the event to which they were called to be faithful. In their theology—and unlike the stance taken by most Jewish Holocaust theologians—the abandoned masses of Latin America are comforted and energized by the presence of Jesus, who, like the God who sent him, has a preference for the weak and helpless. At the very moment of what seems to be abandonment, those who are dying before their time have a theology being written and shared that sees their future here on earth as guided by God.

The question here is less the veracity of their claim of God's presence or even the counterclaim that Jewish theologians make with reference to the Holocaust, but rather the indebtedness of one to the other and the dialogue that can ensue if the boundaries of the traditions are transgressed. Liberation theology without the Exodus is impossible, otherwise Jesus remains a captive to a status quo church. Without the prophets, the announced kingdom of God remains spiritual and on a transcendental plane, again interpreted by a church that helped legitimate a colonial system from which it still benefits.

For the most part, however, Judaism is unnamed by liberation theologians and is too often a backdrop for the more significant work of Jesus who remains, at least symbolically in their writing, Christian. The significant fact that Jesus does not originate in the tradition within which they live is known as a fact but hardly influences the argument of liberation theologians. After all the denouncing of a tradition that has captured and seeks to own the gospels, liberation theologians argue only within the Christian tradition as defined by the church.

The repression by church authorities of those who seek the revolutionary message of liberation theology is fought on the very grounds cultivated by a symbiotic relationship of a colonial system and church. The prophetic is not argued on its own terms. Instead an elaborate argument is constructed which seeks to define the prophetic word in the contemporary world within the framework of a church that has defined the salvific work of a messiah now seen as outside history. Sophisticated theological arguments are elaborated as to how the kingdom of God is built here on earth, at the same time reserving the final kingdom in an eschatological framework. There is only one history of salvation liberation theologians assert, yet they are careful to distinguish different planes of salvific work. Of course, this is after they seek to diminish those same planes asserted by the church because, at least according to liberation theologians, this allows a comfort with an unjust order often legitimated by the church.

The point here is less the details of sophisticated theological argument or the clash between two such arguments than it is the twists and turns of a theology that seeks to claim the very ground of traditional interpretation. In this sense, that which is oriented toward the abandonment of the poor and the consequences of that abandonment—increasing poverty and death—is focused more and more internally to a church and theological questions quite foreign to this abandonment. Theologians called to Rome or the attempt to walk a tight rope so as to prevent church discipline is the news and the worry even as the church hierarchy effectively dismantles the structures that supported this emerging liberation theology.

At the same time that the prophetic call is truncated by the hierarchy and the perceived need of theologians to argue within one tradition for legitimation, the deeper response of liberation theology is blunted and constrained. Could it be that liberation theology is itself legitimate because of its response to the needs of contemporary life?

Outside the limits of the church there is little need to argue its logic and, if argued on its own merits, would liberation theologians have to argue points that seek to reconcile aspects of Christology and ecclesiology that cannot be reconciled no matter how sophisticated the argument? If liberation theology is radical in its own right, in its commitment to the poor and its assertion of God's presence among the poor, would not its field of connection and purpose be more attuned to the questions of the Holocaust that remained unanswered?

In this way reflections on the Holocaust and reflections on liberation can be seen as counterpoints to each other, plumbing the experiences of abandonment and destruction, but also the question of God's presence. Buber's hidden prophets can be found in both the death camps of Europe and the garbage dumps of Latin America, and Steiner's concentric tradition of reading is expanded and gains new resources to continue forward. Even the origins of Judaism and Christianity, when seen as a common resource, take on a mobility and expansiveness without exclusive borders. If the God of the ancient covenant is found wanting in the death camps, can the one who came within that covenant, Jewish but now Christianized, respond in a different manner in the contemporary world?

Covenantal Responsibility

This is hardly a linear progression, as if the claims of Jesus among the poor often made by liberation theologians can escape the experience of the death camps. Both the dead and the living dead are in relation with both experiences influencing each other. A too easy assertion of presence or absence is avoided when both experiences are judged as valid and in a common tradition. On the one hand, this avoids the hoarding of suffering as unique and unreachable by any other people, as is often found in reflections on the Holocaust. On the other hand, the understanding of salvation only through Jesus is mitigated by the Holocaust event.

If the lesson of the Holocaust is the need for power, the lesson of contemporary suffering is that power is too often used to exclude and demean. Holocaust has often paralyzed the search for values and God while liberation movements have often mobilized without thought of the consequences of the revolution's success. The result is less point-counterpoint than the awareness that events seemingly separated by geography, culture, and tradition are in fact common in the deeper questions they pose, and certain values and prospects lost in some events are accentuated in others. Though each particular community may have its own diaspora, the broader tradition of faith and struggle has an enlarged diaspora understanding which allows values and possibilities to surface and speak to whomever and wherever the need is felt.

What does the hidden circle of prophets say within the Holocaust and the struggle for liberation? How does the concentric tradition of reading expand in seeing these events in a relationship of solidarity rather than exclusion? How does the memory of these two events encourage questions and commitment and the movement toward a humanity that refuses atrocity? Perhaps the hidden circle of prophets is simply found in the unfolding of these events without prior definition and the memory is carried along by the recognition of a broader tradition of faith and struggle.

The politics that emerge from the understanding of these events does so like the politics that emerged from other formative events that were recognized by communities in the past. At least for the Jewish and Christian communities, the formative events of Exodus and Jesus were experienced profoundly by the participants and recognized as significant *after* by those who saw them as definitive. It is also true that the recognition of these events as formative meant a break with a normative history that refused disjunction and defined the Exodus and Jesus as peripheral happenings.

It is precisely at the point that the peripheral was seen as central that community formed across the boundaries of the known and powerful. Seen within Egyptian history, then and now, the Exodus is insignificant, in some ways a betrayal of a great and flourishing civilization. So too with the emergence of Christianity from Judaism, a small sect whose chances for survival and expansion were small. That both the Jewish and Christian community would flourish, make significant contributions to the world, and create a normative history that saw, like its predecessors, a break with its continuity as insignificant and even traitorous, was unimaginable at their origins.

Today we are at that same point. Worldliness, spirituality, and the politics that may come from this interruption, which in the larger history of humanity occurs with regularity, is still unnamed and unfocused. So often the politics of interruption is named in previous categories or exists without naming in the lives of participants that seem to be without community. The naming of that community, that is the sharing of values, the pattern of eclectic borrowing, and the gleaning of diaspora fidelity across cultures and religious traditions, is the prophetic tradition that is with us today. This is a politics of intervention, one that fights against injustice, that speaks of global values and a politics of covenantal responsibility, one that seeks to define creation and the human in a framework broader than power and nationality.

A politics of intervention and covenantal responsibility allows particular communities and those already outside them to gather together and work for values that may be seen as within the traditions as we know them, but are actually beyond those traditions. To see the universal within Judaism and Christianity *as a call beyond their boundaries* is in fact to have moved beyond these traditions as sufficient unto themselves. This is true for the secular community as well, whose deepening perspectives are seen as Enlightenment insight, but whose practice, insofar as it engages the spiritual and the unknown, has already moved beyond its initial and well-deserved skepticism.

At the same time, a politics of intervention and covenantal responsibility forces a deeper view of political affiliation. Religiosity is contextual, always within the colonization and evangelization of a particular time and place. So too is politics. A religiosity that crosses boundaries and whose fidelity is found in constantly evolving formations rather than dogmatic assertions and creeds gravitates to a politics that responds to needs rather than ideological or utopian projections.

The limitations and inclusion that the new diaspora finds in its search for fidelity are the same in the political realm; the desire for justice is tempered by the understanding that eschatology in the political realm often neglects the humanity of those it seeks to serve. Neither conservative, liberal, nor radical politics are raised as ends in themselves or sufficient to the task at hand. What is needed is an attention to the details of social and political policies that demean or enhance the human quest for security, health, and well-being. Contextual religiosity is similar to contextual politics in the sense that each age contributes to the possibilities of an evolving commitment and serves as a warning to the overreach of ideals and hopes.

On these issues the prophetic community that has emerged in the twentieth century speaks clearly to those who enter the twenty-first century. Politics without a sense of limits is destined to enlarge the events of atrocity that marred the twentieth century: politics that sees only limits increases the number of those excluded from the protection of society and therefore increases the number of the destitute, another feature of the twentieth century. Instead, the need is to create a politics that increases inclusion, at the same time allowing a freedom outside the political realm. Individuals and communities need protection and freedom to work out their rights and responsibilities.

This is true for the sense of meaning and destiny as well, as each individual and community must search this out. Any overarching vision of society must emerge from a collective experience that continually evolves and is subject to collapse and reinvention. Even the realm of civil religion and public affirmation is suspect here if the claim is larger than a limited and local view of reality. Civil religion and public affirmation is possible only if it too is open to the crossing of boundaries and a contextual defining point.

Covenantal responsibility is thus found in the intersection of a contextual religiosity and a politics of intervention *without a destiny projected beyond either*. Here an understanding of history is involved, emphasizing neither cyclical repetition nor linear progression. The broader tradition of faith and struggle posits a reality beneath and across the surface of religion and politics as usually understood and the hidden circle of prophets is neither of one faith nor one political sensibility. The eclecticism of the new diaspora is purposeful and intelligent as it reflects the understanding of life and destiny as intergenerational, ongoing, and without an eschatological end.

The struggle is within the individual and the always-evolving communal patterns toward depth, inclusion, and the alleviation of suffering. Politics and history are vehicles through which a broader expression of this struggle can be found. Covenantal responsibility is found in the interplay of the personal, communal, religion, religiosity, politics, and history, rather than in the emphasis of one aspect over another. None has a claim that is absolute and all have a role to play in the struggle to be faithful.

When all of these elements are recognized in their proper place, despair and hope are found in their proper relationship as well. An uneasy and troublesome balancing of despair and hope becomes the reality as the individual and community awaken to a history that is made by us and will always be unfinished. The deepest aspects of the human journey are toward an end that cannot be codified, predicted, or celebrated as finished. Instead we are journeying to an end that is unfinished, to a death that is as singular as life itself.

This singularity is also shared, as all human beings live and die in an individuality that is prized and haunting. Thus the communal bond is this singularity and the shared moments of expression that transcend the aloneness that comes with consciousness and conscience. Fidelity too is singular and shared, thus the bonding in a community that is local in time and geography and beyond locality in all senses of the word. Religiosity and politics must therefore be an expression of this singularity and commonality *in our time and beyond*. Politics is also under the sign of colonization and evangelization: its purpose is important and limited, essential and contextual.

13

Speaking of God and the Covenant in the Twenty-First Century

To SPEAK AND WRITE ABOUT GOD is always problematic. God is the most written about subject; because of this one hesitates to add to the body of works already written. Is there any other subject that is defined so often and yet so eludes definition?

In many ways this difficulty is part of the territory. One searches the Hebrew scriptures, indeed the entire bible, for an easy definition of God, and yet in the end definitive pictures of God are shadowed by glimpses of a transcendent and elusive God. An immanent God is also encountered only to be followed by bold portraits of a God who is powerful and sometimes distant.

In our own time the question of God has taken many turns and the images of God that have been offered are often images of brokenness and weakness. The Holocaust raises such images, even the prospect that God is absent. Those struggling for justice after the Holocaust raise the prospect that God is among the poor, once again present to those who need God most, and yet poverty increases and a radical subversive God also comes into question.

God as absent, God as present is almost a mantra in present-day life, at least among those who take the difficult road of humanity during the twentieth century seriously. For who can easily speak of God in a century of mass death, where millions have been condemned to the precincts of the dead and the living dead?

If God is difficult to define in any age and almost impossible to assert in our age, why bother with definitions of God? Why speak of God at all?

As unfinished beings in a universe where meaning and care are not self-evident, God is a way of anchoring our personal and communal life in a structure that lends meaning and support. In a time of crisis our unfinishedness takes on another dimension of hope that a future beyond crisis is possible. Speech about God may in the final analysis be speech about hope, *that history is open, that humanity is possible, that community rather than empire has the last word.*

Such hope is hardly obvious. History as recounted in a modern linear fashion is one where various factors lead from one stage to another. Eras follow upon each other as if a causality determines the next stage of history. The openness of history is affirmed within certain parameters, but the links of history are assumed to come only from within this linear sequence. We are heirs to this sequence and bequeath our own lives to the era that follows. The meaning of living within history, the meaning of history itself, remains unaddressed.

Most theology begins with assertions about the meaning of history or extrapolates a meaning from certain historical events. Speech about God either comes from outside history or within it as a reflection upon history. But what if the question of God comes from outside *and* within history in a contextual form that has a history and is open to new formulations, has roots in particular communities and is available to those in the process of formation? What if God has a predetermined form and yet is always being formed, exists and is always being thought about in different ways? What if the covenant presupposes God and its evolution gives rise to different conceptions of God?

The God of the Exodus and Jesus is a God who is the grounding for the journey of a covenanted people, a God who journeys with that people through historical epochs. Especially in formative events, God is found but also questioned. In the very immediacy of an overwhelming experience and later in reflection on that event, the meaning of life and history is raised to an intense level. All is thrown into motion: the formation and survival of a people, the hope of a history beyond slavery and domination, even the desire for care and affection in a universe that often seems indifferent or hostile to humanity. A time of breakthrough is at hand, as if the very axis of history is shifting.

And yet at this very moment of breakthrough the reality of life reasserts itself. The turning point acknowledged, history returns to its course. Formative events are monumental and yet momentary, at least in the long sweep of history. God is known in the movement of history but history settles in for the long haul. A period of experienced and remembered intensity is followed by a dry period of waiting and sometimes reversal. Openings become closures. Expectations become dulled. If community is at hand, empire often reasserts itself. Closure becomes the way of the world.

The possibility of God is found in both the formative event and in the long haul of history. The dramatic moment points toward God as does the moment of closure. These moments are rarely chosen by individuals or communities; rather they are experienced in history and reflected upon after they pass. Within the experience God is felt as near or absent.

Breakthrough is seen as possible or nearly impossible, but the point is to remain attentive, active, waiting for the next moment when a new possibility presents itself. Rather than the movement itself, God is found in the possibility that history is open and thus a feeling of being connected with God is balanced with calling on God to be that opening.

Closure is real, to be sure. Empire is a reality that often triumphs. *It is the steadfastness that another reality is possible, that an internal sense of freedom and community can be glimpsed in the world around us that speaks of the possibility of God.* Thus the two voices of God—interior and worldly—are important to keep in dialogue, for they point to a dynamic tension that is irresolvable while crucial to continue the journey. If these two voices rarely resound in harmony both the interior and worldly voices of God are also divided, representing the same division within our own voices. We are unfinished and the voices that are our own are discordant as well.

Are the voices of God our own voices in disparate keys? Is the hope for community our own hope elevated beyond the individual? Is the experience of empire by humans in history also the experience of God? This coincidence of voices within and without make the God of rescue and history as problematic as it at the same time renders a purely immanent God impossible. Perhaps the covenant is the mediator internally and externally, a force within and without that carries possibility forward even as it cannot guarantee success.

Yet the content of the covenant remains elusive. If it is not the pact between Israel and God at Sinai or between the new Israel and God through Jesus, what then is it? Can the covenant be less than the promise promulgated in ancient times and remaining in force today? Of course this covenant was offered and accepted at a certain time period, under certain conditions, *in a specific era of colonization and evangelization.* As important, the promises of the covenant have been violated and questioned from the very moment of offer and acceptance. Hence the grumbling of the Israelites in the desert and the long-awaited return of Jesus. And this is only the beginning. The millennia since the Jewish and Christian covenant have seen repeated discordance between the promises of the covenant and the reality of individual and communal life. In many ways, the entire theological enterprise emerges to deal with these discrepancies as do synagogue and church life.

The reduction of cognitive dissonance becomes the lifeblood of Judaism and Christianity from the very inception of these religions to our time. The promise that God will be with the Jews or that in the death and resurrection of Jesus sin has been overcome and eternal life granted is far from obvious. Just the opposite seems to be the case: the promises of God are neither self-evident nor acceptable without an often-convoluted interpretation. In the end faith is needed to resolve these apparent discrepancies, a faith often described as a leap beyond reason and the evidence around us. How often are we advised that what seems confused is really clear, that the end is not an end, that absence is not absence, that presence is available if only our eyes are opened by a force that exists outside ourselves?

What remains after the theology—after the explanations of the apparent failure of the covenant or at least our limited ability to understand the workings of the God who offers the covenant—is the testimony bequeathed by those who struggle with the world and God. This testimony includes the Exodus and Jesus events as well as that which reflects upon these events. But the testimony, canonized, interpreted, and theologized over the centuries is not the last word or the only word.

Testimony found in this vein of history is also testimony in the larger schema of reality that is not contained only within Judaism and Christianity. And even the testimony found within Judaism and Christianity points to questions beyond these religions. What we are left with are testimonies from different times and circumstances that within a certain symbolic and linguistic framework are available to others according to the times and events in which those who testify are living.

The covenant is bound to these frameworks only because we are and only to the extent that we see the possibility of the covenant in no other configuration. Persistence is the watchword here, but also a fear that the covenant will disappear and along with it the two voices of God, which are also our own voices. Looking beyond the language and symbols that we have inherited and are so often inadequate produces an anxiety of void that we seek to keep at bay. Therefore, no matter how inadequate our framework, it is better than the prospect that no framework really exists. Thus faith is often reduced to a fear of no faith, and our belief in God is offered, often stridently, because we fear that there is no God.

After the Holocaust, after the cycle of atrocity that still infects history, after Constantinian Christianity, which has its counterpart in Judaism and Islam, only an agnosticism can be offered to the broader public. Richard Rubenstein, the eminent Holocaust theologian, wrote some years ago that modern society is functionally Godless, that regardless of belief or non-belief, modern society and its advanced technology and sophisticated bureaucracy take on a life of their own, as if God is irrelevant. Even when prayers are invoked or blessings given, the reality of decision making and implementation are completely secular. Like atrocity, the regular workings of society continue on despite the pleas to God for an end to murder or change in social and political life.

Agnosticism, then, may be a mature understanding of the world as it has been, as it is and is likely to be. Perhaps faith, chastened to be sure and humble before the realities of the world, is that element of our agnosticism that prevents the devolution of a healthy skepticism into a cynicism from which there is no return. To project religiosity as *the* answer to the questions of our time is to promote cynicism as well, for who, after this long history of betrayal and the consequent vacuum of religious language, can offer this same language and conceptual framework without courting ridicule? Rather than answers, it may be that religious language, even the name of God, is important in steering agnosticism toward the possibility of faith. This faith is first and foremost in the possibility of humanity and only secondarily in the possibility of God. For would not the possibility of a flourishing and just humanity raise in a new way the possibility of God?

Here the covenant is freed of its particular religious inheritances, and even of the obligation to assert God as foundational to creation and life. Without obligation or a conceptual framework the covenant is allowed its own freedom within the context of our times to appear and disappear at will, to be held by whomever holds it and to flee wherever it needs to flee. Communities who claim the covenant can rise and fall and in falling can reclaim the covenant as well. Other communities that begin in a rebellion against the covenant may find themselves claiming the covenant or living it without naming it. By freeing the covenant of its traditional trappings, political parties and governments will have more difficulty claiming it and Judaism and Christianity will be placed on warning themselves.

Some fear that limiting the covenant's use and effectiveness will limit the ability to choose right from wrong and make it more difficult to lend direction to individuals and society. Yet at this moment the claims and counter-claims only confuse the issue until the covenant is emptied of meaning anyway: it becomes like a football tossed from one side of the field to the other with warriors on each side claiming that God is with them.

Hence the silence of the covenant and of God comes within a world where both are invoked without thought and for partisan purposes. Could it be that this silence is a sign of strength, of waiting, of purpose, of a hiddenness that is private and yet communal? Perhaps the formation of community in the new diaspora is precisely in this hiddenness, in the refusal to use the covenant and God as a wedge or a hammer. Instead a hidden circle, in Buber's sense, one of prophets, gathers to remember the covenants of the past and to search out what the covenant might mean in our own day. This covenant cannot be defined or announced without becoming part of the past itself, and therefore the unannounced nature of the covenant becomes part of its strength and power. The search continues for the covenant *and* a just society oriented toward the person and meaning. Is this not, in its essence and elaboration, a search also for the deeper structures of belief and affirmation, for God?

These deeper structures are the other side of agnosticism, the unannounced, perhaps unnameable side of the spirit that calls us to commitment and fidelity. Rather than dividing us from others, they call us to another level of self and toward an embrace that is difficult to define. The embrace itself is ever expanding, individually and communally, and freeing as well. The covenant beckons us to an inclusive terrain that defies language and creed. The very assertion of that terrain as owned or named—which allows its use over against others—is foreclosed by the nature of the embrace itself. There is no proof of this sensibility or demonstration of it, at least one that can be named in public policy or a religious or political campaign. It can only be hinted at, suggested, probed, and experienced as a possibility in the larger public discussion. It cannot be enforced or prophesied, at least not in its own language and substance.

What can be proposed publicly is that society be responsible for the flourishing of humanity or at least provide a framework in which this is possible. The social order should make it easier for people to be good to one another and here judgment is crucial. Society should be judged according to how difficult it is to carry out the obligation of goodness in the routine of daily living. Expanding the terrain of our embrace may have different foundations for different people or it may, as often it does, rest on inarticulate foundational beliefs and hopes.

Creating a society where it is easier for people to be good to one another is difficult enough with the countervailing ideologies and theologies, not to mention the institutional structures of privilege and scarcity. Is it so important that the foundations of such a society become articulate in a religious way? Just the opposite may be the case. It may be that the common goodness of individuals will give rise to a society that practices the common good, and in the dynamic interplay of personal and communal commitment to this project a sensibility will arise that acknowledges a religious spirit named as God.

Midway between agnosticism and cynicism is this affirmation of the human good. And here again the covenant remains crucial *as the place where practice and fidelity are more important than belief or disbelief.* Constitutional politics in the United States, for example, with all its flaws and limitations, is an example of working out a covenant in the public realm. Here citizenship rather than belief or religious affiliation provides the focus for shared life, and the common good, pursued in diverse ways, is affirmed as more important for society than personal affirmation. And yet it is also true that personal affirmation, the journey of a person within particular communal structures, is absolutely crucial to the larger project. Though the larger society is governed through secular techniques, religiosity can be highlighted insofar as it contributes to the larger discussion of public policy and societal direction. Within this framework both the personal and communal are protected from elements that seek to bend the person and the larger whole into instruments of power and division.

Constitutional politics and covenantal responsibility are joined in a marriage that yields freedom while excluding certainty. It is an uneasy marriage, to be sure, because politics and religion often seek definitions and power that erase doubt and change. Yet constitutions and covenants are always changing, evolving beyond their formation and articulation, interpreted, affirmed and overturned, sometimes held up as the epitome of foresight or derided as documents and beliefs that enshrine injustice or intolerance. In the best of situations, however, constitutions and covenants may function to limit and enhance each other, if not directing us to a final destination, at least warning that if either is enshrined as truth, the balance crucial to life and society will be overturned.

For the religious sensibility, secularity in concept and politics supplies the warning that affirmation of God outside of a covenant is a form of idolatry, attempting to capture for all time that which remains before us. Idolatry is the worship of forms that appeal to us as the definition of the ultimate which, on further examination, is something less than that. Is this not the history of politics *and* religion? In truth politics and religion have and will continue to evolve and most often the difficulty in their evolution is the very assertion, often backed with power, that a final definition and form has been achieved. It is that very moment when the forces of exclusion predominate and the power to censor the thoughts and actions of dissenters is sought.

Those accused of political and religious heresy paradoxically are the ones who ultimately break through idolatry. The cost is high and often the persons and ideas that are persecuted are forgotten in the new configuration that comes into being. Especially in religious life, the very ideas that break through a system of conformity and idolatry are the basis for the evolution of the covenant and covenantal responsibility. The expansion of the terrain of embrace is often found in opposition to the political and religious systems of the day, and the form and communication of that opposition is by nature offensive to those systems and sensibilities.

Here agnosticism veers into atheism, a refusal, as it were, to affirm the institutions and values that present themselves as given and righteous. At certain points in history atheism may be the only vehicle for the covenant to express itself, surrounded as it is by voices claiming ultimate truth. Is this the reasons for Karl Marx's rigorous atheism, the pretense of church, state, and economies of his time to have a monopoly on truth and power? One sees Rosa Luxemburg's atheism in a similar light, as a struggle to live within systems that define their reality as the only possible understanding of life and power. Perhaps the Holocaust provides a form of atheism as well, as an overwhelmingly horrific event that challenges and overturns every belief and ideology that seeks to attain absolute assent and power.

Is it here that the covenant can be found? An agnosticism that veers into atheism suggests opposition to a complacent religiosity, to a God who is deemed present in oppression and injustice. Whatever side God is seen to be present to—on the side of the oppressor or the oppressed—is found wanting. For can God be a legitimator of oppression? Is it possible to posit God's presence among the poor when oppression continues or even accelerates?

Atheism suggests a skepticism that is mature and right if it remains open to new possibilities and configurations. Closed off as it often is, however, atheism simply becomes another orthodoxy, rigid and sure of itself. Open to the world and to surprise, atheism avoids cynicism and becomes the staging ground for a new appearance of the covenant. It may become a foundation for expanding the terrain of embrace.

We arrive here. God and the covenant exist independently of our efforts but await articulation. Existing but unknown, or waiting to become known again within each generation, God and the covenant are powers *in potentia.* The memory of God and the covenant is preserved, at least in Judaism and Christianity, in the synagogues and churches; this is the primary importance of such institutions. That the memory is often presented as living, to be embraced and practiced as it was in earlier days can be both stifling and liberating—stifling in the sense that the God of the past is held captive by these very institutions and is often linked with power and the denial of the prophetic; liberating that the explosive quality of God and the covenant are liturgically rendered and thus made available to the discerning person or community.

The God and the covenant of the past await rebirth in the present without knowledge or interest of the forms that such rebirth will offer. Why would there be such a concern unless the form and symbols of God's presence were fixed, ontologically connected with the struggle to be faithful at one particular time in history? Is it necessary that the language and symbol structure of the ancient Israelites be our own language? Must the language of Jesus, contextual as it was, bounded by the horizon of Judaism, the Romans, and the ascent of colonial power, be our language?

Tradition, as it reminds us of division and the need for repetition of language, symbol, and creed, fails here, for the language of the Israelites and Jesus is not our language, nor is their world our world. And yet the continuity between those two worlds—the reading by Jesus from the prophetic books and his celebration of the Passover—reminds us of the connection between our world and theirs. That connecting link is the struggle to be faithful and the possibility of betrayal, of grasping in our time the reality of God and the covenant, or remaining in patterns that are certain and defining, thus valuing the past over the present.

The connection between their world and our own is the possibility which they acted upon and which preservation of the past warned against: striking out into the unknown with the faith that God and the covenant would become present to them. The risk taken by the Israelites and Jesus can only be minimized by the very repetition they refused. By reciting these stories over and over again, by participating in the kind of religious calendars that they used, reinterpreted, rejected, and transcended, we may miss the radical risk taken by those who sojourned through the desert and those who journeyed with and followed Jesus.

The God and covenant of the past is important here only as each is carried with us and transformed in the future. For those who carry this past as a substantive foundation and strength, risking everything for the future, their contribution to the new diaspora will be in articulating the possibility of God and the covenant. Those without this past or in rebellion against it, along with those who carry a different language and symbol of God and the covenant, will meet in a context ripe with new potential.

The possibility here is less the affirmation or negation of God than it is the exploration of the world and self without prior definition and assertion. Of course, the concepts and values carried within each person and community will be present even while open to reconfiguration in the context of meeting and conversation. Here the new diaspora again looms large: to recognize the other as intimate, as part of a broader community and tradition, the broader tradition of faith and struggle, is to invite expansion of views and sensibilities.

The exterior level of this expansion is easily understood within an ecumenical reality which means that there can be no privilege of any religion or religious sensibility. The more difficult question is the interior life of those involved in this broadening. Is the interior life of a person in the new diaspora also to be open ecumenically in a deep way, beyond acceptance of difference as positive to the very heart of belief and prayer? This addresses the question of the God affirmed within. Could it be that the God affirmed within each person can be untouched by this larger ecumenical thrust? Or does the expansion of the terrain of embrace in the world change the most intimate embrace within?

Here the covenant comes into play again. The covenant within this expanding terrain of embrace is that which reaches out and within, including new spaces of belief and affirmation, and protecting spaces of personal and communal life. Outward and inward are engaged in the new diaspora, while history and formation remain important as well. That which is overcome and becomes articulate in the world affects the interior life of the person but need not be expressed in the same way. Jews who do not see chosenness over against others, thereby recognizing the chosenness of all, do not thereby relinquish a sense of being chosen. So, too, Christians who recognize that other religions have their own validity, and that each proposes a path toward wholeness and salvation, need not end their own belief in the salvific mission of Jesus.

Yet in the end, the public and personal sense cannot be divorced forever. The interaction in the world and the formation of the new diaspora community inevitably challenge the interior affirmation of persons and communities. Ecumenical gestures that are gracious and inclusive cannot be generated over time without an internal assent that is real and evolving. If that is impossible in the generation that embarks on this journey, received patterns determining certain aspects of openness and closedness, the next generation will experience the former before the latter. Ecumenical life as a given, rather than a necessary and forged construct, gives birth to an interior life that sees the gathering of the new diaspora as the starting point for reflection. If the particularity of the previous generation conditioned and limited outreach and internal assent, the new diaspora will be the starting point for the next generation.

Within this context, the desire for the particularity of the *before* can only be retrogressive, not because what occurred historically in the shaping of persons and community was wholly bad, but because the return to the past can only be an attempt to differentiate that which has ceased to exist in the life of the community. The *after* of Judaism and Christianity is the life lived within the new diaspora and thus must be the locus of reflection. In this sense God and the covenant must also be understood as *after*, even if patterns of prior understandings are present because of the previous generation. Those who are rooted in particular understandings but come to the new diaspora expanding their terrain of embrace can contribute the past of God and the covenant to the next generation in their spirit and commitment. Where the new generation will take this is beyond prediction or control.

Part III

THE FUTURE OF ECUMENICAL RELIGIOSITY

14

Thinking and Writing the Holocaust
in an Age of Jewish Empowerment

THE PUBLICATION OF DANIEL GOLDHAGEN'S *Hitler's Willing Executioners: Ordinary Germans and the Holocaust* elicited a tremendous amount of scholarly comment in Germany and America. Much, if not most, of this comment has been negative, even entering the personal realm of motivation and financial gain. The popular reaction to Goldhagen's book has been enthusiastic, as its lengthy inclusion on the *New York Times* best seller list indicates. At a symposium at the United States Holocaust Memorial Museum in April 1996, an overflowing audience enthusiastically endorsed Goldhagen's views and were audibly distressed at the criticism that Holocaust scholars showered upon Goldhagen's book and his own personal standing in the scholarly community. Konrad Kwiet, then Senior Scholar-in-Residence of the museum's Research Institute, began by accusing Goldhagen of having written and promoted the book to become famous; Yehuda Bauer, Professor of Holocaust Studies at Hebrew University, compared Goldhagen's work to that of Arno Mayer, whose work tying the Holocaust to Germany's invasion of the Soviet Union, initially generated much discussion and is now "forgotten." Turning to Goldhagen, Bauer cautioned that his work might end up the same way: "You have started your career the wrong way," Bauer concluded, "You do not begin with public relations, you end with it." While Goldhagen received loud applause for his lecture, Kwiet and Bauer's criticisms were met with near silence.[1]

Since Kwiet and Bauer are known and supported financially by their work on the Holocaust, one wonders at their personal criticism of Goldhagen's success. Both hold positions in prestigious institutions and their status as important thinkers and historians revolves around their writing on this most difficult subject. Moreover, the creation of the Holocaust museum and the funding of Holocaust chairs in university settings is dependent on popular support. Without this support, neither the museum nor the university chairs would exist. Kwiet and Bauer, along with a generation of historians, theologians, and social scientists, have benefited from this support and, in some ways, have helped generate it. One might say that the popular and the scholarly have proceeded hand in hand to make the Holocaust the most remembered and studied subject in history. Why, then, would Goldhagen's continuity in this partnership be questioned so vociferously? After all, the further promulgation of Holocaust study would seem to bode well for Kwiet and Bauer and the entire enterprise.

The substantive criticisms of Goldhagen's work are similarly difficult to understand. Many of the critics charge that Goldhagen has simply cast into popular language what historians have already analyzed, or that he accentuates certain themes of German history at the expense of others, characteristics hardly unknown to historians of the Holocaust or historians in general. Selectivity and emphasis are the bread upon which historians feed. How else does one compress an entire history into a book-length project and create a narrative to order our sense of history?

What seems to run through the criticism of Goldhagen is the charge that he writes from a vantage point that assumes a passionate character. This passion is seen as a threat to objectivity. As Roland Wagner writes in his review of *Hitler's Willing Executioners*: "Under ordinary circumstances, a passion to condemn genocide and a concern for moral accountability would be admirable motivations, but they become serious flaws when they compromise the objectivity of a social scientist." In essence, Wagner accuses Goldhagen of proceeding like a trial lawyer, pressing his point that the peculiar and virulent anti-Semitism of the German people created an "eliminationist" sensibility, one made manifest in the Holocaust.[2]

While Holocaust historians develop a complex Holocaust narrative, an interplay, if you will, of socioeconomic, technological, religious, and political forces that led to the Holocaust and that qualifies the participation of ordinary Germans in mass death, Goldhagen "simplifies" the matter: Germans knowingly and willingly participated in the slaughter of the Jews because the culture they lived in and the world view they inherited and affirmed sought the destruction of the Jews. Contrary to the pleas of many historians to see the multifaceted and complex arena that provided the desire and the means to create a *Judenrein* world, Goldhagen presses the issue of goal and responsibility. Ordinary Germans—not Nazis or bureaucrats or authoritarian personalities—became willing executioners of Jews because the debasement and elimination of Jews gave meaning to their lives. Rather than simplification, Goldhagen's thesis confronts the more "complex" analysis of Kwiet and Bauer with the charge that they are displacing the responsibility for the Holocaust into a series of abstractions that leave one wondering why the Jews and why the Germans.

Goldhagen is relentless on this point. Throughout his analysis, the voluntary brutality and murderous actions of ordinary Germans are emphasized. Even the captions of the photographs in the book illustrate the brutality of the German people. To the picture of a Jew in Warsaw having his beard cut by a menacing figure, Goldhagen appends the caption, "A German cuts a Jew's beard in Warsaw in 1939, while others look on in laughter. " Another picture depicts a similar beard cutting, this time outside of Warsaw, and elicits the caption, "A man from Police Battalion 101 amuses himself and the beaming German onlookers with their German playthings." During a lecture tour to promote the German publication of his book, Goldhagen was lectured by Jurgen Kocka, a professor at Berlin's Free University, on the "sensationalism" of his style and likened his work to movie representations of the Holocaust like Stephen Spielberg's "Schindler's List." Hans Mommsen, a professor and historian of the Holocaust, concurred with Kocka: "I don't think German Holocaust research needs this incentive. Maybe the public and the media needed this, but not scientific research." But again, the criticisms of Goldhagen were made as his book climbed to best seller status in Germany.[3]

One wonders if Goldhagen's main thesis, that the anti-Semitism of Germany and Germans was eliminationist and a conscious choice, that the brutality and murder were voluntary and fulfilled the deepest cultural and personal aspirations of the German people, has simplified or uncovered profound tensions within the study of the Holocaust. Goldhagen describes voluntaristic cruelty as the "grammar of German expression" and chides those who analyze the complexity of the Holocaust in psychological terms. For Goldhagen, they discuss these acts of brutality as if "they were discussing the commission of mundane acts, as if they need explain little more than how a good man might occasionally shoplift," or as if the Germans were childlike and unable to choose their own behavior: "They either ignore, deny, or radically minimize the importance of Nazi and perhaps the perpetrators' ideology, moral values, and conception of the victims, for engendering the perpetrators' willingness to kill. Some of these explanations also caricature the perpetrators, and Germans in general. The explanations treat them as if they had been people lacking a moral sense, lacking the ability to make decisions and take stances." On the contrary, it is exactly the adulthood of the Germans— their ability to make choices—that explains the Holocaust and makes sense of the brutalities and mass murder that is often indescribable.[4]

When the question of resistance is raised, Goldhagen is equally controversial. Though all admit that resistance was minimal, Goldhagen accuses even those against Hitler of sharing the overall anti-Semitism of the culture, even the eliminationist anti-Semitism so important to the Holocaust. Here Goldhagen addresses the issue of Christianity within Germany as part and parcel of the eliminationist sensibility with regard to Jews. "Never once did any German bishop, Catholic or Protestant, speak out publicly on behalf of the Jews," Goldhagen writes, and the Catholic church, which did protest aspects of Nazi policies with regard to the church and the euthanasia program instituted by the Nazis, issued "no official condemnation of the regime's eliminationist persecution of the Jews." As Goldhagen points out, the church did not officially protest the April 1933 boycott of Jewish businesses, the Nuremberg Laws promulgated in 1935, which legalized the separation of Jews from civil society, the violence of *Kristallnacht* in 1938, which saw the desecration and burning of Jewish synagogues, or even the Nazi deportation of German Jews to their death. Those religious figures who did resist the Nazis and even broke with their larger church bodies over the issue of Nazification of German society and the church itself, were often openly anti-Semitic. Martin Niemoller, a Protestant minister and resistor of the Nazi regime, concurred with the Nazis on their understanding of the Jews as "eternally evil"; so, too, Heinrich Gruber, a Protestant minister imprisoned for having protested the deportation of Jews, held views of Jews that were quite close to the Nazis. Gruber felt that Jews were rootless and destructive, that in fact there was a "Jewish Problem" in need of solution: "It was these Jews who from 1919 to 1932 ruled Germany financially, economically, politically, culturally, and journalistically," Gruber spoke in an interview with a Dutch newspaper in 1939. Karl Barth, the great Swiss theologian, leader of the Confessing Church, and ardent enemy of the Hitler regime, held a similar attitude translated into theological language. Thus Goldhagen quotes Barth's Advent sermon of 1933 where he denounced Jews as "an obstinate and evil people." Just as Goldhagen sees Germany as a nation of willing executioners, he also sees anti-Semitism as a corollary of Christianity.[5]

At one level, criticism of Goldhagen's work is understandable, for he writes in a confrontational style that deliberately provokes outrage. His analysis is dependent on other historians even as he accuses many of them of concealing the true nature of the genocide in abstract and academic theory. The public acceptance of Goldhagen's outrage is understandable as well, for if the Holocaust disappears into academic jargon and forums, the memory of the dead can dissipate into trivia and self-important pronouncements. Jewish and German readers, of course, have a special connection to this discussion, a connection that the many books and memorials attest to. However, differing reactions to the book in academic and popular circles point to a continuing struggle to define the narrative of the Holocaust. Will the Holocaust be defined by historians whose academic respectability and status is dependent on applying the rigors of scientific discipline to their study, or by the popular sensibility that sees the writing of the history of the Holocaust as a way of rescuing the voices of the dead from oblivion? At least from the Jewish perspective, there seems to be a need to revisit the Holocaust as a way of expressing the horror of the past that to this day haunts the Jewish community.

The reception accorded Goldhagen's book suggests that the scholarly apparatus and memorial building which has grown so dramatically in the last decades in Europe and America has served to remind *and* to distance the Jewish population from the horrors of the Holocaust. It is almost as if the very naming of the Holocaust and its ascendancy to the center of Western historical and ethical discourse has at the same time diminished the horror that the Holocaust should invoke. Looked at through the eyes of sociology, religion, politics, and culture, the diminution of the horror is part of the price for the elevation of the discourse in academia and in the national life of most Western countries. The greatest example of this price is the United States Holocaust Memorial Museum, created by the Congress of the United States with land and operation funds donated by the government. In this setting, but this applies to the academy as well, moral outrage must be tempered by "objective" history.

Passion has its place on the sidelines of memorials and academic discourse but the standards, the setting, and the financial donors have their say as well. If the university is non-sectarian or has a Christian religious affiliation, the Jewish character of the Holocaust, the question of the culpability of the German people, and the indictment of Christianity for being part of the eliminationist culture, is tempered by an environment that seeks to disperse responsibility for evil into discrete units and preserve elements of the Western and Christian heritage intact. If the government sponsors a memorial museum it is unlikely to react favorably to a wholesale critique of the power and religion that a majority of its citizens holds dear, especially if the lessons of that power and religion can be translated in critical forms back home. Thus the inclusion of the Holocaust in the memory and life of the West means, among other things, a certain caution and domestication of the horrors that Goldhagen writes of so vividly. To throw the horrors of the Holocaust into the faces of those who sponsor the discourse on the Holocaust is to risk the reputation of the narrative itself and the disestablishment of the entire enterprise. Such an event would threaten those who have established this credibility and made their careers within this discourse: it also would raise the question of where Jewish discourse would find a place to retreat to. Could the disestablishment of the Holocaust narrative leave Jews back where they started from, trying to find a voice in a anti-Semitic atmosphere, one where eliminationist anti-Semitism might once again rear its ugly head?[6]

There are other problems beyond the permission of the host cultures, protection of status and prestige, and the fear of a renewed anti-Semitism. An unspoken aspect of this entire discussion is the shadow side of a recently victimized and now empowered Jewish community which seeks to define, maintain, and manage a public discourse on the Holocaust. Though the discussion of the Holocaust is seemingly historical in nature, the speech about and memorialization of the Holocaust takes place in the present among Jews, Germans, and others who live in a world quite different from the one they invoke in writing and symbol. The journey from Auschwitz to the mall in Washington, D.C. covers an almost unimaginable distance. It is difficult to assess such a journey from the nadir to the center of the Western world, even if that journey took place over hundreds of years. That it occurred in less than fifty years is remarkable and almost defies analysis.

At Auschwitz in 1943, could the dedication ceremony of the United States Holocaust Memorial Museum in 1993 been predicted, let alone imagined? That this journey in the West has been accomplished—that the most persecuted people in Europe could survive the German onslaught *and* become a respected, affluent, and powerful community in the United States—is amazing and compounded by the equally unimaginable emergence of a Jewish state that is able to chart its own destiny among the family of nations. One might say that Jewish survival and flourishing in America and Israel after the Holocaust constitute a formative event for the Jewish people, an event that continues to unfold as the century of death comes to a close and the 21st century dawns. Thus the discussion of the death of millions of Jews takes place within the context of a journey from death to life, from weakness to power, from being despised to being celebrated. When Jews speak of Auschwitz, they do so from a distance of years and, as importantly, from a distance of social, cultural, and political context. It is almost as if the Jewish community is in two places at once, on the periphery and in the center, as victim and also empowered.

This amazing journey is complex in the distance traveled and the way in which that travel has taken place. To exist in the camps of Europe is quite different from rising to the upper echelon of America or creating a state where Jews are a majority in the Middle East. Among other things, success in the West demands a strategy of economic development and a politics of engagement; a state demands the formation of Jewish institutions and military power. No people or class are handed these successes, and for Jews the difficulty in achievement can hardly be overestimated. The journey was filled with hope and hard work, at times even a sense that failure would mean the disappearance of an entire history. When looked at from the perspective of the Holocaust, the flourishing of Jewish life at the dawn of the twenty-first century can be seen as a desperate act of rescue which succeeded. However, the struggle to rise in the West and in Israel has also been accomplished through the kind of actions and alliances that accompany virtually all empowerment. To escape the underside of Western civilization, Jews have often identified with the dominant economic classes in Europe and America; to establish a state for Jews in the Middle East, Jews have displaced the Palestinian people. In short, as the victims of the Holocaust are mourned, Jews have reentered the arena of history as a capable *and* culpable people.

So the debate about the Holocaust is carried forth in a necessary and culpable empowerment. To have the Holocaust narrative enshrined in a museum on the mall in Washington, D.C. is itself an expression of that empowerment. Bauer's lecturing of Goldhagen during the symposium carries the threat of banishing the younger scholar to his office at Harvard University where he teaches. The penalty is to be ostracized from the Holocaust establishment not deportation from the Warsaw ghetto, or even being dispatched to contemporary ghettoes in the United States. Emotion aside, the discussion of Auschwitz takes place in a comfort that belies the subject at hand. That others are suffering today—one thinks here of Rwanda and Bosnia—is a subject that is addressed with reference to the Holocaust but always in its shadow. To "confuse" the Holocaust with other events of mass suffering is to warrant the same treatment that Goldhagen has received and that he might be willing to dish out himself. Above all in these discussions, no matter how heated and personal, the Palestinian question is never broached. To speak about Palestinians is to raise the question of the cost of Jewish empowerment and to bring another angle to the question of the Holocaust. For if the lessons of the Holocaust are multifaceted, do they include, among others, the admonition that the displacement and humiliation of a people is wrong? Would they also allow those who have been displaced to lecture, analyze, even argue about the relative merits of historical investigation into the history of those who have displaced them?[7]

Returning to Auschwitz

These questions arose for me well before reading Goldhagen's book and observing the debate it generated. They began in the 1980s as I became more aware of Israeli occupation policies and as I began to meet and dialogue with Palestinians in America and Israel. Actually, I became aware, belatedly it is true, that when I traveled through Israel, I was also traveling through Palestine. At first it was strange to be moving through a landscape that seemed to house two peoples, especially since one, Jewish Israelis, dominated the other, Palestinian Arabs. I had read short pieces about the Palestinians and could even identify with their plight, but as a post-Holocaust Jew it was difficult to know what to think and say to Jewish Israelis, to Palestinians, and to Jews living in America. The emotional high of the 1967 war had influenced Jews around the world, including myself, yet it was clear that the war had led to an extensive and ongoing occupation. To be sure, security was an issue for Israelis. However, by the 1980s it was clear that more was at work than a desire for security. In fact, to a large extent, Israel was living off the occupation, expanding its borders, dedeveloping the Palestinian economy, and integrating that economy into the economy of Israel.

It was one thing after another. My travels introduced a confusing series of geographies and cultures into my view of Israel. At the same time, Israel's nuclear and defense policies with South Africa came to light, as did its military sales to oppressive governments around the world, including Nicaragua, El Salvador, and Guatemala. Israel occupied Palestinian land with the intent to settle parts of it and delay the emergence of a Palestinian state. At the same time, it had become one of the premier arms merchants around the world, benefiting economically and militarily from these sales, and, by serving as a surrogate for the United States, securing a place in the geo-political gamesmanship of the last stages of the Cold War. Of course, these aspects of Israeli policy were rarely spoken about in Jewish discourse, and when they were, such analysis was often denied or dismissed as engendered by self-hate. The questions that arose regarding the actuality of Israeli domestic and foreign policies were regarded as non-questions.[8]

The discussion of the Holocaust, which by the 1980s had matured into a significant, popular, and scholarly narrative, remained essentially untouched by these questions. Buoyed by the 1967 war and a discourse stressing the innocence of Jewish suffering in the Holocaust, it asserted as well the innocence of Jewish empowerment in Israel. For most Jewish spokespersons, Israel functioned as a response to the Holocaust, and the birth of Israel could be seen only within that context. Those survivors of the Holocaust who made their way to Palestine and fought for the establishment of the Jewish state carried their victimization *and* their innocence into battle. Jews were reluctant warriors who with desperation, elan, and perhaps the help of God, succeeded against an enemy who sought their demise. For many Jewish writers and religious leaders, the Nazis had been defeated only to find a new threat of annihilation in the Arab nations. If the Germans were, in Goldhagen's terminology, eliminationist in their anti-Semitism, the Arabs were as well. Why else would they seek to prevent the creation of a Jewish state, if not for their desire to annihilate the Jewish people? The Arabs, and later more specifically the Palestinians, were the contemporary Germans.

To some extent, the Israeli invasion of Lebanon and the bombing of Beirut in the early 1980s, and the policy of might and beatings that sought to quell the Palestinian uprising later in the decade, confronted the Jewish sense of innocence with a brutality shocking to many Jews and non-Jews alike. Earlier wars had been explained in terms of security and, for the most part, disappeared in the rhetoric of Jewish innocence and the dramatic story of a Holocaust people struggling for a new and independent existence against overwhelming odds. If the Holocaust was the nadir of Jewish history, Israel was an epiphany seen within the religious terminology of redemption. For many Jews, Israel represented (and for some still does) the dawn of redemption, a renewed contact with the ancient soil of Israel's birth and with the God who sent this people forth into the world. Yet the indiscriminate bombing of Beirut, and the beating, torture, and killing of Palestinian children in the West Bank and Gaza, confronted that dawn with the cries of another people struggling for their own dawn, for their own land, and for their own redemption from suffering. Could the Holocaust narrative keep these cries from being heard by Jews who sought a dawn and redemption from suffering for Jews *and* all people who struggled for a justice denied them?

The most pressing dilemma, of course, was not a general support for those who struggled for justice. Such support is deeply ingrained in the Jewish psyche and in Jewish history. "Never again" to the Jews is a prominent feature of Holocaust discourse, but a secondary theme is "never again" should *any* people suffer genocidal violence or injustice of a sustained type which denied their humanity. The general theme is an easy one, combining a particular and universal concern that can be adopted by Jews and non-Jews as a moral lesson of the Holocaust. The stumbling block is closer to home. Could it be that those who carry the message of the Holocaust, those who embody the suffering and the hope, are themselves guilty of violating their own injunctions?

That no people can ever be empowered and retain their innocence is axiomatic, obvious even to the casual observer of history. For Jews, however, the obvious is too threatening, as almost the entirety of post-Holocaust Jewish identity is bound to an innocent suffering and an innocent empowerment. For if Jewish empowerment is not innocent, do Jews then lose the right to lecture Germans, Christians, indeed the entire world, on their culpability with regard to Jewish suffering? As important, many Jews are so bound to this identity that admitting culpability seems to threaten the continuation of Jewish life. The fear is simple: if the sole content of Jewish identity revolves around the purity of the Holocaust and Israel in suffering and innocence, then the confession of culpability introduces a dissonance that threatens the entire identity structure. Can a confession of Jewish culpability lessen the Jewish accusation against the world and point that accusation inward as well? Will that internal confession lead to a disappointment with one's own people so deep as to cause a lessening, even abandonment of Jewish identity?

I witnessed this dilemma during my visit to Auschwitz in 1992. As part of a delegation of Jewish scholars and intellectuals organized by the Oxford Centre for Post-Graduate Hebrew Studies, our task was to help the museum at Auschwitz to refocus its narrative to make central the suffering of the Jewish people. Because of the ideological bent of the Cold War years, the victims of Auschwitz had been grouped according to nationality, and the Polish struggle against fascism was the main emphasis. Since approximately ninety percent of the people killed at Auschwitz were Jewish, and since that fact was mentioned only in a peripheral way, the refocusing of the history was essential to the truthfulness and fullness of the museum's presentation.

The crisis surrounding the Carmelite convent and their large and visible cross overlooking the camp was still in the air. For the Jewish community, much was at stake in the narrative and the convent, as the exclusive right to claim Auschwitz was being debated. The explosive rhetoric of

Cardinal Glemp simply fanned the fires of this controversy. As scholars and intellectuals rather than political and organizational leaders, the hope was that our delegation would take a low-key approach to help the Polish authorities reconstruct the narrative without press conferences and condemnations.

The interaction of the Jewish delegation and the museum authorities was, for the most part, constructive. The Polish officials and workers understood the deficiencies and wanted assistance in overcoming them. Their limitations in undertaking this work were obvious, with very little funding available and little in the way of the historical and technological expertise needed to update and modernize their presentation of the story of Auschwitz. While the Poles were accommodating to an extreme, and members of the delegation for the most part courteous and patient, the tension of Jew and Pole was nonetheless evident. For most of the Jewish delegation Auschwitz was a central theme in their intellectual and personal lives, and since for the great majority of the delegation this was their first trip to Auschwitz, the symbol and reality came together in a powerful way.

Walking the grounds of Auschwitz is itself a peculiar experience, as the specter of the mass death of one's own people haunts each step. Coming to Auschwitz felt to many as a return to Auschwitz, but what could one make with this return? One half expected to see the trains unloading their human cargo, hear the cries of mothers and children being separated, or see the blood of the victims flowing from the earth. This was juxtaposed with the reality of a poorly maintained facility and the hundreds of other visitors who were spending the day there; children who were tired and bored, the book shop and the lavatories, all attesting to a factory of death that had become a sight of pilgrimage *and* a tourist attraction. Though all of this was an irritant, a trivializing of Auschwitz, we on the delegation had little to look down on. After all, we were staying at a well-appointed hotel in Krakow and traveled to Auschwitz by charter bus. We frequented the book shop and the lavatories and went through the museum just like anyone else.[9]

In fact, a major point of dissonance had less to do with the tourist quality of the Auschwitz camp then our own bifurcated identity. Though we felt the appropriate seriousness of traveling to Auschwitz and the task we had taken on, our lives were so different from the victims that it felt a chasm lay between us. Most in the delegation were secure, affluent, prestigious, even prominent members of the Jewish community and the broader national community within which they lived. Coming primarily from America, England, France, and Canada, the security of these delegates was assured, and our Western lives represented powerful, wealthy, dominant cultures that had histories featuring great highs and lows, combining, among other things, great literature *and* slavery, the wonder of space exploration *and* the exploitation of native peoples. In short, the delegates benefited from and were protected by cultures and political systems decidedly mixed in their histories.

The reality is that the delegates who visited Auschwitz came and left in a very different way than the Jews of the Nazi period. *They* came as victims and left as corpses; *we* arrived at the center of death embodying a prestige and a power that would have been unimaginable to the Jews of Auschwitz. As awkward as this massive shift would be to any person or people, there was a still more incredible reason for this sense, as the career and prestige of most of the delegates had been aided, sometimes built, on Auschwitz itself. For what separated the Jewish academic and intellectual from other academics and intellectuals than the topic of Auschwitz? And what would the size of the congregation and the prestige of the rabbi be without the Holocaust and the ability to insist on the necessity of Jewish identification after such a horrendous event?

The issue of Israel was also in the air. It was during that spring of 1992 that the Israeli elections were reaching their final phase. Battling for the reelection was Yitzhak Shamir, the reluctant participant in the Madrid peace process, and his campaign opponent, Yitzhak Rabin, who spoke confidently of bringing that process to a successful conclusion. Despite the importance of the election, they were mentioned only once in our week of meetings in Krakow and Auschwitz, and this in regard to the plane crash involving Yassir Arafat in Libya. The report on the BBC, communicated by one of the delegates during breakfast one morning, was initially inconclusive. The plane was lost and Arafat was presumed dead, though the plane and the body had not yet been found. As it turned out, Arafat's injuries were substantial but not lethal, though my initial reaction was to presume the worst.

On hearing the news I was quite shaken. For my Palestinian friends I knew that this would be difficult. Whatever their views on Arafat—and they were certainly diverse—he embodied and symbolized their struggle. The loss of Arafat would occasion a national mourning and reflection among the Palestinians. After the shock wore off, I felt the need to mourn with the Palestinians I knew as a recognition of their integrity and nationhood. However, the discussion among the delegates was quite different, focusing exclusively on how Arafat's death would affect the Israeli election. Would the death of Arafat benefit Shamir or Rabin? Would the prospect of a new Palestinian leadership drive Israeli public opinion to the right or to the center? Most of the delegates were moderates and progressives and thus supportive of Rabin. And no doubt they favored some kind of deal with the Palestinians. What struck me, however, was that for these delegates the nationality of the Palestinians was a bothersome reality that was recognized only to the extent that it touched Israeli politics. Palestinians were peripheral to Jewish concerns and, even as we demanded to be recognized on our own terms, there seemed little desire to recognize the nationality of a people who had been displaced by Jewish power.

It struck me as odd that such recognition was withheld in the very place where the lack of that recognition was being fought retrospectively. We arrived at Auschwitz with the narrative of the Holocaust and the state of Israel as symbols of our recognition in contemporary life, and we remained furious that such recognition had been withheld during the Nazi era, and that in the museum narrative it had yet to be recognized. Any slight—historical, cultural, linguistic—any wording about the Holocaust that was considered by the delegates to be misleading or imprecise, was immediately and forcefully challenged. This applied to the Polish authorities, to be sure, but also to members of the delegation who offered any analysis or narrative that did not comport with the majority view. This is where I began to see more clearly that the contemporary form of Jewish orthodoxy revolves less around God than it does around the Holocaust. Twinning the Holocaust and Israel, or rather seeing Israel only in relation to the Holocaust, had many consequences including the inability to recognize the importance of a national leader to a people laboring under Jewish domination.

In refusing to recognize Palestinians, these delegates in essence refused to recognize an entire aspect of Jewish history after Auschwitz, a history that had seen the movement of Jews from the ranks of the victims to those who created victims. By understanding this consequence, a strange paradox suggests itself: that empowered Jews would rather dwell in the suffering of the Holocaust—and have others dwell in that suffering as well—than face the history that Jews have embarked upon since Auschwitz. The paradox is profound and troubling, as the Holocaust has become a place of safety where Jews can enjoy the benefits of empowerment, claim the status of victim, and thus deflect the questions raised by Palestinians and others about the effects of Israeli policies in the Middle East and around the world.

More important, however, was the general silence on Israel. After the 1967 war, Israel was paramount in the Jewish community, and almost any discussion of the Holocaust ended with the image of Israel. Yet when we discussed how to end the narrative of Auschwitz for those who came to the museum, and Israel was mentioned, the idea was immediately dismissed. Israel is what it is and the Holocaust is what it is; this, at least, was the general tenor of the response. The events were not to be confused or conflated. Yet this is precisely what two decades of Jewish discourse had done. Twinning the Holocaust and Israel was now expected by Jews and non-Jews alike. Disengaging the two would surprise the public.

I wondered at this turn of events. Had the critique of Israel become too much to allow this ending? At one level, the tarnished image of Israel could raise questions that diverted attention from the Holocaust, hence it would be better to leave the end of the Holocaust narrative to silence. At another level, the changing image of Israel could raise questions as to the post-Holocaust actions of the Jewish community, thus challenging the ability of Jews to speak about suffering as if our hands were clean. In a strange twist of fate, the actions of Israel might render Jews silent on the Holocaust. The initial twinning of the events by the Jewish community might then double back with a twinning of unexpected dimensions. Israel would then be a challenge to the moral and political lessons derived from the Holocaust by some on the delegation itself. Had they not spoken of the Holocaust as a suffering visited upon an undeserving and helpless population?

So the Holocaust was alone again. The accusing images of Israeli power could no longer be held together by the Holocaust without tarnishing the Holocaust narrative. A choice was made to support Israel by not speaking of it, and the choice of silence as a gesture of support represented a sea-change in Jewish discourse. Instead of trumpeting the glories of Israel, Israel would be protected through silence. Having witnessed this silence at Auschwitz, I was better prepared when the same choice was made in the narrative of the United States Holocaust Memorial Museum, which opened a year later. Instead of Israel as the final moment of triumph over the forces of Nazism, the museum patron is presented with video testimonies of Holocaust survivors and the rights of Americans to equality and freedom under the Constitution of the United States. When Israel is represented as part of the survival of the post-Holocaust Jewish community, it is represented only within a larger tapestry. Though this also is partially an attempt to protect Israel, it seems, at the same time, to be a warning to Israel itself, that despite the rhetoric of loyalty, Jews in America are choosing their own destiny. If the image of Israel strengthens Jewish identity in America, if it enhances Jewish prestige and status, than so much the better. If the image of Israel makes it more difficult for Jews, then Israel itself is to be downplayed or even abandoned. Jews in America had used Israel for its own advancement. As Israel becomes more controversial, it quietly slips into the background.[10]

Goldhagen in the Time of Netanyahu

Soon after leaving Auschwitz, and as Goldhagen was completing the first draft of his book, Yitzhak Rabin was elected prime minister, and the hope for peace intensified. For many of the delegates, and no doubt for many Jews in Israel and America, Rabin was just the man to push the process forward. After all, his credentials as a military man were unimpeachable. Jews could feel comfortable that in any agreement with the Palestinians, security and peace would be assured. Shimon Peres, as a life-long competitor with Rabin and now his right-hand man, added to the anticipation that a stalled process would soon be energized. Rabin was tough and practical, Peres open and visionary. Perhaps this was the combination of talents needed at this time. Could they bring off the feat they promised in the elections, that is, bring an end to the occupation and, in so doing, allow Israel to disentangle itself from the Palestinian "problem"?

Despite the celebration that the Oslo Accords elicited in the Western world among Jews and non-Jews in 1993, and the outpouring of anger and sympathy over Rabin's subsequent assassination in 1995, Rabin and Peres argued for peace as a victory for Israel and the final separation of Jews and Palestinians. They saw it as the culmination of the ongoing war between Jews and Palestinians, with Israel as the victor and the Palestinians as the defeated. Oslo represents a final surrender by the Palestinians, though the view of that surrender is seen differently by both sides. For the Israelis, the Palestinian surrender is the final step in the long process of settling the land and establishing a Jewish state. For the Palestinians, they recognized that their defeat—that is the destruction of Palestine—could only become more complete if they withheld their surrender and continued to struggle without an agreement with Israel.

Israel's victory was, for all practical purposes, complete, as the withdrawals and redeployment of Israeli troops and the granting of limited autonomy essentially covered areas where Israel had difficulty or no interest in controlling. Palestinians claimed what was left of Palestine as a strategic possibility to reopen negotiations as time went on and confidence measures could be adopted. The Palestinian surrender is thus a negotiated surrender, one that establishes a Palestinian presence and opportunity, as limited and controversial as it seems to many Palestinians. Of course, the ceremony on the White House lawn in September 1993 presented only the glitz and the symbolism of the two warriors, Rabin and Arafat, clasping hands. It was an emotional day for all involved, filled with ambivalence and hope, and darkened only months later when a Jewish doctor of medicine entered a mosque in Hebron and massacred twenty-nine Muslim worshipers in cold blood and with the weapons that had brought Israel the victory embodied in the Oslo accords.[11]

In a powerful speech before the Knesset, Rabin condemned the murderer, Baruch Goldstein, declared him an aberration among the Jewish people, and as a person—and those like him—who needed to be ostracized, denounced, excommunicated from the Jewish people and the land of Israel. Surely Goldstein was, in Goldhagen's terminology, a willing executioner, and the debate among Jews after the massacre in Hebron was how this "errant weed" had come to be among the Jewish people. Was it accurate to say, as Rabin did in his speech, that the murderer was not part of the community of Israel or a partner in the Zionist enterprise? Was he indeed a "foreign implant" and did, in fact, "sensible Judaism" spit him out? Did Goldstein grow in a "swamp" whose "sources are foreign to Judaism"? Or was the murderer born and nurtured in an environment that, again to use Goldhagen's terminology, is eliminationist in nature? Does post-Holocaust Jewish culture deny the humanity of Palestinians and at some level seek their disappearance or elimination?

As Goldhagen might analyze the massacre, Goldstein went beyond specific authorization and exercised choice in his deed. The brutality bore no relation to the victims or their actions: they were assigned to death because they existed as a challenge to the murderer's world view, a world of Jews *without* Palestinians. The violence accelerated as the victims became less able to defend themselves. And Goldstein, condemned by Rabin, was honored by thousands of Jews who make pilgrimages to his burial site. This willing executioner became an inspiration for yet another willing executioner, the assassin of Rabin himself, Yigal Amir. He, too, felt himself fulfilling the cultural and religious mandate of Jewish life, to extend Jewish control over the land of Israel and eliminate the Palestinian presence in the Jewish material and symbolic universe. Was he, too, an errant weed, a foreign implant, which sensible Judaism spits out? After the assassination a banner flew from atop a Jewish settlement proclaiming the opposite. In bold script it proclaimed a solidarity that is startling and instructive: "We are all Yigal Amir."[12]

A year before the massacre in Hebron, I received an unsolicited trial issue of a new journal, *Inquiry*. The cover stories include an essay about the 418 Palestinians who were expelled to Lebanon by the Israeli government in December 1992, and a report on the increasing number of Palestinian children in Israeli jails. As if this were not enough difficult news for Jews to handle—knowing that these stories had been initially reported by such established organizations as the *New York Times* and Amnesty International—the third article is even more provocative. Titled "The War Crimes Record of Yitzhak Rabin," and written by Elias Davidsson, Director of the Center for Policy Research in Reykjavik, Iceland, this article can be described as Wagner described Goldhagen's methodology: a legal brief establishing a position of culpability. Citing the recent call of a number of member states of the United Nations to establish a court to investigate war crimes and crimes against humanity under United Nations auspices, Davidsson charges Rabin with both crimes.

For many the idea of such charges and the appellation of "criminal" to Rabin is startling. Yet the evidence Davidsson cites is well known, some admitted by Rabin himself, others substantiated by such well-known Jewish Israeli historians as Benny Morris. Davidsson cites three charges against Rabin: responsibility for "ethnic cleansing/deportations" during the 1948 war; the destruction of three villages and the expulsion of their inhabitants during the 1967 war; urging soldiers to break the bones of Palestinian youngsters during the Palestinian uprising in 1988. According to Davidsson, the deportation of civilians, the indiscriminate destruction of villages, and the extra-juridical punishment and ill-treatment of protected persons violates in significant ways the Nuremberg Charter and the Geneva Conventions. Davidsson quotes from the Nuremberg Principles to conclude his case against Rabin: "The fact that a person who committed an act which constitutes a crime under international law acted as Head of State of responsible government officials does not relieve him from responsibility under international law—

(Principle III): "The fact that a person acted pursuant to order of his Government or of a superior does not relieve him from responsibility under international law, provided a moral choice was in fact possible for him"—(Principle IV).[13]

It is hard to miss the irony of such an indictment of Rabin, especially when the article appeals to principles created in response to the Nazi years and against the perpetrators of the Holocaust. Could it be that Jewish leaders are accountable to international law as any other leaders are? The opposite is true as well: in general only the defeated are tried in international courts and the victors escape the verdicts of the courts. We might say that Jewish leaders have escaped scrutiny on these counts precisely because of the Allied victory over Germany in World War II and the subsequent alliance of Israel and the countries that formed the alliance. The suffering of the Jews in the Holocaust and the existence of eliminationist anti-Semitism make it doubly difficult in the West to perceive these charges against Rabin as anything but a continuation of anti-Semitism. Thus *Inquiry* is likely to be placed in this tradition and therefore discounted.

Yet from the perspective of those who suffered under Israeli rule, Rabin was a major architect of their displacement. This displacement was not innocent or without its share of brutality. Willing displacers, in Davidsson's parlance, willing practitioners of ethnic cleansing, were easy to find, and this among Jews who had just been "cleansed" from Europe. There were also willing executioners, among them Arieh Biroh, who survived Auschwitz and as an Israeli soldier executed scores of Egyptian prisoners during the Suez war in 1956. Willing torturers also exist among Jews in Israel, as Stanley Cohen frequently documents. As with almost any state, the list of "criminals" is long, replete with those recognized as heroes to many. Rabin is surely among them, but the list stretches back to the founding prime minister of Israel, David Ben-Gurion, and continued through Menachem Begin and Yitzhak Shamir. As the celebrated war hero of the 1967 war, Moshe Dayan, once commented: "We came to this country which was already populated by Arabs, and we are establishing a Hebrew, that is a Jewish state here. . . . Jewish villages were built in the place of Arab villages. . . . There is not one place built in this country that did not have a former Arab population."[14]

What happened to these villages is well known to Palestinians and to the Jewish soldiers who emptied and destroyed them. But the story is hardly known in the larger Jewish world, as it is essentially banned from Jewish discourse. Yet the brutality is in need of recollection, if only to avoid the abstract discussions that reside in terms like the "dawn of redemption." In Lydda, for example, one of the villages Rabin ordered emptied of its inhabitants, Netiva Ben Yehuda, a young female member of the Jewish army, recalled that a soldier went through the streets with "loudspeakers and promised everybody who would go inside a certain mosque that they would be safe." Believing the soldiers, hundreds of Arabs entered the mosque and sat there with their hands on top of their head. Despite their compliance, over eighty of these prisoners were machine-gunned to death. Their bodies were left for ten days decomposing in the summer heat to serve as a reminder of the fate of Arabs in newly conquered Jewish areas. There was also Deir Yassin, where over one hundred Arabs were systematically murdered after the village had surrendered.[15]

The differences in the violence of Holocaust and the violence attending the birth of Israel are significant and hardly need to be enunciated. The point here is of a different magnitude. Both Goldhagen and his detractors analyze, debate, and memorialize the Holocaust *as if nothing of consequence has happened since that event.* Further, they lecture the world and each other *as if Jews and they themselves have escaped the consequences of those actions done on their behalf and that spring from an understanding of Jewish history which, at least from the Palestinian perspective, has been, and in some ways is still eliminationist.* Though the process of elimination is mass dislocation rather than mass death, the effects on the Palestinians as a people have been devastating: perpetual exile in their own homeland and the creation of a diaspora that continues to grow. Finally, it is simply unimaginable to Holocaust commentators and scholars that either the essentialist or "complex" understanding of the forces that led to the Holocaust could be applied at any level to the Jewish people. That the very discussion of the Holocaust without the application of those lessons to post-Holocaust Jewish life could be a way of diverting attention from the crimes against the Palestinian people, thus involving them in a complicity as great as those Jews who displaced and massacred the civilians in Lydda and Deir Yassin, is, in this scenario, outside the boundaries of thinkable thought.

As I came to know some Palestinians, visited with them in their homes, met their children, and listened to their stories, what at first seemed confusing and incredible became understandable and urgent. For Palestinians the "grammar of Jewish expression" is voluntary cruelty reinforced by the power of the state. In general, this is their sole experience of Jews, and they can surely identify with Goldhagen's analysis, though shifted from the Germans to Jews. They can agree with Goldhagen's description of the "underlying German cultural model of 'the Jew'" as comprised of three aspects: "that the Jew was different from the German, that he was a binary opposite of the German, and that he was not benignly different but malevolent and corrosive. Whether conceived of as religion, nation, political group, or race, the Jew was always a *Fremdkorper,* an alien body within Germany." Palestinians can simply substitute Jew for German and Palestinian for Jew. Jews, too, have a cultural model of "the Palestinian": the Palestinian is different from the Jew; Jew and Palestinian should be seen as binary opposites; rather than benign, the difference is malevolent and corrosive. No matter how Jews change in their perception of Palestinians, Palestinians will always be seen as *Fremdkorper*, an alien body within Israel.[16]

With this experience of Jews—an experience wholly different from the German or Christian experience of Jews in Europe—it is difficult for Palestinians to understand how Jews can continue to lecture on the Holocaust. If Goldhagen's charge to other Holocaust historians is that they lose the horror of Jewish suffering and the viciousness of the German attack on the Jews in their ever- evolving complex and abstract theories of human behavior, how can Palestinians experience Goldhagen's analysis if it is not also related to his own people? Could the lack of application to the present render Goldhagen's analysis as abstract and diverting as he accuses other historians of being? Would Goldhagen allow his lecture to be followed by a Palestinian lecturer using Goldhagen's methodology and insights? Could that Palestinian lecturer respond to a German historian's remark—"The specific thing about the Nazi killing of the Jews was that it was not spontaneous emotional killing"—in the way that Goldhagen responded—"Does anyone here apart from Professor Mommsen believe that people who were killing Jews did not have a view of what they were doing?" by confronting the plea of Jewish innocence—"Does anyone here aside from Professor Goldhagen believe that Jews who were displacing Palestinians did not have a view of what they were doing?"[17]

As Goldhagen finds even with those Germans who opposed Hitler on various policies, the consensus on anti-Semitism held strong. There were Germans who opposed particular policies of the Nazi regime, for example the wanton violence accompanying *Kristallnacht*, as uncivilized and beneath the character of the German people, yet the protest was well within the framework of German anti-Semitism. The reason for opposition had nothing to do with an essential solidarity with the Jewish people. Rather, the dissent, often as not, was formed on principles that sought to uphold the moral and ethical principles of German civilization. The goal of a *Judenrein* society could be achieved in an orderly and respectful way. From a Palestinian perspective, the continuing invocation of the Holocaust which Goldhagen now participates in on an international level has, whether intended or not, the same effect. Could the haunting Holocaust museum, the place where Goldhagen initially faced the Holocaust historians—whose purpose is in many ways so noble—symbolize anything other to Palestinians than an argument that diverts attention away from their history and contemporary plight? Palestinians look at the intramural debate on Goldhagen's thesis as Goldhagen looks at protest within Germany: too little, too late, and missing the point.

That this discussion continued in the era of Netanyahu is significant. On his first visit to the United States after his election as prime minister in 1996, Netanyahu deflected critics of his policies toward Palestinians by stating that they were essentially the same as his predecessors, Rabin and Peres. To be sure, the mood and rhetoric is different. However, the caution that Netanyahu counseled is instructive and the example he used telling. On the thickening and expansion of settlements which Western commentators identified as a major stumbling block to peace in the Middle East, Netanyahu asserted that he would basically be carrying out his predecessors' policies. After all, the growth rate of the settler community increased during the time of Rabin and Peres, even as they negotiated and implemented the Oslo accords. To be sure, there were few lectures for settlers on proper behavior with this new government, and the rhetoric of the Greater Land of Israel was more welcome than under Rabin and Peres. The essential policies remained as they form a consensus of the Israeli government and Jewish people vis-a-vis the Palestinians. This leads Geoffrey Aronson, editor of the *Report on Israeli Settlement in the Occupied Territories*, to conclude that Netanyahu was correct: "The Labor-led governments of Yitzhak Rabin and Shimon Peres have bequeathed to the Netanyahu government a settlement infrastructure more secure and sustainable than Labor inherited in July 1992. That consensus is why Yossi Beilin, a key architect of the Oslo process and a cabinet minister in Rabin's government, could take solace after the election of Netanyahu: 'There is not today a meaningful gap between the stands of the two major parties, but rather a joint understanding on the central issues, including a defined timetable for the peace process and a final solution that will be acceptable to most of the right-wing parties.'"[18]

The journey from Auschwitz to the era of Netanyahu and now Barak is short in time, far in geography, and long in consequence. The discussions in the ghettos and the death camps about the contemporary situation and the future of the Jewish people were characterized by a desperation and an awareness that were palpable. Charges against the Nazi—in Goldhagen's sense, the German—onslaught were directed with the ferocity and accuracy suffering often elicits. As time passes and the survivors move on to a protected and welcoming world, the discussion becomes more complex, at times even angrier than it was in the situation itself. Then people were too focused on survival, too busy calculating the casualties and the possibility of escape, to engage in the scholarly and elevated discourse of the present. As the stakes decrease and as Jews are removed from the status of the condemned, public relations, whether, in Bauer's admonishment of Goldhagen, before or after the scholarly investigation, is as much of the process as the emotion evoked. For just as the best-seller list is unreachable without publicity, and the chairs of Holocaust Studies that proliferate in universities of Europe and America impossible without a secure and affluent Jewish community, so are the creation of Holocaust memorials which dot the landscape dependent on a status and prestige remarkable in light of Jewish history.

Yet this publicity and affluence is haunted by the very analysis, study, and memorializing that occur within this success. The fate of Goldhagen's analysis is that one day it will be applied to the very community he seeks to defend against the dilution of its own suffering. The tragedy is that this significant and powerful work, and the debate it engendered, is trivialized by the limitations of the participants themselves and by the Jewish community that seeks to limit the discussion to the past. Freezing Jewish history—and, one might add, German history as well—in the Holocaust is a way of denying contemporary history. Therefore, in the long run, Goldhagen's work is more important in the way that it functions in contemporary Jewish life than it is for the light it might shed on the Holocaust. After all, the debaters are operating in a consensus that belies their antagonism and recriminations.

Goldhagen and the End of Auschwitz

Do Goldhagen and Bauer share the same consensus as Rabin and Netanyahu, Peres and Barak? As Jews with commitments to the Jewish past and the Jewish future, as spokespersons for the Jewish community in America and Israel, they no doubt share an overall perspective produced by the Holocaust and the reality of the state of Israel. Despite their heated arguments and recriminations, they come together on the essential aspects of memory and empowerment. They are poised together against those who would deny the Holocaust, soften its horror, charge Jewish conspiracies, and deny the Jewish right to equality and empowerment. The passion of their commitment is furthered by these denials, but it also makes it more difficult to distinguish between the time of the Holocaust and the dawn of the twenty-first century.

As these figures analyze Jewish history and act on behalf of the Jewish people, they are looking over their shoulders and calculating the price of particular thoughts or actions beyond the thought or action in and of itself. Goldhagen's passionate analysis seems haunted by the prospect that the horror of the Holocaust is being lost and that the victims of the Holocaust will be forgotten or theorized out of existence. Behind his central thesis is the fear that by seeing the destruction of the Jews as a modern, technological enterprise carried out by an elite fascist political movement that involved ordinary people as any state bureaucratic system would, the moral culpability of the Germans is diluted. To dilute their moral culpability is somehow to lose sight of the millions of Jews who perished.

Perhaps in the end Goldhagen's book is a plea to salvage the meaning of these deaths from a meaningless academic chatter. Still, there is an attempt on the part of Goldhagen and the others, as there seems to be a necessity felt by Jewish leaders in America and Israel, to manage the discussions revolving around Jews. Goldhagen appeals to the audiences in America and Germany; Bauer appeals to the academic world. Both seek to manage the discussion as if differences could become anarchy and the entire enterprise might fail. Can one see this same need to manage in the actions, justifications, and appeals of Israeli leaders from Ben-Gurion to Barak? Is this why there remains this exaggerated need for the defeated Palestinians who, more than any people in the world, have experienced the reality of Israel, to acknowledge the right of Israel's existence explicitly and almost daily? Here we also encounter the phenomenon of the recent wave of Jewish writings on Holocaust deniers, and this at a time when more people know about this event than at any time since the Holocaust itself.

The visit of Pope John Paul II to Germany in June 1996 and his visit to the Holy Land in 2000 only fuel these propensities to look over one's shoulder and attempt to manage the issues at hand. A central corollary to the desire to have the world recognize German culpability in the Holocaust is the desire to force Christians to admit their culpability in anti-Semitism and the Holocaust itself. The pressure by Jewish leaders on the various Christian denominations in this quest has been enormous, one might say relentless. And it has increased over the years as churches have issued statements, sometimes confessions, over the role of Christianity in the formation of anti-Semitism and its general acquiescence in the Holocaust, especially as they have sometimes become more critical of the role of Israel in the Middle East. The confession of anti-Semitism and an essential solidarity with the Jewish people has not been enough when coupled with a general critique of Israeli occupation policies.

The "managing" of the Christian understandings of the Jews, anti-Semitism, and Israel is a complex and volatile process, and is perhaps even more important to Jews than the German question. After all, the relationship with Christianity is basic to the last two thousand years of Jewish history. The anger of the Jewish community and the pressing of the Christians to admit unequivocally their historical sins and their contemporary support for Israel is understandable in light of the history of Christianity vis-à-vis the Jews, at the same time betraying this anxiety of recognition. It is almost as if Jews, while proudly proclaiming their independent, self-sufficient and proud identity, are dependent on its confirmation by those accused of defaming and attempting to destroy it.

The relentlessness of Christian triumphalism lends fuel to the fire of this anger. The pope reiterated this triumphalism in Germany by continuing to speak of the martyrdom of the few Germans who resisted the Nazi onslaught as representing "many Catholic men and women who, at the cost of many and diverse sacrifices, rejected National Socialist tyranny and resisted the brown ideology." In a prepared passage which the Pope did not deliver orally, but which nonetheless is part of the official record, he then went on to declare that these Catholics are "thus part of the resistance offered by the whole church to a system contemptuous of God and human beings." Later in his visit, the Pope also avoided reading a passage alluding to the wartime pope, Pius XII, who has been accused of being silent during the Holocaust: "Those who do not limit themselves to cheap polemics know very well what Pius XII thought of the Nazi regime and how much he did to help the countless victims persecuted by that regime." Can one read these words without recalling and understanding the anger in Goldhagen's words on the subject of Christian resistance which the Pope seeks to extend even beyond the individual to stand for the entire Catholic church? It is worth reiterating Goldhagen's angry comment that "never once did any German bishop, Catholic or Protestant, speak out publicly on behalf of the Jews. . . ."[19]

By asserting that the few resistors speak for the many, that in fact the few define the response of the Catholic church, *as if by their opposition the Catholic church opposed Hitler on behalf of the Jews,* is an attempt to falsify the record of the church and manage the crisis of legitimacy which the church's lack of opposition engendered. It fails to come to grips with the culpability of the church in the Holocaust as it has tried to manage its culpability in other areas. One thinks here of the quincentenary "celebration" of the discovery of the Americas in 1492 and the pope's comments in relation to the church's interaction with the peoples of the Americas. Can one imagine the following words being spoken to the people of Latin America after 1492 and the Holocaust? As the pope expressed it in 1992: "We are celebrating, dear brothers and sisters, *the arrival of the message of salvation on this continent.*" Is it any wonder that Jewish writers on the Holocaust seek to keep the plain fact of Christian complicity simple and uncompromising? That is why Goldhagen quotes a historian who writes that the "fearless statements and deeds of individuals on behalf of the Jews should not obscure the fact that the Church became a compliant helper of Nazi Jewish policy."[20]

It seems we are left on all sides with a cycle of argument and counter argument raised to an art form for motives of protection and deflection, and that the debate about the Holocaust, now joined by the pope, functions as much to promote contemporary agendas as it does to explore the past. In this effort the Jewish community confronts the past so as to protect the present from accountability, and the German and church communities seek to deflect the past so as to find a place in the contemporary world. One is forced to ask, however, how long this cycle can continue without so trivializing the Holocaust that future generations will simply dismiss the event as irrelevant or find it so politicized that they turn away from it in disgust. Are we not now, with the passage of time and the process of trivialization, approaching the end of Auschwitz? Can the cycle come to a close by constantly evoking the name of Auschwitz within the framework that has been created for it? Or does the framework of discussion itself signal the end of Auschwitz at least as we have come to know it?

The way forward seems difficult for all the parties involved. In fact, all three communities have moved forward, though in superficial ways. Germany is rebuilt, reunified, and again the largest economy in Europe. Christianity continues to focus its energies on populations lacking the gospel message. Jews have transformed a battered and beleaguered people into a vibrant and empowered community. Though as yet neither the Germans nor the Christian churches have encountered or precipitated another event of this magnitude, the Jewish world has experienced the formative event of the creation of the state of Israel and the displacement of the Palestinian people. Germans reflect on the Holocaust when it is forced upon them, as do the Christians churches, and the people forcing the issue, Jews, do so often to maintain the focus on the past rather than on the present. The way forward is superficial precisely for the reason that there still has not been a reckoning with the reality or the lessons of the Holocaust. Because the Germans and the Christian churches remains virtually untouched by the essential lessons of the Holocaust, lessons that penetrate to the core of German and Christian culture and politics, and because Jews will not allow the spotlight to be turned to their behavior in the present, all proceed with lip service to the horrors while essentially bypassing the meaning of the event itself.

But what if all sides admitted that the era of Auschwitz has come to a close without having taken the event seriously? What if all parties admitted that the core issues of behavior past and present are simply too difficult to face, and that the strategic interests of each community are in reality more important to them than the memory of the Holocaust? What if all parties agreed to drop the rhetorical facade in dealing with the death of six million and admit that the prospect of doing so is too frightening, as it exposes questions of God and humanity that might not have positive answers?

At Auschwitz, when the discussion of preserving the site from age and neglect began, one Jewish delegate objected to the very notion of preservation. For most delegates, preservation is a way of honoring the dead and keeping their memory alive, as well as providing a place for those who mourn the dead and seek to learn the lessons of Auschwitz. But for this delegate, the rabbis were wise in mandating a mourning period and similarly wise in limiting that mourning. There is in Jewish law a ritual surrounding mourning where work halts, black is worn, and mirrors are covered. Yet the wisdom of the rabbis is contained in the need to mourn and the need to resume life. Refusing to mourn or mourning too long carries the risk of trivializing death through forgetting, or allowing the dead to consume life by holding onto death as if it can carry one through life. Thus though the cycle of mourning has different rhythms, the intensity of mourning ends with the passage of time. What this delegate was suggesting is that this ritual apply to

Auschwitz as well. The intense mourning has been completed and the desire to make this the center of Jewish life forever impedes the natural processes of life itself. Memory of the dead has to be in the context of life, lest that memory be used to shield the individual or the community from the challenges of life in the present. His suggestion to implement this plan was simple, if controversial: *let the natural elements decay the site of Auschwitz until Auschwitz itself returns to the earth from which it came. By that time perhaps the decay of Auschwitz will bring forth life, there on its very ground, and allow it to flourish in the world at large.*

As might be expected, this suggestion was met with a silence that signaled rejection. Soon we were on to the technical matters of preservation, including the need to solicit funds to install temperature controls for the barracks that once housed Jews condemned to death. We also demanded that movies about the Nazis stop using Auschwitz as a location for filming, as this hastened the deterioration of the site and even introduced new structures needed for the filming. These structures created a false impression and, as some were left standing after the filming, also left open the possibility of claiming the inauthenticity of Auschwitz itself. For if new structures had been created, could that mean that the original structures were also created after the war? The discussion itself recreated the cycle that the delegates' suggestion hoped to end. By preserving memory against every imaginable onslaught, including time itself, the delegates asserted the need for an eternal vigilance in relation to Auschwitz and to the Holocaust. In a real sense, the decision to preserve Auschwitz was a decision to continue Auschwitz into an eternal future. *Auschwitz as protector, Auschwitz as the silencer of questions, Auschwitz as the refusal of accountability, Auschwitz as the source of all lectures on the culpability of Germans and Christianity.*

Goldhagen's *Hitler's Willing Executioners* functions perfectly in this regard, and so should be regarded as another effort to keep the era of Auschwitz from coming to an end. Yet with all of its passion and argumentation, one cannot help but feel that the ruins of Auschwitz speak more eloquently of the tragedy that befell the Jewish people and the world than Goldhagen's book, his detractors, or even my delegation, which sought to right the narrative of Jewish suffering. Who can dispute the importance of these efforts, save for the feeling that somehow we have betrayed the legacy we seek to preserve. Reading Goldhagen in a time of Jewish empowerment makes one pause and survey the distance Jews have traveled since the Holocaust. Celebration for survival and empowerment is tempered with the knowledge of culpability. Reading Goldhagen at the end of Auschwitz, one wonders whether the cycle of injustice and atrocity can be broken before it is too late. In a paradoxical way, perhaps the jarring disjunction of Jewish accusation and contemporary behavior —the attempt to continue the era of Auschwitz as it comes to an end—will itself help to end the cycle. Then Goldhagen's contribution will be more important and revolutionary than the claims he makes for his own work.

15

Edward Said and the Future of the Jewish People

SINCE THE FOUNDING OF CHRISTIANITY, Jews and Judaism have had many interlocutors, most of them negative and operating from the vantage point of an ideological superiority enforced by material and military power. This is certainly the case in the West and elsewhere over the last two thousand years, as the dominance of Christianity and Christian culture rendered Jews and Judaism both essential and peripheral, visible and invisible, a combination that led to false polemics, exile, and massacre. As is well documented by historians, Jewish history in the West is hardly linear in relation to European Christian culture, with eras of peace and prosperity followed by eras of persecution and degradation. At the same time, the movement from arguments about the superiority of Christianity vis-à-vis Judaism to the racialist movements against Jews, regardless of their religious expression, has accelerated over time, and the mixture of anti-Judaism and anti-Semitism in the middle of the twentieth century provided the worst manifestation of violence against Jews in history, a mass slaughter commonly known as the Holocaust.

In some ways the Holocaust awakened the world, especially Europe and the Western Christian world, to the horror of asserting theological, cultural, and racial superiority. The ecumenical dialogue between Christians and Jews after the conclusion of World War II, with the epoch-making importance of the Roman Catholic Vatican Council II and its statements on Jews and Judaism in relation to its own self-understanding, is the fruit of the Christian discovery of its own culpability in the attempted annihilation of the Jewish people. Though the dialogue and subsequent confession of mainstream Protestant Christian denominations with regard to Jews and Judaism seems altruistic, its main thrust has been one of self-examination and renewal. The horror of the death camps raised the question of Christian authenticity and commitment, in essence the future of Christian faith and institutional presence in the world. In many ways, the attempt to jettison the anti-Jewish and anti-Judaic elements of Christianity provides a new way of looking at the world beyond Jews and Judaism and beyond the West and those state structures that have traditionally supported the churches. Coming to grips with those who created the pre-history to Christianity, and who traveled with them throughout their history, allowed an ecumenical religiosity that culminated in the emergence of liberation theologies around the world.

At the same time that Europe and Western Christianity came to understand Jews and Judaism in a new light, Jews themselves found a voice and affluence in the West far in excess of anything previously known to them. Though the non-linear aspect of Jewish ascendancy and descent remains within Jewish consciousness, the situation clearly changes in the post-war period. As the devastation of the Holocaust became known, Jewish ascendancy advanced both in the United States and in the formation and expansion of Israel. Barriers to Jewish empowerment in the United States fell quickly because of a new sensitivity of the wider non-Jewish culture and because of financial success and a burgeoning intellectual class. At the same time, and for the first time in two thousand years, Jews successfully created a state where a majority of its citizens were Jewish and the power of the state was exclusively in Jewish hands. This dual empowerment and the narrative that emerges from this experience is crucial to Jewish ascendancy and more: it represents the reversal of dialogue about Jews and Judaism and actions taken against them and their religion. From this point onward Jews are central to the drama of the West and Western Christianity in a narrative provided and fashioned by the Jewish community itself. Those who once were spoken to and lectured are now to speak and lecture; those who once were seen as failing and sinful now present themselves as prevailing and innocent.

The emergence of the Jewish post-Holocaust narrative in the West and its connection with the state of Israel is illustrated most vividly by Elie Wiesel. Born in Eastern Europe and a survivor of Buchenwald and Auschwitz, Wiesel assumed a prominent place in Holocaust literature and ethical discussions in the post-war world, so much so that he was awarded the Nobel Peace Prize in 1986. His books and essays, as well as his many commentaries on current events, emphasize the need to speak out against injustice and how silence in the face of injustice becomes complicity. Wiesel's reference point is the displacement and destruction of the Holocaust, and because of his own suffering and loss, his speech takes on the gravity of a moral witness in our time. As a refugee from Europe, his understanding of America is one of welcome and gratitude. As a diaspora Jew, his support of Israel is unwavering, even to the point of refusing to criticize individual policies of the state.

In Wiesel's view, a view that is held by a broad segment of American Jewry, America and Israel are places of refuge for Jews in a hostile world and their fundamental character is one of compassion and goodness. The policies of both nations are shadowed by the Holocaust, with America as the bastion of democracy able to confront injustice around the world and Israel as the place of refuge and renewal for the Jewish people, whose policies exist only to insure both. Those who oppose either America or Israel or critically confront the policies of either are therefore engaged in opposition to an essential goodness rather than an informed and political opposition. By grounding the Jewish narrative in the suffering of the Holocaust and the survival and revival of the Jewish people in the twinning of America and Israel, the policies of both states are shrouded in a morality few commentators ascribe to any nation-state.

If the extension of American or Israeli power is presumed to be innocent, Jewish spokespersons and actions are still farther removed from criticism. Contemporary Jewish life springs from untold suffering, the suffering of the innocent, which informs the speech and actions of Jews who are heirs to the Holocaust. In Wiesel's understanding, Jews who have every right to hate because of what they have been through are incapable of hate. Even Israeli soldiers are witness to this inability, characterized as reluctant warriors who embrace violence only as a necessity thrust upon them. At the same time, they are affected by the suffering imposed on others because of this very necessity. The 1967 War exemplifies this understanding for Wiesel as a war forced upon Israel and whose soldiers fought without cruelty. "During the Six-Day War the Jewish fighters did not become cruel," Wiesel writes, "They became sad. They acquired a certain maturity, a very moving maturity, which I simply cannot forget. And if I feel something towards them, the child-soldier in Israel, it is profound respect." Wiesel concludes that Israel itself represents a moral victory and that its military victories are only secondary to the character that produced them. His pride in Israel reflects this sensibility: "My pride is that Israel has remained human because it has remained so deeply Jewish."[1]

Wiesel's analysis of the 1967 War is crucial to the evolving Jewish narrative in the West because it establishes both a moral sensibility and a religious tone that outweigh the policies of Israel and grounds them in a way unavailable to serious political criticism. The "moral" victory of Israel in the 1967 War is extended to its founding and to its future beyond the war, as it represents a drama, almost cosmic in scope, of a disinherited people being reborn. The drama includes all of Jewish history and penetrates to the very question of God and God's presence in history. "Suddenly all Jews had become children of the Holocaust," Wiesel writes, and the "great mystery in which we are encloaked, as if by the command of the Almighty." Because of this, the Arab armies are defeated. "Millions of the martyrs of the Holocaust were enlisted" in the ranks of the Israeli military and they shielded their "spiritual heirs" like the biblical pillars of fire. With such support as this, how could Israel ever be defeated?

Wiesel is hardly alone in this understanding of Israel. Emil Fackenheim, a European Jewish refugee, post-war citizen of Canada and now of Israel, sees the survival of Israel as a religious commandment, the 614th commandment which completes the Orthodox understanding of 613 commandments to fulfill Jewish practice. For Fackenheim, post-Holocaust Jewish belief in God is uncertain, and secular and religious Jews must come together in the task that defines contemporary Jewry, that is the rebuilding of Jewish life exemplified by the founding and defense of Israel. Thus Israeli soldiers who fought in the 1967 War were warriors with a religious mandate, hearing the commanding voice of Auschwitz. They responded in the only way an authentic Jew could respond after the Holocaust: they gave their lives for the survival of Israel and, in this sense, for the survival of all Jews and Jewish history. Many Christians outside Israel also heard the commanding voice of Auschwitz in uniting for Israel and against the Arab enemy. By doing this, Jews denied Hitler a "posthumous victory" and refused those who, at least in Fackenheim's mind, wanted to carry out Hitler's mandate.[2]

What lurks behind both Wiesel's and Fackenheim's "religiosity," defined by Jewish history and the Holocaust, is the threat of another holocaust, this one signaling the end of the Jewish people. Israel is the guardian of Jewish history, and America, with its power and moral purpose, its guarantor. Anything that threatens Jewish unity around the question of Israel or undermines America's power and purpose in the world is thus defined as enemy and more. Conscious or not, these enemies invite another holocaust. This warning applies to Jews and non-Jews alike, the first accused of self-hate, the second accused of anti-Semitism. If the mission and policies of Israel, even its expansion and wars, are defined in terms of morality and religiosity, then its critics are accused on the same terrain. The circle is complete and Israel and America are brought together in the realm of innocence and redemption, the latter being proposed as the future of a secure and prosperous Israel with the backing of America. Cloaked in the Holocaust, Israel and America are agents of the ultimate reconciliation between God and the Jewish people, between God and humanity at large. The Jewish drama continues this time on the other side of anti-Jewish and anti-Judaic understandings. Yet this drama is continually threatened by a reversal often experienced in Jewish history, shadowed by another holocaust that would bring this history to an end.[3]

The result is the "new anti-Semitism" widely heralded in the 1970s and 1980s by these Holocaust theologians and by other Jewish commentators. The list is long and includes such notables as Norman Podhoretz, editor of the conservative journal *Commentary*, but it also includes liberals such as Nathan Perlmutter, who wrote *The Real Antisemitism in*

America, published in 1982. What is evident in Perlmutter's book is a neo-conservatism emerging among Jews in response to shifting currents regarding Israel's and America's domestic and foreign policy. The specifics and tone of the message are clearly demarcated, naming friends and enemies and suggesting shifting alliances. Liberal commentators and institutions, including those traditionally seen as friends of the Jewish people such as the mainline churches and the United Nations, have become captive to anti-Israeli and anti-American sentiment, while those traditionally seen to be anti-Jewish, such as conservative politicians and Christian fundamentalist denominations, have embraced Israel and the American power that supports it. Perlmutter suggests that a sea-change has occurred within Jewish history, one that Jews have been late in understanding. Indeed, the struggle against anti-Semitism has shifted from those groups on the margins of Western society who espouse traditional Jewish hate propaganda to liberal and revolutionary ideologies and institutions that seek the reversal of an American-centered global economic and military worldview, and with that the decentering of Israel's hegemony in the Middle East. Those toward whom Jews naturally gravitate and who in the past joined them in their quest for dignity and inclusion in the societies in which they live are now seen as endangering Jewish interests and defense. In an age of empowerment political alliances need to be flexible and capable of change. Started in the 1970s, this neo-conservative movement within the Jewish world continues today with the publication of Elliott Abrams's *Faith or Fear: How Jews Can Survive in a Christian America*.[4]

Challenging Jewish Innocence

Those who are critical of understandings and policies supported or carried out by Jews in America or Israel are forewarned. Though the terrain seems to be the engagement of ideas in the clash and compromise of public debate, the reality, at least as seen by many Jewish commentators, thinkers, and political actors, is quite different. The terrain is historical, ideological and theological in a specifically Jewish modality and the stakes are thereby heightened, skewed, in fact, in a direction unknown to most who enter the fray. Jewish discourse is less modern, twenty-first century, Western or even within the context of the nation-state, though these forms are used in a sophisticated manner; it is rather defined by paradigms of thought developed over a five-thousand-year history.

This Jewish sensibility, heightened in our time by immense suffering *and* unparalleled empowerment, is on the world stage in a way that harkens back to Jewish origins and projects itself into the future as the central drama of human history. Other interests and concerns, even if they appear to others to be central to their life and survival, are judged to be secondary and peripheral, allowed only if they do not appear to impinge on the more important Jewish drama. Therefore what seems to others to be a natural assertion of their own interests and rights of critical analysis may be seen by Jews as an assault on Jewish sensibility and well-being. In the drama of suffering and redemption so evident and articulated with the force, though often unannounced, of a history seen by Jews as central to the divine and human journey of humanity, the resistance to critique and the accusation of another threatened event of mass suffering is enough to reduce most critics to silence.

Yet silence on the issue of Jews and Judaism is more than demanded; it is enforced with psychological and material penalties. The charges of Jewish self-hatred, the new anti-Semitism, and the encouragement of another holocaust are complemented by the highly organized and well-financed Jewish political apparatus and institutional structure. Examples abound, and one only need mention AIPAC (American Israel Public Affairs Committee) and the ADL (Anti-Defamation League) to strike fear in the hearts of many who want to question contemporary Jewish understandings in relation to America and Israel. Perlmutter's book itself carries this warning, as his ideological analysis is buttressed by his leadership role in the ADL. The power to pursue political ends as illustrated in aid packages to Israel, with over twenty percent of America's foreign aid going to Israel, a country with less than one-thousandth of the world's population, is striking, but the ability to punish opponents of such support is equally impressive. Witness Senator Charles Percy and Representative Paul Findley, both defeated in reelection bids by organized and targeted Jewish pressure.

This power has had a chilling effect on public discussion regarding Israel, especially in the academic and media arenas. The ADL's infamous anti-Israel list has targeted those who seek to break the silence on issues central to Jewish life. Here, too, examples abound, with the attempt to dishonor and render unemployable those critical of the use and abuse of Jewish power. While Percy and Findley are non-Jews, the attempt to silence in the academic arena often focuses specifically on Jewish dissidents, the most prominent being Noam Chomsky but extending to younger Jewish scholars like Norman Finkelstein and Jonathan Boyarin. In a very tangible sense, the attempt is to eliminate criticism from without and within the Jewish community.[5]

The attempt to marginalize thought and action by the organized Jewish community has been in large part successful. Since the founding of Israel, the Western narrative and policy implementation have been overwhelmingly pro-Israel, and even more so in the years since the 1967 War. Despite the setbacks in the moral sense of Israel in the last years, including the invasion of Lebanon and the bombing of Beirut in the 1980s and the attempt to crush the Palestinian *intifada* in the 1980s and 1990s, and despite the more vocal and expanded debate evidenced because of these events, it remains that those who question the innocent and redemptive features of contemporary Jewish life are on the defensive, liable to accusations and character assassination. For these reasons, Jews and Judaism have lacked voices that can call to account abuses of power, or rather have refused a hearing to those who see the possibility of Jewish life in an alternative way. At the same time, the voices of the suffering, especially Palestinians, have been relegated to a peripheral position, heard only as a reference point for contemporary hatred of Jews. In essence, Jewish leadership has acted to protect its moral standing in a way that all groups with power do: claim the high ground by characterizing dissent as unpatriotic and even demonic and at the same time make the material conditions for dissent difficult, if not impossible.

Within this context two immediate questions arise. How are people who are affected by Jewish power, especially Palestinians, to redress their suffering and concerns? How is the Jewish community itself to be called to account and an alternative way of life proposed? The first question deals with injustice against another people, the second with foundational issues of what it means to be Jewish and what the Jewish future will be. In an immediate sense, these questions may seem unrelated, to be addressed independently, and often this is the case. Palestinians are interested quite properly in their future, which is significantly impacted by policies of Israel with the support of American foreign policy. Their interest in Jews and Judaism ends in the formation and implementation of policies that affect them. The policies of others, say Jordan and Egypt, are dealt with on their own terms and with the same goal in mind: an independent nation that allows the survival and flourishing of Palestinian life and culture. In the long view Jews and Judaism remain important to Palestinians because Jews and Palestinians live side by side, share a history and a future, and will in many ways, as enemies or friends, interact on the economic and political front. Aside from intrinsic merit, the future of Jews and Palestinians is unassailably linked.

For Jews the question is more complicated. Aside from the fact that Jews and Palestinians are and will live side by side, and therefore interact economically and politically, the internal question of dispossessing another people and organizing the community to be silent and complicit in that dispossession has profound ramifications for the internal life of the Jewish people. At stake are the claims of Jewish history and the future path Jews will embrace. The capacity of Jews to do to others what has been done to them profoundly alters the *raison d'etre* of Jewish existence. The embrace by a majority of the Jewish community of Jewish state power in Israel, and the related embrace of the American state, represents a situational shift in Jewish history to rival or even surpass the momentous effect of the Holocaust. Creating a Jewish-state culture fundamentally alters the trajectory of Jewish history.[6]

Of those who have commented on Jews and Judaism within the context of empowerment as interlocutors from outside the Jewish community, two are preeminent. The first is John Murray Cuddihy, an American scholar, who approached the subject, at least initially, in terms of modernity. In his groundbreaking work, *The Ordeal of Civility: Freud, Marx, and Levi-Strauss and the Jewish Struggle with Modernity*, Cuddihy explores the interaction of Jews with the modern West as a series of intellectual maneuvers designed to subvert Christian religious and cultural hegemony and its transmutation into secularized modernity, thus establishing a beachhead for Jewish participation in modernity. As latecomers to modernity, and with a history of suffering and exclusion in Europe, intellectual giants such as Sigmund Freud, Karl Marx, and Claude Levi-Strauss establish ideological arguments and fields of study that have both their own revolutionary scientific merit *and* an unannounced agenda of reversing the established gentile order to provide a path for Jews to transition from a ghettoized and backward culture.

The challenge for these intellectuals is daunting, as they outline this path of assimilation in the West by analyzing European civilization from the perspective of the outsider with modern tools. In doing so, Jews become the interpreters of the West and enter this more powerful, established and often hostile culture on Jewish terms. By advising the West that in psyche, politics, and anthropology, an underground, subversive, and reorienting process is underway, these Jewish thinkers turn the ordinary world on its head and allow Jews to undergo the "hurricane" of modernization with dignity and perhaps even with the advantage of insight. Nonetheless, modernity remains an ordeal, as the Jewish community, with its particular patterns of thought and culture, is left behind to enter this foreign culture. In analyzing these figures, Cuddihy shows the inner turmoil of prominent Jews, and of Jews in general, that accompanies such a transition. Freud, Marx, and Levi-Strauss are great and in some ways tragic figures who parallel the path of Western Jews seeking admission to a modernity that promises and exacts so much. Clouding all, of course, is one distinct destination—the Holocaust—a price that few of these thinkers foresaw and that Freud experienced in the most intimate way.[7]

If the ticket to enter modernity is a civility that breaks apart traditional cultures, Jews are forced, willing or not, to pay the price. Yet the survival of Jewish understandings, the ability to bring aspects of Jewish culture into modernity, even and especially in disguised forms, is established and celebrated in Cuddihy's analysis. Cuddihy marvels at the ability of Jews to in a sense "beat" Protestant modernity at its own game, and in a very short time move from a conversation piece in the West—the Jewish question—to become intellectual giants to whom the West comes for insight. From Cuddihy's perspective these seemingly assimilated Jews carry the burden of a peoples' journey as previous Jewish leaders did in times of crisis.

Cuddihy's respect is clear and his attempt to show the subversive aspect of Freud, Marx, and Levi-Strauss reverses the anti-Semitic stereotype of the insidious Jew so prominent in the West. Rather he emphasizes the Jewish commitment and exploration that exposes the hypocrisy at the heart of a civility seeking to disguise injustice and barbarism. The tragic aspect of leaving behind the old is, in Cuddihy's analysis, complemented by a sense of a heroic struggle that is a gift to Jewish and universal history. The centrality and uniqueness of the Jews, often self-ascribed, is demonstrated and affirmed by Cuddihy in the crucible of the twentieth century. As a Catholic of Irish ancestry, Cuddihy delights in the bravado and courage of Jewish intellectuals and the larger Jewish community, which enters a foreign culture as the despised outsider and creates a home for itself with its own distinctive flavor.

Cuddihy's later work, published in essay form, traces the continuing Jewish journey into modernity after the Holocaust. Cuddihy analyzes contemporary Jewish intellectuals within their present preoccupation of reflecting on the Holocaust and the state of Israel, and finds a continuation of bold thought *and* a new defensiveness. The latter has to do with another shift of Jewish life in the twentieth century, the movement from pariah status seeking survival in Western modernity to an empowered community seeking to fend off commentary about Jewish use of the Holocaust to enhance its status in the West and protect Israel. Asserting the uniqueness of the Holocaust, Jewish thinkers are doing more than remembering the dead; at least in Cuddihy's mind, Jews are using this memory to complete their ascendancy in the West.

Though Cuddihy sees this as understandable, claiming the Holocaust as only Jewish, without comparison or comparability to the tragedies of other victims, is a form of trivializing the claims of the latter. Moreover, the memory of the dead in the present discussion is a claim to superiority in disguise, which has consequences for contemporary intellectual life, denoting entire categories of reflection off limits. Cuddihy reflects on the meaning of Holocaust remembrance as grief work but also as a claim by "cultural status-seekers" who are "engaged in an inner-ethnic and intra-societal *kulturkampf.*" Cuddihy realizes the force of the argument and terrain he is entering, in essence the shift he himself is analyzing and undergoing with reference to contemporary Jewish life, and begins his essay with a statement to his readers explaining that his disputation with the Holocaust is not its historical occurrence, but its use in intellectual discourse. His statement differentiating the history and historiography of the Holocaust made, he emphasizes his own struggle in even raising the issue. Writing of the tears he cried when reading Chaim Kaplan's *Warsaw Diary*, Cuddihy understands that some of his ideas may indeed offend.[8]

In an earlier essay, subtitled "The Incivil Irritatingness of Jewish Theodicy," Cuddihy acknowledges that some of his ideas will offend Jews. Cuddihy wonders how anti-Semitism can only be a one-way street, as if Jews are only victims of others rather than agents of their own history. In this sense Jews see themselves as "morally blameless," escaping the give-and-take of history. This is the contemporary theodicy of the Jewish people according to Cuddihy, the presumption of total innocence in historical and contemporary matters. "Yet, when Jews' own historical actions, in the Middle East for example, create a stateless people who, in turn, blame the Jews and Israelis, what does Jewish theodicy do?" Cuddihy asks: "It blames the victims, the Palestinians, and sees nothing irrational in this." For Cuddihy, blamelessness in terms of weakness (anti-Semitism) and strength (Israel) is "irritating" because it violates reciprocity. What results is "Wieselian bolus," a combination of claiming to be an eternal victim even within empowerment. In this way "public *kvelling* and sanctimonious moralizing" come to be seen by non-Jews as a strategy of avoiding accountability. With great insight, Cuddihy sees this theodicy as emanating from the historic position of powerlessness in the diaspora and so a sense of moral superiority is understandable, even necessary, to survive the dominant culture. However, the "luxury of powerlessness ended with the founding of Israel" when Jews "dirtied their hands." What continues today is a conflict between two rhetorics, one historical, the other contemporary, "between the Diaspora Reform rhetoric of the Jew as ethical, moralistic, and pacifistic and the Israeli rhetoric of Sabra victory and pride, between if you will, the *New York Times* editorial talk and the talk of Menachem Begin and General Ariel Sharon." Cuddihy concludes that Jews come honorably by their paranoia but when it comes to their own behavior "they go on a moral holiday, legitimated by their secular, post-emancipation ideology."9

The second scholar who has commented on Jews and Judaism in the time of empowerment is Edward Said. Unlike Cuddihy, who experiences the onslaught of modernity as a person of Irish Catholic ancestry and thus was born and struggles within the Western tradition, Said, a Palestinian Arab by birth and identification, has lived a life of exile in America. While Cuddihy can identify with the struggle of Jews to assimilate to and survive modernity, and at the same time be outraged by Jewish attempts to have both innocence and power, Said at an early age experienced the loss of his homeland because of Jewish power. As part of a refugee community in America, Said also encounters the West, and Jews within the West, as culpable in his dispossession, and experiences the invisibility of his natural identification. Whereas Cuddihy traces the coming of Jewish intellectual power as a model for his own people's empowerment, the exercise of Jewish intellectual and material power promises Said and millions of other Palestinians a diaspora community without a name, one often identified with weakness and shame. In fact, Jewish ascendancy in America and Israel represents a hurricane for Palestinians, in some ways similar to the hurricane Jews experienced in the wake of modernity. In this hurricane Jews have survived and prospered in the reverse proportion to Palestinians who have experienced the winds and storms of Jewish power as their demise.

In one sense Said, as an intellectual living his adult life in the West and making important contributions to the fields of literary, cultural, and political criticism, is the logical extension of the Jewish journey in the twentieth century traced by Cuddihy. Said raises the next question within this journey, one of arrival, just as Cuddihy addressed the point of embarkation. In his later work Cuddihy begins to analyze that arrival, writing about the confusion of Jewish empowerment in the attempt to maintain the rhetoric of subversion and inclusion even as Jews mobilize to displace Palestinians and others who challenge that empowerment. Cuddihy searches for an intellectual current that can confront Jews in their new stage of empowerment and does so as an outsider whose central insights come from the previous stage. Cuddihy finds the attempt of Jews to have it both ways—innocence *and* empowerment—to be irritating, but surely something more important has occurred. The reversal of intellectual Jewish currents from one of creative subversion to aggressive defense represents the joining of powers that once derided, displaced, and sought to annihilate the Jewish people. What Cuddihy glimpses but is unable to articulate is the end of the Jewish tradition of critical thought, and with that end a final assimilation and assent to that which Jewish intellectuals fought against. In many ways, what Cuddihy glimpses is the end of Jewish history as we know it.

Where for Cuddihy the question is intellectual and deeply felt—if not, why the anger, the disappointment, the almost desperate cry to Jews to look again at what is occurring?—for Said this shift in Jewish life is palpable, embodied as a disorienting and formative experience in his own life, the life of his family, friends, and people. Said and the Palestinian people are victims of the victims, and the claim of innocence is not to be struggled against because for Palestinians it has not existed. The claim of exclusion does not have to be reckoned with because it is Palestinians who have been excluded. Said does not have to struggle with the reversal that Cuddihy begins to analyze, but its opposite, the pretense to innocence assumed in the West. Cuddihy struggles to name the sea- change in Jewish life as Said, with other Palestinians, struggles to name what they have lost because of that change. Whereas Cuddihy catalogues the journey of Jews as they enter the West and become intimate partners in it, Said experiences the West and Jews as partners in an assault that has rendered him and his people refugees without an established identity or country. In this context the interlocutor of the Jewish world has shifted from Cuddihy to Said, symbolically and concretely from Jewish intellectualism to Jewish power.

It is Said's search to understand his own displacement and that of his people that informs his two classic works, *Orientalism* and *The Question of Palestine*. Published within a year of each other in 1978 and 1979 respectively, these books identify the mechanism by which the West has denigrated and dominated the East, and explore the possibility of surviving and reestablishing the identity of the East, with particular reference to Palestine and Palestinians. Using the literature, academic disciplines, and politics of the West, Said demonstrates that Western domination over the last centuries is the result of a careful and strategic expansion of European and American power. Colonialism has many forms, but it is at its surest and most devastating when it can define other areas of the globe, including entire peoples and civilizations, within its own symbolic and narrative system.

Orientalism is a discourse in which a position of authority is assumed by the West in the context of economic and political hegemony. Intellectuals provide the legitimation for this hegemony by creating a dominant narrative. A circulation of ideas, symbols, and physical power is established whereby the Orient is defined as "other" to be studied, invaded, in the broadest sense captured for the use and edification of the West. Thus the "disappearance" of Palestine takes place within the broader context of an Orientalism that reverses the question of the West, often articulated as the Jewish question, to the question of Palestine. Said writes of this reversal: "We were on the land called Palestine; were our dispossession and our effacement, by which almost a million of us were made to leave Palestine and our society made non-existent, justified even to save the remnant of European Jews that had survived Nazism? By what moral or political standard are we expected to lay aside our claims to our national existence, our land, our human rights? In what world is there no argument when an entire people is told that it is juridically absent, even as armies are led against it, campaigns conducted against even its name, history changed so as to "prove" its nonexistence?" At the same time Said recognizes the larger scope of such a negation, the "entrenched *cultural* attitude" toward Palestine and Palestinians that derives from Western prejudices about Islam, the Arabs, and the Orient. It is this attitude that Zionism drew upon in relating to Palestinians and in doing so "dehumanized us, reduced us to the barely tolerated status of a nuisance."[10]

Said's primary interest in Jews and Judaism is in the context of Zionism and Israel but in placing the emphasis on the latter he also focuses on their connection with the West. Though much of this journey is traced with the founding and expansion of Israel—hence reference to the Palestinian catastrophe—his discussion of Jews and Zionism prior to the founding of the state is illuminating and provides another perspective to that of Cuddihy. For while Jewish intellectuals in the West were forging a future for the Jewish people in the West, other Jews were preparing the ground for a state in the Middle East. Said cites Chaim Weizmann, a leading advocate of Zionism, negotiating with Arthur Balfour, then British Foreign Secretary and in certain ways an anti-Semite, and establishing a common understanding of Arabs and the Orient which spoke to British superiority and Jewish concerns.

With Balfour, Weizmann plays upon the myth of Semitic backwardness while changing places with the Arab. Weizmann's burden as a Semite is to demonstrate that Jews, under the beneficence of the West, have altered their nature while the Arabs in Palestine remain the same. In fact, from this moment on Jews are considered to have a special insight into the Semites of the Arab world, identifying with the West as opposed to the East. As Said so aptly writes: "By a concatenation of events and circumstances the Semitic myth bifurcated in the Zionist movement; one Semite went the way of Orientalism, the other, the Arab, was forced to go the way of the Oriental." This division of Semites into Orientalist and Orientals is fundamental to the creation of Israel, to create a network of realities—language, colonies, and organizations—that leads to the conversion of Palestine into a Jewish state. Jews acquire a legitimacy for this effort by giving it an "archeology and a teleology that completely surrounded and, in a sense, outdated the native culture that was still firmly planted in Palestine." Zionist Jews proceeded in two directions: by appealing to the West to restore Jews to their "native land" to which they feel themselves entitled as Semites *and* degrading the Semitic inhabitants of Palestine as backward and interlopers. Both depend on the Jewish position within the Christian West, arguing from a premodern perspective within the context of a modern, or at least modernizing people.[11]

What Cuddihy identifies as a Jewish schizophrenia, the rhetoric of diaspora innocence and Sabra power, Said identifies as narrative that inserts Jews into a sympathetic solidarity with the West as a cover to policies that systematically displace his own people. The narrative gains adherents because of Jewish suffering in the West and because of the superiority the West feels with regard to the East. Yet this same narrative is inherently unstable, because the assertion of Arab backwardness as well as the essential absence of Palestinians needs to be continually proven to others and to Jews themselves. Argument is constructed in which Palestinians are visible in order to be degraded and invisible so that no hue and cry can be raised with Jewish settlement. Jews thus pose as civilizers of the backward and return to their ancient land which is "unsettled." Palestinians are continuously derided *and* removed from Western and Jewish consciousness because their mere presence and humanity challenge Jewish claims and power.

Because Palestinians do in fact exist, and in great numbers, and because Palestinians are native to Palestine and the Arab world, a competition over "native" status ensues. This Zionist claim to be native demands a physical and ideological apartheid system that aims to create and sustain a vision of righteousness and apartness. Any challenge to the Jew as native, such as the very presence of Palestinians or discussion of Palestinian nationhood and culture, must be debased or erased. Furthermore, the native presence of Palestinians can only be seen as a threat to the entire Israeli, and later Jewish, narrative in the Middle East and the West, thus transposing resistance to displacement into a threat of annihilation. An explosive contradiction enters Jewish life precisely at this moment, as the apartheid vision is as disastrous for Jews as it is for Palestinians. Because Arabs are seen as synonymous with everything degraded and irrational, Jewish institutions that are humanistic and progressive for Jews—and here Said cites the kibbutz, the desire to take in immigrants, and the Law of Return—are "precisely, determinedly inhuman" for Palestinians. By Judaizing territory, even with a European and progressive sensibility, Jews de-Arabize the same territory and produce a contradiction of massive proportions between the assertion of innocence and the practice of politics.[12]

What follows is Said's charge that those who refuse to face these contradictions have become, in the terminology of Antonio Gramsci, "experts in legitimation," that is "dishonest and irrational despite their protestations on behalf of wisdom and humanity." Describing this shift in Jewish sensibilities—and including those non-Jews who are equally uncritical of Israel—as "one of the most frightening cultural episodes of the century," Said names some of those who function as experts in legitimation: Senator Daniel Patrick Moynihan; novelist Saul Bellow; but most startling, Jewish philosopher and binationalist Martin Buber. Said cites Buber as approving, or at least not protesting, the story told to him of Israeli soldiers who in the 1956 war with Egypt were ordered to kill any Egyptian soldiers who became prisoners. When Buber was told of the difficulty that Israeli soldiers had in carrying out the order—a difficulty with reference only to the Jewish soldier's internal sensibility rather than the agony and humanity of the Egyptian soldiers who were executed—Buber spoke of the greatness of the story rather than the horror of the executions. Said, who characterizes Buber somewhat sarcastically as "moral philosopher, humane thinker, former binationalist," makes clear the transposition of Jewish thought in the context of empowerment: Jewish vision is clouded by an internal reference point and dramatic narrative that leaves others outside, diminished, peripheral actors in a drama that Jews narrate. There is a blindness in the experts of legitimation, a necessary blindness that once afflicted those who consigned Jews to the status of victim. Buber exemplifies this transition, for the discussion of these executions occurred in 1962, less than twenty-five years after Buber was expelled from Nazi Germany.[13]

Said addresses the fact that Zionism and Israel have as their primary victims the Palestinians and the Arab world, but other victims are also to be found, including Jews who dull their intellectual ability to legitimate actions that once adversely impacted their own community. Or perhaps better stated, Jews now hone their intellectual ability to conceal rather than expose, to cover-up rather than enlighten, to participate in an intellectual game that such thinkers as Marx, Freud, and Levi-Strauss once subverted. Those thinkers and activists who speak out against injustice around the world—for example, in the 1970s, human rights abuses in Argentina, Chile, and South Africa—are silent about preventive detention, torture, population transfer, and deportations of Palestinians. This silence is a complicity, to be sure, but it also amounts to an act of aggression within the Middle East and in areas of the world, especially the West, where the Palestinian cause and narrative is diminished and demonized.

Jews and the Ideology of Difference

Said understands that the discourse and power that displaces his people and seeks their disappearance is not solely sponsored by reactionary or even conservative elements, but often is a liberal undertaking. In one sense the conservative elements are easier to confront and expose because of their jingoistic Americanism or overt racism. The liberal speaks in more sophisticated terms, travels in circles where jingoism and racism are frowned upon and condemned, and typically leans toward internationalism and empowerment of oppressed peoples. In fact, the peculiar aspect of the question of Palestine is that it is seen differently from other struggles and has difficulty claiming its rightful place in the solidarity network often frequented by progressive thinkers and activists, among whom are many Jews. Not only has this had a deleterious effect on the actual struggle of Palestinians to reestablish Palestine, it has also had an almost catastrophic effect on the formation of Palestinian identity, at least in the West.

This is the reason for Said's strong and ironic description of Buber, but closer to his new home in the West there are other contemporary Jews who figure prominently in his later, more polemical interventions. Among those whom Said singles out for special approbation are the Orientalist Bernard Lewis and the ethicist Michael Walzer. With regard to Lewis, who attempts to sum up the Arab world for his Western readers as never-changing and mired in mythology, Said writes that he is a "perfect exemplification of the academic whose work purports to be liberal objective scholarship but is in reality very close to being propaganda *against* his subject material." In an exchange with Walzer—whose book-length analysis of the Exodus is triumphal toward others who the Israelites ultimately vanquished and is profoundly Western in orientation, claiming, among other things, that the Exodus legend is Western, liberating, this-worldly and linear as opposed to other ideologies that have the opposite origins, values, and results—Said writes as one on the other side of the Exodus tradition, if you will, as a Canaanite. Noting Walzer's reading of Exodus as a contemporary one whose purpose is to place contemporary Jewry and especially Israel as a flowering of this tradition, Said responds in the context of the Exodus story with contemporary import. "But the one thing I want Walzer to remember," Said writes, "is that the more one shores up the sphere of Exodus politics the more likely it is that the Canaanites on the outside will resist and try to penetrate the walls banning them from the goods of what is, after all, partly their world too. The strength of the Canaanite, that is the exile position, is that being defeated and 'outside,' you can perhaps more easily feel compassion, more easily call injustice, more easily speak directly and plainly of all oppression, and with less difficulty try to understand (rather than mystify or occlude) history and equality."[14]

Said outlines the underlying sensibility to this liberal discourse in his essay "An Ideology of Difference," written in the wake of Israel's invasion of Lebanon. In some ways, the question Said raises—how Jews can hold fast to a notion of Israel's innocence and mission when its behavior contradicts these notions—is the same question found in his earlier writing, but now more sharply honed. It is almost as if the sheer blatant quality of Israel's behavior engages Said's sensibility; or perhaps the contradictions, known by Palestinians since the founding of Israel, are now more identifiable in the public discourse of the West. If Jews were justified in their need for a state, thus framing the 1948 War as an example of a struggle defying the odds of history and geography, and the 1967 War as a miraculous response to the Holocaust and final return to Jerusalem, what could be said about the invasion of Lebanon and the bombing of Beirut? Could Lebanon be seen as a defensive war, one fought against great odds and only with the most basic necessity? How could this war be justified within the Western and Jewish narrative? How would the experts in legitimation place the war in its proper context? Or would the truth finally be told, and if so, how would it be told? Would the invasion of Lebanon become a place of denial, or be admitted as a transgression to keep the larger denial in place, or would the invasion become a place of reckoning, and if so, what might that place look like for the West, for Jews, for Israel, and for Palestinians?[15]

Cuddihy's shift in sensibility, his labeling of the "Wieselian bolus," comes in the wake of the invasion of Lebanon as well. Cuddihy's understanding of Jewish intellectuals as a subversive force and their movement to one of defensive maneuvering is accompanied by his sense that the Jewish use of chosenness, already secularized in the twentieth century and used as a wedge to enter modernity while retaining a particularity unrecognized by non-Jews, is now attached to the Holocaust and Israel. Therefore, the argument for the Holocaust as unique and Israel as innocent has a latent, unannounced quality, and the assertion of Jewish chosenness, though framed in fine and logical arguments, is unavailable for rational critique. In essence, as Said points out, a religious assertion is promulgated with the power of the university, the social sciences, and the state behind it.

Said focuses on this point of chosenness in the theological realm as the positing of "difference." The translation of this theological concept to the actualities of Israel is impossible for Said to understand through reason because it proposes a unique bond to the land of Palestine/Israel, "distinguishing Jews from all other peoples." Jews are somehow different from others in an essentialist manner, always and everywhere, and thus those who are not Jewish are posited as "radically *other*, fundamentally and constitutively different." Policies in Israel are based on that understanding as fact established beyond argument. Thus land is reserved for Jews only and held in trust for the Jewish people. Even the kibbutz, the herald of European socialist liberation, is only for Jews. Within this understanding separation is not racism— hence the outcry against the United Nations' resolution that asserts Zionism as a type of racism—and the policy of separation is rarely argued and more often assumed. Even the peace movement in Israel assumes elements of this ideology of difference, and thus in Said's view helps perpetuate the political and state forces that, despite their protest, carry out this ideology. So, for example, Peace Now, an Israeli peace movement formed in the wake of the invasion of Lebanon, actually prevents a "true critique" of Israel from taking place, at least one that touches the essence of the dispute between Israelis and Palestinians and its possible resolution. The ideological premises that Zionism acts out toward the Palestinians, that is the origins of Palestinian displacement, the colonization of Palestine, the creation of Israeli identity in the negation of Palestinian identity, all remain untouched in the narrative of the peace movement.

In some ways, the articulation of the need for peace and the belated recognition of Palestinian nationality and rights preserves the ideology of difference and thus allows the essential division of Jews and Palestinians in thought and practice to continue. A false symmetry is asserted by those who ostensibly argue for peace: "In the first place, the conflict between Palestinian non-Jew and Israeli Jew was never discussed in the theoretical or philosophic terms that might have elucidated its core as ideology imposed upon a 'different' (i.e., non-Jewish) population." Alternating between discussing Palestinians in pragmatic terms (let us forget history and just solve the contemporary problem) and essentialist terms (the division between Jew and Palestinian is to be taken for granted, otherwise a threat of displacing Jews is evident), Said feels that both understandings conclude with "Zionists berating Palestinians for not being forthcoming enough, for not recognizing Israel, for not renouncing violence, for not being like Peace Now, as if all of these things were equal in magnitude to the destruction of Palestinian society and the continued ethnocide waged by the Israeli government, in possession of all the land and all the weapons, against the Palestinian people."[16]

False symmetry denies the damage done to Palestinians and other Arabs, in this case Lebanese civilians, but it also denies the very rights Jewish liberals and progressives are now ready to recognize. The recognition itself is predicated on Jewish assumptions and needs, and Said illustrates this by the insistence of many Jews, including Michael Walzer, on denigrating the leadership that Palestinians recognize as their own.

Palestinians are thus recognized *and* dismissed at the same time, both defined within a Jewish framework. Analyzing the war in Lebanon as an aberration from the pristine history of Israel, hence articulating a desire to jettison the present war and return to an innocent Israel, is itself part of the denial of Palestinian history and aspiration *and* part of the conundrum unto which Jews have fallen. For Said it is only by recognizing that Israel has always been and continues to be a disaster for the Palestinian people that the hypocrisy of Jewish thought can be exposed and the possibility of Jewish practice can undergo a radical change. By understanding this thought and action as the ideology of difference, no way out is allowed. Instead a sophisticated and circular level of argumentation jettisons insight for a moral posture that reality cannot justify.

"Difference, in short, can become an ideological infection and a generalized *traison des clercs*," Said writes, especially when it becomes a cover to prevent the understanding of massive socioeconomic and political problems. Fraud, deceit, and utter contempt for the truth are the results of difference when reified in commentary on questions that are diverse and interconnected. Zionism is not the only ideology to suffer such truncation, to be sure, and, according to Said, Palestinians must be wary of the same trap, that is "essentializing" Israel, Zionists and Jews, and thus imputing to them unchangeable characteristics. Israel and Zionism are not stable and essentialized objects anymore than Palestine and Palestinians are, and the appearance of draft resistance, an incipient civil rights movement, public debate, and ongoing historical revision, are all real efforts by Jews to come to grips with this history. There are Jewish figures who honestly grapple with Israel, Noam Chomsky and Israel Shahak preeminent among them, and Said feels that the common humanity of Jews and Palestinians will always assert itself, at least on the margins of personal and public discourse.

The task is to continue to hammer away at the ideologues who mask their chosenness argument in political speech that legitimates injustice. In fact, the challenge is less to dispute difference, though on close examination any detailed definition of difference is difficult, if not impossible, but to deny difference a political meaning and especially political power. One can be for difference and at the same time be against "rigidly enforced and political separation" of population groups. As Said writes with regard to the Palestinian argument: "Not only is it manifestly the case that different national, ethnic, and religious groups exist, but no one has the inherent right to use 'difference' as an instrument to relegate the rights of others to an inferior or lesser status." Palestinians have learned this prohibition not only in the face of Israel, but also in their experience with Arab states that similarly essentialize Palestinians through ideology and practical politics. The reality of life is different and this is what must be emphasized in the coming years: that far from separation and purity, life actually involves "mixing or crossing-over, of stepping beyond boundaries, which are more creative human activities than staying inside rigid-ly policed borders." To raise these questions is existentially important to Palestinians in their struggle to overcome their defeat and to Jews who ultimately must overcome their victory, which on the moral level is also a defeat. Indeed a new logic is needed if Jews and Palestinians are to live together with respect, justice, and peace. Said defines this logic as one where "'difference' does not entail 'domination.'"[17]

In 1988, three years after Said's essay on difference, Daniel and Jonathan Boyarin responded with an essay seeking a new level of dia-logue. The Boyarins are Jewish scholars active in Jewish affairs, the for-mer, at that time, living in Israel, the latter in the United States; both are affiliated with progressive Jewish politics and have substantive questions about Israeli policies. Further, both realize that Said's challenge to Jews and Israel is important to engage, to affirm at some points and dispute at others. Their argument is sophisticated and nuanced. On the question of racism for example, Said's discussion of Israeli apartheid is challenged with the following statement: "Apartheid is a racist ideology *tout court*; Zionism is an ideology that has racist aspects and effects, and also is a response to racism." Though apartheid and Zionism share some common roots, the difference with Zionism is that it is a flawed response to oppres-sion in Europe and, unlike apartheid in South Africa, it is possible for Zionism to be purified of its racist aspects. To see Zionism as unable to be cleansed of racism, as the brothers Boyarin claim Said is in danger of positing, is to become part of a "totalizing thrust toward the utter delegit-imization of Zionism." In their view Said stops short in his analysis and simplifies the difficult position of Jews vis-à-vis the West and Israel itself. Though for the Boyarins Israel is deeply problematic as the post-genocide embodiment of Jewish identity, Israel remains important because "Jews have been victimized in ways analogous (though obviously not identical, and the difference once again must be specified) to the victimization of Palestinians." As Jewish nationalists, who believe that Zionism is a national liberation movement for Jews and who respect other national movements of liberation, including the Palestinian national movement, the Boyarins believe that Said shortchanges the desire of Jews for a homeland where Jewish renewal and cultural development can take place alongside Palestinian renewal and cultural development in their home-land. Thus, difference can be respected and projected in its own spheres, Jewish and Palestinian, without denigrating the other. Therefore it is pos-sible while critiquing Zionism to see the possibility of a commitment to Zionism entailing a commitment to Palestine. For the Boyarins such a commitment is "a direct consequence of Zionism properly understood."[18]

Said's response is written against the backdrop of the Palestinian intifada and the brutal repression of this movement of national liberation by the Israelis. For Said, the "Wieselian bolus" identified by Cuddihy had already issued into a Walzerian jumble where the history of the victor is claimed as a passport for the victim to oppress another people, and here, in the midst of this continuing and escalating oppression, the Boyarins, brothers whose intellect and active life are committed to the left, are engaged in a further act of symmetry. Beginning with the bold statement that they are "fully committed to national liberation for the Palestinian people" as part of their commitment to Zionism, and ending with the three interrelated issues that fuel their argument—Israeli repression of the Palestinians, the historical predicament of the Jewish people, and the Jewish struggle for self-determination—Said is almost overcome with the self-referential aspect of their argument.

In five pages of closely reasoned and carefully worded text, the Boyarins manage to traverse the entirety of the struggle that has been waged for almost a century, explaining and committing themselves to both Jews and Palestinians in the process. To the point that historically the Zionist movement was one of liberation because there were no other historically feasible alternatives at the time, Said asks if this is "somehow to mitigate the suffering imposed by Jews on non-Jews and obligates us always to recall and write extensively about the travails of Europe." To the Boyarins' sense that Said does not deal sufficiently with anti-Semitism, seeing it as a subordinate term in the formulation of his argument, Said responds that this sensibility is "staggering in its impropriety," especially at this moment: "Can they not get it into their heads that as Palestinians, whose total dispossession and daily—I repeat, daily—torture, murder, and mass oppression by 'the state of the Jewish people' occurs even as the Boyarins speak, we are not always compelled to think of the former suffering of the Jewish people. Can you imagine the brothers Boyarin standing next to the residents of Beita as their houses were being blown up by the Israeli army, and saying to them, 'It would help you to know and remember that the Jews who are now killing you were once cruelly and unfairly killed too'? Or consoling the parents of a Palestinian child just shot by an Israeli soldier by saying that the soldier may have had relatives who were exterminated by the Nazis." Said concludes strongly by asking how the Boyarins can write these things, as if "dialogue with the Palestinians was completely separable from the outrages taking place in the Occupied Territories." Said's criticism of Jewish intellectuals remains in place: "What they cannot accept is that the Palestinian and Israeli positions are not symmetrical today, and that whatever the horror of Jewish suffering in the past it does not excuse, abrogate, or exonerate the practices of the *Jewish* state against the Palestinian people."[19]

The Jewish Assimilation to Power

With the essay on difference and the response to the Boyarins, Said's discussion of Zionism and Israel and the role of Jewish intellectuals with regard to both comes full circle. His two important insights—that Jewish intellectuals have, in the main, become experts in legitimation, and that the ideology of difference, no matter how carefully disguised and argued, is ultimately an assertion of chosenness reinforced with the apparatus of the state of Israel—are clearly and forcefully enunciated. For the most part, and in light of his experience and that of the Palestinian people, Said's tone is analytical and remarkably restrained. Said's anger as seen in his response to Walzer and the Boyarins is born of commitment to his own people; there is only one other point where Said demonstrates such anger and that is in response to Palestinian leadership signing and implementing the Oslo accords. What Cuddihy chides the Jewish community for, a lack of reciprocity, Said fulfills in the Oslo era. In light of his essays and editorials since 1993, Said's honesty in addressing the Jewish people becomes even clearer: power and the abuse of power, the necessity of intellectuals to honestly evaluate that power regardless of where it emanates from, is Said's hallmark. When he feels that his own people are being neglected or abused by their own leadership, he is forthright, rigorous, and vigilant in the same tone and manner as when he criticizes the abuse of Jewish power. Even in the most tenuous of situations, where Israel clearly has the upper hand, there is a responsibility to refuse to be experts in legitimation and to refuse the ideology of difference that blinds one from the follies, shortsightedness, and corruption of power. By refusing to essentialize the Palestinian cause, by airing his critique of the Palestinian leadership in exactly the same way he has encouraged Jews to do, and, in doing so, jeopardizing his standing among Palestinians and Palestinian leadership, Said embodies his ideas in a way that removes them from any hint of suspicion of ulterior motives or special interests.[20]

In the entire body of Said's work there is never a hint of overt or covert anti-Semitism, or even the construction of an argument that cleverly conceals such a view. From the beginning of Said's writing on the subject of Orientalism and Palestine, there is a sensitivity to Jews and Judaism that is evident and a willingness to take both seriously in the forms that affect the Western perception of the East and the Israeli perception of Palestinians. While the dominant practitioners of Orientalism, at least historically, are not Jewish, those who are Jewish are analyzed like the others and without rancor. Zionism and its adherents are criticized for their practical policies and the ideas that legitimate them; mystification, whether in charges of Jewish aggressiveness or conspiracy, are, in Said's work, completely absent. Rather than being absent for strategic purposes, however—for example to avoid aligning oneself with a fringe anti-Semitism in America or to gain a better hearing in a context that is openly pro-Israel and, at least to some extent, though not without ambivalence, pro-Jewish—Said's critique of paternalism and injustice is highly principled and biased only in the most natural of ways. Perhaps because of his disposition, upbringing, context, and character, Said seems to identify with those on the other side of power and clearly would, were the situation different, identify with Jewish suffering.

Because Said deals with Jews, Zionism, and Israel in a principled manner and in a broader framework of ethics and justice, he addresses the Jewish people and Jewish history in a variety of ways. First and foremost, Said decenters Jews and Jewish experience by looking at Orientalism from the perspective of the East and the West and by looking at Palestine and Palestinians from the perspective of their history and aspirations. The question of Palestine arises in history for Palestinians because every people in each generation must search for its identity, and the recent experience of dispossession and diaspora demands a new commitment to that search. That the dispossession has occurred at the hands of Jews with the support of the West is a detail of absolute importance because it frames a concrete context for the Palestinian struggle, not because of any intrinsic Jewish sensibility or blame. No doubt, if another people had dispossessed the Palestinians, the particulars would be different but the challenge would be similar: the reconstruction of Palestine and Palestinian identity in the wake of catastrophe.

Decentering Jewish experience and history is important for Palestinians in that they recognize their struggle as against invaders and occupiers rather than a mythicized community, thereby refusing to essentialize Jews as Palestinians have been essentialized. At the same time, decentering Jews is an important contribution to the Jewish community because it reverses the blindness that the ideology of difference demands. For Said, though Zionism and Israel are *the* problematic for the question of Palestine, it is simply because of the power of the West and Israel at this time in history. Though Jews do indeed have a particular and special history in Said's eyes, this lies outside his interest. In fact, that Jews hold this view of their history, that Jewish hsitory is central and unique, is contradicted by the very normality of their abuse of power and the attempt to hide that abuse. If there are to be any claims about Jewish history, they will now have to proceed through the filter of this aggression.

Said neither affirms nor denies Jewish self-understanding. Rather he challenges it by refusing abstraction and by paying attention to the details of Jewish history vis-à-vis his own people. That there is no other agenda in Said's analysis is problematic for Jewish intellectuals because it does not allow a retreat into a specialness via negation of Jewishness or exaggeration through the myth of the Jew. Jews in the guise of Zionism and Israel insofar as they operate as experts in legitimation must be opposed just as any others who dispossess and legitimate dispossession must be opposed. If, for Cuddihy, the attempt on the part of Jews to have both power and innocence is irritating, the opposition to dispossession that is caused and furthered by Jews without any other motive or agenda is confusing, even disorienting, as it undermines the very concepts that Jews, often unconsciously, employ. It cuts to the very heart of Jewish identity.

Whereas Cuddihy uncovers the foundations of Jewish identity as Jews move in and through modernity, Said probes the reality of Jewish practice in the context of communal empowerment. For the most part, Cuddihy analyzes the movement of Jews into the twentieth century; Said traces their trajectory into the twenty-first century. In some sense Jews are in both of these contexts at the same time, and here is a difficulty that has two aspects: an unconscious and unintended suspension between differing and to some extent overlapping situations—emancipation and empowerment—and a conscious desire to maintain innocence within empowerment as a strategy of self-interest and lack of concern for others. Whatever the instances, and in some cases there is a mixture of the unconscious and intended, Said calls Jewish intellectuals and public actors to account, to realize the change in Jewish status, influence, and power and to respond accordingly. In lieu of this, Jewish intellectuals at least have the responsibility to end the moralizing from and emphasis on their suffering and to begin to simply state the facts of Jewish empowerment boldly. It is almost as if Said is challenging Jews who believe in the dispossession of Palestinians as a right to say so boldly, to say that Israel is right in humiliating, torturing, and murdering Palestinians, and that anyone who criticizes those policies should be fought to the end. Is this not the policy of Israel and the Jewish establishment from 1948 to the present?

For Jews to admit this power and its use, and for Jewish intellectuals to admit their role as experts in legitimation, is to perforce surrender on the question of difference. Jewish soldiers are like any other soldiers, even in the 1967 War, and in a larger sense a Jewish state is like any other state. The military and the state, especially one marked by colonialism and expansion, needs intellectuals and theologians to legitimate its policies. Thus Jewish thinkers like Bernard Lewis and Michael Walzer are intellectuals in service to the state as were many intellectuals who supported governments that displaced and murdered Jews. Said does not articulate this connection as Noam Chomsky does, but the implications of his analysis are clear. As a Palestinian, the aggression of Israel and those who justify its policies—even, as Said points out, by maintaining the overall thrust of the state through selective criticism and false symmetry—are agents of doom that must be confronted and struggled against. The agony of Jewish intellectuals and their often twisted arguments are, as Said suggests in his response to the Boyarins, ultimately irrelevant and absurd.

If the entry point of Jews into modernity is an intellectual and ethical probity, thereby allowing the claim of distinctiveness in secular terms, what is left of that distinctiveness when Jewish intellectuals are found, like many non-Jewish intellectuals, to be in service to the state, and when Jews who wield power are found, like non-Jews who wield power, to be unjust, coercive, and self-aggrandizing? If there is no difference, is there any content to Jewishness in the contemporary world? Said's challenge is deepened because, though born outside of the West, he, like Jewish intellectuals before him, has penetrated the West and made a home for himself at the center of Western intellectual life. Said thus is an outsider/insider who has experienced Jewish power in its raw and objective rather than distant and mythical reality. Contrary to the assertion of anti-Semitic propagandists in Europe, Jews did not control European life or participate in a global conspiracy to control the world's wealth, but Jews *did* (and *do*) displace Palestinians and destroy Palestine. Jews are in control of a state that sponsors, among other things, a systematic policy of settlement, expropriation of land, torture, and creation of refugees. In Said's generation, a Palestinian diaspora has been created by Jews in Israel with the support of Jews around the world. Though Jews have continually and with great difficulty fought the myth of anti-Semitism, Said presents, indeed embodies, a nightmare of epic proportions, because his criticism is of a Jewish power that is abusive *and* real.

Thus Said presents Jews with the other side of Jewish life in our time. The consequences of that presentation are intended to unmask oppressive power and to challenge chosenness, uniqueness, and ethical character articulated in a secular and modern form. Once that critique is accepted, the consequences are immediate and long-range. As Said remarks in his exchange with Walzer, instead of demanding their place in the West as if nothing has happened in Jewish history since the Holocaust except the lamentable need to defend Jews against new enemies, Jews should express compassion and atonement for what they have done and what has been done in the name of the Jewish people. This compassion and atonement means, among other things, an honest confession that goes beyond what is normally found in intellectual discourse and a desire to rectify as much as possible the dispossession of the Palestinian people. To do so is to highlight the truth of what has occurred, a rarity to be sure, but a truth that has been articulated by those Jewish intellectuals and activists that have broken through the acceptable discourse and suffered at the hands of the very thinkers who are now called to confession. Confessing is an opening to the Palestinians *and* to the Jewish tradition in pursuit of justice and to a renewed sense of dignity and honest discourse. It entails the end of privileged testimony; the ideology of difference would be disconnected from the state and the power it wields. Instead of defending Jews from the vicissitudes of history, understandable in the wake of Jewish suffering, Jews reenter the risk of history, of "mixing," beginning in the reconfiguration of Israel/Palestine.[21]

Without specifying this trajectory, and always in a completely secular manner, Said asks for a decentering of Jewish experience and the re-embrace of an authentic diaspora sensibility in the West and in Israel/Palestine. By pulling back the "curtain of sentimentality and casuistic argument drawn around Israeli-Zionist brutality and inhumanity," the "only hope," a community of Palestinians and Zionist and non-Zionist Jews, can take root on the land of historical Palestine. The choice of prolonging the now mutual antipathy between Jews and Palestinians inherent in Israel's exercise of power is challenged by a vision that refuses to "privilege the experience or the contemporary situation" of either peoples. Difference is acknowledged as a bridge to sharing insight and the rigid enforcement of separation, so necessary for a state that claims to embody the essence of Jewish history, can be relaxed.

Stepping beyond the boundaries of the known where the more creative human activities are found is then a challenge rather than a danger. One wonders, and again Said does not address this directly, whether this crossing-over is the way out of the isolation that many Jews feel and Jewish intellectuals often operate from. The shadow of the Holocaust, used as a protection but also deeply felt, may then become more distant in time and feeling. To realize and admit the capabilities of Jews to suffer *and* to cause suffering and as intellectuals to subvert *and* legitimate injustice, to experience the Jewish claim on the world to be just *and* unjust, all depending on the historical era and context, is to realize that being a victim or a victor is not pre-ordained. Whether underneath or riding the wave of history there are situations that can be fought and refused in light of the possibility of an interdependent journey with others. Seeing power as univocal, either being without it or having it, is the way of legitimation and difference as a survival of power or use of power over the "other." Seeing power as an avenue to interdependence, to mutuality in politics and thought, is a way of using difference to heighten and deepen a joint enterprise where no one is alone and where the infringement of one is the infringement of all.[22]

Where does this humility and confession lead? What if the Jewish state became a joint homeland of Jews and Palestinians? Would the Holocaust as a central aspect of Jewish identity then recede? Would Jews in the West care about a homeland that increasingly oriented itself to its actual geography and history? If Jews saw Zionism from the perspective of Jewish history *and* its victims, would the Jewish claim of uniqueness and ethical character suffer a death blow? After the mobilization of the Jewish community around the world in terms of Holocaust and Israel, what would become the center of Jewish identity in their stead? Are the Holocaust and Israel, the secular equivalent of Jewish religiosity, the only religiosity that can be embraced by the majority of Jews in contact with modernity? Would the head-long flight to rescue Jewish history from the prospects of annihilation in the Nazi era then fail in an era of peace and normality where Jews have no reason to embrace the Jewishness they may have left anyway, except for the Nazis and the founding of Israel? Could the fear of giving up the Holocaust and Israel as *the* center, twinned and invoked together, be a fear that there is nothing compelling left of Jewish life and that without this center the final assimilation is at hand?

One wonders if Said's statement to Walzer—that from the position of exile ideologies of difference are a "great deal less satisfactory than impure genres, people, activities; that separation and discrimination are often not as estimable as connecting and crossing over"—can be received as a truth about life in general and still remain within the formative identity of Jewish history as carried forward in the modern world. Or do Jewish intellectuals fear this sensibility, struggle against it, and in different ways attempt to argue their way out or around it? That is why in the end Said needs to shout out the reality of Jewish life in its empowerment, distinguish its intellectual argument from the reality of its power to displace, and expose it in its sometimes ludicrous sensibility. When Said confronts the Boyarins with the imagined statement of Jews explaining to Palestinians who have just had their house blown up by the Israeli army—"It would help you to know and remember that the Jews who are now killing you were once cruelly and unfairly killed too"—the absolute absurd reality of such a statement in the face of that suffering nonetheless rings true.[23]

As much as Said's sophisticated analysis, this statement of creative license resounds in the history of the Jewish people. It is a final caution, indeed statement of fact, that Jews are not pure or innocent or even different, and that the assimilation that Jewish thinkers fight has already occurred. That assimilation is to power and the injustice that results from its abuse.

The Future of the Jewish People

Those who seek to chart a future for the Jewish people must start with this startling fact that Said confronts us with: Jewish assimilation to the state and its culture has already occurred. The trajectory analyzed by Cuddihy has come full circle, and the intellectual power of subversion has become the intellectual power of legitimation. In an era when Jews are called upon to build and defend the state, Jewish participation and dependence on state culture is expected as the norm. In this sense, and in the span of less than a century, Jews have moved from a pariah people to a people commemorated, celebrated, and empowered in the West and in Israel. The normalization of the Jewish people, a goal of Zionism and even some Holocaust theologians, has taken place. In a symbolic and literal sense, Jews are now among the nations.

Who could fault Jews for such a desire, especially after the travails of their history? Has there ever been empowerment without bloodshed? Should Jews be denied empowerment or called to a purity that no one else can claim? Does the need to survive override the ethical idea, religious or secular? Now among the nations, what is the responsibility of a Jewish state to others? Is it any greater than other nation-states? Does one expect a Jewish state to listen to the cries of its victims or even its own dissenters more than other nation-states? On the practical level, is the struggle within Israel now, especially after the post-1967 expansion of the state, a civil rights struggle seeking equal rights for Palestinians within the borders of what was once historic Palestine? Has the battle shifted from one of justice and accountability, and thus the ethical imperative to do what is right and redress the grievances of those who have been wronged, to acknowledging that the struggle has been lost and the new entity is here to be reckoned with in a completely different manner? The language of innocence and redemption is lost to be sure, but is the language of identity and struggle already dated as well? Said is quite right in demonstrating that Jewish discourse in its assimilation to power has lost its foundation and substance, but has the language of resistance, in light of the continuing inability to stop the expansion of Israel, also lost its bearings? Do the two questions, the Jewish question and the question of Palestine, remain in force, or have they been transformed in ways that are as yet without articulation? If this is so, if the Jewish and Palestinian questions within an expanded Israeli state have become one question, what will become of the Jewish and Palestinian diaspora communities? How will they form their questions, to what foundations will they look, and how will their identities maintain a substantive focus?

Said's disdain for the "pure" and his option for "mixing" is important here, as is his understanding that the future of Jews and Palestinians in the land will be shared. His distinction between secular and religious criticism, articulated in *The World, the Text, and the Critic,* is also important. For Said secular criticism is the continual opening to reality, especially the opening provided by distance to origins, contemporary claims and power. By introducing circumstance and distinction where conformity and belonging reign, a distance is projected from whence criticism is born. This distance is from the ivory tower *and* from movements demanding absolute allegiance.

Nonetheless there is a closeness to reality that portends and involves commitments, a state of vigilance which Said defines in this way: "To stand between culture and system is therefore to stand *close to* . . . a concrete reality about which political, moral, and social judgments have to be made and, if not only made, then exposed and demystified." Thus secular criticism deals with "local and worldly situations" and is opposed to the "production of massive hermetic systems," a production Said identifies as religious in its orientation. Consciously or unconsciously, religious criticism reinforces these hermetic systems by indulging in "unthinkability, undecidability, and paradox together with a remarkable consistency of appeals to magic, divine ordinance, or sacred texts." The secular deals with a "knowledge of history, a recognition of the importance of social circumstance, an analytical capacity for making distinctions," all of which trouble the religious who long for the acceptable, the known, and the comfortable. The secular is close to the world as it is and how it might be, while the religious create a world above reality and seek to protect it through retreat and mystification. The tension that Said sees in the world—between filiation (birth, nationality, profession) and affiliation (social and political conviction, economic and historical circumstances, voluntary effort and willed deliberation)—is one that needs to be struggled with rather than resolved. Closure is a form of mystification just as the pretense to be without roots and context is. Connection *and* distance, a sense of identity *and* openness, fosters criticism that is intelligent *and* compassionate. Because of this, secular criticism is life-enhancing and opposed to all forms of tyranny and injustice: such criticism acts to develop space where alternative acts and intentions can flourish. In Said's view, this is the path of advancing human freedom as a fundamental human obligation.[24]

How can one remain close to the Jewish community, especially its normative discourse, and remain attentive to the facts as they have and continue to unfold in Israel? Said's sense of the intellectual as oppositional—as one who refuses a patriotism that is blind and blinding, who is open to the diversity of life especially when a univocal commitment is demanded, and whose larger commitment is to humanity even when group survival is invoked as an emotional brake on intelligence—draws one to an exilic position. Could it be that Jews are called to side with the Canaanites, participate in a Canaanite reading of contemporary reality, to be among the Canaanites *as a sign of fidelity to Jewish history and contemporary reality*? It may be that Jews who have opposed the experts in legitimation and use of difference as a form of domination are in fact in exile. Still, many have argued their exilic position as a way of confronting the community, calling it to an alternative sensibility, and hoping that in doing this they will once again join the ranks of the community in good standing. Though understandable and in many cases laudable, this position may itself become a form of mystification whereby the ethical propensity of Jewish life can be reasserted *while the abuse of power continues*. The confrontation with state power is thus affirmed *and* jettisoned at the same time. A new comfort level can be achieved, a new innocence proclaimed, a renewal of Jewish life celebrated as the Palestinian diaspora grows and Israel reaches ever deeper into the last reservoir of Palestinian life and culture. This, too, is an assimilation to power by which celebration of renewal occurs in the protective embrace of the state even as displacement and destruction continue. Thus claiming exile is not enough. The rigors of exile must be attended to so that exile itself does not become part of the pattern of domination.

In our time, and for the foreseeable future, the exile of Jews and Palestinians will continue and perhaps even escalate. The foundations of Jewish life, already seriously undermined, will continue to erode until the exilic situation will become the norm. Of course nation-states can operate, at least for a time, on coercion and bribery, and there are intellectuals enough who will sell their thought and be honored for it. They will claim continuity with the Jewish tradition, dismissing the exiles as those who threaten to unlock the gates of power. If it is true that we have entered the terminal phase of Jewish life, if indeed we have come to the *end of Jewish history as we have known it*, this does not mean that the rhetoric of Jewishness or Judaism will grow faint. Just the opposite. The voice of Jewish life resounds as never before in history and it does not seem to matter, at least to those in power, that it returns as an empty echo. That emptiness is deafening both for those on the other side of Jewish power and for Jews who through birth and commitment seek a fidelity now shrouded in darkness. It is strange, perhaps, though on deeper reflection absolutely fitting, that a modern Canaanite, Edward Said, lights that darkness with his own intelligence and compassion. One wonders if this light will one day become a beacon of recognition and reconciliation for Jews as it has been all these years for his own people.

16

Dorothy Day, the Jews,
and the Future of Ecumenical Religiosity

JEWS HAVE ALWAYS BEEN CENTRAL TO CHRISTIANITY and the embrace of the Christian faith. In many ways, even until the middle of the twentieth century, this centrality has been defined negatively and with corresponding results. For Christians this has meant a combination of rigidity and militarism, a triumphalism of the spirit and the crusades. The travail of the Jews is historic within this negative definition, realized in ghettoization, pogroms, and holocaust. The Nazi terror, seemingly so distant but reaching closure only some fifty years ago, is a horrific expression of this negative definition, for if the death camps were built within the framework of a political fascist ideology, the singling out of the Jews for destruction came from those who claim to believe in the messianic journey of the Jew who Christians name Christ.

Throughout Christian history Jews have been seen in a dual role, as those who prepared the way for the coming of the messiah and those who refused to accept the messiah once he appeared. Carrying the word of God, the Jews also refused that word, and in the body of the messiah crucified it. The promise, which Jews once alone embodied among the world's peoples, passed with that crucifixion to a new people who walked in the footsteps of the one who brought salvation. The Old Israel was replaced by the New Israel, with catastrophic results for Jews. As those who betrayed the messiah and thus God, Jews were condemned for eternity to live with their choice, humbled, chastened, wandering without solace or home. Jews were important as symbolic reminders of the fate of those who reject God as well as the sign of the end times. In their betrayal and stubborn adherence to their crime, a crime at once human and ontological, they also represented the possibility of recognizing the salvific act of Jesus Christ. For if one day even the Jews recognized their mistake and assented to the messiah, if even the stubbornness of the Jews broke with a bow to the truth, then the second coming of Christ was assured. Condemned and broken, with license for those of the New Israel to further abuse Jews for their crime, Jews were also to be watched and evangelized so to monitor the closeness of the end times.

Paradoxically, those who held the keys of the Kingdom and then threw them away for thirty pieces of silver continued to hold them for those who accepted the Kingdom but waited for its manifestation on earth. The definition of Jews by Christians, the very designation of Old and New Israel, therefore, held a tremendous tension and anxiety for Christians. Jews embodied failure and must be seen to have failed, hence ghettoization and violence against them. However, the despised also embodied the possibility of salvation, then and now. Those who followed Jesus were perpetual latecomers, dependent on those despised. Furthermore, the messiah himself was one of those who embodied this tension. Worshiping a Jew and proclaiming one's superiority within that proclamation could only elicit a variety of unresolved tensions and ambiguities. The polemic and violence that occasioned this dilemma force another question as well: How did those who received the messiah and worshiped him act so violently against this lesser and condemned people without incurring the wrath of the God they worshiped? If the covenant was broken with the Jewish people because of their actions and blindness, could the new covenant also be broken by the actions of Christians against Jews?[1]

Suffering and the Question of God

When I first met William Miller, the biographer of the Catholic Worker movement, I had encountered various aspects of these understandings. As a Jew and as part of the first generation born after the Holocaust, I knew very little about Christianity. In my college years I majored in religious studies and it was through courses in New Testament and the history of Christianity that I learned the details of what had existed in the background of my upbringing but had lacked articulation: that Christianity was foreign and an enemy, at the least to be avoided and, if the situation worsened, to be opposed with our lives. Though this seems a dramatic rendering of the 1950s in America (and in North Miami Beach no less), Germany in the 1920s had also seemed hospitable to the Jews. Whatever the objective circumstances, the turns and twists of Jewish history served as a caution, certainly in a time when the ovens of Auschwitz were only recently destroyed.

With this as background, my meeting with Miller and the importance of his book was in an existential sense connected to the Holocaust in another way. The formative teacher of my college days was Richard Rubenstein, a Holocaust theologian who, in light of the Holocaust, saw the bond between God and the Jewish people severed. If God is a God of history as Jews believed in their trials and tribulations through the centuries, where was God in the death camps? If the rabbis had believed that

Jewish suffering in the diaspora was caused by God as a lesson to heed God's word and return to the practice of the Law, could one believe that the massive suffering of the Holocaust was part of that punishment and desire to return? How could one continue to pray to such a God?[2]

The question of God's existence and goodness was complemented by a further and equally disturbing question as to whether Jews could continue to work for an interdependent world where all would be safe and secure. If one of the lessons of the Holocaust was that Jews could not expect help from God in their time of need, another lesson, at least for Rubenstein, was that Jews could not expect a solidarity with other human beings and communities in time of need. Rubenstein found a dual violation in the Holocaust by God and humanity, and therefore posited power as the only remedy for Jews, indeed any people, who hoped to survive the vagaries of God and the world. This was the lesson of the Holocaust as Rubenstein saw it, and the vision of a world bereft of solidarity struck his students, as it did me, with a force that to this day remains with us.

As a Holocaust theologian, Rubenstein also explored the realm of Christianity, especially its role in the degradation of Jews and the groundwork it laid for the Holocaust. Here, too, there were twists and turns; Rubenstein saw the Nazis as anti-Christian but caught in the very dynamic of Christianity itself. As rebels against Christianity, they affirmed its hold on the European continent and battled against its effeminate aspects, which they ascribed to its Judaic background. For the Nazis would accept a Christianity masculinized by rejecting its Judaic elements, a step that many Christians were all too willing to take. The other side of this was the laying of the groundwork for singling out Jews. This obsession with the Jews was similar to and dependent on the Christian obsession. In this respect, Nazis and Christians shared a world view that converged on the Jews, and thus even those elements of Christianity that resisted Hitler and the Nazis were often anti-Semitic.

My encounter with Miller and the Catholic Worker occurred within this background but I was moving toward the next question posed by Rubenstein's analysis. If Rubenstein understood the world I inherited at midcentury, was this the world I would inhabit and pass on? There was an earned bitterness in Rubenstein's manner and thought that was both attractive and frightening: attractive because it called history to task and faced that history unflinchingly; frightening because Rubenstein's world was void of comfort and love. Rubenstein, like all great teachers, issued a summons to accompany him on his journey and then to return to one's own with the questions his journey posed.

Yet at that moment I was too young to return only to my world or to embark on my own journey, and instead found an equally powerful figure in Miller. Like Rubenstein, Miller had also encountered history, and his defining moment could be found in Dorothy Day and the Catholic Worker.

As I listened to Miller and read his first book on the Worker, *A Harsh and Dreadful Love: Dorothy Day and the Catholic Worker Movement,* the very title proposed another perspective on history. Here in a life and a movement, the horrors of history were confronted by a commitment, especially to those who suffered, and a commitment to build a world of mutual solidarity. In this solidarity, a beauty is found, and so too a God who is with those who are suffering and those who are working toward that solidarity. This solidarity is found in the Christian and specifically Catholic faith, but the resources for the journey moved within and far beyond those confines. For me, the encounter with Miller and his work, and later hearing and meeting Dorothy Day, had this quality of posing a different perspective and path in the same world Rubenstein had evoked. The broken solidarity could be reestablished and the connection of God and humanity and humans with each other could be affirmed in a committed life. Moreover, the protection of life did not come through the exercise of political power but through a kind of power that no longer existed in Rubenstein's world: the power of love lived in the world.

The People Israel

In Miller's biography of the Catholic Worker a chapter title appears seemingly out of nowhere. Placed between chapters on the depression years and Dorothy Day's pacifist stand during World War II is a chapter entitled "Israel." I can remember wondering what that title might refer to. The modern nation-state came immediately to mind, but the first pages made it clear that this was not the case. In fact Israel was the religious definition of the Jewish people and for Miller, at least, the Worker sensibility toward the Jews was as defining of its intent and direction as any other issue. The 1930s and 1940s were of course defining moments for the Jewish people as well, and Miller captures this phase quite well by beginning his section on Israel: "As the Jews moved into the most agonizing phase of their history. . . ."[3]

My own copy of Miller's biography is well marked, especially in this chapter. Here a range of Catholic thought on the Jews was brought to my attention, from Charles Coughlin, the anti-Semitic priest and radio commentator, to Jacques Maritain, the influential Catholic philosopher. In fact, as Miller points out in that book as well as in his later biography of Dorothy Day, Dorothy's experience with Jews predates the 1930s, as her closest friend in college, Rayna Simons, and a man she was briefly engaged to during her early years on the lower east side of New York, Mike Gold, were both Jewish. Both were revolutionaries and atheists wanting to build a society and world where injustice perished and community was established as the essence of human striving.[4]

This experience of being drawn to the ideals and personality of Jews was one that served Dorothy well and because of this she rarely entered the theological discussion regarding the relationship of Jews and Christians until after the Vatican II Council. In confronting anti-Semitism, however, she was clear and forthright from the beginning. In response to a particularly offensive broadcast of Fr. Coughlin's in December 1938, Dorothy wrote a statement that she circulated to local newspapers and the *New Republic* asking Jews to consider this a case of "extraordinarily bad manners." In May 1939, she helped organize the Committee of Catholics to Fight Anti-Semitism. A paper, *The Voice*, was created to promulgate the views of this committee and was distributed along with the *Catholic Worker* newspaper.[5]

The early discussion of Jews in the *Catholic Worker* was carried forth largely by Peter Maurin and others associated with the movement. One is drawn to the Easy Essays of Maurin on the subject and the startling artwork of Ade Bethune that becomes more and more prominent in the paper as the tragedy of the Holocaust begins to unfold. One thinks here of Maurin's essay, "Let's Keep the Jews for Christ's Sake," which is central to the front page of the July-August 1939 issue, followed by Bethune's depiction of the baby Jesus within a prominent Star of David in December 1939. On top of the star in Hebrew is the statement rendered in English on the bottom of the star, "the Son of God, the son of man, God is with us."[6]

Maurin's essay is interesting in a variety of ways. Combining and condensing insights from Leon Bloy and Jacques Maritain, Maurin first asserts the "mystery" of the Jews. He begins with what they are not:

> They are not a nation
>> although the Zionists
>> try to build up one
>> in Palestine.
> They are not a race
>> for they have intermarried
>> with many other races.
> They are not a religion
>> since their belief
>> calls for one Temple
>> and the Jewish Temple
>> has not been in existence
>> for nearly 2,000 years.[7]

If Jews are not a nation, race, or religion, what are they? That indeed is the mystery. Jews have survived for millennia in their dispersion and remain a mystery even to themselves. Maurin quickly shifts to an abridged history of Jewish survival where the mystery of the Jews is again addressed. In Spain, for example, and later in the papal states, Maurin asserts that Jews found protection in the "shadow of the Cross." Historically, the attempt to convert Jews went hand in hand with the protection of Jews, which contrasts significantly with the desire of the Nazis to persecute them. The shadow of the cross compares favorably with the swastika partly because of what both symbols stand for: the first salvation, the second perfidy. Moreover, the church recognizes the mystery of the Jews as a "reminder to the world of the coming of Christ." Though they did not recognize Christ, the Jews remain chosen, "for God does not change." Thus the Jews who "refused to accept the Cross find their best protection in the shadow of the Cross" and surely this refusal of the cross does not excuse actions that are non-Christian in their manner and intent. Maurin closes his essay with the contemporary need for Jews to find refuge, and even identifies Jews, against their economic stereotype as parasitic middlemen, as those who can work the land and build urban centers. America is "big enough" to welcome Jews who need refuge, and their work on the land and in the cities of Palestine shows their ability to contribute to America.[8]

The situation of the Jews continued to weigh on Maurin, and in two subsequent essays, "Why Pick on the Jews" and "Judaism and Catholicism," published in the winter of 1940, he again tried to sort out the issue of Judaism and its relation to Christianity and divorce this relationship from the anti-Semitic racial and economic propaganda emanating from Europe and America. The most obvious battle reigned in Europe with the Nazis and their racialism, but Maurin also understood the tendency of Christians to mistake a significant religious dialogue with persecution. In these essays Maurin argues for the superiority of Christianity only insofar as it completes Judaism. Thus when Jacques Maritain, a convert from Protestantism, is accused by some of being a convert from Judaism, Maurin reports that rather than being ashamed of this possibility, Maritain would be proud of a Jewish background, as is his wife, Raissa, who is a convert from Judaism. In fact, Raissa claimed that in her conversion to Catholicism "she is now 100% Jewish." Other Jewish converts felt the same way, and Maurin names some prominent academics and priests who have become Catholic as a way of completing their Judaism. The converts who have become priests may have been rabbis if they had not accepted the cross, and Maurin comments on this without denigration. Though as priests "they announce the good news that the Messiah announced by the Prophets died on Calvary" as rabbis they would be "commenting on the Jewish prophets." This corresponds with Maurin's understanding that Judaism contains within it the "doctrine of a personal God as well as sound social ethics." Several years later Maurin used Leon Bloy's own words to express his solidarity with Judaism and the Jewish people and to accelerate his outrage at the anti-Semitism of his day. Titled, "Salvation is of the Jews," Maurin quotes Bloy:

> The history of the Jews
> > damns the history
> > of the human race
> > as a dike
> > damns a river
> > — in order
> > to raise its level.
> The Jews
> > were the only people
> > from which came forth
> > all the recording secretaries
> > of the commandments of God.[9]

Of course, the authenticity of Judaism and the Jews continues when Jews are Jews, or in Maurin's terminology, "when the Jews are themselves." When the Jews are themselves they believe in and live within the framework of the covenant, especially with reference to the prophets. When Jews are no longer Jews, that is when they adopt bourgeois understandings and practices or a belief in being Jewish solely through race identification, they become a "nuisance," for Jews were a "chosen people but they were never a superior race."

Maurin applies this sensibility to all who come into his purview. A charge laid to the feet of Jews is that they seek to separate religion and business, but for Maurin that is the assertion of many Christians as well. If Jews turn "sharp corners" in business, so do Christians. Capitalism itself is thought to be founded and promulgated by Jews—and here Maurin addresses the larger critique of Jews having created the liberal and rootless society—but as Maurin reports "Adam Smith and Ricardo, the theoreticians of Bourgeois Capitalism were not Jews." Rather than blaming Jews, the basic problem, the drift of peoples around the world from their roots in religion and ethics, needs to be addressed.

When a separation of religion and economic and political life occurs, the result is totalitarian systems that breed oppression and resentment. When the Jews are blamed for a wider and more substantial failure, this simplifies the analysis and excuses those from all communities who have participated in this failure. Though Maurin believes in the cross as the preeminent salvific act to which all are called to share in belief and action, Jewish religion and ethics are sufficient in and of themselves to critique the wayward drift of the world and to provide the foundation for a new society. If the Jewish people were never a superior race, they were a chosen people, Maurin relates, but the Nordic people are neither superior nor chosen: "Hitler needs to read the Old Testament and the New Testament if he wants to lead men into the Promised Land where people no longer try to cut each other's throats and where the lion comes to lie down with the lamb."[10]

In this time of great crisis Maurin argues that Jews are tied to the heritage of Christianity, are essential to the faith of Christians and a test for Christianity and individual Christians. Jesus Christ is of the Jews, historically and in the present, and the fate of Christianity is tied to the treatment of Jews by way of Jesus. What is done unto the Jews is done unto Christ. Therefore to persecute Jews is to pervert Christianity, in essence to do what Christians accuse Jews of having done in the past, that is to refuse to recognize the messiah. The attempt of Jews to assimilate into German culture is a political and religious failure on par with the attempt of Christians to assimilate into the bourgeois and totalitarian state. Indeed, what makes man human, a title of a subsection of an essay Maurin published in September 1939, is exactly this refusal of assimilation and the recovery of the original covenants, old and new, in what Maurin terms the "unpopular front." In this front are theists, Protestant Christians, Catholics, humanists, and Jews, who can affirm what makes us human: to give and not to take, to serve and not to rule, to help and not to crush, to nourish and not devour.

For Maurin it is ideals rather than deals, creed rather than greed, that ensure the possibility of a humane social order. When brought together, these communities can also confront a totalitarianism on the verge of triumph. Moreover, each community has something particular to contribute to this unpopular front, and the Jewish Jubilee, where every fiftieth year debts were remitted, land returned, and slaves set free, features prominently in his analysis. The foundation of that jubilee is clearly anchored in the Jewish belief in the God who created the world and the "Brotherhood of Man, for God wants us 'to be our brothers keepers.'"[11]

If the theological centrality of Israel was primarily carried by Peter Maurin, the *Catholic Worker* newspaper made Jews visible in ordinary and political ways. In a March 1934 column, Dorothy wrote of meeting with a minister, priest, and rabbi who had just finished a speaking tour of the United States to uproot religious prejudice. Though she was encouraged by their stories of people they had met, Dorothy had received earlier in the day a three-page, single-spaced letter "full of carefully reasoned religious prejudice" that left her "pessimistic about attitude of Gentile to Jew." At the end of her column, Dorothy thanks Mrs. Gottlieb, a Jew, who on fast days feeds the Catholic Worker staff with a "pile of potato pancakes or fish and her cooperation saves the editors a great deal of time and effort." In December 1938 an article appeared entitled "Catholic Church Has Defended Jews During Times of Stress," which quotes Martin Luther's diatribes against the Jews and counter poses these with a book by a Catholic priest defending Jews. The *Catholic Worker* of July/August 1939 reports on a letter written by Archbishop Samuel Stritch of Milwaukee to Rabbi Joseph Baron of the same city decrying anti-Semitism and pledging the sympathy and active work of the Catholic community to confront this "wicked movement." The following month a similar story was reported of a priest, Charles Owen Rice, at the Catholic Worker house in Pittsburgh, who condemned the exaggerated accusations against Jews as "damnably un-American, un-Christian and antisocial." In May 1940 a long article about the Hebrew Immigrant Aid Society appeared which detailed the travail of the Jews of Europe and reflected upon the charity of Jews to one another and concluded affirmatively: "Though HIAS may not call it such, it is what we call the works of mercy. All those who have passed through the agency are benefiting through the charity of others. . . . We cannot praise too much the work that caused this writing and we ask you to think of them in prayer."[12]

The inclusion of Jews on a variety of levels in the *Catholic Worker* at a time when Jews were under increasing pressure in Europe and America made little tactical sense, especially as the United States moved toward war and the Worker adopted an unqualified pacifist stance. Why take on the controversial issue of Jews and Judaism *and* the most popular war in American history? At the same time the seemingly contradictory stance of support for Jews *and* arguing for their conversion stands out boldly. The situation is even more complicated by the clear sense found in the Worker newspaper that though Jews should be candidates for conversion, they remain the chosen people and are sufficient unto themselves. If the Jews are a mystery to the world and to themselves, Maurin argues that they are candidates to help implement his synthesis of cult, culture, and cultivation. Candidates and more, for the centrality of the Jews remains in their physical being today. For Maurin, at least, their destruction and rescue are central signs of the times in which he lived.

The balance of inclusion, respect, rescue, pacifism, and conversion has been a difficult one, especially as the years passed and with the discovery of the extent and nature of the Holocaust. Yet the Worker clearly understood the dimensions of the destruction and argued that only a negotiated peace rather than a conclusive victory could save the Jewish communities of Europe. The May 1943 *Catholic Worker* featured a front page article, "Peace Now Without Victory Will Save Jews," that summarized a talk at the Catholic Worker by Jessie Walker Hughan, secretary of the War Resistors League: "If we persist in our present war aim of unconditional surrender; if we promise only executions, retributions, punishments, dismemberments, indemnities, and no friendly participation with the rest of the world in a post-war world, we shall be depriving not only the German people of all hope, but we shall be signing the death sentence of the remnant of Jews still alive. If, on the contrary, we demand the release of all Jews from the ghettoes of Europe and work for peace without victory . . . then there is a chance of saving the Jews." The following month in an essay "Where is Sanctuary?" Dorothy directly confronted the blindness of a person who attended her own talk on the subject of Jews and the war and refused to believe the plight of Jews in Europe: "Against such astounding unbelief the mind is stunned. And yet we of America and

England who read and believe, do nothing to oppose the restrictions against immigration of Jews, their seeking sanctuary in this country. Who does not remember and shudder at the thought of that ship that sailed the seas, looking for a haven for its load of sufferers and turned away from these shores, refused by England, and finally rescued by such little Christian countries as Belgium and Holland?" Dorothy outlines in vivid detail reported massacres of Jews in, among other places, Bessarabia, Odessa, Kiev, Pinsk, Brest-Litovsk, Mariupol, and Smolensk. Her cry is clear: "Do we believe these facts and then do nothing? Where then is sanctuary for these suffering ones?"[13]

Jews and the Critique of Bourgeois Christianity

We know of course that the world did nothing about these "suffering ones," and Jews were not saved for "Christ's sake." Nor was the war fought for the Jews, as is often thought today. The attempted annihilation of the Jews was part of a broader destruction, of civilization, of Europe, of humanity, and this is how the Worker approached the question. This is how we can understand that though the prominence of Maurin's essays on Jews and the art work depicting the Christ child within the context of the Jewish people—as well as the other articles decrying anti-Semitism and even organizing against it—are startling, the central focus of the Catholic Worker was the demise and reconstruction of the social order in its broadest sense. Other issues, the plight of labor and the argument for pacifism, for example, played a much larger role in Worker ideology and coverage in the newspaper. African Americans, then called Negroes, had far more attention paid to them than Jews, and after the war ended the dropping of the atomic bombs on Hiroshima and Nagasaki assumed a central place in Catholic Worker concern. A large part of this concentration on African Americans and atomic warfare flowed naturally from the Worker's sense of its own place in the domestic reality of the United States. Though the coverage of world news was extensive, and in many ways remarkable, the struggle of the Catholic Worker was decidedly in America.

After the war, coverage of and comments about Jews declined markedly and much that remained were just repeats of Maurin's earlier essays and the Christ child drawing. The issue of Zionism was addressed in several issues of the paper, most extensively in the fall of 1948 and the summer of 1951. In the first essay, Robert Ludlow sees those non-Jews who support Zionism as distancing themselves from Jews who remind them of their own vocation to follow Jesus Christ. "There continues to be among some Christians a persistent and never dying detestation of the Jew," Ludlow writes. "Our God, who as a man was a Jew, would be unwelcome in the homes of these Christians." That is why Christians find Zionism acceptable: because they welcome a solution that would "relegate the Jews to some portion of the earth where they would no longer have to rub elbows with them in the subways nor be disturbed that other than Gentiles eats, sleeps, walks in white Gentile America." Ludlow is clear on the desire of Christians to distance themselves from Jews, which he relates, like Maurin, to the desire to distance themselves from Jesus himself: "Christ walks in white Gentile America, walks as a spectacle to the nation, walks by the side of His Jewish blood brothers, fills the ghetto on Manhattan's Lower East Side, rubs elbows with white Gentile Americans in the subways—eat, sleeps, walks in white Gentile America to the disgust of those who worship him as God."[14]

In fact, the attempt to distance themselves from Jews is more than an attempt to create distance from the one they worship; rather, it is to place this God at such a distance that they do not bother to follow the precepts of Christ's teaching. Many Christians would not only exclude Jesus from their apartment buildings, occupations, and schools, they would lynch him as a Jewish radical. The only way to redress this calamity and draw closer to the Jewish man they worship as God is to welcome Jews who live in the United States and those abroad still displaced by the war. The worthy experiments conducted by Jews in Palestine should be conducted here, sparing the survivors of the Holocaust the increasing violence in Palestine. Therefore, immigration of Jews to the United States should be facilitated and land should be given to them free.

This was the demand of the hour. Insofar as Jews were welcome, the God who Christians worship was welcomed. Clearly, however, Ludlow saw the Jews and the God who comes from the Jews as a subversive presence, questioning what Christianity had become and the social order it upheld. To see Christ among the Jews is to subvert the notion of a white Christianity and a white America as dominant and superior. Here Ludlow closed his essay by linking Jews and Negroes in their common subversion of a Christianity in service to race and the state: "The Christian who does not want the Jew or the Negro for his next door neighbor does not want Christ for his next door neighbor. It is as simple as that. There can be no evasion. The Catholic who objects to intermarriage because of race objects to Christianity. It is as simple as that. The Catholic who is to the least degree anti-Semitic denies the incarnation of Christ, profanes the humanity of Christ, blasphemes the Holy Eucharist. There can be no evasion. On that issue alone we stand or fall in the Judgement. It is as simple as that."

The second essay on Zionism was written by Hector Black, who went to the new state of Israel to experience life through the agricultural experiments of the moshav and the kibbutz. These were the agricultural settlements to which Maurin and Ludlow had referred and their existence affirmed Maurin's sense of the need to live in a communal environment. After arriving in Haifa and Tel Aviv and experiencing the frenetic pace of these cities reminiscent of life in America, Black traveled to a kibbutz and experienced first-hand community on the land among Jews. He reports on his acceptance as a person and a Christian and the international atmosphere of the settlement, with volunteers from around the world. He perceived the agricultural and educational methods of Jewish communal life in Israel, and the lack of overt religiosity as a positive connection with Jewish history. After reporting that there was no religion as such on the kibbutz, Black predicted that the concern for one another and the revival of ancient agricultural festivals would gradually become more recognizable as religion. "I shall never forget celebrating Passover with them," Black writes. "It was a beautiful cool evening as we walked out to the fields to meet the community choir in their folk costume. . . . I thought of how the Israeli folk song embodies the vigor of the spirit of their people as we followed the singing choir out into a field of new wheat where, with choir still singing, four men cut the first of the grain." A feast followed and at the beginning of the meal the traditional reading of the Book of Exodus took place, a reading modified to include the "subsequent movements of Hebrews including the present exodus from Europe to Israel." Black engaged the members of the kibbutz on the subject of nonviolence, a topic he felt, because of present circumstances in the country, they could not agree on. Regardless, the time Black spent in Israel was quite fulfilling: "Their strong idealism, their sense of mission, their sensitivity and the way they received me, a Christian, among them as so few Christian communities would have received a Jew—these are beautiful memories."[15]

In this same issue is a review by Michael Harrington of Martin Buber's *Paths in Utopia*. Harrington sees this book as containing a "brilliant" analysis of the revolution that the Catholic Worker seeks in its own way. Harrington sees Buber as describing in the most "concise and lucid" way the communal ideals that many in the Christian world are now striving for: "Buber's ideas are close to, if not identical with, the concept of the Christian 'leaven' in society which Maritain has written about. And in light of the clear papal pronouncements on the social and non-political character of Catholic Action, they deserve to be considered as an important contribution to the philosophy of the lay apostolate." In fact what Buber has done intellectually, according to Harrington, is what Black's journey through Israel has done on the practical level: to reconstruct the social order in a personalist way. While Black links the Jewish expression of community to ancient and contemporary history, Harrington sees Buber as a philosophical mentor in the exploration of the future for all humanity.[16]

This discussion of Zionism in the context of combating anti-Semitism at home and the embrace of Jewish work on the land held the dynamic of Catholic Worker discussion of the Jews in a pattern similar to its pre-war discussion. The challenge for Christians was to accept those who gave birth to their faith and in that acceptance to redefine the parameters of Christianity itself. The force of Jewish life, with its dialectic of assimilation and recovery of the prophetic, mirrored the course of Christianity and Christian commitment. Those who recover the "dynamite of the Church," as Maurin often expressed it, could recognize the dynamite inherent in the Jewish message and in the Jewish people. Though Christianity furthered and completed the message of the prophets, the faults of the Jewish people, including their inability to recognize the messiah, were no different from the faults of Christians who worshiped the messiah and turned their backs on him at the same time. In both the pre-war and post-war era, Jews are presented as biblical people who bequeathed the messiah to the world and whose history continues into the present in its own authenticity.

Thus Jews are not presented as foils for the Christian message or as biblical fossils whose history ends with the appearance of Jesus. Even with the message of Jesus completing the words of the prophets, Jesus without the prophets becomes an empty abstraction. Jews are necessary as a reminder of the promises of God *and* serve today as witnesses to Christians in the deep embrace of their own faith and as pioneers in the reconstruction of the social order. As often as they are written about in their relation to theology and salvation, Jews are also addressed in their living reality as models of serving one another and as intellectual pioneers. Through their productivity they represent the very vision that Christians should be embracing.

In the non-theological realm, Jews are seen alongside African Americans. African Americans challenge white supremacy as Jews challenge gentile arrogance. Moreover, when Christianity is discussed in relation to African Americans, the challenge is to follow the radical teachings of St. Augustine, himself an African, rather than assimilate to white Christianity. Indeed in an essay in May 1938, Maurin made the same point that Ludlow made after the war, calling African Americans back to there roots just as he did with Jews:

> The Jews think
> > that they are better
> > than the Negroes.
> The Germans think
> > that they are better
> > than the Jews.
> I don't think
> > that the Jews
> > are better than the Negroes
> > or the Germans
> > better than the Jews.
> The way for the Jews
> > to be better
> > than the Germans

> is to behave
> the way the Prophets
> want the Jews
> to behave.
> The way for the Negroes
> to be better
> than the Jews
> or the Germans
> is to behave
> the way St. Augustine
> wants everybody
> to behave.[17]

The point that Maurin seems to be making by connecting African Americans and Jews with their "enemies," racist whites and racist Germans, is that only through a dynamic of recapturing the essence of their history and embodying it in the present can these peoples witness to who they are. This witness is the way forward for all peoples rather than a superficial assimilation to the ways of the enemy. It is a self-contained witness and always one beyond itself, not as a question of superiority but rather as a mark of authenticity. Authenticity is the way toward a grappling with self and the social order enfolded in a people's history. At the same time it advises the enemy of the distortion of self and community undergone when a sense of superiority leads to domination and oppression. African Americans and Jews serve as reminders of the need to acknowledge particularity in the wider umbrella of universality. They call for justice and a new social order that will allow them to fully participate in a newly conceived universality where neither superiority nor inferiority exists.

Toward an Ecumenical Religiosity

The transition, or perhaps better stated, the revolution, embodied in Vatican II was relatively easy for the Catholic Worker. In many ways Peter Maurin and Dorothy Day, along with others who affiliated with the Worker over the years, anticipated the council and, when promulgated, radicalized it as well. For many Catholics, at least in the United States, the call of Vatican II was one of modernization and assimilation to a bourgeois mainstream. Openness to modernity and the goodness of the world led to a celebration of affluence and a participation in the world without guilt or restraint. The Catholic Worker saw the changes in the church in a different light, as a further possibility of engaging the world in pursuit of justice and peace. Rather than modernization and assimilation, the Worker embraced Vatican II as a call to witness to the possibility of goodness by being present to those outside the core culture of modernity.

The emphasis on inclusion in the early years of the Catholic Worker illustrated a tendency toward ecumenism. Thus Jews, but also Protestants and atheists, were encouraged in their sensibilities even as they were called to a deeper reality. So, too, African Americans were encouraged in their struggle for justice and their inclusion into the larger society. In the post-war world, this inclusion extended to what later became known as the third world. Hence Gandhi was venerated and the struggling people of Latin America, Africa, and Asia were reported on in sensitive and perceptive ways. The coming of liberation theology was anticipated by the Worker, especially by Dorothy, and her travels to Cuba and reflections on the death of Camilo Torres were an early and moving recognition that an era of revolution was upon us. The only question was whether religion would play a positive role or would be relegated to a peripheral and reactionary role.

What Vatican II did for the Worker is as important as the vanguard role the Worker had with the coming of the Council: it allowed a freedom to name that which it had anticipated and helped create. In relation to Jews, the freedom now was to accentuate the positive side of the tension the Worker had already articulated. The authenticity of Jews and the Jewish tradition came to be emphasized. The calls to conversion dwindled. The struggle against anti-Semitism had existed from the very origins of the Worker, and crimes against Jews were also seen as theological transgressions against the very substance of Christianity. Now a further embrace could occur, as ancient Jewish texts and contemporary Jews were now viewed as distinct and yet part of the Catholic tradition without being anticipated or transfigured by Jesus. Or better stated, even when the anticipation and transfiguration is asserted, the Jewish dimension is retained, is independent, and becomes in a way interdependent with the continuing life of the Jewish people.

The declarations on Jews and Judaism in the Vatican Council were taken almost as self evident, and because of this little space in the Worker newspaper was devoted to this momentous event. With Maurin's death in 1948, the theological speculation on Jews and Judaism essentially ended and Dorothy's comments on both were few and interspersed in her reflections on life and her own journeys. Elie Wiesel, the Holocaust survivor and writer, was mentioned, as was the great theologian Abraham Heschel. Their message was for everyone and the assumption was that reading and contemplating Jewish reflections of suffering, celebration, and God are ways of deepening the human and Christian journey. Yet, paradoxically, it was this sense of inclusion that made it difficult, if not impossible, to engage in a critical dialogue with Jews. Just as the call for Jews to convert to Christianity ended with the Vatican Council, so too the Worker was silent on an increasingly militaristic Jewish state. The critique of Zionism, fashioned in the context of safeguarding the rights of Jews in the diaspora and as a critique of white Christianity, ended as the emergency situation of the Holocaust years grew distant.

Since the Worker showed a mostly positive emphasis on contemporary Jews during their time of crisis and an atypically even-handed position of dialogue on religious affirmation when most Catholic thinkers and institutional representatives did not, it is paradoxical that this sensibility does not carry over into the period of Jewish empowerment. In fact a reversal is evidenced in the post-Vatican II era of Worker commentary on Judaism and Jews. Whereas in the era of crisis the suffering *and* capability of the Jewish people was emphasized, in the era of empowerment, Jewish suffering is emphasized almost to the exclusion of contemporary Jewish achievement. Of course, in this way the other side of Jewish achievement, Jewish militarism and even criminality in the exercise of state power, can be downplayed or ignored. Thus the "mystery" of the people Israel, complicated as it was in Catholic theology and projected so prominently in the 1930s and 1940s in the *Catholic Worker* newspaper, remains as the demystification of state power in Israel becomes an issue. The Worker correctly fought against the myth of Jewish power promulgated by fascists and demagogues, but when Jews achieve an objectively quantified power, the Worker, as happened with many others, is unable to speak to the issue.

In this sense, the Worker's pre-Vatican II solidarity with Jews is, within the context of the historical and theological currents of the time, a critical solidarity, emphasizing the inclusion of a people in distress, whereas the solidarity with Jews after Vatican II is relatively uncritical—a reversal of what seems on the surface to be quite the opposite. At a time when the desire to convert Jews could be combined with respect and protection, the Worker intervened in a forceful and analytical way against a wave of religious and political anti-Semitism. At a time when a desire for conversion would be seen even retrospectively as anti-Semitic, the embrace of Jews is without critical force or content. The very focus of the Worker and its spirituality, to be with the least and the outcast and to criticize the state and economy that cause dislocation and death, focused on the Jews during the war years, is almost completely abandoned after the war. The Jews remain a special case, to be sure, but the mystery is less and less clear as it affects the contemporary world of the believer.

If Jews provide a critical insight into societal exclusion and white Christianity, those days are fading into the past, especially as Jews take on more and more of the attributes so criticized by the Worker. During the 1930s and 1940s, Maurin especially called assimilationist Jews back to the prophets as he called assimilationist Christians back to Christ, but the post-war years seemed too confusing as almost the entire Jewish community opted, as a religious act, to support and speak for the state of Israel. On the face of it, Maurin's criticism of bourgeois Jews in the 1930s would call forth a similar criticism of state Jews in the 1960s and beyond, that is calling the Jewish people back to the prophetic task of creating a world where no one is excluded or denied. Perhaps Maurin's death explains the lack of carry through on this obvious point, as from that point on in Worker history Jews are not discussed in a theological way. The practical fight against anti-Semitism led by Dorothy was, in the post-Holocaust years, less and less needed in Catholic circles and in the larger Western world. Here must be added the new understanding of Jews and Judaism that emerges from Vatican II, a positive evaluation to be sure, but one that also minimizes the critical engagement with the Jewish world that needs to emerge in our ecumenical era.

Perhaps it is here that the limits and possibilities of the new ecumenical religiosity are to be understood. A critical understanding of Judaism and the Jewish people served the Worker well in forcing a critical evaluation of Christianity in the 1930s and 1940s, but a critical understanding today might force yet another evaluation of Christianity beyond the confines of that religion itself. In former times, Jews and Judaism helped in the confrontation with a cultural Catholicism that was increasingly assimilationist. Peter Maurin and Dorothy Day in particular saw Jews and Judaism as a way of proclaiming a radical center to their faith and therefore calling the Catholic community back to that center. Were Christians really following Jesus the Jew, a Jew who also stood in line with the prophets, even when they persecuted Jews and denigrated Judaism? Blaming Jews and Judaism was symbolic of an entire bourgeois ethos that Christians were, at one and the same time, benefiting from and blaming Jews for inaugurating and encouraging. To blame Jews and Judaism was to take one's critical eye off the behavior of Christians themselves and *their* betrayal of the message of Jesus and the church. To discuss the chosen people then meant to discuss the ramifications of being the New Israel. Jews and Judaism became a clarion call to the Catholic tradition, to its origins and meaning. The mystery of Israel was really the mystery of the church.

In a time when the mystery of the church has been demystified, even abandoned in some quarters by those seeking to be faithful as Christians in the contemporary world, the mystery of the Jews has little meaning. In fact, as Jews and Christians have followed the path to the deepest assimilation, that is assimilation to power and the state, the very assimilation the Worker warned against, the ability to establish a center of either faith has diminished. This is often passed over in religious journals and newspapers because the lack of such a center brings into question the religious enterprise itself. Instead an ecumenical brotherhood and sisterhood is simply asserted, Judaism and Christianity together, as if both religions are joined in a redemptive mission. Refusing to question Jews and Judaism removes Christianity itself from questioning, at least at a fundamental level.

The Jewish covenant remains in place and so, too, does the Christian covenant. These covenants provide a promise to which Jews and

Christians are heirs, but the validity of both together or either separately *as demonstrated in the actions of their adherents* is left unaddressed. Whereas Peter Maurin and Dorothy Day risked much in the assertion of the importance of Jews and Judaism to the fidelity of Christians, today it can actually be a protective procedure, part of the banquet circuit, a dialogue that in some cases becomes a deal of silence and complicity. In this sense the Worker has become a passive participant in that which it originally and passionately argued against, a cultural arrangement benefiting both Jews and Christians as a way of bypassing the central questions of both faiths. Perhaps the Worker does this less because of a desire to mainstream itself than because it does not know how to take the next step in the journey of faith. In action the Worker is beyond reproach and without fear, but in its own theology it is relatively stagnant. Is the fear that the culpability of Jews and Judaism is neither mythic nor related to redemption but all too normal, pointing to the same demystified culpability of Christians and Christianity? Could it be that to understand and affirm that we have come to the end of Judaism *as we have known and inherited it* is to affirm that we have come to the same end of Christianity?

With these results the future of ecumenical religiosity comes into question. It cannot begin with the mystery of Judaism or Christianity or even their journey together. To claim the center of each, as the Worker once boldly did, is to retreat into the past. We are somewhere else now, as the assimilation of Judaism and Christianity and Jews and Christians attest to. Where is this "somewhere else," and how can it be defined and embraced? What labels will we attach to it and how shall we celebrate its victories and mourn its failures? These are questions that today lie beyond Peter Maurin and Dorothy Day, indeed beyond the Catholic Worker itself.

17

Questioning Conversion:
Gillian Rose, George Steiner, and Christianity

ON DECEMBER 9, 1995, just hours before her death, the Jewish philosopher Gillian Rose was received into the Anglican church. As one of the premier young British philosophers whose work was known and respected throughout Europe, her death at the age of forty-eight was greeted with sadness. At the same time, her last book, *Love's Work: A Reckoning With Life*, autobiographical in nature and published during the last stages of her illness, was destined to reach an audience beyond the esoteric confines of philosophic discourse. Though there is no lengthy discussion in any of her philosophical writings, or even in her autobiography, of embracing the Christian faith, the long and beautiful obituaries in the leading British newspapers featured Rose's conversion and quoted prominent religious figures with regard to it. John Milbank writes of Rose's struggle with faith in a perceptive manner: "She bequeaths us difficulties and mysteries. The thinker who denounces the modern Jewish retreat from the law in the name of the formalism of love was finally led to embrace Christianity. . . . At the threshold of her own, eternal consummation, Gillian Rose leaves us to reflect further on the conditions, both political and metaphysical, under which healing may at last supersede rupture." In her funeral address, Margaret Archer, a Catholic sociologist, colleague, and friend, spoke of Rose's embrace of Christianity as a fulfillment rather than a repudiation of Judaism.[1]

Milbank and Archer refer to two aspects of Rose's conversion, one philosophical, the other religious, each in its own way controversial. As a philosopher, Rose cultivated the "broken middle," a terrain between the conservative status quo and the revolutionary utopia proposed by those on the right and the left. For Rose, suffering and possibility in history bequeath us something richer and more complex than either acquiescence or perfection. The broken middle recognizes the inherited past and the limitations of the present, as it seeks a future that evolves from both. The projection of a past reborn or a future that appears untested in history frightened Rose; the broken middle allows for a new configuration to come into being as a human creation, with the flaws, limitations, and hopes that characterize the human journey. In religious terms, the broken middle placed Rose between Judaism and Christianity, and she remarked to her confessor some years earlier that she was "too Jewish to be Christian and too Christian to be Jewish." Clearly, with her conversion to Christianity, this middle was broken through, at least in the religious sphere. As Rowan Williams, an Anglican bishop, remarks, a decision by a Jew to become a Christian always involves an act of violence. Perhaps Rose felt that this act was necessary to move beyond a place of paralysis where the broken middle had left her. Was it because her salvation lay at stake that Rose was forced to this act of violence seemingly against her own philosophy?[2]

Surely more was at stake than her own philosophy, for many Jews consider public conversion an act of violence against the Jewish people. Even the attempts of her Christian friends to be respectful to the Jewish community as they discussed her conversion highlighted this danger. The view of Christianity as a completed form of Judaism, an understanding popularized by the French philosopher and theologian Jacques Maritain in the 1950s, has long since been repudiated by Jewish theologians and institutional leaders. In some ways, the asserted completion of Judaism through conversion can be seen as more offensive than the complete break with Judaism that for most Jews conversion to Christianity represents. The first is a call to all Jews to recognize Christianity as the natural destiny of an incomplete faith; the second can be seen by Jews as an unnatural break, an apostasy that severs the convert from Jewish history.

To complicate matters further, Rose's situation was unusual in that she was a public figure. Confronting death is hardly a simple matter, and an early death through disease is more difficult still. For most of us, coming to grips with death is a private matter, and the religious affirmations we make rarely extend beyond the immediate family. As a person known within her academic field but essentially unknown to the broader public, Rose could have kept her final resolutions private. However, as a philosopher engaged in the questions of our time, she undoubtedly felt, as did others, that her reflections in the face of death were important to explore and discuss. This is the point where controversy enters, for who could deny a personal need to affirm Christianity if it did not come from a figure who in her death had access to a larger public than she had in life? And what would it matter if the person converting had little to say to others about the significance and destiny of our personal and communal journey?

Rose was a compelling figure in life and death. The obituaries are clear in this respect. Her students loved her both for her thought and who she was as a person. In a rare way, Rose combined complex thought with personal attention to others, especially their sufferings. Rose recalls in her last book published when she was alive, how she cared for her first philosophy teacher as he was dying of AIDS. When she discovered his situation—a dire one of illness, abandonment, and hunger—Rose periodically flew to New York and nursed him. Yet it was not just the extraordinary situation that attracted Rose's attention. Rose was interested in the ordinary aspects of people's lives. In her obituary, Marina Warner comments on this aspect of Rose's personality: "Unlike some people of her intensity of intellect, she was very interested in others and their ordinary lives—in their past loves, in their children's doings."[3] I experienced this in my meetings with Rose. When we first met on a delegation at Auschwitz in the spring of 1992, my own situation was precarious. I had been invited by a person to whom I had been recommended, but who knew little of my work on the Holocaust. Because I raise the issue of the lessons of the Holocaust in relation to Israeli policies of occupation and displacement, my work is seen as controversial, even reprehensible, by some. Rose went out of her way to greet me, congratulate me on my work, and be seen with me in public settings. At the same time, she inquired about me personally, asking about my life and, in general, showing a personal interest beyond my public persona.

After commenting on Rose's interest in the lives of others, Warner adds that Rose was "uncommonly brave, too." This also was evident at Auschwitz, both in her relation to me and to the other delegates. At a crucial moment in our deliberations on the historical knowledge of the Polish guides, Rose spoke, out of turn and off the subject, of the nearness of God. This was a violation of etiquette, and worse. Rose was suggesting that the anger of these delegates, for the most part Holocaust scholars and rabbis, was a retrospective one that, paradoxically sought the Holocaust past as a safe haven from inquiries of the present conduct of the Jewish people. Rose's suggestion about God was her way of pointing to the need for a different attitude and direction in Jewish life, emphasizing the present over the past, or at least showing compassion for those, like the undertrained Polish guides, who were struggling in contemporary life. It was Rose's only intervention during our deliberations, and one she delivered softly, in one sentence, and with an assurance that belied a need for explanation. After her intervention, tea time was declared and the delegates avoided her as they had earlier avoided me.

It was clear in our private discussions that Rose was ambivalent toward her Jewish background and toward Judaism itself. It was not, as is so easily and frequently asserted, a case of self-hatred. She came to the study of Judaism late in life and approached it as she approached other subjects, in a critical manner and in particular through the lens of Jewish law and philosophy. In her essays on Judaism, published under the title *Judaism and Modernity,* Rose explores the terrain of modern Jewish expression without professing or demonstrating a relationship with it. Reading her essays, one has the feeling that Rose is testing the best of contemporary Jewish philosophy against the philosophy of Europe, or, perhaps better stated, seeing whether the modern Judaic sensibility adds to or transcends the European philosophy she knew so well. Rose maintains the same distance that characterizes her philosophic method, which, while part of the accepted academic discourse, is unlikely to bring a person into a closer proximity with one's inheritance. At the same time, Jewish establishment figures, while no doubt welcoming Rose's philosophic interest, were wary of a person of her critical abilities. The delegates at Auschwitz were simply unable to understand her and thus dismissed her out of hand. In Britain, a small, divided, and nervous Jewish community is wary of powerful Jewish thinkers unless they are clearly identified with Jewish institutional life.[4]

Could Rose's ambivalence toward Judaism have been intensified by her experience of contemporary Jewish life and leadership? Clearly, the answer is yes. At Auschwitz, for example, the catered Kosher food, flown in from Switzerland and at considerable expense, and almost inedible at that, seemed ludicrous to her. Most of the delegates ate non-Kosher food on a regular basis, and Rose saw this as an artificial attempt to show that Jews maintained their tradition of separation from the larger population. Moreover, Rose thought that the delegation—or at least the most vocal of the group—were using the Holocaust as a sign of superiority in suffering, even though the majority of delegates lived in a manner that to most Polish people is affluent and unattainable. Though she had lost distant relatives in the Holocaust, Rose found many of the delegates to be smug and uncritical of their own attitudes and place in the world. Rose wondered how these men, so sure of themselves and angry at the world, could create a future for the Jewish people or be contributors to the larger project of life beyond the Jewish world.

Rose and her generation of Jews experienced the after-effects of a world in turmoil. The Holocaust was no stranger to Rose in terms of family or the wider Jewish discourse. Still, in her formative years, the Holocaust had yet to be named as the signal event of the century; as importantly the state of Israel, formed in her lifetime, similarly lacked the central place in Jewish life that it would assume after the 1967 Arab-Israeli war. While these core events of contemporary Jewish life awaited naming and the attendant mobilization of Jewish institutional and intellectual energies, Rose's generation stood in a kind of limbo, with no way back to the Jewish life of the past and, as yet, no path to a future. For most Jews, choosing a life outside the Jewish community was experienced as both challenge and freedom. In fact, Jews had been acting upon this freedom for more than a century. The Holocaust made this choice mandatory, especially in Europe, since large Jewish communities structured around Jewish culture, language, religion, and politics were eliminated.

The desire to taste the fruits of the larger society with roots in the particular and alien Christian community and culture became a need to integrate without roots. What we now see as Jewish roots is retroactively established through the events of Holocaust and Israel, which in Rose's formative years were, paradoxically, close and yet unavailable to form identity. Continental philosophy was therefore a natural subject for a precocious Jew who was searching for the meaning of life. The language and conceptual framework were German and European, and even her choice of the German Jew, Theodore Adorno, for her dissertation topic, illustrated the fate of Rose's generation. Adorno could be read as an intellectual subverting the mystifications of European and American culture and politics rather than in the Jewish framework from which he emerged.[5]

In this context, the mobilization and militarization of Jewish life after the 1967 war was quite foreign to Rose. The crystallization of Jewish identity around the Holocaust and Israel may have seemed too easy, too militant, or even perhaps superficial for a thinker of her caliber. Gathering everything into itself and redefining all that is Jewish around the events of Holocaust and Israel may have struck Rose as a force of violence against critical thought and activity. There is little doubt that this new and limiting definition of Jewish life which Rose rebelled against also drew her in mid-life to consider the Jewish framework as it had been and as it is today. The relationship she assumed as a virtual outsider to the Jewish material should be seen in this light. With her generational background, there is little chance that Rose's conclusions could have been anything but a distant critique and respect for the struggle of Jewish philosophy and theology after the Holocaust.

Rose's ambivalence toward Judaism does little to explain her ultimate conversion to Christianity. After all, a majority of Jews identify only in a peripheral way with Jewish life, and ambivalence toward Jewish authority, institutions, and religion are the hallmarks of modern Jewish life. The force of the Holocaust and Israel only covers over that ambivalence, and perhaps even demonstrates its importance. In adopting the Holocaust and Israel as central to Jewish identity, Jews essentially depose traditional Jewish leadership and institutional life, and, it can be argued, adopt a new religiosity. It is almost as if Jews decided that their identity would henceforth be embraced outside any power of the Jewish elites. New texts emerge as central to Judaism, including Holocaust memoirs like Elie Wiesel's *Night*, and new Jewish leadership emerges from the death camps and Middle Eastern battlefields. Still, this only delays a deeper reckoning, for most Jews who adopt this Holocaust/Israel religiosity are neither survivors nor citizens of Israel. Diaspora Jews who, after the Holocaust and founding of Israel, remain in Europe and America, choose a religiosity in which they participate in as interested observers. One wonders if this choice is itself part of the ambivalence Jews feel toward their Jewishness, wanting to remain Jewish and to be free of the demands of traditional Judaism, Jews choose a vehicle of identification that can be affirmed with donations of time and money. Articulated in a certain way, this religiosity can also function as a way of integrating into the larger Western world.

Paradoxically, the articulate voice of Jewish suffering after the Holocaust becomes a claim on Western conscience and raises the status of Jews around the world. The story of Israel linked to the Holocaust also resonates in the West, as the story of a defeated people who, through their own effort, become a moral and empowered nation. That this nation is seen as endangered by Arab countries bent on its destruction simply heightens this narrative of destruction and rebirth to the level of drama. It is this dramatic narrative that Jews and others identify with and that carries the Jewish people through their ambivalence toward and revolt against traditional Jewish life. Yet the mobilization of a people is fraught with anxiety, and beneath the rhetoric and the status of the events of suffering and empowerment lies the fear that this new identity is a void from which there is no rescue. The past has been swept away. The present is a life raft from which a future cannot be born.

The best-kept secret of the Jewish world is a fear that there is nothing compelling left of Jewish life and that, if the events of Holocaust and Israel recede, as in time they must, the symbolic center of Jewish life will be empty and incapable of regeneration. A further problem is that the most recent mobilization of the Jewish people has, for most Jews, been external, a projection of pride and strength, but one that has left entire areas of the human psyche untouched. The anger with God, initiated with the Holocaust and articulated in theology reflecting on the Holocaust, has exaggerated this externalization, because the more internal, spiritual questions have been so difficult. Once articulated and affirmed, and with the distance from traditional resources for dealing with such questions, anger with God has taken on a life of its own. Indeed, over time a reckoning with God in a different, more conciliatory way becomes part of the fear, for an internal healing might lead to an external one, jeopardizing the mobilization of Jewish life, and therefore introducing that fundamental anxiety once again.

The cycle is clear and devastating. Life involves the desire for security and empowerment and also much more. There is a fundamental desire to embrace and be embraced here on earth in a personal way, and there are questions of destiny and God that are beyond the communal and political. The desire for embrace in the religious sphere is a human hunger known to all religions in all times. For understandable historic reasons, contemporary Jewish religiosity has failed its own community in this fundamental human quest. Was Rose's conversion the culmination of her search for an ultimate embrace unavailable to her in contemporary Jewish life?

Rowan Williams is correct: the event of a Jew crossing over to Christianity is something of a violent act. Clearly, Williams is referring to the history between Christianity and Jews, a history that can be characterized as an almost relentless assault of a powerful Christianity against a weakened Judaism. Of course, the assault increased in the modern era as Jewish life rather than Judaism itself came under attack. After more than 1500 years of this assault, the distinction between the religion and life becomes almost impossible to distinguish, so that becoming a Christian in religious terms is seen as contributing to the impoverishment and destruction of Jewish life. Thus, an assent to Christianity is judged by the Jewish community to be a violent act, and the person herself a traitor to the community. What the person intends, what she finds in Christianity, how she judges Christianity vis-à-vis Judaism, is lost in the communal fear of an oppressed community.

This threat continues after the Holocaust because the community, having just survived the Nazis and now speaking of that suffering to alert Christians of conscience to the equality of Judaism and Jewish life, is struggling to rebuild a Jewish presence in the world. In an era when Jews are slaughtered for being Jews, and when the Nazis have almost annihilated the Jewish people, is not abandonment of the Jewish people tantamount to continuing, even finishing Hitler's work? Emil Fackenheim posits a 614th commandment regarding the abandoning of Jewish life after the Holocaust, that is, the refusal of Jews to grant Hitler a posthumous victory. In the present, then, the violence of conversion can be seen in a variety of ways, including granting a retroactive right to Christian and Nazi violence against Jews and abandoning the Jewish people in their process of rebuilding after the Holocaust.

The weight against a Jew affirming Christianity is thus substantial in its external ramifications. Internally, the struggle can be equally violent. A history of this ferocity cannot exist simply on the outside, as if long-standing communal clashes are not internalized as well. Breaking with Judaism and the Jewish people involves an internal violence, too. In Rose's case, some members of her extended family were killed because they were Jewish; she was denied their presence in her life. Thus the external battle of religion and the communal nature of warfare were intimate to Rose. Her embrace of Christianity could be seen as an embrace of a religion that laid the groundwork for the death of her family members. Could such an embrace be an affirmation of their murderers?

The internal struggle has still other levels to operate within. When a Jew first encounters Christian symbolism in the public realm, it is placed in the category of the majority population and culture. With the explanation of what, for example, a Christmas tree represents, or what a frequently heard Christmas carol refers to, the category of "other" with whom Jews live is created. After a while the religious category is lost and it simply becomes part of a cultural background within which a Jew moves with ease. It is almost like background music played as one works around the house or in a large department store—it is relegated to the corner of the mind, forgotten as it is heard, and almost impossible to recall even if queried about it.

A church is much different, for the setting is religious and the rituals performed there necessitate a different kind of explanation. Though culture is found here as well, religiosity and theology are primary. The difference between shopping and praying is obvious, because what in the department store is background becomes primary in the church. The images of the cross, of Mary, of the saints, even the smell of incense, cross the boundary into the internal life of the person. For most Jews, the setting itself is foreign, even unwelcoming. Of course, a simple visit to a church means little compared to participating in the life of the church, especially participating in the Eucharist. The taking of the body and the blood of Jesus into the body of the Jew represents the extreme in this crossing. Here an entire Christian history and theology comes into a Jewish body whose ancestors have been denigrated, tortured, and put to death by those who consumed the same body and blood, announced the same creed, and read from the same texts.

If the external and internal violence of Christian history and ritual are not enough to persuade a Jew to remain within the Jewish fold, the attraction to Christianity must be strong indeed. Of course, the historic violence of Christianity is hardly limited to the Jewish people, since the majority of Christians in the world today, especially Christians of the third world, have also experienced this violence. I saw this in my years as a professor at Maryknoll, where my students came from various countries that had been conquered by Christianity or were currently facing conversion to Christianity. After many years of teaching these students and visiting the countries in which they live, I have come to see the violence that Christianity visited upon the Jews of Europe as similar to the violence perpetrated against native peoples outside of Europe.

At Auschwitz, I thought of this connection and even shared this understanding with Rose. Here again we agreed on a subject taboo among the other members of the delegation. Though our suffering at the hands of Christian theology and symbolism can hardly be overstated, the argument that it is unique, without parallel or comparison, is naive and self-serving. Moreover, the Jewish sense of uniqueness in suffering also serves as a way of isolating the Jewish people from the struggles of today. For if we are unique in all things, including our suffering, than we are superior to others and excused from the critical thought about the world and ourselves that comes with the recognition of our commonality with others. It also excuses us from the understandings and theologies emerging from those conquered by Christianity, specifically liberation theologies, which challenge all forms of domination, including Christian and Jewish ones.

Could these theologies of liberation contain a message for the Jewish world, especially about the relation between empowerment and domination in Israel and Palestine? Freezing Christianity in its Holocaust formation allow Jews to freeze Jewish history at that same point. Thus for most members of the delegation, the Jewish people are still boarding the trains destined for Auschwitz. It is a troubling image, but as troubling is the sense that this image, in a paradoxical and horrible way, is also a comfortable one. If the trains are still unloading their human cargo at Auschwitz, Jews are still innocent victims. If the image of the trains is a historical one propelling us into the present, then other issues are before us, including the fact that Jews are, in the main, affluent and empowered, and that this new status has complicated our innocence and replaced it with a new culpability.

The Deeper Crisis

Rose is hardly alone among Jewish thinkers of our time who have been influenced by, even drawn to, Christianity. One thinks here of the great French mystic, Simone Weil. But today the most notable of these thinkers is the literary critic George Steiner, a refugee during the Nazi era who is now a professor of comparative literature at Cambridge University.

Steiner is a fascinating thinker in a variety of areas but the distinguishing mark of his career as a literary critic has been his ability to probe the deepest questions within the European philosophical, religious, and literary traditions in the context of contemporary history. Steiner's encyclopedic grasp of these traditions has been noted often, yet his genius lies in the interplay of the traditions and history, relating in our time, and as a Jew, specifically to the Holocaust. For Steiner, the Holocaust raises questions about all of these traditions and the civilization they gave rise to, as they gave birth to the classics of literature *and* the Holocaust. Steiner has gone further to suggest that the relation between the classics and the Holocaust is less one of dichotomy, as many would wish to believe, than it is a haunting intermingling of the two. The Germans were hardly barbarians: many were highly educated and motivated by the words and music at the heart of Western civilization. As Steiner writes, the "eruption of barbarism" that characterized the Holocaust did not "spring up in the Gobi desert or the rain forests of the Amazon. It rose from within, and from the core of European civilization. The cry of the murdered sounded in earshot of the universities; the sadism went on a street away from the theaters and museums."[6]

For Steiner, there are many ramifications of this eruption of barbarism within European civilization, among them the ability of language and religion to carry forth the deepest values and aspirations of humankind. German has been infected by atrocity since this is the language that imagined and carried forth the death camps; Christianity in its traditional anti-Semitism and with its complicity in the Nazi era has entered a "terminal" phase. For how can German be spoken today without hearing and bearing within its own being the words of Hitler and orders of the commandant at Auschwitz? This is true for Christianity as well. As an institutional presence representing a religious belief system, the churches were largely silent if not actively complicit. Could this historical failure, located through anti-Semitism at the very heart of the Christian life, carry on after the Holocaust as if the belief system and the words and ritual that embody that system are unsullied?

Judaism is involved in this crisis because the suffering of the Jews directly affects the efficacy of the God who stands at the pinnacle of Jewish belief. Steiner acknowledges the question of God's presence, or lack thereof, in the death camps and poses an even greater difficulty than the possible negative answer about that presence. The greater difficulty lies in the possibility of the magnitude of the Holocaust destroying the ability of Jews to address God with their questions relating to the Holocaust. Again the problem is highlighted in the language of address: "In what conceivable language can a Jew speak *to* God after Auschwitz, and in what conceivable language can he speak *about* God?" To those who suggest that the dilemma is resolved through the creation of Israel—that is the founding and building of a Jewish commonwealth after Auschwitz—Steiner is stridently argumentative. Contrary to most post-Holocaust Jewish thought, which sees Israel as a new beginning for a suffering community and as offering the possibility of renewed contact with the divine, Steiner sees the state of Israel as a counter-sign. Like any other state, Israel is a creature of power and deception. For Steiner, Israel represents a desertion and distortion of the Jewish vocation in the world. That vocation, defined by Steiner as the "pure hunt for truth," cannot be found within the "barbed wire and watchtowers of national dogma."[7]

Yet even as the pure hunt for truth is denied access to the transcendent because of the Holocaust, and the historical claims to reestablishing a framework through the birth of a nation-state are declared fraudulent, Steiner continues to experience the transcendent, or at least intimations of the transcendent, through literature and music. In the arts there is an intimation of something beyond. One feels drawn into a sphere of meaning and beauty that can be analyzed, even deconstructed, but nonetheless retains a power beyond limitation and definition. Referring to the mystical tradition, especially the poems of St. John of the Cross, Steiner writes eloquently of this transcendence: "It is just because we can go no further, because speech so marvelously fails us, that we experience the certitude of a divine meaning surpassing and enfolding ours. What lies beyond man's word is eloquent of God."[8]

Steiner has written extensively on the Jewish contribution to the world in terms of the prophetic voice. This voice represents a form of transcendence because, like literature and music, it is found within a context and, because of its depth and power, transcends any particular context as well. Prophetic speech can be read and interpreted well beyond the immediacy of the spoken word because it calls us beyond our limitations and points to an area beyond definition. This power to speak forcefully to a particular time and beyond intimates that the ground of the prophet's speech and the ground of our hearing is within and transcends the known. How else could the discovery of monotheism be made and how else could the messengers of the ideals of that monotheism—Steiner cites Isaiah, Jesus, and Marx—live beyond their time and place if the ground of the Jewish contribution was only local and limited?

For Steiner, the prophetic is a contribution to humanity and a confrontation with it. This confrontation is with the limited scope of human understanding and action, in essence a confrontation with refusal of the offer of a transcendence that is embodied and ethical and therefore demanding. That Jews developed a tradition of contextual reading and interpretation around this possibility of transcendence made them targets for abuse and opened them for a violence found in the Holocaust. As "pure hunters of truth" the Jews were rejected because the option for an embodied transcendence was too difficult for humanity to embrace. To kill the Jews was one way of rejecting that offer as if the difficult questions they raised would somehow disappear.[9]

Today, after the Holocaust and in light of the terminal condition of Jewish and Christian belief, Steiner is still confronted with transcendence. Though he, with many others, can no longer define that transcendence within a particular tradition or even name the source of that transcendence as God, the stubborn reality continues to exist. At the end of historical and textual analysis, Steiner confesses that "reason as I can, there are passages in the Old and New Testaments which I am unable to accord with any sensible image, however exalted, of normal authorship, of conception and composition as we seek to grasp them in even the greatest thinkers and poets." He is at a loss, for example, to place even at the "far edges of the ordinary," the speeches of Job out of the whirlwind or certain sequences in the Psalms or Ecclesiastes. Nor can he explain in a "wholly rational hermeneutic" such lines in the gospels as Jesus' "Before Abraham was, I am" or of chapters 13-17 in John. In such cases, Steiner feels himself backed up against the "harsh radiance of the scandalous." The terminal belief in Judaism and Christianity remains, even as Steiner affirms a transcendence that haunts him. This makes it even more difficult to keep to the most demanding of tasks assigned to our history, or rather the task that flows from our history of barbarism: "to keep quiet about God."[10]

While Steiner's constant hunt for truth takes place outside any particular religious tradition, his prophetic searching of the entire corpus of Western literature flows from a deep humanistic tradition within Judaism. Just as Steiner is distinctly Jewish in his universalism, he also carries forth this particular aspect of Jewish culture by refusing to embrace a simplistic theological concept to overcome a deeply critical attitude toward history and religion. What is different about Steiner within the context of his Jewish universalism is the search for transcendence itself, albeit all but abandoned in the contemporary aspect of this tradition. That is, even as Steiner affirms the universal and critical aspects of the Jewish tradition, he refuses the easy answer that many Jews have come to within this tradition: that the entire idea of transcendence and God is simply a cover for an indifferent universe. Steiner finds both those who can name God and those who refuse to explore avenues to God, as missing elements of history and depth. By refusing to acknowledge the evidence that contradicts transcendence *and* that which suggests an affirmation of transcendence, the pure hunt for truth is aborted. In short, though the resolution to the chasm that separates contradiction and affirmation is unlikely to be found, the continuing search is an imperative, perhaps suggested by the very chasm itself. In the end, Steiner finds himself in a dilemma that provides little clarity. Reasons to deny and affirm transcendence abound.

Very few commentators are able to walk the fine line between denial and affirmation of transcendence. In fact, in his later work, Steiner has been moving closer to the affirmation of transcendence, though the defining content of that transcendence remains vague. Yet in the few moments when he comes closer to embracing a defined position, a Christian aspect is suggested. This Christian tint to Steiner's later work is remarked upon by Mark Krupnick when he analyzes the Jewish writers that Steiner celebrates as those who continue the tradition of central European humanism, a tradition that through much of its history was explicitly Christian and, when secularized in more recent times, continues to evolve within the matrix of Christian patterns and feelings. Thus, in Krupnick's opinion, Steiner's "lifelong devotion to the classic texts of European humanism has produced a personal culture that is as much Christian as it is Jewish." The paradox is clear as Steiner, who as a child during the Nazi period was made a refugee, in defense of the literature and culture of old Europe comes "close to the edge of a specifically Christian affirmation."[11]

In his response to Krupnick, Steiner affirms this "new coloration" that, with the help of two well-known Christian theologians, Hans Urs von Balthasar and Donald MacKinnon, has found the "echo chamber indispensable to my uncertainties." However, this indispensability carries with it a cost. As Steiner articulates it: "I had not in any way foreseen this modulation, and it troubles me." It remains for Steiner the fact that no other visionaries of the "long midnight of our century" surpass those of Franz Kafka and Paul Celan, both of them Jews. Still, for Steiner, the "legacy of iconoclasm" and "juridical rationalism" in Judaism inhibits the approach to transcendence. Iconoclasm and rationalism, celebrated by Steiner as Jewish contributions to the world in their prophetic and rabbinic sensibility, "inhibits an idiom that endeavors to come nearer the transcendent possibility of informing unreason in the arts." Instead of the prophets and the rabbis, Steiner has drawn closer to the "pulses of metaphor" and the "analytics of mystery" in Augustinian, Thomist, and Pascalian schools of thought. In so doing, he has begun to "glimpse the sickening wellspring of Jewish self-refusal" in the French Jewish-Christian mystic, Simone Weil. Steiner refers to this identification with Weil as "somber ground."[12]

Somber ground it is, for Steiner is acknowledging a debt to Christian thinkers and theologians beyond an academic courtesy. Rather, these Christians are pointing a way out of the dilemma Steiner faces as a Jew who was a refugee from Nazi Germany, and upon which Christianity, which helped pave the way for the Holocaust, built much of its foundational philosophy and polemic. Steiner, of course, is aware that Christians have traditionally seen the superiority of Christianity over Judaism precisely in this area of iconoclasm and rationalism. Translated by these Christian theologians into the broad dichotomy of law and love, works and grace, the argument was that Jews were blocked to transcendence because of idioms that were blinding. Christianity, on the other hand, had the key, the idiom to unlock the transcendence that Jews were blinded to by their stubborn refusal to acknowledge the need for salvation through Jesus Christ and their adherence to the Law, which bound them in a slavish and myopic way. The somber ground that Steiner feels himself to be treading upon is not an acceptance of these interpretations, which are suspect both in their theological and historical claims, and which have been murderous in their crude interpretation and implementation, but seems rather to be an understanding that these Christian theologians, indeed Christianity itself, were right at least in their theological argument. Judaism cannot open Steiner's world to the transcendence that he needs to probe to answer his "uncertainties."

It is interesting that when Steiner looks toward culpability in history it is Christianity that he focuses on; Judaism is the religion of contribution and continuous elaboration and the only culpability of Jews—importantly Jews rather than Judaism—is contemporary with regard to the state of Israel. Even here, Steiner's critique is that the state is a sad compensation for the majesty of the diaspora condition, a condition that allows the freedom to be prophetic in the search for truth. In some ways, Israel represents the end of the Jewish tradition, at least that part of the tradition with which he identifies. Perhaps it is more accurate to say that for Steiner the Holocaust and Israel represent the final shattering of the Jewish culture and way of life that gave birth to and have sustained him.

Steiner's judgment on Judaism is therefore built on a foundation of a positive Jewish identification that gives way because, at least in his personal life, it is inadequate to answer the questions that confront his own explorations. Nowhere does he compare the two faith systems outside his own personal biography. Still, Steiner realizes that his own personal journey is a matter of public interest. No doubt the somber ground is felt internally on both levels, personal and public, for the affirmation that one needs to move beyond iconoclasm and rationalism is also a judgment that Jews and Judaism are caught in a trap from which the light of transcendence is eclipsed.

Steiner does not deal in any detail with these ideas. His comments are interspersed, issuing from the works he is analyzing, often at the end of essays or, as in his book *Real Presences,* approached indirectly through the larger concept of transcendence. Still, the urgency is there because Steiner believes that the human enterprise is in great jeopardy to a large extent because the traditions that have guided the West are under assault. "Our grammars, our explications, our criticism of texts, our endeavors to pass from letter to spirit are the immediate heirs to the textualities of western Judeo-Christian theology and biblical-patristic exegetics," Steiner writes, and the critiques of the Enlightenment that continue today "borrow vital currency, vital investments and contracts of trust from the bank or treasure-house of theology." The borrowing continues apace and Steiner, with others, has made very little in way of a "return deposit." That is why Steiner can characterize much of the academic debate about meaning and authenticity as a "more or less embarrassed act of larceny." Discourse and inference, hermeneutics and aesthetics in the secular, agnostic civilization of the West is in danger of depletion. The refusal to wager on transcendence, when in fact the critical work of the modern scholar is dependent on traditions that affirmed transcendence, is moreover an act of duplicity that colors the work of criticism itself. As Steiner points out, the old adage that nothing comes of nothing is instructive: only by repaying these loans can the enterprise continue with some hope of resolution or at least integrity.[13]

In Steiner there is no indication of how that loan can be repaid or the currency needed to replenish the account. Perhaps Steiner is simply at the beginning of the journey himself and as yet unable to specify how to accomplish the necessary mission. Does the currency need to come from one tradition, Jewish or Christian? Can it come from the Judeo-Christian tradition, or is there a new tradition beyond the singular or the two combined? Clearly for Steiner the Jewish tradition and the prophets and writers who issue from it are seen retrospectively rather than prospectively: the Holocaust predominates with writers either prefiguring or reflecting on the event. The brokenness they reflect on, indeed invoke with power, is one that Steiner affirms. Still, these writers are unable to suggest a transcendence within the brokenness. Steiner admires this refusal to ease over the chasm of our century and struggles for light within this chasm. It may be that the penetrating insight that these writers have is the reason for their refusal and in this sense Steiner is with them. However, the hints of transcendence Steiner finds elsewhere confront the Holocaust without providing an answer to the initial question.

Here Steiner enters the most difficult of questions for a Jewish thinker. Could it be that there is no answer to the paradoxical element of suffering in the Holocaust and the existence of transcendence that he finds in the depth of the written word and art, except the formulation of the cross? As Steiner writes: "There *are* those—they need not be Christians or even religious believers—for whom the nature of Golgotha is the irreducible crux (let the pun be allowed) at the heart of our moral and political condition. There are those who feel that there can be no responsible, indeed and paradoxically, no *rational* endeavor to grasp the collapse of European values in this century and the regime of the inhuman which obtains since 1914, without reference to Christ's agony." Indeed, there are those who perceive a relationship between Golgotha and Auschwitz, between the suffering of Jesus and the suffering of the Jews, as the only way to explain the terror at the heart of twentieth century and its movement, perhaps in a less horrific way, into the new millennium. It is unclear whether Steiner places himself among those who see the relationship between the agony of Jesus and the agony of the Jews in the theological sphere, but even to broach the possibility as Steiner does is already to cross a line heavily sanctioned by the contemporary Jewish community. Certainly, the possible relationship suggested by Steiner is unaccompanied by any specifically Jewish alternative. Thus the burden or hope involved in a choice between a Jewish and Christian alternative reading of the Holocaust and the post-Holocaust world is missing. However, Steiner asks implicitly what future there could be for Judaism if it does not present an alternative reading of its own tragedy that might respond to the past as a path to the future.[14]

Steiner is aware of the Jewish literature that seeks to cope with the tragedy of the Holocaust and finds it wanting. Jewish Orthodoxy continues in its "jejune formalism," in its devotion to "ritualistic minutiae," and in Israel the Orthodox establishment has done far worse by fueling "state savagery and corruption." In its treatment of Palestinians the Orthodox establishment has reversed Emil Fackenheim's plea that Jews not hand Hitler a posthumous victory by abandoning Judaism, Jewish commitment, and Israel. For Steiner, when a Jew humiliates, tortures, or makes homeless another human being, Hitler's posthumous victory is assured. On the liberal side, and in Judaism at large, metaphysical exploration and spiritual development are at a standstill. The standstill is found in the inability to produce truly revolutionary insights into the Jewish and human situation at the close of the century. This leads Steiner to the startling conclusion that the only possibility to advance inward in Judaism's sense of purpose—defined by Steiner as grasping the mystery of its survival and the obligations the mystery entails—is for Jews to "grapple with the origination *from the heart of Judaism* of Christianity." That is, Jews are tied to a religion that originated within its household not only because the history between Jews and Christians has been so bloody but because the logic of such a development has been lost in a polemic that now needs to be understood.[15]

Behind all this analysis—the criticism of Judaism and Christianity, the sense that after Auschwitz, Jew and Christian "go lame, as if the wrestling-bout of Jacob had been well and truly lost"—is the sense that only an exploration of the moment of separation of the two faith communities can respond to the crisis of our time and to the echoes of transcendence that still resound. Neither Judaism nor Christianity as religious systems or institutional realities has responded or perhaps can respond to this crisis and possibility. Rather, the issues "defy the ordering of common sense. . . . They are extraterritorial to analytic debate." Only the question of God, the question of God's existence or nonexistence, can reorder our sensibilities, and for Steiner, Judaism and Christianity are too ordered and rational, set in their ways with too many questions for their own survival, to participate in a helpful way. Having said this, however, Steiner still offers the cross and Golgotha as possible because once separated from the religious systems that rejected and accepted Jesus as the messiah, the suffering of Jesus fulfills both the need to defy ordering and to be extraterritorial to analytic debate. The stumbling block to probe this question is Judaism's inherent need to say no to Jesus and the cross and Christianity's need to own and domesticate both. Because of this, Steiner suggests that it might be salutary if words failed both Jews and Christians.[16]

Steiner suggests the terminal nature of Judaism and Christianity and the survival, perhaps even a renewed significance, of Golgotha and the cross. Since the West is a culturally saturated and demographically Christian culture, and since Judaism has existed within the Christian framework for well over a thousand years, if in the future any religious symbolism has significance, the possibilities are clear: the religious future of the West will be specifically Christian. Steiner's own analysis and proclivities over the years demonstrate this trend. For if a Jewish thinker who is a refugee from the Nazis and remains in Europe as a sign of the survival of the Jewish people and its traditions can end his days ruminating on the cross, what future is there for the Jewish people?

As a public person who is more than aware of the failings of Christianity and the fragility of Jewish life in Europe, and one who has already broken with the state of Israel, which many Jews see as a response to that history and as the future of the Jewish people, the responsibility for accepting the limitations of the contemporary Jewish world is immense. In light of this history, some might counsel Steiner to search out his own uncertainties and find his own conclusions in private. No doubt there is an internal voice within Steiner that cautions him as well. This is why a public conversion remains unlikely, even if the ceremonial aspects of such an event would be appealing to Steiner. Perhaps such a public confession would be repulsive to Steiner because of the history between Jews and Christians and the symbolism involved. Yet it hardly needs to be done. Though always elliptical, reading Steiner the direction is clear enough.

Conversion at the End of Auschwitz

If Rose and Steiner do not represent the majority of Jews or Christians, they point to a series of questions that are difficult to deny. As writers and critical thinkers they focus on aspects of contemporary religious life that are present among many but for the most part remain unarticulated. They report on the ever-widening distance between the Jewish establishment and ordinary Jews, on the desire of Jews to hold onto the Holocaust as an anchor of Jewish identity even as it becomes more distant in time and experience, and on the inability of the rabbis and Jewish theologians to articulate a spirituality that speaks to the person on the level of her "uncertainties." They also illustrate the possible failure of Jewish religious organizations to combat assimilation.

Though on the popular level assimilation is often analyzed within the confines of intermarriage and the loss of Jewish membership in the Jewish community, Rose and Steiner point to an even more difficult problem. In the search for spirituality, the failings of the Jewish community can be addressed by Christian literature, theology, and symbolism that pervade the West. Rose can become a Christian and Steiner can identify with Christian theology while abjuring formal entry into the Christian communion. Furthermore, Rose and Steiner can be drawn to Christianity in the search to respond to their most intimate queries, while at the same time critiquing Christian anti-Semitism and predicting the end of Christianity, at least in the way it has existed historically. By critiquing Christianity and becoming a Christian in membership and outlook, Rose and Steiner can cross the boundary between Jew and Christian by emphasizing *and* minimizing the boundary at the same time. The contemporary establishments of both Judaism and Christianity are attacked and declared irrelevant as are the historical frameworks of both religions. In this sense, Rose and Steiner embrace a faith and a symbolic structure that has a long and tortured history against their own people by jettisoning that history and its carriers.

The charge of assimilation is thus transformed by Rose and Steiner into an embrace denied them within Judaism. There are at least two ways of looking at their perspective: either the burden of Jewish history is too much to bear and its post-Holocaust incarnation too restrictive and angry, or it leads away from Judaism to a Christianity without a history. Still another way of looking at this question is that a certain strand of Jewish life is interpreted as wanting while a certain strand of Christian life is embraced. In this sense, Rose and Steiner leave one arena and enter another one with both arenas being defined by them. Yet, as distinctive as each thinker is, they remain within a cultural and religious world that they can interpret only through their participation in it. The distinctive quality of their thought cannot hide the fact that they are part of a Jewish stream of history that is moving toward a Christian destination defined by them. Both are interpreters and reporters, creating and mirroring aspects of contemporary Jewish and Christian religiosity in the West.

If the destination is Christian, at least in the broadest outlines of religiosity, this does not mean that Jewish identification is waning. In fact, just the opposite is the case: Jews now identify themselves more readily and assertively than at any time since their emancipation in Europe began. And contrary to the sense one receives from Steiner, Jewish renewal movements abound, especially in America. Still, Jewish identification and renewal occur within a context that is less and less distinctively Jewish. The paradox is that Jews assert their differences from their Christian neighbors and the Christian culture they live within as these differences are more difficult to find. The important assimilation has less to do with religious affiliation than it has to do with the practical aspects of domestic and public life.

That Jews are integrated into the public life of the West signifies at the same time the more important integration into its religious and symbolic universe. In essence, Jews are now claiming a Jewish space in a Christian world that once denied them that space. Though Jews claim to be the engines of that redefinition that is only partly the case. A more accurate picture of this change in the Western Christian psyche can be found by looking at the changing nature of Christianity. After the Holocaust, the necessity of Christian renewal has allowed, encouraged, and needed Jewish renewal. For how else has Christianity defined and redefined itself through the centuries, except through its changing understanding of Jews and Judaism?

Thus, remaining Jewish and cultivating Jewish identity in the post-Holocaust West is at the same time and paradoxically an assertion and cultivation of Christian identity. The Christian need for Jews is historic in its anti-Jewish aspects; in the contemporary world it is part of an alliance that seeks to demonstrate the confession of the past sins of the churches and the possibility of faith in a secular age. Jews continue to function for Christianity, albeit in a more positive way, as proof of its vocation to the world. For the promise made to the Jews—to be a covenanted people for all time—is now affirmed by the main denominations of Christianity, which assert that the same promise was also made to those who follow Jesus Christ.

In contemporary Christian theology, God's promise to the Jews remains valid and has never been revoked, despite the earlier insistence by Christianity that the attitude and behavior of the Jews had led God to choose another people to be the new Israel. In the same way, God's promise to the Christians remains valid despite the attitude and behavior of the new Israel to the first Israel, the Jews. One need not push the psychological interpretation too far to see the obvious benefit and dependency of Christians on Jews after the Holocaust. For if God could withdraw the special relationship with a people over actions in the world, would it be possible to believe in a just and compassionate God and still believe that God would continue to embrace the Christianity that laid the groundwork and provided the workers to build and operate Auschwitz?

The dependency of Jews on Christians is equally clear. If Jewish identity and space were, to a large extent, generated and maintained over the last fifteen hundred years by a militantly anti-Jewish Christianity, the dependence on Christianity for self-definition remains today in an altered atmosphere. For if Christianity had not existed in the past and somehow disappeared today what pressure would there be on the Jewish community for defining and maintaining itself? A hostile Christianity demands that attention and energy and a positive Christianity encourages the same. However, an ideology that simply has no interest in, has no special place for, and does not define itself positively or negatively in relation to Jews and Judaism is a more dangerous place for Jewish identity and continuance. For how do Christians and Jews define themselves without each other? At least in the West, whether in negation or affirmation, there is no contemporary historical record that allows conjecture of whether Judaism or Christianity would survive the demise of the other. Whether affirmed or not, and certainly with great ambivalence, Jews have chosen to depend upon and to assimilate to Christianity in the struggle for affirmation and survival.

Both Judaism and Christianity have also chosen assimilation to a larger and more powerful force than either religious system for their mutual survival, that is the Western cultural, capitalistic, and modern model of life. Though both Judaism and Christianity claim systems of redemptive power they also realize that the primary ideological system of redemption operating in the world today is the system of modernity. In short, there is no salvation outside of modernity, and Judaism and Christianity have assimilated to this motto precisely because this more powerful system of modernity allows both to survive and assert a distinctiveness that is largely symbolic. Like Jews, Christians speak more and more about their special mission in the world as that mission becomes almost indistinguishable from the modern world it has assimilated to.

So the question of assimilation shifts as the assimilation of Jewish and Christian religiosity to modernity is completed. Or rather, it becomes more complicated as religiosity takes two directions in its modernizing tendency: one toward a celebration of modernity, where religion is essentially a way of affirming the status quo; the other acclimating to modernity in style of life while assuming a stance of opposition to modernity in religion. The former can be seen within the Catholic middle- class embrace of Vatican II, the latter, often described as fundamentalism, is a way of carving out a place of meaning while allowing, despite the rhetoric, the world to go on as it is. One can see these tendencies in Judaism and Christianity as renewal movements within the framework of the more powerful ideology of modernity. Of course, both progressive and conservative renewal movements are ways of becoming comfortable, or signaling discomfort with aspects of contemporary life in a religious language that is not intended to be taken seriously outside the religious space. For if modernity is to be seriously challenged, then its primary challenge would have to take place outside the weakened, almost ineffectual realm of traditional religion, and the livelihood of the congregants as well as the sustenance of the synagogue and church budgets would be seriously threatened. In short, the proclamation of the prophets and the gospels must be spoken and left within a space that has little power except on the psyche of the members who are then free to resume their normal life in a more adjusted manner. Having heard the "truth," and perhaps even chanted and sung that truth, the clerics and the laity are free to resume their lives in the world.

Regardless of this reality, those who seek to leave the confines of these forms of religiosity are seen as assimilationists because their religious affiliation is questionable, over time perhaps even unidentifiable. As people who protest what is and seek to make that protest effectual in the world, the progressive and conservative currents of modern religiosity seem static, hypocritical, perhaps even helping to solidify the injustice and sin that both currents ostensibly condemn. Those who leave these religious currents are without a religious home and language. By leaving the safety of contemporary religion they are truly exiled from religion, both as judged by the religious themselves and through internal acceptance of the definition laid down by those who affirm religion in our society.

The exile is practical and psychological. There is no longer an affiliation where these issues can be discussed and the internal acceptance of the definition of religiosity makes it more difficult to see an alternative view. Most of these exiles are lost to the question of religion in our time, and quickly at that. For the next generation the question is lost, and when the longing for a language to express the deepest part of life and that which transcends life appears, it is assumed to be a momentary phase that should not be pursued. Even the framework for such a pursuit is lost—the language and symbols of religion are in disrepute and distant for the following generation.

Here Rose and Steiner are again exceptions. Both are schooled in history, literature, and philosophy so that their escape from contemporary religiosity is informed and deep. Their conversion or tendency toward that point has a complexity about it as well as an aura of unreality. It is their very education and deep thought that allow both Rose and Steiner to embrace *and* escape the very problematic they know so well. In fact both embrace religious ideas and symbols that are essentially archaic and without roots in the contemporary period. Instead of leaping into the unknown, joining the many Jews and Christians who are searching in exile, instead of exploring a new religious language, both tend toward a past that cannot be brought into the present and certainly cannot challenge in any realistic way the course of European or world history.

It is fascinating that both Rose and Steiner are profound critics of contemporary history and society but their ultimate religious embrace lacks that critical edge. Both seek to avoid assimilation to the mainstream of philosophy and literary criticism, in fact both establish streams of thought that fight that assimilation, and they further avoid assimilation to contemporary religiosity by embracing religious realities that in effect no longer have a community basis for existence or extension. Their philosophy and literary criticism is as unique as their religious embrace, though moving in two seemingly contradictory directions: the former far in advance of the field, the latter by its very nature archaic.

In short, these Jewish subversive intellectuals embrace and are drawn to a Christianity that persecuted their own people *and* has no future. One wonders if this is their final protest against assimilation even as it appears to Jews to be an apostasy and to Christians as a reinforcement of their own path. For to embrace a religiosity that has a future is to cross into a transgressive territory, a place where refusal becomes betrayal. Crossing into the Christianity that draws Rose and Steiner appears to be the ultimate transgression, especially with their communal and familial history, but upon closer inspection is an embrace without historical consequence. It neither denies nor affirms what it appears to be. The ultimate assimilation turns out to be a refusal of both Judaism and Christianity, at least the way they are practiced today.

After Auschwitz, what can the refusal of the limitations of Judaism and Christianity *and* the refusal of assimilation to contemporary religiosity and modernity mean? Is there more than a personal meaning to these acts and propensities that define these great Jewish thinkers? Are we here speaking of conversion in its traditional sense, or do Rose and Steiner enter into a new arena of conversion, using traditional affirmations to define a territory that remains without geographic and communal boundaries? Is this the only path open to those who take Auschwitz seriously and who also are attempting to come to the end of the era of Auschwitz? It seems that Rose and Steiner are acting as if fidelity to the dead of Auschwitz and affirmation of a reality beyond destruction and death cannot be pursued within a reality that is present *in our time.* Fidelity to death and beauty, horror and love, critique and affirmation, for those who come after Auschwitz, is to affirm an imminent transcendence and a transhistorical symbolic formation that grounds the person in a vision that has not been realized in history and will not be realized *in our time.* Nonetheless, for both Rose and Steiner, it is a betrayal to pretend that what is beyond our reach cannot be embraced by the person who is drawn to this reality in spite of the barriers of history and tradition.

Here they leave us, one in death, the other, at least for now, in a posture of fragments and hesitation. Rose and Steiner are drawn, and indeed draw us, beyond the boundaries recognized by authority and history into a realm that is deeply personal and yet has consequences for those who are drawn to the religious question. That the twentieth century, so full of promise and death, produced the likes of Rose and Steiner, is remarkable, and the journey they leave to us is just as remarkable. Their "conversion" is as important as it is a mystery. After Auschwitz and at the end of the era of Auschwitz, these Jews are drawn to Christianity *and* refuse assimilation, embracing a path in history so destructive of Jews that it has no future. Yet realizing that the Jewish path has also come to an end *and* has come into complicity with injustice, perhaps they had little choice. Could it be that their embrace of a distant and subversive Christianity is the only path available to a Jewish intellectual who is drawn to God?

An Ecumenical Religiosity

Though Rose and Steiner represent the latest of a trend in the Jewish search for God after the Holocaust, they are neither alone nor without precedent. In fact a number of Jewish thinkers have sought out this path or one very close to it, among them some who perished and some who survived the Holocaust. One thinks here of Edith Stein, Simone Weil, Anne Frank, and Etty Hillesum, all of whom died in the Holocaust, and Viktor Frankl, the Austrian psychologist, who survived Auschwitz.

Frankl developed a new branch of psychology, Logotherapy, that emphasizes the search for meaning even in extreme cases of human deprivation. In *Man's Search for Meaning,* published in 1946, Frankl asserts that the possibility of meaning is the barrier between the human and destruction of the human, and that this possibility of meaning must be affirmed to survive the reality of the camps. Even if a fantasy, meaning must be asserted, otherwise death is imminent. After the Holocaust, that same meaning exists and must be reasserted if the human is to triumph over evil. The search for meaning is constant: the Holocaust is a breach in human history that must be fought like other breaches before and after. Frankl's work is neither explicitly Jewish nor Christian and affirms any system, including humanism, that can hold out meaning in the face of adversity.[17]

For Stein and Weil, that meaning was explicitly found in Christianity. In 1933, Stein converted to Catholicism and became a Carmelite nun. Weil, though never officially converting to Catholicism, wrote a series of letters to two Catholic priests in the 1940s which contain elements of a powerful Christian testimony. Stein's witness to the Holocaust as a Catholic who affirmed her Jewish heritage and who died as a Jew in Auschwitz has received the sanctification of the Catholic church by her beatification. Weil's autobiography, *Waiting for God*, was heralded by such luminaries as T. S. Eliot and Albert Camus. More than fifty years after the Holocaust, her autobiography and other writings continue to be issued in new editions, and biographies of Weil proliferate.[18]

Anne Frank and Etty Hillesum, both of whom are known through their diaries discovered after the war, share aspects of Frankl's search for meaning and Stein's and Weil's Christianity. What is fascinating about these figures, however, is their exploration rather than their destination. Neither formally declared their Christianity or accepted this identity as their own. In *The Diary of Anne Frank* and *An Interrupted Life*, Frank and Hillesum engage their deteriorating personal situation as individuals in the Netherlands by identifying as Jews in a communal way while searching for answers to the coming Holocaust freely and with their own interior and cultural resources at hand. The power of Frank and Hillesum is in their respective searches, which involved the Jewish, Christian, and humanist traditions that were under assault by the Nazis. The assault against these traditions is found within the individual and collective, and Frank and Hillesum respond to deportation and death by searching and reconfiguring the human elements and potential of this unprecedented assault. Like Rose and Steiner after the Holocaust, Frank and Hillesum, and for that matter Frankl, Stein, and Weil as well, take seriously the depravity that has overcome the world in order to prepare for a time beyond suffering and destruction.[19]

It is important to note that these testimonies within the Holocaust are often disparaged by those writing after the Holocaust. Lawrence Langer is typical in this respect when he criticizes Frankl for covering over the destructive aspects of the Holocaust with imagery of meaning and purpose. "It is as if Frankl approached the crumbling edifice of twentieth-century humanism in Auschwitz armed with intellectual and moral props from an earlier era," Langer writes. "He is determined to shore up the ruins and to reassure his readers that in fact there has been no irreparable damage to the architecture of thought about the human spirit from Spinoza and Lessing to Nietzsche and Rilke, and up to the present." For Langer, Frankl and others try to rescue humanity from a reality too hard to bear, the fact that suffering in the Holocaust is without meaning or redemption. The Holocaust did not produce martyrs or heroes and there is no meaning to be gleaned from these years of utter destruction. Rather, the Holocaust exposes a rupture in human sensibility that resists our attempts to carve out an order beyond the destruction itself. Langer confirms this with the testimonies of the survivors themselves, as most of their stories "nurture not ethical insight but confusion, doubt and moral uncertainty." Instead we are left with those who try to piece together a moral tale of survival for those who cannot face the meaningless Holocaust universe. Langer is blunt in his critique of those who try to construct a world of resistance and meaning in the Holocaust: "Sandwiched between a vocabulary ("redeeming" and "salvation") that prods us away from the event toward a consoling future (a vocabulary, one might add, with a distinctly Christian flavor) lies the predicament of a son involuntarily sending his mother to her probable death." In a world where choice is choiceless, where moral choice is infected with atrocity, the structures of meaning and possibility are foreclosed.[20]

Langer's charge against Frankl is leveled with anger at those who affirm aspects of the Christian and humanist message. With regard to Hillesum, Langer writes that though she does not "repudiate her Jewish identity, neither does she particularly acknowledge it; it lies uneasily on her shoulders like a burden she might wish to discard." Thus, at least in Langer's view, Hillesum is virtually unique among the victims of the Holocaust by "dissociating her Jewish heritage and her fate and searching for sources of strength and consolation in a Christian vocabulary and attitude that to many will seem alien to her special dilemma." Langer is by no means alone in this sensibility. Other Jewish scholars, like Sander Gilman and James Young, criticize Anne Frank for her lack of "Jewish accent" in her writing and her use of Dutch rather than Hebrew in her diaries. According to Young, Frank was part of an assimilated Jewish culture and should be seen as a "member of the human community and not as one who identified herself as part of a collective Jewish tragedy."[21]

In her book, *Writing as Resistance: Four Women Confronting the Holocaust*, Rachel Feldhay Brenner disputes this claim by these post-Holocaust critics. In fact, she finds that Frank and Hillesum confronted the Holocaust by identifying completely with the Jewish people when their background and circumstances allowed other options. Brenner cites Frank's diary entry: "We are Jews in chains, chained to one spot, without any rights, with a thousand duties. . . . If we bear all our suffering and if there are still Jews left, when it is all over, then Jews instead of being doomed, will be held up as an example." Frank affirms that it might be from "our religion" that the "world and all the peoples learn good" and she even speculates that this may be the reason for Jewish suffering in the present. Despite this suffering Frank affirms that "we can never become just Netherlanders or just English or any nation for that matter, we will always remain Jews, we must remain Jews, but we want it, too. . . ." These sentiments are also present in Hillesum's diaries as she not only identifies with the Jewish people as one of them but sees a specific Jewish mission to the world within the context of suffering and with the world that comes after the destruction. As Hillesum writes of the suffering and the witness it involves, "It is not easy—and no doubt less easy for us Jews than for anyone else—yet if we have nothing to offer a desolate post-war world but our bodies saved at any cost, if we fail to draw new meaning from the deep wells of our distress and despair, then it will not be enough."[22]

For Brenner, the response of Frank and Hillesum as Jews within the Holocaust render "ironic" and self-righteous" the critics' questioning of their identity. It is as if there were a correct response to the Nazi persecution that these Jews failed to carry out and as if a language of resistance unfamiliar to these critics invalidates their witness. Both Frank and Hillesum rediscover their Judaism, probe it more deeply and assign new meanings to it within the tragedy. They establish affinity with Judaism through identification with historic and contemporary persecution. In doing so they accept the concept of Jewish chosenness in its ethical ramifications for Jews and the world at large. As Brenner points out, when their own lives were in danger, these "assimilated" Jews, "who spoke neither Hebrew nor Yiddish, spoke unknowingly in the language of the old Jewish tradition of *tikkun olam*, mending the world, combining its universal message with their Enlightenment heritage." In so doing, they affirmed the Jewish place in the world as their lives and the lives of their families came to an end. This Jewishness was emphasized in their diaries in the face of personal, familial, and communal death in dialogue with a world on the verge of its own destruction. Can one judge this or any other response as incorrect, not Jewish enough, or a failure, especially by those who have never faced this tragedy and who themselves embody many of the aspects of these "assimilated" Jews, writing in English in American universities?[23]

It is interesting that Brenner identifies the connection of Frank and Hillesum with the tradition of *tikkun olam*, a tradition reinvigorated in the post-Holocaust era by Holocaust philosopher and theologian Emil Fackenheim. In fact, Brenner uses their witness as confirming Fackenheim's central assertion that the repair of the world after the Holocaust is possible because there were those within the Holocaust who continued to resist the Nazis attempt to destroy human dignity. "The women expressed solidarity with the victims of the Nazi oppression, even though each knew that, as a Jew, she herself was destined to death," Brenner writes. "In the 'illogical logic' of resisting the 'irresistible logic of destruction,' in the words of Fackenheim, the women continued to care."[24]

For Brenner, these women embodied the *"tikkun* of ordinary decency" that Fackenheim sees as ontological in nature, confronting the ontological rupture that the Holocaust represents. If the destruction of the Holocaust is the abyss from which there is no rescue, if that abyss ruptures the Jewish covenant with God and the possibility of human trust, then the *tikkun* of ordinary decency is the place of healing, or at least a response to the abyss that portends a healing in the future. Furthermore, Brenner finds these women invoking Fackenheim's strategy of rediscovering meaning in a meaningless world through the invocation of a "mad midrash," as the only possible story and action left in a world where God and God's order have been silenced and so violated. The "mad midrash," in Fackenheim's words, "points to acts to restore a world which ought to be but is not, committed to the faith that what ought to be must and will be, and this is madness." Brenner concludes that each of these women in her own way "anticipated Fackenheim's paradoxical directive." Writing their own "mad midrash," Frank and Hillesum believed in and in fact succeeded in conducting a humanizing dialogue with the world in the midst of the Holocaust.[25]

Edith Stein, another woman analyzed by Brenner, was identifiably Christian in her orientation and thus much more suspect of crossing important boundaries in the Holocaust. Still, Brenner holds forth her right and responsibility to express her spirituality as she experienced it rather than being condemned for it. In fact, Stein expressed a solidarity with others who were suffering during those years and expressed that solidarity at great personal risk. Stein's witness is compelling. Despite her ability to blend into her new Christian faith community, the Carmelite order, in the face of increasing anti-Semitism expressed in Germany, she wrote and published a book of memoirs about her Jewish upbringing specifically to undercut such prejudice. Titled *Life in a Jewish Family* and published in 1933 on the eve of her departure for religious life, she identified with her own people. In her memoir of 1938, Stein recalled the increasing hostilities directed against her own people: "God's hand lay heavy on His people, and the destiny of this people was my own." As Brenner points out, Stein's solidarity was hardly confined to the writing of memoirs, as she requested private papal audiences in order to intercede on behalf of German Jews—requests that were refused—and when deported from the convent to Westerbork, she went with her sister, Rosa, with these words: "Come, Rosa. We're going for our people."[26]

Stein's God was identifiably Christian, and there are some of her Carmelite biographers who feel that part of Stein's witness to the Jewish people was for their conversion to Christianity, an issue that has made the beatification of Stein so controversial in the Jewish community. Clearly, as Brenner points out, Stein's later identification with the Jewish people came through the Jewishness of Jesus and her acceptance of the cross as essential to her own life and to the life of the world.

In a note from Westerbork to her prioress in Echt, Stein reiterated her connection with her own people through the cross, experiencing the suffering of Jesus through her own suffering and the suffering of her people. Nonetheless, Brenner remains adamant on her point. Stein was faithful to her Jewish identity to the end and felt a continuity of Judaism and Christianity in her own life. Rather than a conversion from one identity to another, Stein felt a convergence of Jewish and Christian identities in her life and death.[27]

Though Frank and Hillesum have a Christian sensibility, it is quite different from Stein's. In fact, the designation Christian is itself problematic if by Christian one means the centrality of Jesus Christ and the cross. Rather, both may be seen as embracing a God that is neither identifiably Jewish nor Christian in the mainstream tradition. For example, Hillesum writes of God as being part of her inner self: "I shall always feel safe in God's arms. They may well succeed in breaking me physically, but no more than that. I may face cruelty and deprivation the likes of which I cannot imagine in even my wildest fantasies. Yet all of this is as nothing to the immeasurable expanse of my faith in God and my inner receptiveness." This interior God is unable to protect her or her people from destruction. Just the opposite is the case, as God needs our protection: "I shall try to help You, God, to stop my strength ebbing away, though I cannot vouch for it in advance. . . . You cannot help us, but we must help You and defend Your dwelling place inside us to the last. . . ." For Frank, God is also an interior reality and though connected with nature is unable to rescue her or others from their historical plight: "I know that I am not safe, I am afraid of prison cells and concentration camps, but I feel I've grown more courageous and that I am in God's hands. . . . Without God I should have long ago collapsed."[28]

As Brenner understands it, both Frank and Hillesum pray to a God who is no longer powerful and authoritarian but rather a God of loving attention and consolation. Rather than a God who rescues the victims of atrocity or even prevents atrocity, their God is one who sustains those who suffer, helping them to maintain dignity and self-respect for as long as possible. The communal God has become a personal God; the God who commands obedience is a God whose "presence depends on our readiness to find him." Thus, the God of Frank and Hillesum is neither a Jewish nor a Christian God, neither a God of history nor of salvation. Transcendence and power become immanence and weakness as dogma and salvation become the preservation of dignity and the protection of the space for God in the person and nature.[29]

Frank and Hillesum enter into a discourse with God that stresses the universalist values of the Enlightenment in dialogue with Judaism and Christianity. By affirming a God whose essence lies in the ethics of dignity, self-respect, and responsibility and whose self-revelation allows the person to transcend fear and despair, they draw on an ecumenical theology that sees them through the darkest of days in service to others who are suffering. This ecumenical God is weak to be sure, but in another way powerful almost beyond words, accomplishing, for Frank and Hillesum, *tikkun olam* within death and destruction. "Hillesum thus defines God as the redeeming moral value that needs to be rediscovered and rescued in the reality of moral collapse," Brenner writes. "God is the divine spark that constitutes the essence of humanity and therefore must survive. And as the divine spark in us, God is more powerful than ever, because the illuminating spark of the Divine compels us to resist the dehumanizing logic of destruction and affirms our courage in the reality of the apocalypse."[30]

Thus for Frank and Hillesum, the possibility of mending the world in the future is connected with guarding God in the present, the interior God that allows our humaneness even in the logic of destruction. It is this connection of self and God, this mutual and interconnected reality, that allows Frank and Hillesum their witness *as Jews*. The *tikkun olam* realized through the *tikkun* of ordinary decency in the midst of the Holocaust is carried by women who affirm an ecumenical theology and pray to and with an ecumenical God. Though Stein is identifiably Christian, even her witness is seen, at least by her, as a continuity of Judaism and Christianity. With Stein, of course, because of her conversion and her choice of institutional religious life, there is a need to justify this continuity in philosophical and theological language. For Frank and Hillesum, there is little, if any, justification at all. It is as if the catastrophe that awaits both draws them to an unfamiliar yet intimate realm. Hillesum, for example, begins to pray in the period of anxiety before her internment and in a position "not handed down from generation to generation with us Jews," that is, on her knees with folded hands. In this prayer, elements of Judaism and Christianity, as well as the works of Dostoevsky and Rilke, enter, as if the boundaries of Hillesum's inheritance have been burst asunder. As the world is being destroyed so, too, are the boundaries of literature, religious tradition, and life. Yet the importance here must not be overlooked: the embrace of these three women of God *and* their Jewishness, which takes them to their deaths with dignity and in service to others, especially to other Jews, is found in the crossing of boundaries or, even more to the point, by calling on resources that are Jewish in origin and Jewish in tradition and culture.

Could this witness, therefore, be properly placed in the genre of non-Jewish, Christian, or gentile? Could Stein, Frank, and Hillesum be seen retrospectively as crossing over to Christianity and therefore somehow betraying the Jewish people? In that these figures blur the distinction between Jewish and Christian in their own time and in response to the Holocaust do these distinctions need to be restated in our time to define their betrayal in theirs? Does this help us to understand the *tikkun* of ordinary decency in their time and thus in our time, or does a rigid classification of Jew and Christian then serve to force us to reassert one now, one that was hardly followed by most Jews then? The combination of universalist Enlightenment values with Jewish particularity is the way of life for most Jews after the Holocaust, as it appears to be the way of life for many Jews who died in the Holocaust. Could the ecumenical theology and the God found especially in Frank and Hillesum be the future of the Jewish people and therefore be fought by those who see their witness as a possible future? Or rather, one might speculate that the Jewish world has come to a standstill in ethical and spiritual ways precisely because the future appears to move beyond Judaism and Christianity. Thus the voices within the Holocaust who found their way in this sensibility have to be censored or declared outside of the community.

If in their lives and spirituality these women resisted the logic of destruction, they also provide a counterpoint to Langer's analysis that the attempt to reassert the possibility of affirmation and meaning in the face of the Holocaust is impossible. Just as the *tikkun* of ordinary decency must be taken into account in Fackenheim's sense of the ontological rupture that the Holocaust caused, thereby repairing the world as it was shattered, so too the voices of those who held onto meaning in the world must also be heard. The words of Frank and Hillesum, for example, are not mere palliatives issuing from an ivory tower transcending suffering, nor is Frankl's analysis of the search for meaning. Their vocabulary is less one of the redeeming or salvific aspects of a people's suffering. They represent instead and communicate in their writing the possibility of living with dignity, being present to history, and being available to others in a humane way in a time of inhumanity.

Frankl, Frank and Hillesum, do not use a distinctively Christian vocabulary but instead are ecumenical in the broadest sense of drawing upon resources available and relevant to their experience. At the same time, they also see in their experience a way toward a future that, at least in Frank's and Hillesum's cases, they will not live to see. Langer's understanding is contradicted as these writers provide a counterpoint to his absolute sense of the end of moral and ethical reasoning because both are infected with atrocity.

Within the universe of choiceless choice, there was indeed a choice that is more than theoretical or pious in its annunciation. We can establish possibilities because there were those who made a choice within atrocity. Because of this choice, including how to exist within the structure of forced death, a world is possible where that possibility is chosen again. For these witnesses, the coming world would have to choose the path of morality and ethics in an ecumenical spirit; a choice otherwise is at too great a cost. This is how, just days before she was transported to her death at Auschwitz, Hillesum could write: "All I want to say is this: The misery here is quite terrible, and yet, late at night when the day has slunk away into the depths behind me, I often walk with a spring in my step along the barbed wire. And then time and again, it soars straight from my heart—I can't help it, that's just the way it is, like some elementary force—the feeling that life is glorious and magnificent, and that one day we shall be building a whole new world."[31]

Crossing Boundaries

The desire to build a new world and even more, the hope that a new world will be built in light of your own suffering and that of your people, reflects a generosity of spirit difficult to ignore. The resources that allow the bitterness of suffering to give way to hope are important as well. These resources are diverse, to be sure, and include Orthodox Jewish piety and secular atheistic defiance as well as Christian themes. Those diaries that are considered authentically Jewish, such as the diaries of Emmanuel Ringelblum, are now expanded in tone and sensibility. For is Ringelblum, as the great commentator on the Warsaw ghetto, authentically Jewish whereas Frank and Hillesum are not? Those Hasidic Jews who bargained their food rations for tefilin and prayer shawls, in essence affirming their spiritual dignity in the face of starvation, as well as the secular existentialist poet who arrived at the place of deportation wearing prayer shawl and tefilin, are also witnesses to the Holocaust.

What we have is an evolving tapestry, an incorporation of old and new themes, a bridging of barriers, a series of interpretative journeys that respond to the moment rather than worry about the purity of tradition or even the future of Judaism. All respond as they can in circumstances of distress and destruction. With the witness of care and support, with the acts and writing they bequeath, in short with the testimony of witness we inherit, who is to judge the authenticity or lack thereof of these people? Could it be that the judgment is retrospective, having to do more with the problematics of our time than theirs?

18

"Other Teachers, Other Paths":
Martin Buber, Abraham Joshua Heschel,
and the Future of Jewish Life*

I FIRST ENCOUNTERED THE WRITINGS OF MARTIN BUBER in the early 1970s as a student at Florida State University. My course in religious studies was taught by a professor from an evangelical Christian background who had embarked on a journey among the world religions to answer questions of meaning and purpose for himself. Among other books, he assigned Buber's *I and Thou*. He also made audio tapes in which he extended his lecture discussions on Buber and his philosophy. Each night I read Buber and listened to the tapes. A world of dialogue and presence opened to me, one that I scarcely knew existed.

A year later I encountered Richard Rubenstein, another member of the faculty, and his own understanding of Buber in relation to the Holocaust and the political and religious task of our century. I heard then what Rubenstein presented several years later in Germany on the occasion of Buber's centenary celebration. For Rubenstein, Buber's understanding of dialogue and presence introduced a mystical and misguided interpretation of the political nature of power and powerlessness, as well as the consequences of such an approach. What Jews needed during the Holocaust and after was a power of protection and retribution. Buber confused the issue then and now: relationship to God and each other could only be secured through naked power, a power wielded without attention to ethics and morality.

These diametrically opposed understandings between two of my teachers were challenged by my experience at the Catholic Worker in

---

*An earlier version of this chapter appeared in *Perspectives in Religious Studies,* *26* (Spring 1999): 67-78. This review essay engages the following books: Dan Avnon, *Martin Buber: The Hidden Dialogue.* Lanham, MD: Rowman and Littlefield, 1998; and Edward Kaplan and Samuel H. Dresner, *Abraham Joshua Heschel: Prophetic Witness.* New Haven, CT: Yale University Press, 1998.

New York City a year after my graduation. Begun in 1933 with the meeting of Peter Maurin and Dorothy Day, the Catholic Worker was then and remains committed to a life among the poor and the reconstruction of society emphasizing equality and human dignity. Among the patron saints of the movement are those who have argued for a communitarianism that flows from the spirit into social and political life. Those outside of the Catholic tradition who are often quoted and deemed worthy of study and emulation are Mohandas Gandhi and Martin Luther King, Jr. And of course Martin Buber.

In some ways my own encounters with Buber mirror the extraordinary complexity and richness of Buber's life and writings. Buber is a magnet for those who seek depth and those who are critical of "utopian" sensibilities, encouraging, on the one hand, acts of gratitude and, on the other, accusations of naivete. My fourth encounter with Buber some years later on the issue of Israel/Palestine illustrates this sensibility at its highest level. Buber's understanding of dialogue and presence led him to a communitarian hope for a mutual homeland for Jews and Palestinians in the Holy Land. For this too he has been heralded as a prophet of justice and condemned as a naive moralist.

The strength of Dan Avnon's analysis of Buber is to search out the foundational elements of Buber's thought, especially with relation to scripture. The "hidden dialogue" that Avnon finds in Buber's writings on religion, philosophy, and social reality illuminates the more surface readings from which Buber has suffered among both his admirers and his critics. Those who have encountered Buber can only be grateful for this sustained and brilliant analysis. Rare among books on seminal figures, Avnon's work deepens our encounter with the figure at hand and becomes part of the ongoing encounter itself. In Avnon's critical analysis, Buber comes alive with a depth that surprises both admirers and critics and places Buber's thought in the context of his and, paradoxically, our time. Thus, Buber's thought and life are contextual, allowing us to see how he worked through the difficult crisis of the first half of the twentieth century, and futuristic, demanding that we grapple with Buber's breadth and limitations as we enter the twenty-first century. Because this contextual and futuristic aspect is, for the most part, unannounced in the book, Avnon himself engages in a hidden dialogue as well. The power of Avnon's book rests here: exploring Buber's hidden dialogue and engaging in one himself, Avnon asks us to understand and articulate our own hidden dialogue on the threshold of the twenty-first century.

The Hidden Dialogue

What was Buber's hidden dialogue? To begin with, Avnon surfaces various ideas and visions embedded in Buber's writing throughout his long and public career. Though there is an evolving ideational development over time, Buber's underlying ideas and, more importantly, the source from which his ideas come, remain constant. The task is to make explicit what Buber hints at but often disguises in language more accessible to the ordinary reader, whether religious or not. Buber's two-fold audience, Jews and humanity at large, were often unaware of what Avnon calls Buber's "hermeneutic code" and in large part, at least in Buber's mind, were unprepared to name the source behind the vision.

Quite simply, Buber's source was the Hebrew bible, especially Isaiah 49:2. Here Isaiah speaks: "He made my mouth like a sharp sword, in the shadow of his hand he hid me; he made me a polished arrow, in his quiver he hid me away." For Buber, Isaiah here speaks of the prophets and the student of the prophets; once they spoke boldly to the people Israel and to the world of a history of relation to God, humanity and creation. That history, the one proposed in the original covenant, had been violated and buried, often by the very heirs of the covenant. Instead, a history of states and institutions, among them religious institutions, betrayed this history by the use of power and objectification to distance Jews and humanity from the original revelation. Buber understands this original revelation to be associated with the primal voice of the Hebrew bible and the essential insight of philosophical contemplation. In fact, history as we know and record it today is for Buber simply a facade that masks rather than reflects reality. Avnon posits Buber's alternative view of history as the "chronicle of an ongoing relation to being that exists in diverse cultural forms and is characterized by the agent's ability to relate directly to being, without the prior mediation of thought."

Isaiah's sense of history is different, and because Jews and the world have not accepted this path, "real" history is in exile as are those who carry this history forward. Those who move beyond the facade are therefore hidden like the history they embrace. The hidden history is carried forward by hidden students. Avnon refers to Buber's understanding of the "hidden circle of prophets" who in biblical times opposed the tendency among the Israelite tribes to circumscribe faith within the confines of cult and ceremony and today oppose the tendency of the state and religion to dehumanize humanity through war, oppression, and the legitimation of injustice. These hidden prophets carry forth a tradition that seeks the personal and social recovery of the deeper history of humanity. Avnon crystallizes Buber's foundational understanding of the prophetic voice then and now in the following words: "Social and political forms of association and structures of authority should be commensurate with the overriding goal of transmitting the teaching that serves as the opening to revelation. . . . As social structures reflect ontological presuppositions, meaningful renewal of social structure is necessarily determined by personal ontological change."

Buber distinguished between the history known to the larger world and the history known to the few. He disputed the idea that the division was between the political and the religious, eschewing the distinction often found in organized religion between the profane and the sacred, as if the political were of this world and the religious were of another realm. This false dichotomy represented, at least for Buber, the failure of politics *and* religion, for the realms of social and spiritual life are one. It is this immediate and unmediated connection—or at least the attempt to approach and renew this connection—that found Buber writing about such seemingly diverse topics as the bible and social reconstruction in the aftermath of the Holocaust and the height of the cold war.

This was also Buber's entry point into the difficult realities of the Middle East. As a life-long Zionist before his forced departure from Germany in 1938, and as a resident first of Palestine, then Israel until his death in 1965, Buber argued forcefully and repeatedly for a Jewish homeland that would embody his search for the renewed connection between humanity and God. It was Buber's hope, one he held on to despite repeated disappointments, that the hidden history found in Isaiah and the students of Isaiah, those prophets in exile throughout Jewish history, would speak to the Jewish people of their need to return to the source of their founding and existence. The challenge of the Jewish homeland was clear, at least to Buber. In the crisis of Jewish history, represented by the Holocaust and general drift of modernity into objectification and oppression, the Jewish homeland could model an alternative way of living with one another and with God. Of course, as with all of Buber's writings and vision, the Jewish return to authenticity could become a model for those of other communities to return as well. Addressing the Jewish crisis was also addressing the world crisis.

That the Jewish homeland would interact peacefully and justly with the Arab inhabitants of Palestine was axiomatic for Buber and the essential challenge of Zionism. If Jews could not be just to their neighbors, how could they create justice among Jews in the Jewish homeland? If Jews acted in a militaristic way against the Arabs, how could they avoid the militarization of Jewish society? Buber was vocal on these issues in ways that would surprise contemporary students of Jewish life. On various occasions he debated and lectured the prime ministers of Israel, especially David Ben-Gurion, and opposed from the beginning the partition of Palestine and the formation of a Jewish state. He also argued repeatedly for the return of Palestinian Arab refugees and against the confiscation of Palestinian Arab land within the newly found state of Israel.

In short, Buber fought for the Jewish homeland as the place where his alternative view of history would be realized. At the same time he clearly saw the transformation of his dream into a new exile, as the heirs of the prophets once again marginalized that hidden history of the circle of the prophets carried forth by Buber and other Jews of his time.

Buber's "Failure"

Though Avnon spends most of his energy describing the hidden aspect of Buber's public rhetoric, the deepest strata of Buber's mature public interventions, he does not hesitate to criticize the social application of Buber's philosophy. For Avnon, Buber ascribes an inarticulate foundation to the emerging Jewish homeland. The Jewish settlers see themselves as secular and estranged from the Jewish tradition: they want to be Jews freed from the past and from God. Their experiments in social living, most notably the kibbutz, are attempts to realize the European socialist vision in a pioneering Middle East context. Those who created the state came to Palestine for ideological and security reasons, but Buber sees them instead as reestablishing the original vision that occurred at Sinai.

So, too, in other non-Jewish social experiments. Buber tended to confuse historical moments and the people involved in them with the manifestation of his theological vision inculturated into a social and political reconstruction. Avnon believes Buber misunderstood Jewish and international politics because of the very dichotomy Buber saw underlying reality, that is, the division between history as understood by the world and the hidden history carried on by the hidden circle of the prophets. In the case of the state of Israel and the Palestinians, Buber felt that the hidden history of the Jews would unfold and become manifest, when in fact the triumph of force and oppression continued to operate. If, indeed, the Arabs of Palestine were the litmus test for the ontological turning of Jews to the deepest calling of the Jewish history and revelation, then the hidden history remained hidden and a different confrontation with state power had to occur. Avnon cites Rubenstein's criticism of Buber in relation to the Holocaust. Buber could not bring himself to understand that the forces of power had to be met with the same kind of power or, more simply, that the history of power and oppression was *the* arena of history that freedom is to be found in the arena of history that Buber spurned. Paradoxically, it may be that the exploration of Buber's hidden history can only occur within this other arena of history as a subversive hiddenness that can influence but not dominate the history of power and oppression.

Instead of a legacy of social reconstruction, Avnon concludes that Buber's "lasting achievement was his bringing to light and transmitting the remembrance of the original 'teaching' and 'testimony.'" For those who have encountered Buber in the past and seek his counsel for the future we are left with these questions. Is it possible to rest easy with Buber's failure? Can we count his legacy a success within a larger failure? Is there a way to promote Buber's legacy into a sustained program for social and religious reconstruction? Is the alternative history Buber proposed destined to remain in exile as are the prophets who carry forth this message?

Well before liberation theology, Buber discovered that history could be viewed from above—the history of power and oppression—and from below—the history of relation and revelation. And well before liberation theology, Buber also experienced that the power of the suffering and the prophets was often, and perhaps always, tested. Even in movements of liberation the tendency toward objectification and abuse of the very symbols of liberation often triumphs. Like liberation theology, but again in anticipation of it, Buber saw religion and religious sensibilities as serving two masters: history as known by the world and history understood by the prophets. Buber's option for the suffering and for relation to the world and to God was recognized by movements such as the Catholic Worker as the path forward. But like liberation theology and Buber himself, the Catholic Worker remains an alternative view of the world that has not been emulated to any great extent and in the larger world remains unknown or a curiosity.

Perhaps we are at a moment that Buber only glimpsed, and his failure speaks eloquently that the particulars of each community's hidden history must join in an expanded circle of prophets. Buber saw the particular and the universal as separate and connected with the strength of each particularity leading somehow to a community of communities. Therefore each community plumbed its history and returned to its primal origins in order to reconstitute itself in the contemporary world. Each particularity had an original revelation that when embraced in a creative and open way contributed to itself and the world. It was almost as if the peoples of the world each carried a destiny within them. That destiny was hidden, waiting to be unfolded and embraced. The only way forward for each community and the community of communities was the embrace of that destiny.

Yet across communities, the hidden history and circle of prophets are engaged in the same task and, for the most part, experiencing the same failures. For Buber, the ecumenical spirit was the recognition of this common work and in many ways has become part of the ecumenical spirit of our time. Still, one wonders if the destiny of each community adds up to the destiny of all and whether in fact the destiny of each can be contained or even explored only within the framework of a particular community. What if the proposition is reversed, that the original revelation of each community is itself unoriginal and eclectic and thus the hidden history and prophets are themselves products of the interaction of different communities in different historical time periods? If, as Buber correctly points out, hidden history and the circle of prophets struggle within their own particularity, which is itself conforming to power and oppression, why not see all those who continue the struggle as a common patrimony that might one day lead to a new particularity? Stated differently, the hidden history and the circle of prophets are part of a tradition that is broader than each particularity and await an articulation that even Buber could not identify. Perhaps there is a broader tradition of faith and struggle that is part of a larger destiny that each particularity contributes to but in the end transcends.

One wonders if Buber's limitation was less his ability to translate his ideas into reality than his inability to see that the destiny of humanity is no longer to be realized within the dialectic of particularity and universality or even in the dichotomy of the history of power and the history of relation. Buber's limitation seems to be his inability to name the broader tradition of faith and struggle, that is the interpenetration of all those throughout history who, in their own time and context, have embraced the values and visions that Buber celebrated. Instead of the prophetic struggle within particularities giving birth to a community of communities, the broader tradition of faith and struggle is itself a particularity that transcends the communities from which the struggle emerged.

The strength of this evolving tradition countcracts one of Buber's weakest points, as he saw the loneliness of the circle of prophets constantly battling the community to be heard. If the broader tradition of faith and struggle is itself fighting a losing battle, then at least there are more resources and people to wage the battle. For is it not the case that the struggle to be faithful across communities is part of a larger destiny awaiting us? And does not this struggle, wherever it appears across time and geography and faith community, deepen our own struggle?

Many questions remain, of course. Does a destiny beyond Judaism, or for that matter Christianity, Hinduism, and Islam, weaken the particularities and thus the initial carriers of revelation? Does the rooting afforded by a defined identity, one that Buber certainly carried with him, end in a universality without roots? Does the broader tradition of faith and struggle encourage a superficial eclecticism, almost a new age sensibility now so familiar to us?

Avnon does not address these questions, as his task is to interpret the challenging life of Martin Buber. As I encountered in my earlier life the different responses to Buber, so, too, this book calls us to search beyond Buber himself.

Buber, Heschel, and the End of European Jewry

Soon after my introduction to Buber, I encountered Abraham Joshua Heschel. In fact, the similarities I found in these two men were exhibited in their personal and public lives.

As with Buber, I encountered Heschel in a religion course, though he was only referred to in passing. At the Catholic Worker, Heschel was quoted often and in the line of Buber, though Buber was emphasized more in the communitarian aspect of the movement and Heschel in its spirituality. Dorothy Day was especially fond of Heschel and told me once of a meeting with him at his apartment. At the end of their time together, she asked his blessing and he gave it willingly and in Hebrew.

It was a moving event for Dorothy and as she recalled it one could tell its significance for her.

As with Richard Rubenstein's intellectual involvement and critique of Buber, so, too, Heschel played an important role in Rubenstein's life. At Jewish Theological Seminary, Heschel had been his teacher. Over time, their relationship broke down, in part because of a personality clash but mostly because of different understandings of the Holocaust and its meaning for Jewish life. If Rubenstein broke with Buber over his utopic understanding of an unmediated relationship with God and decentralized communities of conscience and spirit, he broke with Heschel over understandings of Jewish law and covenant.

For Rubenstein the Holocaust calls into question the utopian understandings of religious and social life that Buber offered *and* the more traditional understandings of Jewish continuity and God's presence that Heschel articulated. After Auschwitz, a phrase that is common today in the discussion of post-Holocaust Jewish thought but was introduced by Rubenstein in his ground-breaking, now classic work, *After Auschwitz: Radical Theology and Contemporary Judaism,* both Buber and Heschel were found wanting. Utopian and traditional understandings of Jewish life could not be asserted after Auschwitz, and traditional Jewish life with the covenant at its center, no matter how beautifully translated into contemporary language, could not be honestly contemplated. For Rubenstein, at least, Auschwitz was the end of belief in goodness and God, at least the God of history symbolized by the covenant at Sinai.

Buber and Heschel encountered each other in their own lives. As Edward Kaplan and Samuel Dresner point out in the first volume of their projected two-volume biography of Heschel, the similarities between Buber and Heschel were profound. They were both born in Poland and experienced the diverse social and religious life of pre-Holocaust Jewish life; both were educated in religious and secular institutions of higher learning in Germany; both spoke to the Jewish community, the ecumenical community of Jews and Christians, and the larger world; both fled Germany in the 1930s. Their connection was more than background, for when Heschel emerged on the religious scene in Germany, Buber was already a highly respected theologian. Thirty years Buber's junior, Heschel appealed to him at the beginning of his career for acknowledgment and later for employment. As Buber prepared to leave Germany for Jerusalem in 1938, it was Heschel whom he entrusted with a leadership role at the Frankfurt Lehrhaus. This allowed a close working relationship, almost a mentorship, as they both experienced the final moments of European Jewish history.

From the broader contours of Jewish history, Buber and Heschel seem quite similar in their theological perspectives. Both were religious Jews who called Jews to take more seriously their religious commitments and saw religiosity as a spiritual and social force for good in the world. Like Buber, Heschel saw Jewish particularity as a bridge to other faith communities and to the secular world as well. In Germany and then later in Palestine/Israel and the United States, both were seminal figures in the ecumenical dialogue. In different generations and in the same period, Buber and Heschel sought desperately to impart spiritual meaning and strength to a beleaguered community and world. With their combination of religious and secular learning, Buber and Heschel searched for and articulated a spirituality that laid the groundwork for future Jewish generations to work out with others, especially Christians, who found a deeper sense of spirituality in the theology of these two Jewish thinkers.

But as Kaplan and Dresner point out, the differences between Buber and Heschel were significant. Though both were deeply religious Jews, their religiosity differed in significant ways, so much so that it was only the crisis of Nazi Germany that finally brought them together. The difference can be found in Buber's understanding of God and human response as relational and contextual, thus releasing Jews from strict observance of the Law. Buber insisted that a person should feel called by the Law in order to accept its obligations, thus subordinating the Law to human initiative; the mitzvot were not prescriptive expressions of divine will, but rather a way of response found in turning to mutuality and God. Buber himself was not an observant Jew, at least in the traditional sense of that term. For Buber, the practice of Judaism prescribed in advance and codified by authority too often blocked Jewish response to the God he described as Thou.

Unlike Buber, Heschel was an observant Jew in the more traditional sense and he saw regular observance as the path to Jewish renewal. For Heschel, God was more definable than Buber's Thou, and the relation between Jews and God was found less in dialogical terms than it was in responding to the call of the God who had called the Israelites from Egypt and sent the prophets to Israel in their journey as a people. Rather than a relational encounter with Thou, Heschel saw the prophet's awareness as a response to a divine incursion. For Heschel, Buber's God was too vague, almost a symbolic presence that therefore could not respond to this incursion. Without the traditional God and the framework to channel this divine incursion, Heschel thought that Jewish continuity would be endangered. Kaplan and Dresner cite this as perhaps the essence of Heschel's and Buber's difference and wariness of each other.

Heschel boldly claimed the prophets and the prophetic voice as emerging from the practice of Jewish life. Rather than finding this voice in dialogue and relation, Heschel's prophets were in a sense seized by God. This accounts for a difference in the thought, work, and personality of Buber and Heschel. As Kaplan and Dresner portray it, Heschel was bold in his personality and in his assertiveness. In his early years at least, Heschel was often to himself, convicted by a mission he boldly asserted, a prophetic mission that he called others to as well. This could and often was seen as a distancing from others, an aloofness, even an arrogance. Surely, Buber's hidden circle of prophets was less Heschel's style and vision.

For Heschel the continuity of the prophetic voice was expressed in public and without disguise. If the prophetic voice was not heard in contemporary life, the failure could be ascribed to institutionalized religion, the trivialization of belief, and diminished moral courage. The need was for religion, belief, and courage to be revitalized and proclaimed in words and deeds, especially at the twilight of European Jewry when the dark clouds were enveloping humanity during the Nazi era. Heschel believed that only through piety could this revitalization take place. As Kaplan and Dresner understand it, this piety combined "faith, belief, attachment to God, observance of the mitzvot, loyalty to the Jewish people—all leading to practical action in the world."

Kaplan and Dresner recall an incident in 1930 that helps illumine Heschel's personality. Heschel had sent some poems that he had written to an editor for publication and the editor responded favorably. When the poems were published the editor sent along an honorarium and in the accompanying letter asked if Heschel had been influenced by Rainer Maria Rilke. Heschel, feeling that his originality had been questioned, responded without hesitation: "I didn't have to study in Rilke's *heder* to recognize that there is a God in the world. I had other teachers, other paths, other images."

In encountering Buber and Heschel after the Holocaust, perhaps this understanding of different paths is the most startling and instructive aspect of their lives and theology. The first volume of Heschel's biography ends with his emigration to the United States in 1940, thus the second half of his life was shadowed by the destruction of European Jewry and much of his family. Later Heschel would write of his escape and continuing commitment to justice and compassion in the United States: "I speak as a person who was able to leave Warsaw, the city in which I was born, just six weeks before the disaster began. My destination was New York; it would have been Auschwitz or Treblinka. I am a brand plucked from the fire in which my people were burned to death." In the 1960s, this brand spoke boldly for the struggle to gain civil rights for African Americans and against the war in Vietnam and for an ecumenism that recognized particularity and the universality of God's call.

These other teachers, paths and images were proclaimed by Buber and Heschel alike, though in different styles. And they continue to be proclaimed today as Buber and Heschel are widely celebrated in Jewish and Christian circles as powerful voices for faith and justice in the world. Avnon, Kaplan, and Dresner are clear about their continuing importance as larger-than-life theological figures who continue to dominate Jewish thought and reflection, even when they are mentioned only in passing.

This is true in the Christian community as well, where certain insights of Buber and Heschel are taken for granted, even assumed, and where often those who promulgate their insights are unaware of their original authorship.

Still, the question remains as to whether these other teachers, paths, and images that influenced Buber and Heschel and which they subsequently, in their own distinctive ways, bequeathed to the world, continue to provide subversive messages at the dawn of the twenty-first century.

On the Future of Jewish Life

In 1972, shortly before his death, I met Heschel. He had been a featured speaker at the university lecture series and afterwards, as was the custom, students were invited to a reception for the speaker in a small Methodist chapel adjacent to the campus. Usually only a handful of students came to these receptions and that night was no exception. So for an hour or so our small circle sat with Heschel. He responded to our queries mostly with patience, but sometimes with irritation, especially when questions were asked about topics he had written much about. His suggestion was no doubt sensible: read what I have written on the subject and then come with questions. To me it was a great opportunity to meet him, if only in a group; some months later when I learned of his death, it reminded me of how tired he looked that evening.

Richard Rubenstein was not on campus that evening, neither at the lecture nor the reception, and I was aware that he did not invite or publicize Heschel's appearance. As a sophomore, listening to Rubenstein in class and reading his work, I was only becoming aware of the furious storm that Rubenstein had unleashed in his theological commentaries. Holocaust theology was in formation at that very moment and Rubenstein and his respondents—Elie Wiesel, Emil Fackenheim, and Rabbi Irving Greenberg—were centering Jewish theology in a new and difficult way. Though they differed sometimes vehemently in their outlooks, these theologians placed the Holocaust and the state of Israel at the center and affirmed Jewish empowerment as a necessity where belief in God was in doubt.

Continuity of Jewish life was seen in this empowerment in contrast to the desire of Hitler to end Jewish life. The prophets, hidden in Buber's theology or boldly proclaimed in Heschel's innovative orthodoxy, seemed distant, as if they had been nurtured in a world that no longer existed. In many respects this was true, as both Buber's and Heschel's perspectives, though experiencing Nazism and the Holocaust, were formed before and within the onslaught. Holocaust theologians were doing theology *after* Auschwitz, to a generation of Jews who were formed in a different world and could no longer accept—in some ways did not have access to—the continuity Buber and Heschel embodied. With Buber's death in 1965 and Heschel's in 1972, the field of theology was dominated by others. Many Jewish religious thinkers, including Rubenstein, increasingly saw Buber and Heschel as beautifully expressing a Jewish world that no longer existed.

If all theology is generational and contextual, if Buber and Heschel were bypassed by a theology that emphasized the absence of God and the boldness of empowerment, Holocaust theology is likewise defined by time and circumstance. Empowerment in Israel has been achieved, but at a cost disappointing to most Holocaust theologians, at least those who emphasized empowerment as the path of Jewish continuity. Theologians have been largely silent on the complexity of Israel, especially its treatment of the Palestinians, preferring to reassert Jewish innocence in establishing a state in the wake of the Holocaust.

Rubenstein, of course, has had little problem with Israel, as empowerment supersedes morality, and his refusal of the moral question after the Holocaust was part of his break with Buber and Heschel. Wiesel, Fackenheim, and Greenberg have taken up the moral question without certainty about God, demonstrating a continuity with Buber and Heschel, even as they have left behind those formed before and during the Holocaust. Unfortunately, a current revival of interest in Heschel, demonstrated by the series of essays in Heschel's memory in the progressive Jewish periodical *Tikkun*, seek to recapture Heschel's voice for a prophetic Judaism by essentially passing over the question of Israel and its mistreatment of Palestinians.

The conundrum of Jewish theology can be found here. With the disappointment in Israel and the subsequent drift of Jewish social thought to the right of the political spectrum, progressive Jews have shown a revived interest in Heschel and sometimes in the more mystical aspects of Buber's writings. In essence the path created by Holocaust theology has been found wanting. Unfortunately, this has often been a way to circumvent the central question facing Jews today: the need for peace with justice in Israel/Palestine. The respective crises facing Buber and Heschel in Nazi Germany and Rubenstein, Wiesel, Fackenheim, and Greenberg after the Holocaust are two different crises, connected by history and tradition to be sure. Still, one arose in imminent and horrific danger; the other in an attempt to unify a people for survival after the cataclysm. At the close of the twentieth century, the crisis is neither one of imminent danger nor of survival, but of asserting a power that dislocates another people. The Nazi era threatened Jewish continuity in a physical sense. On the threshold of the twenty-first century Jewish continuity is threatened in a moral sense.

It is clear now that the "other teachers, other paths, other images" Heschel embodied and the hidden circle of prophets whom Buber thought would arise in the Jewish homeland have not been sufficient to awaken the Jewish people, or the world for that matter, to an alternative way of life lived with God and each other. The arrival of Jewish-State culture in Israel and the United States—that is, a Jewish government in Israel and an intellectual class in service to the state in America—has changed, perhaps irrevocably, the landscape of Jewish life. In an era of Jewish empowerment, the resources and energy of the community and the tradition itself must be mobilized in support of that empowerment. Thus the tradition moves from the resistance of Buber and Heschel and the lament and assertion of Holocaust theologians to a silence on the major and unexpected question of our day. With all the concern about assimilation, Jewish theology faces today an assimilation to the state and to power, an assimilation, as with Christianity, that can use the symbols of continuity for its own purposes.

Of course, the assimilation to the state and power itself creates a wave of dissent, and there are Jews in Israel and the United States who oppose injustice and therefore refuse this assimilation. In the main and almost without exception, these Jews are outside the synagogue and positions of leadership in the Jewish community. For the most part, these Jews are in exile from mainstream Jewish religious and social life, as they have been forced from public life by a Jewish establishment who sees the alternative future they embody as a threat to post-Holocaust security and affluence. Like Buber's prophets, they are hidden, and unlike Heschel's prophets, they are unable to name the source from which their activity emerges. In their profound and unremitting secularity, Jews in exile protest assimilation but are unable to articulate the depth or destination of their journey. One is left with the question of whether these Jews in exile are carrying the covenant with them. Is this the last exile in Jewish history? If so, Jewish history as Buber and Heschel knew and practiced it, has come to an end.

Do Buber and Heschel speak to Jews in exile? Are they teachers for them? Do they provide other paths, other images in an era close in time but far different from their own? Can they speak within a time when survival as Jews has less to do with the physical than the spiritual? Where the state is not oppressing Jews but when some Jews use the state to oppress others? Can they speak to Jews who live out the ethics of the tradition without religious speech partly because those who speak religiously too often refuse to confront their own culpability?

On the threshold of the twenty-first century, Jews come after the Holocaust *and* Israel. In some ways Jews are experiencing an ending in Jewish history, a closing of a chapter in the long journey of an ancient people. Within the context of state power and the religious legitimation of it—or at least the silence surrounding it—the tradition itself, or at least the tradition's representatives, is mute. It speaks more easily about that which is outside the Jewish community. Hence Elie Wiesel's prophetic words about world issues and his virtual silence on the plight of the Palestinians.

Placing the prophetic critique inward toward Jewish power is the unexpected of Jewish history, and Buber and Heschel are of little help here. While bold on civil rights and Vietnam, Heschel romanticized the Jewish return to the land of Israel, especially after Israel's victory in the 1967 war. In some ways he was spared the test that others after him failed: confronting Israel's policies that have gone far beyond the need to establish and secure a Jewish homeland. Living in Jerusalem, Buber did confront a state in the making, worked tirelessly to steer its course toward justice, but he was also spared the final expansion of Israel in 1967 and beyond. Neither Buber's nor Heschel's prophets, hidden or boldly proclaimed, prevented then or now the joining of Judaism and the state. Just the opposite. Buber and Heschel were the last giants of Jewish theology and religious social action who lived in the shadow of the Holocaust and the promise of a Jewish homeland before the state of Israel defined itself, at least by its actions, as a state like any other state.

Still the presence of Buber and Heschel haunt the Jewish landscape. Both assimilationist and exilic Jews ought to hear their voices as a call away from uncritical service to the state and to the necessity of articulating one's resistance in religious language. If Buber and Heschel wrote often of the message of Judaism and the prophets, what message is there to be spoken today? Certainly the hiddenness of the prophetic voice is once again in evidence and the bold prophetic speech to the identifiably religious is even more important today.

The difficulty is that both hiddenness and the proclaimed word are internal to the Jewish community and, at the same time, almost unrecognizable to the community itself. Neither Buber nor Heschel can be heard within Judaism today except to legitimate the present agenda. More often they are passed over as irrelevant. Even Jews who might hear their word and apply it now are either silenced or disciplined by the selective use of their words or the meaning they might carry in the contemporary world.

Such are the times in which we live. What Avnon, Kaplan, and Dresner have done is represent these prophetic figures to the Jewish community and the world. There will always be some Jews attentive to the spirit of these men, and Christians too. Perhaps the minority of Jews who can hear these words today simply mirrors the minority of Jews who could hear Buber and Heschel in their lifetime. And Buber and Heschel were minority figures, against the tide in the tragedy of the Holocaust and beyond. Perhaps without intending it, Avnon, Kaplan, and Dresner bring the most poignant of points home for Jews and Christians who encounter their volumes and the men they bring to life so vividly: that the time for thought and action, indeed the struggle to be faithful, is always contextual and dangerous. The legacy of that struggle is a fidelity to the past and the present embodied for a future that continues to unfold.

19

On Revolutionary Forgiveness: Practicing the Covenant in a Time of Colonization and Evangelization

A LITTLE MORE THAN A DECADE AGO IN IRELAND, I taught a week-length course on prospects for the development of a Jewish theology of liberation. On the second day, the subject of forgiveness was broached in an unexpected and almost violent manner. Having spent the first day lecturing on the Holocaust, I started the second day in like manner. A Catholic sister from California attending the course became angry with the subject at hand and, in reference to Adolf Hitler, blurted out the following: "You hate Hitler in your heart, don't you?" Her tone was almost bitter, as if my personal opinion or heart-feeling about Hitler overshadowed the Holocaust event itself.

Behind her words and tone lay a vast tradition. Christians were those who forgave their enemies; Jews were those whose hearts were hardened. And in their hardness of heart, Jews had crucified Jesus. This same hardness of heart lay at the root of the refusal of Jews to forgive those who persecuted and murdered them. I felt the violence behind her words, as if I were implicated in the crime of deicide. My refusal to forgive was equated with the horrible crimes of the Nazi era.

I was stunned into silence by the force of her words. Did I hate Hitler in my heart and, if so, was this itself a crime? Was her ability to forgive Hitler counterbalanced by her inability to forgive my feelings of distaste and condemnation? What struck me at that moment was that I actually had no feelings toward Hitler at all. When his name was mentioned or I spoke of him it was as if a vast emptiness enveloped me.

I stood silently in front of the class for what seemed like an eternity. Then I noticed another student, a Sudanese priest, rise. Being unable to respond myself, I waited anxiously to hear what he had to say. Recalling his own community's struggle with Sudanese of Islamic background, he offered the following comment as a defense of my position: "I refuse to forgive as well. If a Muslim comes into my village I will take a gun and blow his brains out."

The contrast was so startling as to provoke a further silence. A religious woman whose violence against the Jewish people is spoken of in an internal language of the heart is confronted by a priest whose imagery of violence is so blatant as to picture the brains of another person spilling at my feet. The assault and defense rendered me unable to continue the lecture. Excusing the class, I felt drained and at a loss. I felt like weeping.

That confrontation remains with me to this day and the image of forgiveness and murder presented by the sister and priest still resonates in a painful way. She, of course, had never experienced violence on a mass scale, nor had she inherited this suffering from her ancestors. He had experienced violence, perhaps would experience more in the days and years ahead, but seemed unable to offer an alternative path. As a Jew, I was caught in the middle, assaulted and defended without consultation and without probing. I could not endorse either position as stated, and felt distant from both.

Still, the issue of forgiveness continues to present itself in other fora, as I am asked often by Christians if it is not possible to forgive Hitler, the Nazis, the German people, and in a particular sense Christians themselves. Yet I am struck by a fated irony: the tradition of the sister who assaulted me and the priest who defended me helped to create the violence I am now called upon to forgive. A cycle of violence has enveloped Jews, one that we are now accused of or encouraged to continue.

The previous year I had embarked on two projects that related to this encounter in Ireland. The first was travel to Germany; the other to Israel. In Germany I spent time with Germans who were repenting their countries involvement in the Holocaust and the subsequent inability of their fellow citizens to come to terms with this historical event. In Israel I met Palestinians who suffer displacement and exile at the hands of Jewish Israelis who, often as not, use the Holocaust to justify their military and expansionist policies.

In Germany the theme was a repentance without a desire for forgiveness, for how, my hosts conjectured, is forgiveness possible when the Holocaust is buried by affluence and the desire to embark on a new history without guilt? Remarkably, the people I spent most of my time with in Germany are Christians themselves, part of the large and growing network of Pax Christi members who, with the end of the war, and after the mass slaughter of each other and the Jewish people, determined that a chastened and pacifist Europe was a necessity.

The Israeli-Palestinian conflict is an historical and continuing event. The Palestinians ask for justice and the Israelis, even those in the peace camp, are far from the desire to confess their transgressions. For the most part, and despite the agreements and even a Palestinian state, Jewish Israelis feel that their cause is justified and that the suffering of the Palestinian people is secondary to the struggle of Jews to find their place in community of nations. But in meeting Palestinians and journeying with them through checkpoints and under occupation over the years, the question of justice was tempered by the call for confession.[1]

Will Palestinians one day call on us as Jews to confess and will we one day ask them to forgive us? What will that confession and forgiveness look like and lead to? In one sense, the challenge of Israel is greater than the challenge of the Holocaust, because Jews and Palestinians face one another and thus there is still time. The Holocaust is alive only in memory and Germans have the added challenge of dealing with the memory of Jews who have been eliminated from their country. This transforms the most horrific crime into an abstraction that nonetheless gnaws at the heart of German history. In these two journeys I ask if confession, forgiveness, even reconciliation are possible without a living community at the very place of violation.

At the heart of an evolving Jewish theology of liberation stand these important issues: the Christian ethos that still pervades the West and indeed large areas of the globe; the wounds of the Holocaust, which remain open and unhealed; the division between Jews and Palestinians in the Middle East, which is both a response to the violence of Christianity and the Holocaust and a furtherance of violence against a people that have not been involved in the historic suffering of Jews.

A triangulation of history and contemporary life has evolved which, if it continues, threatens the healing of these histories—Christian, German, Jewish and Palestinian. Is there a way forward, and if so, can that way forward be found in the very confrontation that rendered me silent in Ireland? A Jewish theology of liberation, written during this time, could only begin to touch on these points, weaving together the seemingly disjointed histories of peoples and religions within the context of their historic and contemporary struggles.[2]

Surely we as Jews cannot move forward within the present impasse. Jewish empowerment, so necessary in light of the Holocaust, has not healed us as a people. When I visited the hospitals in Jerusalem in 1988, just months after the beginning of the Palestinian uprising and the policy of might and beatings instituted by then-Minister of Defense, Yitzhak Rabin, and saw the Palestinian children lying in beds from which they would not soon leave, some paralyzed for life, others brain- dead, existing on antiquated life-support equipment, the point was driven home. Instead of the healing and normalization of the Jewish condition, the force of Israel has deepened our wounds. In a paradoxical way, by externalizing our pain and inflicting it on another people, we have become more distant from the sources and resources of our own possible healing. By seeing power as the only way forward, by feeling that with power comes dignity and respect, by projecting power as the only line of defense against a further violation, another holocaust, that very power

is unraveling the tradition, culture, and religion that had itself been violated.

What the Nazis had not succeeded in accomplishing—the undermin-
ing at a fundamental level of the very essence of what it means to be
Jewish—we as Jews have begun. I witnessed this in the hospitals and in
the streets where Palestinians, struggling to assert their own dignity, were
being systematically beaten, expelled, and murdered by those who had
suffered this indignity less than fifty years earlier.

After Auschwitz and Nicaragua:
A Dialogue on Revolutionary Forgiveness

As I was thinking through this seeming conundrum, I came across a
book of feminist reflections on Nicaragua with the provocative title
Revolutionary Forgiveness. Read in light of the confrontation in Ireland,
my travel to Germany, and the witnessing of the Palestinian children, this
book had a strong impact on me.

As with my own writing on a Jewish theology of liberation,
Revolutionary Forgiveness is also part of a journey. Carter Heyward, an
Episcopal priest and professor at Episcopal Divinity School, with a group
of her seminary students, traveled to Nicaragua in the 1980s at the height
of the United States-financed war against the Nicaraguan government.
Expecting to find hatred against citizens from the country that was
financing this costly war and had produced so many casualties and hard-
ship, they found the opposite: a welcoming of those American citizens
who opposed their government's policies and who risked traveling to a
country in the midst of war. Instead of vilifying Heyward and her students, the Nicaraguans they met were open to those who confessed the
sins of the American governmental policy and sought a way beyond the
cycle of violence these policies furthered.

When forgiveness was sought by one of the students it became clear
that such forgiveness could only come within a commitment to justice.
"People cannot simply 'forgive'—invite back into their lives on a mutual
basis—those who continue to violate us," one student wrote, "otherwise
'forgiveness' is an empty word. Forgiveness is possible only when the violence stops. Only then can those who have been violated even consider
the possibility of actually loving those who once brutalized and battered
them. Only then can the former victims empower the victimizers by helping them to realize their own power to live as liberated liberators, people
able to see in themselves and others a corporate capacity to shape the
future." It is in the ending of injustice and the journey toward a mutual
and just future that forgiveness becomes revolutionary.[3]

This understanding of revolutionary forgiveness, though Christian in
inspiration, is also Jewish in its demand for justice. By placing forgiveness in motion, the static and superficial request—even demand by the
powerful—to be forgiven *without embarking on a new social and political*

project of inclusion and justice, is placed in perspective. In Heyward's sensibility forgiveness is less the end of the matter than it is a process of conversion to a future different from the past.

Being in right relation allows a forgiveness that is not devoid of memory. Rather, memory of past injustice becomes a shared memory of victim and victimizer. This memory, coupled with the desire to create a society beyond injustice, allows a new societal foundation to evolve. In revolutionary forgiveness, a new freedom is found, a freedom that also evolves over time into a new social and political identity. No longer victim and victimizer, both parties are freed to become whom God calls us to be.

Thus, a personal transformation is accomplished as well. In the movement toward justice, persons are freed from having to assume the role of victim and victimizer, a role that cuts to the heart of human dignity and potential. Beyond the cycle of violence is the embrace of the human, flawed and finite to be sure, but flourishing in a social and political order where right relation is struggled for and attained.

Revolutionary forgiveness is far from the teachings of Richard Rubenstein, a mentor of mine and one of the first Holocaust theologians. Thinking through the aftermath of the Holocaust in the 1960s, Rubenstein writes of the end of the Jewish tradition of belief in a God of history. Simply though powerfully articulated, the Jewish covenant has been abrogated by God who either through neglect or weakness forsake the Jews of Europe.

For Rubenstein it is not so much the existence of God, but the kind of God one can posit after Auschwitz. If God exists, where was God in the Holocaust? If God is all-powerful, an essential belief in Jewish history, why did God refuse to act? If God is not all-powerful, if God is unable to rescue a suffering people, why worship such a God? As for the traditional Jewish belief that suffering is punishment for neglecting Jewish law and God's teachings, who can hold fast to a God who reckons such disproportionate suffering from the people God chose and promised to protect? Were those millions who perished in the Holocaust guilty of a crime? If so, did the punishment hardly fit the crime?

Rubenstein's response to the Holocaust is disbelief, a defiant agnosticism or atheism, if you will, that is a refusal to believe in the God of Jewish history, and this disbelief has social and political ramifications. If God is not to be relied on, who is? The solidarity of God with the Jewish people has been irrevocably broken. On the human level, solidarity is also deeply questioned, for if God was absent from the Jewish people during the Holocaust where was humanity?

Thus both the solidarity of God *and* humanity cannot be relied on and only power, the power to protect and punish, can be efficacious in our world. Theories of the righteousness of God and the goodness of humanity—the prospect for revolutionary forgiveness—for Rubenstein are blinders to the reality of the world. After Auschwitz we know better. Those with power flourish and those without power are condemned to the margins of society, segregated into ghettos, and sometimes threatened with annihilation.[4]

Listening to Rubenstein, first as a college student, later in discussions at conferences on the Holocaust and, in 1992, at Auschwitz itself as part of a delegation on the future of the Auschwitz camp site, I experienced almost a mirror image of the Catholic sister and Sudanese priest I encountered in Ireland. After Auschwitz, internal and external violence has merged into a protective shield that allows little room for exploration. Views of the world outside of power are relegated to the periphery, as if to entertain these views is a form of violence itself, *as if contemplation of a world journeying toward revolutionary forgiveness can only lead to another Auschwitz.*

The views of the Catholic sister conjure up the world of Catholic and Christian piety, often experienced by Jews as a form of violence, and the need of the Sudanese priest to defend through murder the integrity of his people provokes the memories of a world collapsing around the Jews of Europe. On the one side is a forgiveness that can only come from an internal violence against the Jewish people; on the other, a struggle that starkly places the future of a people at risk.

For Rubenstein, after Auschwitz only the organization of an empowered state can shield Jews from both risks. It is only in the power of the state, a power used to exclude the Jews of Europe, that Jews can protect themselves. Instead of revolutionary forgiveness, a forgiveness that raises the question of solidarity and God in right relation and justice, Rubenstein feels compelled, despite the risks, to choose the power of the state. The struggle for power is all and the winners take all: Jews and Jewish leadership, indeed the leadership of any community, has the responsibility never to lose again.

Forgiveness and Promise:
The New Beginnings of Hannah Arendt

In *After Auschwitz,* but even more so in *The Cunning of History,* Rubenstein cites the writings of Hannah Arendt. Arendt's sweeping survey of contemporary European history and the crisis of values and traditions she finds there, are crucial to Rubenstein's political argument and conclusion. The whole of Western civilization has come "toppling over our heads" Arendt writes in *The Origins of Totalitanisnism,* and the lesson of our century is that those on the margins of society are declared superfluous and condemned. Rubenstein takes these themes and expands upon them; as a theologian, he also explores the culpability of theology and God. But the social and moral reconstruction that Arendt envisions in *Origins* and pursues in her later work is absent from Rubenstein's analysis.

It is almost as if Rubenstein is stuck in the absence of God and solidarity. With this absence the cycle of power can only continue on its foreordained path. While Arendt, herself a refugee from Europe, analyzes the horror and then embarks on a reconstruction of the values so violated in the Holocaust, Rubenstein is not so inclined. Perhaps Arendt could not afford the break that Rubenstein sees as so definitive. As a refugee rather than an American analyzing the effects of the Holocaust, Arendt had to construct a world for herself in another place.[5]

It is not surprising that the possibility of forgiveness is present in Arendt's work, though it is only peripherally connected to the question of God. Arendt rarely writes about God, for her main theme is a social and philosophical reconstruction of a world where the death camps are still visible and the cold war is in full bloom. Even her discussion of Jesus of Nazareth as the "discoverer of forgiveness in the realm of human affairs" is couched in non-religious language. Arendt's view is that too many contributions from religious thinkers and actors have been lost to contemporary public discourse because of their religious nature. Her point, especially on the question of forgiveness, is that the contribution itself, even when shorn of its specific religious nature, can assist in the reconstruction of the public realm after the catastrophe of the Nazi era.[6]

What does Arendt mean by forgiveness? What role can it play in personal and public affairs? To begin with, forgiveness is linked with promise, and both are seen in the context of the ability to create and secure a stable public realm. Both forgiveness and promise, while often thought to be in the private realm, are, for Arendt, also public in nature.

Here the concept of respect rather than love is the currency, and the private realm where love may indeed suffice is transcended. For Arendt, respect is defined by the Aristotelian *philia politike,* a friendship without intimacy and without closeness, "a regard for the person from the distance which the space of the world puts between us, and this respect is independent of qualities which we may admire or of achievements which we may highly esteem." Love, often thought of in regard to the Christian aspect of forgiveness, is, when transported into the public realm, dangerous. "Love, by its very nature, is unworldly," Arendt writes, "and it is for this reason rather than its rarity that it is not only apolitical but antipolitical, perhaps the most powerful of all antipolitical human forces."[7]

If forgiveness is public because of the distance it allows so persons may function in the public realm, promise is also public in nature because it creates the possibility of meaning and stability in a world where neither is self-evident. The unpredictability of human affairs and the unreliability of human beings necessitate a "promise" into which "certain islands of predictability are thrown and into which certain guideposts of reliability are erected." Forgiveness and promise come together because without either the dynamic of finitude and the search for meaning and coherence collapses. Though both forgiveness and promise are never assured, both are necessary if we are not to become lost in violation or in uncertainty.

To create order means to allow people and institutions to transcend their natural tendency toward inwardness and selfishness. This is an ongoing process of trial and error, for action in the world is unpredictable. Only through a willingness to risk, to promise, can a future be envisioned; but only with a willingness to forgive can the risk, stymied by error, be taken again. Since trespassing is an everyday occurrence and is directly related to the establishment of new relations within a broader web—Arendt's definition of the constantly evolving public realm—trespassing "needs forgiving, dismissing, in order to make it possible for life to go on by constantly releasing men from what they have done unknowingly." For Arendt the role of punishment can be seen together with this dynamic of forgiveness and promise, as the act within the public realm that reminds the person and the community of the frailty of the human enterprise and the ability, once the punishment has been carried out, of the person to reenter the process that sustains life.[8]

Forgiveness and promise interact in Arendt's system of thought as a way of responding to and insuring the essence of human activity. All acts are themselves beginnings, and the way those acts interact with other acts are, in their unpredictability, also beginnings. Our acts soon have a life of their own or, better stated, assume a different life as they intersect with other acts.

Chains of action and speech evolve, and since both determine identities, identities are always evolving. Identities are therefore constantly being formed and unformed. That is why the interaction of these three elements is so crucial. Adi Ophir, a Jewish Israeli historian and philosopher, explains the dynamic of Arendt's understanding: "The one who forgets cannot forgive, but the one who forgives (or is forgiven) is free to forget; forgiveness unties. Similarly, he who fulfills promises is free to let his memory loose and untie the knot that promise creates. Before forgiveness, or before the fulfillment of a promise, forgetfulness acts like a virus in the network: it prevents the untying of old entanglement and loosens ties necessary for successful coordination and cooperation among actors. After forgiveness has been granted or a promise fulfilled, it is memory that becomes the virus: it infects the network with unnecessary ties that block new beginnings; it distorts identities; and it increases the burden that the past and the others who represent it exert on unforgetful actors."

Arendt's view of forgiveness, promise, and new beginnings coincides with her view of the structural elements of human action and the public realm in which it occurs. Ophir describes Arendt's vision in this way: "Plurality, new beginnings, open-endedness, uncertainty, the weaving and unweaving of flexible, loosely structured networks of interrelations embodied in the spaces of mutual visibility, in which identities are never fixed, and no pre-established teleology resides."[9]

A New Saving Alliance:
Crossing the Boundaries of the Religious and Secular

This question of forgiveness haunts the contemporary world, as does promise, the twin complex that Arendt believes makes possible new beginnings in a fragile, humanly constructed and meaningful world. Throughout her work, the limitations of life are stressed; teleologies when brought into the public realm signal totalitarianism. Instead, Arendt stresses plurality, interrelation, visibility. New beginnings mean that the old is neither to be swept away nor preserved, and traditions are constantly being remade even as they are being proclaimed as eternal. Her watchword is a freedom born of commitment and restraint. Memory, like commitment, evolves.

The anchor of memory, especially the memory of violation and suffering, is waiting to be brought into a new relation with the wider public realm. Only by releasing one's hold on this memory, by forgiving through accepting a new promise, can one's horizons open again. The freezing of memory, the inability to forgive and accept a new promise (as one is forgiven and welcomed back into the arena of promise as well) betrays the very structure of social existence. But even more important it betrays the promise of life, for without forgiveness and promise there is no future.

At the same time, it is clear that Arendt believes that certain acts cast one outside of this structure and therefore make one unfit to participate in the public realm. Eichmann, one of the masterminds of the Final Solution, is one such person. Arendt believed that through his actions he disassociated himself from the rest of humanity. As Ophir points out, for Arendt there is a point beyond which forgiveness is impossible, "for *what* one *does* destroys whatever is left of the respect for *who* one is." Here we encounter radical evil, an evil that can only be fought with violence. This struggle with radical evil, especially as routinized and legalized in the modern state, has to be systematically opposed *as a crime against humanity and the future.* Thus by inference the memory of radical evil against individuals and communities cannot define the possibility of life experience. Radical evil takes place within the world but is also outside the world of discourse and action that can support meaning and life.

To define the future by the radical evil experienced in the past is to delimit the possibility of new beginnings; it is to bury the possibility of forgiveness and promise that unleashes that which is static and old. The way out of these memories is not to forgive the perpetrator or to dwell on him. Rather it is the acceptance that life is more than radical evil and those within the public realm can, through struggle and compromise, create a future beyond that evil.[10]

Here Arendt and Carter Heyward join their respective analyses. A new beginning is possible if the promise—to enter into the public realm with a sense of mutuality and justice—is authentic. Though there are no guarantees in the future, the ability to move forward, to transpose the memory of injustice into a call to freedom, is dependent on a commitment to move beyond past violation and crime. When the crime has removed the individual or community from the ability to participate in the public realm, then others must be found who will carry on. Even in the darkest hour there are those who refuse injustice or repent of past injustice. Those who are violated must also recognize the possibility of a new beginning in those former persecutors.

To break the cycle of violation and memory, forgiveness and promise must be engaged by both parties. Risk is inherent, of course, and there are no guarantees that a new configuration that seeks to dominate the same or other individuals or communities will not arise in the future. And as Ophir points out in relation to Jews in Israel, his analysis of Arendt has contemporary significance. Citing Arendt's life-long fight against totalitarianism and the presence of totalitarian elements in contemporary life, Ophir quotes Arendt and then follows with his own provocative comment: "'Totalitarian solutions may well survive the fall of totalitarian regimes. . . .' Indeed, they have survived, even in the State of the survivors."[11]

Thus revolutionary forgiveness, found in right-relation and the commitment to justice, with memory and promise joined in a dynamic that allows new beginnings, is always haunted by reversion to injustice, by abrogated promise, by a memory that refuses to risk. So revolutionary forgiveness is always provisional, prone to movement in unanticipated directions, hopeful, risky, challenging identities and theologies so often thought to be unchanging.

Forgiveness is revolutionary in that it allows new beginnings, but in its constantly evolving status it refuses the totalitarian impulse, or rather is constantly in battle with that impulse even when it arises from the former victims. New beginnings are shadowed by totalitarian fragments and solutions that survive the end of one configuration of totalitarian rule.

What does this analysis have to do with the question of faith and faith communities? Is revolutionary forgiveness possible with faith or without it? Can forgiveness take place, can promise take hold in secular or religious communities? Are new beginnings illustrative of faith or in contradiction to it? Do particular secular or religious communities lend themselves more readily to forgiveness and promise, to open teleologies and new identities? Do others lead away from these possibilities? Surely those mentioned and analyzed from the Christian community—the Catholic sister, the Sudanese priest, and Carter Heyward—and from the Jewish community—Richard Rubenstein, Hannah Arendt, and Adi Ophir— are diverse in their understandings, beliefs, and directions. They also cross boundaries.

Could it be, in this instance, that it is the religious Christian, Carter Heyward, and the secular Jew, Hannah Arendt, who help us see the possibility of a forgiveness that leads to justice? Is it simply coincidence that perhaps the most haunting statement of religious reconciliation in the post-Holocaust era has been made by Johannes Baptist Metz, a German Catholic theologian heavily influenced by the Frankfurt School of Jewish secular thinkers? Metz writes the following of a new beginning of Christianity: "We Christians can never go back behind Auschwitz; to go beyond Auschwitz is impossible for us by ourselves. It is possible only together with the victims of Auschwitz."[12]

Metz names this a "saving alliance" and refers back to the origins of the Christian community when both Jews and Christians were "outside" the Roman imperium. But what can be said today when so often Jews and Christians are "within" the imperium? Is it possible that those Jews and Christians who affirm their religious faith and those who are secular in their orientation are often divided, some outside and others within the new imperiums?

Surely religious identification—Jew, Christian, or for that matter, secular, agnostic, or atheist—does not tell us where individuals place themselves with regard to revolutionary forgiveness. As Ophir correctly points out, totalitarian solutions can survive among the survivors and violence as I experienced it in Ireland can be expressed by those who see forgiveness as the center of their faith. Theologians like Rubenstein can deny the possibilities of new beginnings while Arendt, as a secular philosopher, can place it at the center of her philosophy.

Often as not these boundary crossings are seen as fascinating engagements or contradictions; they are explored for a while and then forgotten. The lines of Jew and Christian, secular and religious, are then redrawn incorporating these insights *as their sources and significance disappear or are rendered invisible.* For Christians these influences become invisible when, for example, a theology of the cross is explicated. Jews are guilty of the same offense when Jewish particularity is asserted.

Who remembers the tremendous influence of Reinhold Niebuhr on Will Herberg, Abraham Joshua Heschel, and Irving Greenberg, or the influence of Karl Barth on Michael Wyschogrod? The separation of religious and secular is equally as interesting, for the theologies of liberation and renewal are significantly affected by secular thought and justice movements. One thinks here of the influence of Marxism on the initial writings of Peruvian liberation theologian Gustavo Gutierrez, the Black Power movement on the African-American liberation theologian James Cone, and the civil rights struggle on leaders of Jewish renewal such as Arthur Waskow and Michael Lerner.

Does the interdependence of religious and secular thought and the interpenetration of Jewish and Christian theology ask of us a new articulation of what it means to be created, to be human, to forgive and to promise, in short to engage in revolutionary forgiveness? Does, then, the crossing of boundaries raise the question of God?

Thomas Merton and the Covenant
in an Age of Colonization and Evangelization

On his journey to Asia, just months before his death, Thomas Merton wrote in his diaries quotes from two Asian mystics. The first was from Milapera, an eleventh century Tibetan yogi: "It is the tradition of the fortunate seekers never to be content with partial practice." The second combined his own reflection with one from the Astavakra Gita: "Song sparrows everywhere in the twisted trees—'neither accept nor reject anything.'" Merton had reached a place in life where he was so deeply rooted in his faith that the doctrines and dogmas of Catholicism were simply there: his struggles with censorship, his ability to speak on social and political questions, the changes in the church and even his own vocation as a monk, became background to an openness without fear. Instead of filtering ideas, propositions, and actions through his own situation—certainly a major preoccupation in his diaries—Merton allowed his own practice to deepen to a place without boundaries. On his Asian journey, he tried to absorb the great wisdom he encountered without judgment and without comparison with his own Christianity. Strongly rooted in his Christianity, Merton sought an accelerated spiritual practice with what would became his mantra: "neither accept nor reject anything." Longing to leave behind "partial practice," Merton embarked on his last and fateful journey.[13]

Speculation about Merton's final days, and even more so the future he would choose had he lived, has continued over the years. Was Merton leaving his Christianity behind? Upon return from Asia, would Merton have left the monastery, the priesthood, even the Catholic church? Had Christianity itself become too confining for a monk-mystic who was no longer content with partial practice? His political interventions over the years—atomic weaponry, the civil rights movement, freedom of conscience and speech, his stand against the Vietnam War—could these be continued and deepened within the folds of the monastic and Christian life?

In another sense, however, Merton's journey mirrored the journey of many Christians and, in some ways, Jews as well. Through his voluminous correspondence and writings it is clear that Merton had grappled with Christianity to the point where there was little left to mine. To move forward, to proceed to a deeper level, to approach God beyond the God he had found and embraced, Merton continually crossed religious, political, cultural, and geographic boundaries. Most of this crossing took place within the confines of the monastery, but there was a need to move into the world on a physical basis.

Merton's journey to Asia is significant in many areas, but his physical engagement speaks wonders to the future of religious life: engagement had to be physical as well as spiritual, touch as well as theology. His engagement with Hinduism and Buddhism began with an inquiry into their religious and metaphysical understandings but ended with the absorption of their wisdom in face-to-face encounters with those who embodied these teachings in the cities and countryside where the religion and spiritualities took hold and evolved.

Still, within Merton's search was a reality as important as his particular religiosity and journey. Merton's journey is also relevant in the context of anthropologist Clodomiro Siller's reference to the evolving spirituality of native peoples in confrontation with the powerful political, economic, and religious forces of their day. Siller describes the type of Christianity that evolved among native peoples in Mexico as the "indigenous comprehension of their own living religious tradition in new circumstances of colonization and evangelization." When analyzing peasants in the countryside of Mexico, the hybrid Christianity that has evolved since the arrival of Europeans and European Christianity is easy to understand, but was Merton doing the same thing as a sophisticated and learned monk? The colonization and evangelization of the *conquistadores* is obvious, but could Merton have been struggling with the colonization and evangelization of the most powerful religion of our time, modernity, a religion which has created new empires?[14]

Merton's entry into the monastery was preceded by a conversion from a Protestant agnosticism to a fortress Catholicism; his promise of fidelity was occasioned by an overwhelming need for forgiveness. One cannot escape the sense of covenantal embrace in Merton's original commitment to the monastic life. But if Merton's ongoing journey is characterized by one overall theme, it is the continuous expansion of that embrace. In his refusal of a partial practice, in his movement to the place where he neither accepted nor rejected anything, Merton expanded the Catholic tradition, even Christianity itself, to a broader tradition of faith and struggle, where all those struggling for justice and peace were counted, drawn upon, and included. Merton raises the question of whether there can be revolutionary forgiveness in the most inclusive sense of the term without embracing this broader tradition of faith and struggle.

Though many theologians believe that fidelity to their own traditions can only be accomplished by converting the culture or by standing against it, Merton exemplifies a journey of an initial withdrawal from and then an embrace of the world. This embrace, however, was within the context of the "colonization and evangelization" of modernity, imbedded in certain forms of Christianity and Americanism. Thus, Merton's understanding of the religious task is to pursue commitment, fidelity, and God wherever they can be found in contemporary life. From his hermitage, through prayer, correspondence, and writing, and then finally through travel, Merton tried to embrace all those through history and in the present who struggled to define an elusive covenant that nevertheless could be found.

How did Merton define that covenant? In the first years of his monastic experience, he knew quite well its contours; a traditional Christianity defined by ritual, place, and continuity. By the end of his life the contours of the covenant had expanded considerably. Had they been relativized in this interval? Had Merton moved away from a well-defined Christianity to a relativized religious experience?

The thrust of Merton's later years seems to be a recognition that the task of Christianity, indeed the challenge of faith, had shifted precipitously. *The task of Christianity, of faith itself, became for Merton the crossing of boundaries in search of a covenantal promise within the new circumstances of colonization and evangelization.* The world in which he made his youthful promise no longer existed, and yet the promise continued in new circumstances. Likewise shifting was his initial choice to sequester himself against the world. Merton's final commitment was to move deeper within the world to find the broader tradition of faith and struggle, a tradition that could bring him with others to a new place of covenantal fidelity.

Practicing Revolutionary Forgiveness

The temptation is to continue on point counterpoint, expanding the circle, lengthening the linear years of struggle and fidelity. One could add here Abraham Joshua Heschel, the late Jewish theologian and philosopher, with his understanding of the Sabbath and the prophets, his sense of radical amazement *after Auschwitz.*

Emil Fackenheim, the German, Canadian, and now Israeli philosopher comes to mind as well, especially his *tikkun* of ordinary decency. For Fackenheim, the diabolical actions of the Nazis cause an ontological rupture that is a *novum* in human history but acts of ordinary decency during the Holocaust—giving food and shelter to a hungry pursued Jew, coming to the aid of a Jew who was being beaten, speaking the truth to the Nazis in public—all testify to the possibility of healing the universe. Fackenheim sees the righteous gentile in this philosophical category repairing a universe torn by evil.

In Fackenheim we hear Metz's "saving alliance" and Heyward's "revolutionary forgiveness," or do we hear Fackenheim's voice in Metz's work? Can either now be seen alone without the other, as if Jews and Christians in the West have not themselves embarked on a largely successful, and from the standpoint of the difficult history of Jews and Christianity, a remarkable program of revolutionary forgiveness?

Elie Wiesel, the Holocaust survivor and Nobel laureate, who writes so movingly in his autobiographical *Night* of the Jewish plight in the Holocaust and the difficult questions of God which he, with other Jews, faced, buried his quarrel with God on the fiftieth anniversary of the liberation of Auschwitz. Can the time be so long before Jews as a people combine the prophetic impulse of Heschel with Fackenheim's *tikkun* of ordinary decency and Wiesel's narrative power to engage with the Palestinian people? Will then the dynamic of forgiveness and promise, the possibility of new beginnings outlined by Hannah Arendt be cited or simply appropriated in the movement toward justice and reconciliation?[15]

One thing is certain: there can be no revolutionary forgiveness that is insular, protective, closed in on itself or, at least in our time, fashioned within one community. The boundary crossing that is necessary for revolutionary forgiveness is constitutive of forgiveness itself, for how can one be forgiven and how can one forgive without moving outside and beyond ourselves and our community? Even the process of personal and communal healing is a going out and a witness to others; it is reinforced or made more difficult by its reception by communities ostensibly outside the process.

In the very crossing of boundaries, without which forgiveness is static, even, as in the case of the sister in Ireland, a form of violence, the covenantal promise is itself found and embraced. Revolutionary forgiveness is on the move, always on the verge of collapse and in need of constant support, shifting in alliances and solidarity, with promises once made broken and other broken promises being reformed. If God is found in and is an aid to the movement toward revolutionary forgiveness, or at least the hope of such forgiveness when there seems to be no hope, then God and the covenant are constantly on the move as well, always before us, calling us to continue on.

Can God be embraced in this search for revolutionary forgiveness across borders and in the realization that no community owns God, even those that claim chosenness, whether described as the old or new covenants? The broader tradition of faith and struggle informs us that God is where God wants and needs to be, here and there, in the wind and spirit, in the very breath of life and movement, as the ancient Hebrews understood it.

If the sister and the Sudanese priest I encountered in Ireland rendered me speechless, it is not that I am without speech. Rather it is because through their speech and imagery they invoked a God that has been claimed and owned and desecrated for so long that the likes of Hannah Arendt could introduce Jesus of Nazareth as the bearer of forgiveness in the public realm but only if shorn of his religious implications. This religious Jew who, in his actions, bore a revolutionary forgiveness that crystallized parts of the Jewish tradition and gave birth to a religion that hoped to carry forth that impulse, becomes the pivotal point of a great Jewish philosopher in the twentieth century, who can see Jesus only as a Christian whose contribution must be seen without the covenant and God. The irony is profound and tragic, and yet if we see Jesus in a similar situation to the one we are in today, then the distance and the tragedy may be somewhat abated.

For one way of seeing Jesus is as a Jew, with other Jews who followed him, seeking an "indigenous comprehension of their own living religious tradition in new circumstances of colonization and evangelization." This follows John Dominic Crossan's understanding of Jesus as living within and confronting Roman commercialization and Herodian urbanization, Greek cultural internationalism, and Roman military imperialism. Crossan describes the mission of Jesus as embodying the "'new world' of the Jewish God incarnated as human justice opposing the pagan God incarnated as Roman imperialism."

At this level, is this so different from what we are called to be and do? It seems that Jesus was a Jew not content with partial practice and that he embodied, at the deepest level, Merton's final mantra—"neither accept nor reject anything." But he did so, like some before and after him, by crossing the boundaries into a revolutionary forgiveness that deepened his embrace of the covenant and the freedom that this embrace bequeaths, even as it led him, as it has so many others, to an untimely and tragic death.[16]

For us, of course, the question is life rather than death. Partial practice reflects the fear that on the other side of creedal affirmation lies an abyss; ritual and pious affirmation become a form of protection against the unknown. In partial practice, crossing boundaries is seen as a threat to one's identity, as if the movement to the "other"—who in that movement may no longer be "other"—threatens to dissolve one's rootedness and commitment.

But what if enlarging the terrain of embrace, both internally and externally, is the movement beyond partial practice? What if it was exactly this movement in the life of the Jewish Jesus and those who accompanied him that made his life so momentous? The practice of revolutionary forgiveness refuses partial practice because the entirety of faith and life is placed in motion *as a movement of the heart, mind, and body toward the "other," especially the suffering, without reserve and in deep humility.*

The physicality of revolutionary forgiveness is, at the same time, a spirituality, for how can a person, let alone a community, move within and outside itself without earthly *and* divine assistance? Here the moral gap, the gap between our desire and ability to lead a moral life, and bridged, according to John E. Hare, through divine assistance, is itself assisted by the experience of embracing the "other" who has harmed or been harmed by persons or a community.[17]

The experience of Jesus seems to point in this direction. Was he not touched and changed by his own practice as others were transformed by him? Seen in this way, the practice of Jesus, the discipline found inside and outside the canonical gospels, is a practice on the move. Rather than deriding or denying his Jewishness or the tradition he inherited, Jesus found the practice of contemporary Judaism partial. The error of the generations that followed him was, on the Jewish side, to mistakenly believe this fuller practice to be outside Judaism and, on the Christian side, to see this fuller practice as a new covenant that could only be seen in opposition to the very covenant Jesus embraced.

Yet in the broader tradition of faith and struggle, Jesus should be seen as embracing a practice that comes within Judaism and exists outside it as well, because, as Thomas Merton realized almost two thousand years later, *the refusal of partial practice is itself a fidelity that moves within and beyond any particular tradition or community.* Even the beginning of this fidelity, and in our limitations and finitude, we experience a freedom that is found in the ancient scriptures and recorded (and unrecorded) lives that have gone before us.

One thinks here of Etty Hillesum, the Dutch Jew who, in Weterbork and on her way to Auschwitz, wrote of and lived the birth of a new world beyond suffering and oppression, and of Archbishop Oscar Romero of El Salvador, who spoke out against the repression of his people and died for that witness. Is their refusal of partial practice separated by historical divisions of creedal affirmation or joined by their practice unto death? Are they separated from Jesus by his divinity or joined with him in a communion of saints and prophets who have struggled to be faithful in their own time? Both Hillesum and Romero enlarged the terrain of their embrace by practicing revolutionary forgiveness and, in that process, enlarged our terrain of embrace as well.

Practice, Tradition, and the Covenant

Perhaps it is possible to define fidelity in this way, *as the constant practice of revolutionary forgiveness which focuses our lives and the lives of others on the deepest calling of material and spiritual reality.* Only in this way can we approach the covenant as it appears in our time, as it is in every generation, in a physical and spiritual dynamic that moves inwardly and outwardly. As revolutionary forgiveness is a process and its practice a dynamic that continually leads us to unexpected and difficult places—birthing new beginnings—so too the covenant. *The covenant itself, far from being ancient, is itself a birthing, an exploration, a territory that, though experienced in every generation, is always new.*

By creating a canon and preserving it, the ever-new is seen to be ancient and the experiences of the prophets and Jesus, for example, are distinguished and privileged. In their canonized version, they become models, unfortunately and too often seen as the experience of embracing the covenant done by them for us. As covenantal models, they may thus remove the risk for us that they themselves experienced. Having embraced the covenant to its fullest in their testimony of word and action, and with the consequent experience of exile and death, our remembrance of their experience rendered liturgically, can be cause for passivity and sometimes arrogance.

Are we not the inheritors of Sinai and Jesus, God's chosenness and sacrifice, that we are justified by and through? The events of Sinai and Jesus, representing the enlarging of the terrain of embrace, thus shrinks, at least for those persons and communities who enter into these events as observers. New beginnings become codified and relegated to a transcendental sphere where security replaces danger and the unknown becomes the always known. The religious calendar, so dramatically and sometimes beautifully rendered, is mistaken for the religious journey itself, as if Sinai and Jesus were possible without the expansion and often violation of the religious calendar of the time in which these events took place.

Of course, the religious calendar can itself be a prompting beyond itself, forcing us to consider avenues of action, of border crossing, of an embrace that is revolutionary in its forgiveness and promise, by informing us of those who refused partial practice in the past. By preserving, canonizing, and liturgizing these personalities and events we can gain insight into the calling of our own time. But when those who overcame their own tradition's contemporary partial practice are presented in a fragmented and exclusive way—that is, within only the tradition that evolved from that experience or person—then partial practice is again enshrined even when the rhetoric is to the contrary.

Jews and Christians tend toward this syllogism only too often by portraying Sinai and Jesus as dramatic breakthroughs with no antecedents or precedent. In fact they crystalized and focused elements of their own time by refusing segmentation and separation, by refusing the canon they were presented with and by refusing to mistake partial practice for the practice requisite to their time. Tradition here was respected and incorporated in a movement that completed and subverted it, birthing new possibilities that were seen as so threatening as to force a people to flee a country and a righteous Jew to be executed.

Tradition, then, preserves narratives of radical embrace and dissent *and* domesticates these same narratives, allowing the congregation to gather to listen to scripture and participate in its ritualization. The latter is important if it recalls for us our own possibility and obligation to transcend partial practice, or better stated, allows us to carry our partial practice into another dimension of practice with others struggling in the same direction.

Here the Jewish ritual of taking the scrolls from the Ark and parading them through the standing congregation—with each congregant touching the covered scroll with a prayer book or talus—presents the paradox of tradition in stark relief. One is either awed and subdued by the Torah in front of you or galvanized to contribute to the continual unfolding of Torah in our time. The prophetic is either recorded, read, and consigned to ancient times or raised up as a challenge. To recall the ancient prophets as impetus for today is worthy of a tradition that is unfolding and turned outward to the need to cross new boundaries. However, tradition usually functions as a caution against our own action, especially actions that subvert the preaching and teaching of tradition as a closed system.

The challenge here was understood by Walter Benjamin, the German Jewish literary critic and philosopher who committed suicide during the Nazi period. Benjamin was neither a believer nor an atheist but a person on the edge of both affirmations, in-between and over the boundaries of traditional belief and modern belief, and critical of both. For Benjamin, tradition carried with it two aspects: on the one hand, divine sparks that call forth the messianic; on the other hand, a conformism to unjust power.

To embrace tradition as it is presented is to tend toward the latter, for Benjamin a temptation and permanent danger. To allow the fragmentation of tradition to speak to us is to glimpse the divine sparks that are understood in the dual movement toward the past and future. Fragmentation allows the past to be seen within the image of "enslaved ancestors" and the future to be open to the revolution of an ongoing reconciliation, i.e., a dynamic of revolutionary forgiveness, though Benjamin does not use this term. The messianic sparks emerge from the refusal to conform even to the power that emanates from the revolution, which also has a tendency to conformity and power. Theologians and philosophers as well have the task of identifying the messianic sparks and fanning their flame so as to prevent a premature coalescence and certainty.

For good reason the covenant is rarely mentioned by Benjamin, for he frees the power of the tradition precisely by refusing its religious language, and thus the dynamic of the messianic in its physicality and spirituality is restored. Or perhaps better stated, this dynamic is reasserted in its plurality and open-endedness, becoming reinvigorated, experiencing another new beginning.

As importantly, Benjamin does not see the locus of the messianic within any one community or shared among communities. It is almost as if the messianic, in its confrontation with the angel of death—and here Benjamin raises the poignant Klee painting of that title to a symbolic height—is to be found wherever it appears in the struggle for visibility and survival. Without a predetermined site of appearance or known avenue of embrace, the covenant, in a sense, is always escaping the desire of tradition to define it and conform it to expectation and power.

Perhaps Benjamin's suicide can be seen in this light, as the Nazi era embodied a conformism to power that destroyed the messianic sparks of renewal or rendered them useless in the battle against totalitarianism. Benjamin's suicide can be seen as a rejection of his friend Hannah Arendt's sense that beginnings, through forgiveness and promise, arrive during and after a darkness that seemingly consumes everything.

And yet Benjamin's writing on a philosophy of history, written in the late 1930s and discovered after the war, is itself a new beginning. It can now be seen as part of an evolving matrix that refuses partial practice and the traditions that define practice as full despite its partiality. This inversion disallows overt religious language and category unless used in opposition to the very tradition that claims it. The very naming of this practice remains in tension with the tradition itself.

It is almost as if Benjamin refuses to name the very struggle with tradition and God he embarks on because of the misuse of both and the dangers to conformity he seeks to avoid. Over time, however, if the inability to name the struggle becomes a tradition itself—*with its own tendency to conform to power*—then the radical edge is blunted even as it is asserted. The very connection of physicality and spirituality that Benjamin sought to reconnect in the Nazi years can become a partial practice itself, a tradition of post-modernity that develops its own liturgies and rituals to protect itself from the critique that it enshrines as gospel.

20

Toward a Prophetic Memory of the Holocaust: A Meditation on *We Remember: A Reflection on the Shoah*

THE VATICAN DOCUMENT *We Remember: A Reflection on the Shoah*, written by the Commission for Religious Relations with the Jews and accompanied by a short introduction by Pope John Paul II, was released in March 1998. Coming as it did just two years before the third millennium of Christianity and toward the closure of John Paul II's pontificate, the document was highly anticipated. As it turns out, it was also highly controversial. Few commentators, Catholic or Jewish, found the document satisfying, and the praise was, for the most part, limited to the understanding that the issues of anti-Semitism and the Holocaust raised in the document would require further study. Reverend Richard McBrien, a professor of theology at the University of Notre Dame, summed up many of the feelings toward the document when he commented, "Even if you analyze it rhetorically the language is very, very cautious, very restrained, very diplomatic." McBrien holds out the hope that the pope himself will at some point "write a much stronger, heartfelt statement than this commission did."

The present document notwithstanding, the history of relations between Jews and Catholics before and after the Holocaust has been strained, even to the point of violence. Though the violence was in turns sporadic and concentrated, occurring before and during the Holocaust, and reflecting the dominance of the Catholic church and Christianity in Europe, the strain after the Holocaust, even within a process of reconciliation, remains. An understandable and residual anger of Jews toward the Catholic church flourishes even as relations between Jews and Catholics on the individual, local, and regional levels appear cordial and increasingly intimate. Jews and Jewish leadership seem to harbor a resentment toward the Catholic church that inexplicably increases as letters and statements from the Vatican over the years map out a theological terrain of rapprochement and reconciliation.

Paradoxically, the more the Vatican addresses the historic relations with the Jewish people, the higher becomes the degree of disgruntlement. Referring to *We Remember*, Eugene Fisher, director of Catholic-Jewish Relations at the United States Catholic Conference, remarks that the document was intended to foster a "reconciliation of memory" and "spark some discussion." That discussion will be historical—with "massive data to be worked through, that should be worked through together"—but one wonders if Fisher is correct. Is the problem historical in nature, a matter of researching and judging the "facts" of Catholic anti-Semitism and the complicity of Catholics and the hierarchy in violence against Jews, culminating in the Holocaust? Is the memory that both Jews and Catholics invoke, explore, agree and disagree on, primarily historical? Or are we dealing with a more primordial, theological argument that reaches back to the origins of Judaism and Christianity, a division whose scars are assuaged in the rhetoric of ecumenism only to erupt in the most unexpected of times and places, when one community ostensibly is reaching out to the other?

Surely the historical discussion in *We Remember* is fraught with theological overtones. The reason for remembering the Holocaust itself—as a collective and Christian act—emerges from the special relationship between the Catholic church and the Jewish people. Hence the recitation of the prehistory of the Holocaust begins with the birth of Christianity, and tracing anti-Semitism is important for the modern period of persecution because of the intimate relationship between Jews and Catholics. This relationship is followed here, as elsewhere, in post-Vatican II reflections on the shared covenantal promises of Jews and Catholics as well as the divergent paths taken by both communities after the first century of the common era. The document is clear on this point: "The Church's relationship to the Jewish people is unlike the one she shares with any other religion. . . . [The Holocaust] cannot be fully measured by the ordinary criteria of historical research alone. It calls for a religious memory and particularly among Christians, a very serious reflection on what gave rise to it." Moreover, memory of the Holocaust itself is crucial for Jews and Christians, as a future grounded in history and faith is impossible without such memory. "History itself is *memoria futuri*" the writers of the document posit. More specifically, they say that memory must be seen in relation to John Paul II's apostolic letter *Tertio Millennio Adveniente*. At the close of the second millennium of Christianity and in preparation for the new millennium, Catholics should become "more fully conscious of the sinfulness of her children, recalling all those times in history when they departed from the spirit of Christ and his Gospel and, instead of offering to the world the witness of a life inspired by the values of faith, indulged in ways of thinking and acting which were truly forms of counter-witness and scandal."

Placed in the perspective of John Paul II's apostolic letter, *We*

Remember and the theological ramifications of the Holocaust as *memoria futuri* come into focus. Here history is servant to a narrative more important than history, and the church's witness within history is to a calling beyond history itself. Memory as a path to the future is in actuality a path to the past as well, to the old and new covenant, to Moses and Jesus and the life to be found within the communities that carry their message of hope and salvation. At the dawn of the third millennium of Christianity, a purification is necessary so that Christianity can be carried forward in a way that is compelling and faithful. Counter-witness and scandal harm the body of Christ, then and now, and only through confession and repentance can the Catholic church and Christianity itself continue the pilgrimage that their founder embodied and set forth. This memory is utilized by the Jewish people, who were mistreated and killed, and it is for Christians to set aright their own house and mission.

Tertio Millennio Adveniente sets this framework from the start. Section one is introduced with the quotation from Hebrews 13:8: "Jesus Christ is the same yesterday and today." In this section, John Paul II explains the meaning of that statement for today's Christians: "*Jesus Christ is the recapitulation of everything. . . . Christ is thus the fulfillment of the yearning of all the world's religions and, as such, he is their sole and definitive completion.*" Later in this same section, after tracing the development of the Jubilee tradition beginning with the Hebrew bible, John Paul II asserts the following: "*The words and deeds of Jesus thus represent the fulfilment of the whole tradition of Jubilees* in the Old Testament. . . . The prescriptions for the jubilee year largely remained ideals—more a hope than an actual fact. They thus become a *prophetia futuri* insofar as they foretold the freedom which would be won by the coming of the Messiah." The repentance sought within the coming Jubilee, the "Great Jubilee" of the year two thousand, is thus set in motion: the salvific act of Jesus Christ already accomplished and awaiting its final consummation, the history of salvation marked out and to be lived in fidelity to that salvation, is backdrop to the sins and infidelity found in history. Confession and repentance is to redress a movement away from the path that has been set out for all time; it is to bring Catholics and Christians of all denominations back to their belief and hope. If Jesus Christ is the same yesterday and today, so, too, is the church. The confession and repentance is called upon by the church for those of its communion who have strayed from the church's essential message of love. In *Terito Millennio Adveniente* and *We Remember,* the message of Jesus Christ and the Catholic church which embodies that message is innocent.

Because of this distinction between the innocence of the church and its message on the one hand, and the sinfulness of Christians on the other hand, *We Remember* is fraught with ambiguous statements that compromise its message, or, using its own language, render unclear how the Holocaust will function as *memoria futuri.* After discussing the different forms of anti-Semitism from the birth of Christianity to the Nazi era, for example, the document offers the following sentence: "Thus we cannot ignore the difference which exists between anti-semitism, based on theories contrary to the constant teaching of the Church on the unity of the human race and on the equal dignity of all races and all peoples, and the long-standing sentiments of mistrust and hostility that we call anti-Judaism, of which unfortunately, Christians have also been guilty." This statement leads to the following controversial conclusion: "The *Shoah* was the work of a thoroughly modern neo-pagan regime. Its anti-semitism had its roots outside of Christianity and, in pursuing its aims, did not hesitate to oppose the Church and persecute her members also."

The controversy that these two statements ignited, and which drew a wide variety of commentators to conclude that the document was deeply flawed, comes not so much from the total inaccuracy of these statements on a historical level but from the compression of the historical facts into a symmetrical and defensive tone. Few scholars dispute the difference between a religiously based anti-Judaism and a racially based anti-Semitism. Few scholars would deny the neo-paganism of the Nazi regime or that in certain instances the church and some of its members were also persecuted. What many scholars and interested observers cannot accept, however, is the strict separation of anti-Judaism and anti-Semitism and the seeming equation between anti-Semitism and the sufferings of the church under Nazi rule.

What is missing in *We Remember* is the complex interplay of anti-Judaism and anti-Semitism and the difference in quality and quantity between the sufferings of the Jews and the sufferings of the church and its members. In a sense, the document initially states theologically what should inform its later analysis historically: "The Church's relationship to the Jewish people is unlike the one she shares with any other religion." In the history of Jews and Christians, in Europe at least, the theological and historical relationship between these two communities is essential to understand so the compromised position of the church is not explained away by neat divisions and symmetries that do not exist.

After more than a thousand years of theological and institutional anti-Judaism, is it possible to make the case that Nazi anti-Semitism "had its roots outside of Christianity," or that the anti-Semitism of the 18th and 19th century was "essentially more sociological and political than religious"? Christians were guilty of anti-Judaism *and* anti-Semitism because the theological and institutional carriers of Christianity, including the Catholic church, were historically—and in the Nazi period—providing the foundation that led to views of Jews that were derogatory and denigrating. Though the institutional church often sought to mitigate the more violent expression of these views, the foundations of both anti-Judaism and anti-Semitism in the church and in society were laid and constantly renewed through a prejudicial and often violent rendering of

Jews and Judaism *in mainstream Catholic theology, imagery, and institu-tional practice.* The point here is that Christians have been "guilty" of anti-Judaism and anti-Semitism because the church itself has been guilty of both.

Memory and Forgiveness

In a speech to a symposium on the roots of anti-Judaism in October 1997, Pope John Paul II stated: "In the Christian world—I do not say on the part of the Church as such—erroneous and unjust interpretations of the New Testament have circulated for too long, engendering feelings of hostility towards this people." Quoting this statement, *We Remember* remarks: "Such interpretations of the New Testament have been totally and definitively rejected by the Second Vatican Council." But if it is true that anti-Judaism and anti-Semitism have been rejected by the church, citing as erroneous interpretations of the New Testament that have been used for centuries to promulgate views and actions that the church now rejects and condemns as sinful, the understanding of Jesus as messiah, as the same yesterday and today, as the recapitulation of everything, as the fulfillment of the whole tradition of the Jubilees, as the "*one Mediator between God and men,* [where] there is no other name under heaven by which we can be saved," the certainty of salvation as initiated by Jesus Christ and carried by the Catholic church and by Christians who adhere to the message of Christ, remains. While on the occasion of the coming millennium, Pope John Paul II earnestly desires confession and repen-tance for the sins of those who betrayed Christ's message, errors by Christians in history remain peripheral to the message of the church. Sin is a distortion of the message of Christ and the church itself calls all to repent that sin. The possibility that the church and history, the living of Christianity in the world, indeed even the salvific mission of Jesus itself, are transcendent *and* historical, prompting a reevaluation of how the Christian life is understood and lived and how the message is received and proclaimed, seems off limits to this analysis.

But can memory, especially the memory of suffering, give birth to a future without a reckoning with behavior *and* belief? Johannes Baptist Metz, the German Catholic theologian, writes of the challenge to Christianity of the memory of the Holocaust in this way: "We Christians can never go back behind Auschwitz; to go beyond Auschwitz is impossi-ble for us by ourselves. It is possible only together with the victims of Auschwitz." The question Metz raises is how Christians can journey with the victims of Auschwitz. Can Christians journey with their victims by taking on the questions that the victims themselves embody? Surely Jews have experienced what *We Remember* speaks of as sinful behavior on the part of Christians, but Jews have experienced that sinful behavior as part of the belief structure of Christianity itself. In the violence perpetrated against them, Jews experienced the violence of anti-Judaism born in a certainty that Jesus Christ is the messiah of all, as the pope states it, the recapitulation of everything. These claims are challenged by the victims of atrocity at a foundational level and ask whether the claims that give birth to the violence are not themselves suspect. After the Holocaust, is it enough to assert the sinfulness of the violent without somehow asking further questions of the claims that continue to be made?

To assent to the need to rethink the fundamentals of any community, especially a religious community, is to affirm that revealed truth is found in history and ultimately judged by it. A historical analysis of the church finds this to be the case; if not, why, then, the need for councils of the church, including the Second Vatican Council? There are few historians who can affirm the statement made in *We Remember* of the "constant teaching of the Church on the unity of the human race and on the equal dignity of all races." Rather, this vision has emerged over time, through conflict and influences outside the church as well as internal sources responding to the signs of the time. If Jesus Christ is the same yesterday and today, the interpretations of Jesus have changed over the years, as have many of the rites and dogmas that surround these changing interpretations. Can we honestly say that the fundamentals of belief have or should remain the same? Rabbi Irving Greenberg has written of the most difficult of challenges after the Holocaust: "After the Holocaust, no statement, theological or otherwise, can be made that is not credible in the presence of the burning children." Would the division between anti-Judaism and anti-Semitism, the separation of the church and its congregants, Jesus as the recapitulation of everything, be credible to these children? In their presence, can the case be made for *We Remember* or even *Terito Millennio Adveniente* as *memoria futuri* and *prophetia futuri*?

Greenberg's challenge is seemingly impossible. After all, what Christian, or for that matter, Jewish theological statement, could make sense to burning children? Greenberg answers that only a commitment to end the cycle of violence that produces burning children is a response: this may one day make the possibility of God real again. Metz responds in like mind though with a proviso that discussion of God, the entire theological enterprise, can make sense only if the victims of Auschwitz are "assigned" to Christians in an "alliance belonging to the very heart of saving history." The victims of Auschwitz are to be mourned and listened to because they provide the only way through the questions that Greenberg asks. Faith is possible after Auschwitz because there were Jews who embraced their faith even unto death. According to Metz, that is why Christians can pray after Auschwitz: "We can pray *after* Auschwitz because people prayed *in* Auschwitz."

Metz is correct in that people did indeed pray in Auschwitz. However, those prayers were chastened by the death surrounding prayer and the death even of those who did pray. Moreover, if this does establish a continuity of prayer and the depth of prayer within and after atrocity, there were many who prayed before the Holocaust and lost their ability to pray within the Holocaust. Does their witness speak to the possibility of religious affirmation after the Holocaust? In light of the questions posed by those who remained believers and those who refused belief, Greenberg posits the possibility of "moment faiths" as the only response after the Holocaust. Moment faiths maintain a tension between belief and unbelief, between hope and horror, *in fidelity to the burning children.* For Greenberg, the religious act is saving the world of burning children; religious certainty is sacrificed to the deeds of humanity, including the church and Christians who laid the groundwork for the Nazi period and looked away when the moment of challenge appeared.

In *Terito Millennio Adveniente*, Pope John Paul II seems to respond to part of this challenge posed by Metz and Greenberg. In the spirit of repentance, the pope counsels Catholics to be aware of acquiescence to "*intolerance and even the use of violence* in the service of truth." The church of today needs to examine itself "*on the responsibility which they too have for the evils of our day.*" Here the pope cites the role of Christians who have been silent in response to the violation of human rights by totalitarian regimes and the responsibility "shared by so many Christians *for grave forms of injustice and exclusion.*" There has been a response to this injustice by Catholics and other Christians, hence the pope's assertion that at the end of the second millennium of the church, martyrdom, as in the first centuries of Christianity, has become a defining characteristic of the church's witness. "*The Church has once again become a Church of martyrs,*" the pope writes, and this martyrdom has an ecumenical character to it. According to the pope, this martyrdom "cannot fail" to have such an ecumenical character and expression, and for him "*the ecumenism of the saints and martyrs*" is the most convincing form of ecumenism. "The *communio sanctorum* speaks louder than the things which divide us," the apostolic letter concludes, though the pope adds that these martyrs are defined in our time, as historically, by those who lived fully by the "truth of Christ."

Thus the pope responds *and* steps away from the challenge posed by Metz and Greenberg in the presence of the burning children. At the very heart of saving history are the victims and those who become martyrs, and at some moments victims and martyrs are one and the same. The ecumenism that Metz suggests is touched upon by the pope but without the consequences of the unity found therein. Does not the ecumenism of the saints and martyrs, stretching well beyond the Christian world to include Jews and many others, call for a reevaluation of the foundational understanding of those who lived fully? Though the "truth of Christ" may be an explanation for those Christians who embraced martyrdom, is this explanation sufficient for those non-Christians who also embraced martyrdom? Of course, there were those with no faith at all who died for others. Do they not respond as well in the presence of the burning children? They make it more possible today to respond in faith to those children and therefore become part of the religious journey of our time. Do they not also deserve a special place in the *communio sanctorum* of our time? What truth did they live fully and does that speak to the "truth" of the church?

The challenge here is to incorporate the testimonies of the victims and those who resist injustice and death in an ecumenical search for the "truth" of our time in dialogue with revealed truth as interpreted by the church and other communities of faith. By emphasizing the ecumenical quality of the cycle of atrocity and resistance, the claims of all—the burning children, the martyrs, *and* those who carry on after the Holocaust— are reviewed and chastened. Rather than the assertion of the truth of the church's teachings, often positing a continuity where little can be found, or separating theology and history, when the strict division between the two falsifies the interconnective quality of belief and action, a new listening can occur. If indeed the victims of the Holocaust and those who come after the Holocaust are assigned to the very heart of saving history, as Metz understands it, and if the true ecumenism can be found here, as the pope asserts, then Jesus Christ can no longer be seen as the culmination of all, and the church as carrier of Jesus' message can no longer be seen as innocent. If the terrain of victimhood and martyrdom are expanded, a *prophetia futuri* can only move in that same direction. Confession and repentance is static if both are enjoined to returned to a way of Christian thought and belief, institutionalized over the last two millennia in the church, that has led to a cycle of atrocity that stretches before and after the Holocaust. Is it possible to neglect the fact that *after the Holocaust* apartheid in South Africa, ethnic cleansing in Bosnia, and mass slaughter in Rwanda were carried out either in the name of Christianity or by Christians?

The ecumenical fraternity and sorority of burning children in the twentieth century, which in many ways gives birth to the ecumenical fraternity and sorority of martyrs, challenges the "truth" of the church to be sure, at the same time forcing a naming of the community that could bring confession and repentance into a dynamic reformulation of saving history. If we know that Christians can persecute others *and* give their lives for others, and if we know that this is true for all communities, citing for example the ability of some post-Holocaust Jews to persecute Palestinians while others seek a solidarity with them, then we are asked whether our communal loyalties are with a divided community who "follow" the "truth" or whether we stand *in repentance and confession* with the burning children of all times and places *and* with those who have resisted injustice and atrocity, even unto martyrdom.

Here the question of fidelity, or the struggle to be faithful, takes precedence over foundational theology, and history becomes the arena through which our ultimate values and hopes are tested. The task is less preserving the "truth" from the onslaught of complicity and silence, or even defending that truth from the doubts and anxieties inherent in human experience. Rather the task becomes one of balancing rootedness and openness, being bound and free and allowing saving history to evolve in the ongoing testimony of the human journey. That testimony is less to "truth" than it is to diversity, less to the messianic than it is to the unfinished, less to division along lines of truth and falsehood, than to actions and disciplines that foster atrocity or justice. On the threshold of the third millennium, is there instead a broader tradition of faith and struggle that lies at the heart of saving history, awaiting to be named and embraced?

This new ecumenism, or rather the discovery of the truly ecumenical in the history of faith and struggle, does not minimize the question of God or place it on the periphery. The diverse expressions of covenant found in this tradition, whether religious or secular, point to a God whose presence is more subtle and unfinished, as if fidelity itself is part of the evolution of God. Stated more precisely, our naming of God is always unfinished, especially when we claim God as understood and defined. The broader tradition of faith and struggle allows those who have struggled to be faithful across time, tradition, culture, and geography to speak to all of us in the present, as it allows the understandings of God embraced in this tradition to speak to us as well. Our understandings of fidelity and God thus broaden together. Is this not true in our lives, that our own struggle to be faithful in our encounter with others on the same path deepens our embrace of and our need for God? This helps us to accept the almost mystical statement found in the writings of the Catholic priest, Joan Casanas, who, in accompanying those who fought the dictatorship of Augusto Pinochet and relating their diverse religious experiences, came to the following conclusion about fidelity and God: "It is difficult for us to live underway—always on the move—even when we have knowledge of the goal to which we are heading, the name to be given to it, and the manner of expressing it. But God is not; God will be. And if God does not exist yet, then ours is the task of making God exist (the task of intrahistorical justice), even without knowing what God is, or is like."

Perhaps the Holocaust is the preeminent challenge to knowing or proclaiming God, and even the remembrance of the suffering of the Jews is a danger if the suffering of the present is left unattended. Forgiveness for the Holocaust cannot be nuanced or static or found within one tradition, as if the resources for forgiveness and healing can be found in one or even two traditions. *The third millennium of Christianity can only become a time of reconciliation and healing if this broader tradition of faith and struggle is seen outside and within the church itself.* But this is true for Judaism and the Jewish community as well. Only when the limitations of Jewish life and its own propensity toward power and injustice are recognized and addressed can a Jewish future be secured. That future, like the future of the church, will be chastened by a history that continues to issue into atrocities that neither humanity nor God seems able to end.

21

On Worship and Proclamation:
Piecing Together a Jewish Life
After the Holocaust

IT IS TELLING THAT THE TERM "worship" has meant little to me; indeed, I have even at times found it to be off-putting. Perhaps it is the formality of the term or simply the way "worship" entered my life: through Hebrew school at too young an age and in a foreign language or through Christian church advertisements on billboards and signs in front of imposing and, yes, foreign, church structures. Official synagogue and church ritual has always struck me in the wrong way, as if God is boxed within a service where the seasons of religious life are known in advance and order of prayer is in some ways the order of God.

I thought this way as a child when I tried to escape the rigors of Hebrew school and Shabbat services to play sports and read. I wanted the open air, to breathe and run with others, to read words of history and imagination, to be free.

And then came the Holocaust—not the event itself, for I was born well after the end of World War II—but the naming of the Holocaust as an event of significance and horror. What did this event say to the order of worship, to the buildings and leadership that invoked God with an unthinking regularity? If God had chosen us as Jews, if God had promised to be with us in our struggle for liberation and in our suffering, where was God in Auschwitz? If indeed Jesus was the savior, the redeemer of all humanity, and if Jesus had a special gift of being with those who were suffering, healing them of their wounds and brokenness, where was Jesus, himself a Jew, at this moment of loss? Where were those who followed him as their salvation? In Europe, at least, so many Christians were involved in anti-Semitism or were silent in the face of it.

The language of God was, from my perspective, too easy to speak. And yet I was drawn to those who were religious, preferring their company to overtly secular people. Religious orthodoxy lacked the freedom and the questioning I needed to find my way, but secular orthodoxy struck me in a similar manner: there was a certainty of denial whose failings paralleled the certainty of belief.

For many years I remained between the religious and secular, or perhaps I combined the two. Most of my public life, which is largely an articulation of my personal journey, can be found in searching out a space and a language, a freedom if you will, to speak of God and humanity with integrity after the Holocaust.

I cannot find my way as a Jew only or as a non-Jew. I must instead listen to the voices of fidelity in every language, culture and religion that I encounter. For me, fidelity, or the struggle to be faithful, is the key to spirituality. When the doors of worship were closed to me, the struggle to be faithful spoke to me. It was and is the key that unlocks the doors that can confine religious language and ritual.

It was at the Catholic Worker in New York City that I first experienced Christian worship. As a community that lives and works among the poor and raises its voice in critique of a social order that produces poverty, community members gathered for worship in the dining room where during the day they served meals to the hungry. The setting was austere: pots and pans for cooking were visible, and the community gathered around the tables where the men and women of the Bowery ate their food. No prayers were said before these meals nor was religious instruction provided or demanded. The only prayers were at Mass, which everyone who wanted to could attend.

I remember sitting at the back of the room listening to the priest welcome the congregation and then solemnly begin the liturgy. The community was diverse and included those who volunteered at the Worker and those who affiliated with it in the neighborhood, the Lower East Side of Manhattan. Often people from the soup line were present, sometimes as communicants, sometimes interrupting the service in need of food or clothing. Occasionally, a brick would be thrown through the window or a person from the street, friendly when sober, would arrive drunk and angry, ready to dispute, at the most inopportune time, the words of consecration.

It was here that I met Dorothy Day, the founder of the Catholic Worker, and Daniel Berrigan, the radical Jesuit priest who then and now continues to present a radical vision of God and the social order. For Day and Berrigan, as for others who gathered at the Worker, worship was prayer in the very heart of their work and struggle. Though the dining area was cleaned before the service, it was cleaned in the same way that the room was cleaned before serving meals: it remained as it was for the work or, if you will, the life lived during the day. No separation was allowed or desired. Liturgy emerged and flowed with a committed life lived out in the world.

Life here was difficult for everyone and living at the Worker for a year was the most difficult time of my life. Witnessing suffering close-up, without escape, and living in the context of poverty and destitution was not easy for a person from a middle-class background. I never became used to it nor was I good at attending to the suffering. The smells and horror of some lives I encountered has never left me, nor has the essential lesson I learned at the Worker, that the poor and destitute are no different from the affluent except in circumstance and possibility. There is a thin line between hope and despair, affluence and poverty, well-being and destitution.

When we pray in affluence, what do we pray for? Does the God who blesses us deny to the poor and destitute his blessing? Do the prayers of the poor counteract the prayers of the affluent? Are the affluent and the poor divided in life but united in God? Is it true that unity through Jesus overcomes the disunity among Christians in the world? Is salvation found in God or in the world? What is salvation? What does it mean here on earth?

These questions remained with me as I embarked on a journey with the Maryknoll Fathers and traveled the world among the poor and with liberation theologians who spoke for the poor. Here I encountered again the worship of those on the outside of worldly power, those who were segregated into the precincts of the living dead. I often wondered in my travels and conversations in Latin America, Africa, and Asia whether those of the living dead were so different from those of my dead, remembered in Jewish theology.

The echoes of Jewish life I found here were startling: a recovery of the Exodus and the prophets, even the Jewishness of Jesus. Here God was among the poor, or at least this was the assertion of the theologians and the people themselves. Could it be that God was among the poor in the garbage dumps of Lima, Peru, but not among the Jews of Auschwitz? It could be that God was with both these Peruvians and the Jews. And it could be that God was among neither peoples, then or now.

For many years I remained stuck on this question of God's presence, as if the question itself was all-determining. Yet I was also called to form a religious practice, because of my personality and perhaps because of the circles I traveled in. I was both an observer and a participant without knowing it, and my place in either dimension was unknown, even as it was at the same time deepening. At this time I made a decision to form a discipline that allowed these two dimensions of my life to coexist and come into a new configuration. The decision was neither rational nor irrational. I was not able to articulate or even define what this discipline might be. Traveling among others who were not my own, I also decided to travel to foreign territory within myself.

Like transporting oneself to a foreign country, the development of a discipline is dependent on the means of transportation available. For me the known vehicles were from my own Jewish tradition and from Asian spirituality, especially Zen Buddhism, which I was introduced to in my university days. Though known intellectually, these practices were still foreign in the same way that visiting another country is different from reading about it.

Thus I began with Shabbat and Zen: on Friday nights reading with my family the Shabbat prayers and each morning sitting in silence. The two practices are seemingly disparate in extreme, the first speaking of God's creation and the covenant at Sinai, the second, entering the self to experience nothingness. Still, both helped to transport me to a different landscape and allowed me to appreciate the world in a different way. The questions remained. The colors of life changed.

I could not have embarked on Shabbat if I held to a rigorous honesty. And even today when my oldest child, Aaron, who now shares the invocation of the Shabbat blessings, asks if I believe all that we read, I admit my limitation of belief. "Did God create the world?" Aaron asked me some years ago. When I began a lecture on the complexity of the question he stopped me short. He informed me that a simple yes or no would do. I told him that I was unsure.

Did God choose the Jews? Has God accompanied us through history? These also are affirmations that I choose to speak to, but whose answers yet elude me. Still, I continued in the service until the affirmation of truth became less important than the questions the words raised. After more than two decades of Shabbat observance, certain passages of the service continue to provoke. Is it right to thank God for choosing us and setting us apart as a people? And what does "set apart" mean in our day, especially at a time when Jews are integrated into American life and Christian friends share our Shabbat table? If Jews are set apart, can we also thank God for that at other times in history, at Auschwitz for example? Does our sense of being chosen and set apart also allow some Jews to act against others, Palestinians for example, in a manner that too closely resembles ways that others have acted against us?

For most people it is difficult to understand a religiosity that is unsure of itself, a faith shadowed with doubt and questions. Can a believer question the creation of the world as an act of God? As important is the affirmation of God's presence in the world. But who, after the Holocaust, can be certain of this presence?

Often it is said that faith is a gift and those without that gift must simply struggle along. Yet even the biblical stories are full of doubt and many seem without a clear destination, or one that many today would find difficult to accept. Can I worship a God who tests Abraham's faith by his willingness to sacrifice Isaac, or a God who judges the ancient Israelites' fidelity with a reign of death?

I entered faith through doubt, or perhaps I embarked on a practice that embraces doubt but refuses to be paralyzed by it. This provides the luxury of choosing aspects of the tradition and allows a critical attitude toward parts of the biblical journey. Formative events for me occurred then and now, and Jewish religiosity is an opening to continue to search history for acts of fidelity that inform my own desire to be faithful. Even on Shabbat, "then" and "now" are in relation, as creation and chosenness are confronted by suffering and Holocaust.

As I read the words of blessing I also have in mind Palestinians who experience these words as hypocrisy and as instruments of violence and exile. Shabbat speaks of the end of exile even within exile, but I experience Shabbat in the comfort of affluence and security. Does the hope of ending exile speak to all those on the other side of powers that too often invoke religious language and symbol to legitimate the cycle of atrocity?

Doubt can be a critical element of faith, relativizing all claims, including our own. Silence enters here, at least in my own evolving practice. Sitting quietly, regularly, and within a discipline, is an opening without claims or doubt. Shabbat is an assertion, albeit a beautiful one, and the questions that Shabbat raises for me are speculative, no matter how deeply experienced. Zen seeks a reality beyond words and a presence to life without judgment or name.

To reach this point is a lifetime journey, and the goal is itself an assertion of destination. At least for me, the silence is a place of rest that refuses destination and destiny. To be here in the moment, attentive but not captive to that which surrounds us, to listen to what is inside of us but not to be captive to it, is to practice a freedom that connects me to the world in a way different from Shabbat. Perhaps they work in tandem, as voices of self-correction and as postures in the world, one with words, the other without, one with others, the other alone.

Still the questions remain. Often I am asked about fidelity as I have come to understand it. What is fidelity? To what or whom are we faithful? In an earlier time I would respond that the call is to be faithful in and to history. Usually the person asking the question is religious in a more conventional sense, knowing that fidelity is to God and the ability to be faithful comes from God, and so my definition of fidelity is seen as either a challenge or a superficial response to a deeper question.

But after the Holocaust, with God in fragments, as it were, or at least the possibility of faith in fragments, how can one posit a sure anchor from which answers, power, and strength flow? How can one assert a God that is whole and holy, when our experience is one of despair and waiting?

If for Jews the Holocaust remains the ultimate shattering, a further fragmentation has occurred in response to the Holocaust in the formation and expansion of the state of Israel. To many, the birth of Israel is a reformation of Jewish life, asserting life where death reigned and even holding open the possibility of the renewal of God's presence in the life of the people. And so it may be. But for many Jews, and I include myself here, the dispersion and oppression of the Palestinian people makes this view impossible to hold. Empowerment is necessary to maintain one's integrity and survival; it can be the place from which a new interdependence can grow. But when a state is built on exclusivity and the exclusion of others, then isolation and militarism is the norm. Ingathering can become another form of shattering, and Jewish redemption from the Holocaust in the creation of a Jewish state is a disaster for Palestinians and for Jews as well.

I remember well the shattering that the recognition of injustice toward Palestinians caused for me. As I began to break through the difficulties of worship, as I began to move beyond a paralysis that needed assent before ritual, the most beautiful holiday of the Jewish year, Passover, became impossible for me. How can I celebrate our liberation when another people is enslaved? Taken to the entire world the celebration would never be possible. However, here was a most specific case of direct Jewish responsibility that was being evaded. Our fervent desire for liberation, experienced in our time after the Holocaust, was being perverted in the oppression of another people.

Paralysis of belief, the inability to enter into another space so as to see religiosity from another perspective—for me the movement toward Shabbat and Zen—was different from what I experienced in the waning Passover celebration. Passover became impossible for me because the contradictions of real oppression were too great, and it was precisely the other vantage point, the vantage point of the Palestinians, that brought Passover to an end.

Could fidelity be seen as a movement beyond the historical and then within it, as a place from which to judge history in a critical manner? Shabbat and Zen would then be possible as a way of looking at Passover and judging the community's assertion of liberation at the expense of another people's oppression. It at least asks a question of history from a vantage point that deepens as it becomes more experienced. Stated another way, the critical examination of Passover as liberation in our time becomes more articulate as an internal affirmation of spirituality is explored in more depth.

Here again resolution is elusive, and contradiction is present as well. There is a choosing, Shabbat over Passover for example, that can be turned on its head. Why not celebrate both or abandon both as a point of consistency? Is one holy day exempt from critique while another deepens it?

Perhaps this is simply another aspect of the fragments of Jewish life left after the Holocaust and Israel. Each Jew pieces life together in a particular and eclectic way. Boundaries are crossed and often intersect like an unplanned tapestry. It is untidy, to be sure, and the contours of the tapestry are uneven. Yet in meeting with other Jews and those from different traditions who are also experiencing a fragmentary life, a sensibility does emerge beyond the individual. One encounters a diaspora sensibility in more than a geographic sense or even the traditional Jewish sense of commonality within diversity. The diaspora encountered is a reality where the fragments of different traditions and lives are coming together in new ways. There is a particularity found among Jews in this new diaspora and a particularity that is evolving among the various peoples found in the diaspora. Jews, then, form a particular aspect of a larger community that is forming around a condition of exile and fragmentation experienced by many peoples. Which is to say that Jewish particularity in this evolving diaspora is in dialogue with two foundational realities, the Jewish world from which we come and this broader community within which we find ourselves.

I have found this to be true in my own life. It is almost as if I am traveling the diaspora, carrying with me my heritage and history as I encounter others. The interaction is one of solidarity and confrontation, forcing an expansion of my capacity for belief and action and a focusing of the interior life that is formed and unformed, affirmed and challenged in the encounters. Piecing together a post-Holocaust Jewish life is hardly static and traveling the diaspora becomes a spiritual vocation in and of itself.

Over time the need for an anchor is experienced, or so it seems in my life. Exploration of fragmentation can lead to subsequent levels of fragmentation until the experience becomes foundational itself. A fragmentation that is foundational is quite different from a fragmentation of a foundation; the danger is that fragmentation becomes less a search for wholeness and more an experience that has no place to return from or journey toward. The former has a place of depth from which it is jettisoned and a desire to find meaning even if the original foundation is inaccessible; the latter ultimately loses the possibility of depth, as the resources from which it came recede into the distance. At some point the resources of tradition become inaccessible and even the quest for depth recedes. Then a refusal to continue on the journey takes place. Either the ability to see a journey or a destiny at all is lost or, in fear, the attempt to embrace the former reality takes place as if the shattering had not occurred.

But what allows that movement forward? What allows the continuation of the journey into the unknown? What allows for the courage to continue to piece together the fragments after the Holocaust and Israel? What allows Jews to travel the diaspora without fear of losing our own identity or even the possibility of further shattering an already fragmented identity?

Looking back to the difficulties I had with worship and the subsequent creation of an admittedly eclectic discipline, what has been present since the beginning is the covenant. Not a whole covenant without question and doubt, or even one that can be called by one name or found in one tradition. This covenant has accompanied me even as I searched for it. It has been with, around, and beyond me, all at the same time.

I often question where this covenant comes from, where it resides, and by what name it is to be called. On Shabbat it is found within the

Jewish tradition; sitting Zen it is within the silence. In Peru among the poor, I experience the covenant when God is called on to empower the people. When I think of Dorothy Day and the Catholic Worker movement, the covenant is palpable, and in the pictorial representation, so often published in the Catholic Worker newspaper, of Christ on the breadlines among the poor, the covenant is invoked with an intensity that is haunting.

In my own experience of traveling the diaspora, the covenant takes center stage as an almost unknowable yet intimate reality, at moments so close to me and yet just beyond me at the same time. It is the covenant of the bible, revealed and embraced, yet one that is also evolving independent of revelation. Embraced initially in the desert and often betrayed, the covenant holds forth possibility and engagement wherever people grapple with history at its deepest level. Rather than answers, the covenant embodies the questions and tensions of personal and communal life: it is not a place of rest but rather a calling forth.

The covenant is multifaceted, experienced in different ways when approached from various perspectives. Shabbat and Zen become two vantage points on the same path, at the same time a point of fragmentation and integration. The motion is forward, as if both point beyond themselves and transcend their own particularity. Here the answer is unimportant and truth ceases to be an objective to be pursued. The covenant does not propose a truth; it is an accompanying inner voice without destination or destiny, except, perhaps the destiny of the path itself, the traveling that never ceases. In the covenant, endings are beginnings, and the discipline of searching and seeking to embrace the covenant is itself valuable.

Perhaps the fragmentation of so many traditions is itself a call forward. So often during Shabbat and sitting in silence, I feel a gratitude that comes from the possibility the brokenness of tradition affords. How else would I have experienced this diaspora and the beauty within it? How else would my fidelity have been tested and strengthened? The suffering that has brought about the fragmentation we inherit is beyond words and continues today in so many countries and cultures. Still within the horror the journey continues, the covenant beckons and fidelity is called for. I have often wondered if it is possible to be grateful for a journey that is uneven, discontinuous, even violent, and yet the theoretical question is belied by the experience. It is precisely in the brokenness that gratitude comes into view with a power that sometimes overwhelms and other times is so subtle that the experience is missed.

Do we often miss the overwhelming and subtle experience of gratitude because we seek to place it within a framework that no longer exists? Do we seek to place a reality that is beyond naming into a historical naming, or mistake a historical naming for our own vocabulary? Does the search for order and certainty replace the possibilities inherent in a dynamic experience that elicits names but eludes a final naming?

It may be that the world has always been fragmented beyond the order imposed upon it by humans in search for certainty and that the covenant has always traveled freely and been embraced by people searching beyond the confines of the known. The mystical path, found in every tradition, is testimony to this, but the reality I experience is beyond the esoteric and the few. The fragmentation and the search is found within ordinary life, among the many and at the very heart of evolving disciplines of spirituality and everyday life. It is not beyond intact traditions, but is at the very heart of traditions fragmented by history.

To travel the diaspora is to enter into another evolving sensibility and connect to another history. It is a move forward and backward at the same time, embracing diversity in the present and past. The struggle to be faithful is found in many places today, and with that recognition that same struggle can be found historically in many places as well. If fidelity cannot be confined in the contemporary world to any one place or community, this is true for the past. Thus the struggle to be faithful is nourished in this two-fold movement and the terrain of embrace, the resource of nourishment, is expanded.

My fidelity is informed by Jews and others struggling in the present. One thinks here of Ari Shavit, a Jewish Israeli journalist, who protests Israeli state power when it abuses Palestinians, and Sara Roy, a child of Holocaust survivors, who has traveled among Palestinians and is a world expert on Gaza. But I am also nourished by the witness of Archbishop Romero, who stood with the poor of El Salvador and was murdered for speaking on their behalf, and Gustavo Gutierrez, who has lived with the poor of his native Peru and founded the theology of liberation which speaks of a God active in the liberation of the marginalized and dispossessed. So, too, with history. I am nourished by the German Jewish philosopher Franz Rosenzweig and the German Christian resistor to Hitler, Dietrich Bonhoeffer. And further back in history I am nourished by the founders of the great religions, including Buddha and Jesus.

Should I be denied their insights and struggle? Should I deny the resources that are available to me and carried by others in the new diaspora? By denying them I diminish my own sensibility of others around me. And since in so many ways those who have struggled to be faithful are connected together, through borrowings, cross influence, and common trajectories, my denial would be a denigration of their contributions in a common history.

The broader tradition of faith and struggle can be found in the imagining of a diaspora that is continuous over time, searching through history for justice and love, always incomplete, even in its depth, and somehow complete in its effort. Whether Buddha or Jesus, Rosenzweig or Bonhoeffer, Shavit or Romero, all have sought commitment and community. In this search the covenant has been present and the particular language of their search, whether theological, philosophical or secular, sheds light on the struggles of our own day. Within our particularities to be sure, but also well beyond them, we take our place in a broader tradition that calls us to, and provides resources for, our own journey.

As we move deeper within the broader tradition of faith and struggle, the charges of relativism, of abandoning particularity and claims to truth ring hollow. A critical understanding of the people and communities that have struggled over time to be faithful uncovers strengths and weakness in their witness. This informs us of the complexity of our own search and witness, including the too-easy criticism of those who remain within a particularity or those whose particularity has become inarticulate to them.

The broader tradition of faith and struggle is expansive in our time as it was in the past, and a dialogue between those within and outside of traditional particularities is essential. Recognizing the diversity of commitment and perspective allows a humility regarding our own choices. Rather than relativizing each other's commitments, respect is needed across lines of division. Thus, Judaism and Christianity may be wanting and limited, and so they are, but the new diaspora and the broader tradition of faith and struggle are also in need of criticism and augmentation.

A new ecumenism comes into view. One aspect is historical, recognizing the divisions in the past and the commonalities that are clearer in retrospect; the other is contemporary, expanding the partners for dialogue beyond the denominational and faith divisions to a more diverse and complex field. Ecumenical here includes the monotheistic faiths and those outside that category. It also includes those within the broader tradition of faith and struggle, both those who articulate themselves in religious language and those whose secularity is defining. The new ecumenism does not privilege or disparage any particular sensibility, but includes all perspectives in a spirited search and debate.

At the center of this ecumenism is the search for the covenant. In its diversity and variety the ecumenical dialogue takes on a forward momentum, breaking through the parameters of the dialogue as it has evolved. Dialogues between traditions, which seek common ground within a context of differing truth claims, can only travel so far. Areas that are declared off-limits increase over time or cease to be of interest. At the end of decades of discussion many of those involved in the ecumenical dialogue have agreed to disagree or simply retire to other issues. The new ecumenism forces a different agenda, one that is less easily defined and defended. Rather than truth claims or even defense of particular traditions, the issue is fidelity in the broadest sense of the term. A listening takes place and a gratitude for resources that come from the most unexpected places, even places within one's own tradition that were buried and come to life in the dynamic interchange across boundaries.

Will the crossing of these boundaries lead to the dissolution of all traditions? Will there come into being a confusion about the center of fidelity, including the abandonment of particular understandings of the covenant and even particular understandings of God? The risk is clear if one believes that there is an ontological connection between certain claims about the covenant, their embodiment in traditions with their symbolic and ritual frameworks, and that without these claims and the communities that carry them in history the very truth that our lives depend on will be lost. Passing the tradition on to the next generation is paramount here and future generations must be formed in the same way we were. To many, this means the same formation that has existed since the beginning of the community.

Yet we are advised in so many arenas that what is understood as traditional is often quite recent and that the layers of tradition are many. For Roman Catholics, Vatican II addressed this reality, calling the hierarchy and the laity to recover the original impulses and liturgy of the early Christians as well as founders of religious and lay communities. The dynamic Vatican II unleashed is still being confronted by those who were attached to the tradition they inherited—often dating from the 19th century—seeing change as liberal, influenced by modernity rather than faith. Those who embrace change find traditionalists caught in a time warp, seeking to separate faith and life and often mistaking a contemporary synthesis of culture and religion with apostasy, though their traditionalism once represented the same attempt in a different century.

Still, there is another group within the post-Vatican II generation, one that has "left" the church or remains only on the fringes. They are searching for another way of life and many can be found within the new diaspora. Will this latter group be incorporated into the Catholic church posthumously, as it were, calling the church forward into the twenty-first century? Or will they be excluded from the church as it continues on, lost to the community through malice or apathy? A further question is whether this Catholic diaspora community can carry its own resources into the new community and whether or not their children will be interested at all in the search that fueled their parents' exodus. Will the Catholic sensibility that prompted their parents' journey be available to the children who, unlike their parents, have no reason to rebel? Of course, a phenomenon recognized in different parts of the world and in different religious communities is the return of the children to the very community their parents left. If the parents needed to rebel in order to find their own way, the children's need is to find an anchor, a sense of certainty and order that their parents found stifling.

Could it be that this leave-taking and return, the identification with traditions and the formation of new ones, is simply representative of the human search for goodness, love, justice, and God? Is our journey always made up of fragments and the attempt to overcome them? Could we live in a world where only fragments were in evidence or only a known order? Could the covenant survive only fragmentation or only certainty?

Between fragmentation and certainty is a fidelity that is steadfast in its questions and its commitments in the world. That "between" is a place from which fidelity can grow and be nourished, even as it is deprived of the answers so often proffered by those who know the "truth" and seek to mold others in that singular vision. Fidelity here is broader and narrower, listening to the testimonies of others and one's own testimony as a grounding of openness and possibility. After the Holocaust, fragmentation cannot be confronted by "truth" or answers. Rather, responses are worked out in the world, offered, synthesized, projected, humbled. The covenant can only be glimpsed here or pursued on a journey that is life-long and in process. The covenant cannot be owned or proclaimed, lest it flee the possession that, often as not, has as its core injustice and pretension. Thus the new ecumenism and the broader tradition of faith and struggle are relativized as well; a path on the way that can also lose its way.

We all await a new beginning, especially those of us who have experienced an ending. New beginnings come from endings, emerging from the least expected places, ending themselves and providing room for other beginnings which we may not even witness. Is the covenant that place of beginning, so often, once disclosed, mistaken for an ending? Do traditions exist only for the beginnings that can emerge from them, even as the guardians of tradition seek to foreclose those beginnings? Thus the contradictory aspects of experience: tragedy and beauty, death and birth, commingle, haunt each other, as if one could not exist without the other.

To flee worship as a child and flee answers as an adult are thus rebellions against a unity that is shattered. And yet an acceptance of fragmentation as the way of the world is to be refused as well. Is there not wholeness in brokenness, and brokenness in wholeness? Perhaps a refusal of either without the other is the faith we are left with, honest to experience and the world. We are left then with prayer and silence and activity, in different combinations, in different parts of the world, among diverse cultures and religions.

What then do we proclaim? In both Judaism and Christianity proclamation stands at the center and even those who rebel against the certainty of these traditions proclaim their defiance. Zen also proclaims, as do other non-monotheistic religions, a way or path. And within all these traditions are those who, throughout history, stand as a witness to these proclamations.

How often these proclamations become weapons against others, as if proclamation itself is a type of religious warfare. And how often behind these certainties and violence is a void, a zone of uncertainty that is filled only when others assent to what is doubted by the proclaimer. Of course the hypocrisy and violence found within individuals and communities at certain times of history do not invalidate the message itself. While not invalidating the proclamation, a permanent warning is established. Proclamation as a weapon is the mask we wear in a life of uncertainty and ambiguity, and the violence that has often resulted is a further masking of the complexity of life and history.

When will we understand that our path is not *the* path, that a resolution of the deeper questions of humanity and God are not resolutions to be found here during our journey on earth? To some this might mean the end of proclamation, of the prophetic word or the messianic coming, but this too would be a false resolution. Ecumenical inclusiveness and even the between of fragmentation and certainty do not deny the inherited proclamation or even the inbreaking of the Word. Without knowing or proclaiming *the* truth, the moment of relation and dialogue, the glimpse of a higher purpose and reality, the obligation to respond to these realities, remains. It is almost as if the prophetic and messianic call asserts itself within doubt and complacency, even within rebellion, and emerges from the most unexpected places.

Witness is the embodiment of proclamation and its carrier. It is the physicality of a message that is so deeply personal and mysterious that attempts at codification and creeds can only touch but never capture. The communal celebration of this witness in its original form, whether it be God's choosing of the Israelites or Jesus' suffering and resurrection, can only point to a place of encounter that faced individuals and communities historically and faces us today. Patterns and interpretations of these original encounters are presented to us in the traditions we affirm but they can only be guides on the path: to substitute their experience for our own is to place an impossible burden of substitution on the Exodus and Jesus. Is that why we are often so confused and why we mask that confusion with violence in word and deed?

Epilogue

I Am/Not a Rabbi!
A Meditation on Jewish Leadership
in a Time of Crisis

THREE DAYS INTO THE PASSOVER HOLIDAYS, I realized that for the first time in several years I had neglected to write a Passover meditation. In previous years I had written short essays either because an issue was on my mind or because it had been requested by a group or a journal. These urgings and requests were new to me, as was the title rabbi, a title attributed to me with increasing frequency.

At first I was surprised by the meditation requests and the rabbinic references. I complied with the former and vigorously denied the latter title, though at times I was too tired to constantly define myself by what I am not and let the appellation pass. Still, I began to wonder why people were asking for Passover meditations and using a religious title to address me. The final straw occurred when, listening to a progressive radio station in New York, I heard the familiar voice of Edward Said speaking of the crisis in Palestine and referring, in a positive way, to the "eminent Jewish rabbi, Marc Ellis." Later at a conference in Bethlehem that Said and I were both addressing, I thanked him for his kind words about me but alerted him to the fact that I was not a rabbi. He apologized for being inaccurate but in a moving way continued, "Perhaps you are not ordained as a rabbi, though you are a rabbi in the deeper sense of the word."

The Passover meditations, and lack thereof, when joined with the rabbinic references, are important points of reflection. For over the last decade the Passover season has become increasingly problematic for me, to the point where the Passover seders are conducted in my home only for the benefit of the children. How can I celebrate our deliverance as Jews from the house of bondage while we have placed the Palestinian people in bondage? One might argue that the seder itself would remind Jews of what it means to be in slavery, therefore raising the subversive question of what Jews have done to Palestinians, and some progressive Jews do just that in their Passover liturgies. But the reality of state power in Israel, with the complicity of Jewish leadership in the United States, dooms this subversive hope to a prayer without substantive meaning. Thus Passover, once the most meaningful Jewish holiday for me, becomes an empty deception.

So, as I started to write Passover meditations with the theme of Jewish oppression of Palestinians, I could no longer practice the seder with any conviction. Were the meditations themselves a desperate attempt on my part to rescue the season that had meant so much to me as a child and in many ways had opened the world of Judaism and spirituality to me? And was this attempt, coupled with my other writings on Judaism and the challenge of Israel and Palestine, the reason that people were referring to me as rabbi?

In my reflections I note a curious paradox: over the years I have become more overtly religious and articulate on the question of God at the same time that I have become convinced that the Jewish tradition as it has been passed on to us is coming to an end. In the oppression of the Palestinian people, and despite negotations and agreements, we have come to the end of Jewish history as we have known and inherited it. For can we as Jews claim a tradition and a history forged in suffering and struggle that raise the questions of power and ethics in a peculiar and important configuration while permanently dislocating another people?

As with Constantinian Christianity, the original twinning of religion and the state in the fourth century and beyond, claims can be made and, like Christianity, religion can flourish in its ties with power and the state. But as with Christianity, a Constantinian Judaism is gutted of its ethical traditions; it becomes something other than originally intended or at least as it has been practiced for the last 1500 years. Constantinian Judaism undergoes an assimilation so similar to that which befell Christianity in its Constantinian synthesis that as the millennium turns, the difference between the two religions is negligible, relegated to ritual and belief. The practice of the two communities, at least in their mainstream variants, is almost exactly the same: heralding the American dream, seeking wealth and status, joining together in thought and theology that serves affluence and power.

In Israel, Constantinian Judaism is even more obvious, driving a wedge between religious and secular Israelis. Some have even questioned whether in the coming years a civil war will erupt between these two groups, one claiming authenticity as religious Jews, the other an Israeli nationality without reference to Jewishness. One Israeli sociologist, a secular Jew himself, has even gone so far as to claim that secular Israelis are not Jewish at all: they are so divorced from the Jewish tradition and so deeply identified with the nation-state that he refers to Israelis as "Hebrew-speaking Gentiles." Of course then one must ask about the claim of the religious themselves. So identified with the messianic claim of the land and so untroubled by the injustice done to the Palestinians—can this be the Judaism of the future?

And where is Jewish leadership on these questions, the institutional and religious leaders, or if you will, wealthy Jews involved in Jewish life and the ordained rabbis who proudly display their hard-earned credentials? Jewish institutional and religious leaders are found either happily and militantly pursuing Constantinian Judaism, deflecting criticism of such a path from Jews and non-Jews, or turning inward to Jewish spirituality as if Judaism and Jewish life can be practiced as the Palestinian people are denied the right to be free in their own homeland.

Perhaps that is why two prominent progressive American Jews, Michael Lerner and Arthur Waskow, have recently taken on the honorific "rabbi" without benefit of ordination. Were they also referred to by this title so often that they simply assumed it as bestowed by that part of the Jewish community that will not accept Constantinian Judaism and its consequences? Did Lerner or Waskow simply acquiesce to the constant reference and, in doing so, identify with a part of themselves recognized by others? Of course, in their case, as high-profile personages who claim the center of the Jewish religious tradition, the rabbinic title may represent a status due them and necessary in the battle against what Lerner calls "settler Judaism." In this case, "rabbi" becomes part of the civil war within Judaism and stakes a claim that is also a chasm: choose which Judaism you want to be a part of for that choice defines you and the future of the Jewish people.

A Jewish civil war is like any other war, fought with armaments and authority, and Jewish renewal is like any other subversive movement that claims the center, a fight unto death to forge the future of a nation or people. And yet the reality is always more complex. At this point in Jewish history, calling the state of Israel and the people Israel to an innocence long-since compromised and preparing for a future as if the dislocation and humiliation of the Palestinian people is to be noted and bypassed so that a renewed and expanded piety can be embraced, is to accept the fate of Palestinians as peripheral to Jewish history. It is the other side of Constantinian Judaism, the shadow side if you will, that believes Jewish continuity and presence to be more important than the dislocation which, after the fiftieth anniversary of Israel, has, for all intents and purposes, become permanent.

What does it mean to be a rabbi in this situation? Perhaps it means accepting the title or even appropriating it to wage the battle, no matter the prospect of victory. Or it could be that the meaning of rabbi here is outside of the known religious framework, en route to a place that ordained rabbis rarely venture or even know exists. Could it be that a rabbi today must articulate what is felt by many Jews, albeit Jews who are outside of institutional Jewish life, that the Jewish tradition as we have known and inherited it is over? Could it be that a rabbi today is called less to be an official representative of the community or even to wage battle for the forces of good over evil, than to be with those on the margins of the Jewish world, in exile from silence and complicity and even from progressive Judaism and the war raging for the heart of Judaism?

Since most Jews in exile are secular, unwilling to entertain the question of God or, perhaps as important, no longer able to articulate a spirituality even when drawn to it, the rabbinic function is less a religious instruction than accompanying witness. Being with those Jews who are in exile for the very reason of justice and compassion, two centers of the history and tradition we inherit, is the task of the rabbi, a task that can be joined only if the rabbi himself is in exile.

Where does this exile lead? What is the practice of exile? What can we say about God in this exile? Does the rabbi embody these questions, become articulate about them, share them with others on the journey, help name the exile for those who are searching to explain to themselves and others the difficult road they have embarked upon?

I wonder also if a rabbi is, at least at this moment in time, for Jews only. Or can the articulation of the journey into exile also be for others in exile, those from every religion, culture, and nation-state who have also embarked on this journey? These exiles are also part of the Jewish exilic community, an emerging community that needs each other's voices for support and light. Does the rabbi here, like the Jewish exilic community in general, become listener as well?

I am/not a rabbi. This has become a mantra of sorts and remains so. Exploring the themes that emerge from the appellation is helpful so long as one is not caught up in the honor of being thought to be such a person. Being a rabbi in exile, perhaps the last exile in Jewish history, is a title that can make sense only if it is substantive, humbling, inconclusive. If it is true that these Jewish exiles carry the covenant with them in their journey, then the prospect of being a rabbi on this journey is even more daunting. And if the destination of these exiles, as it surely must be, is a solidarity with those whom we Jews have dispossessed, the Palestinian people, then the journey is bound to a place where all of Jewish life is questioned and transformed.

How strange the transposition over the course of the century: rabbis accompanying their own communities to death in the killing centers of Nazi Europe; rabbis accompanying an exilic community into solidarity with the Palestinian people.

One can spend a lifetime pondering this transposition at the heart of Jewish life, even denying that it is possible. One can spend a lifetime meditating on the title bestowed by those inside and outside of Jewish life who unwittingly or perhaps with insight spark this reflection. For what right do they, or for that matter I, have to such a title?

At the end of Jewish history, in the last Jewish exile, these thoughts do not come without a cost. I am/not a rabbi, to be sure, unless I grasp the solidarity at the center of this exile that I share with so many other Jews and continue on, whatever the burdens that lie ahead. On the threshold of the twenty-first century, the challenge is fidelity, whether for a rabbi or not.

Notes

Notes to Chapter 14:
Thinking and Writing the Holocaust in an Age of Jewish Empowerment

[1] Daniel Jonah Goldhagen, *Hitler's Willing Executioners: Ordinary Germans and the Holocaust* (New York: Knopf, 1996). For a report on the symposium that includes these quotes from Kwiet and Bauer, see Maria Mitchell and Peter Caldwell, "Symposium on Goldhagen's *Hitler's Willing Executioners*," H-Net List on German History, April 11, 1996. The authors of this report are faculty members at Franklin and Marshall College and Rice University, respectively.

[2] Ronald Wagner's review appeared on H-Net List on German History. He is a faculty member at San Jose State University.

[3] Goldhagen, *Hitler*, 93, 245. Also see Alan Cowell, "Author: Nazis Weren't Only Cause of the Holocaust," *New York Times*, September 8, 1996.

[4] Goldhagen, *Hitler,* 377, 21, 13.

[5] Goldhagen, *Hitler,* 110, 113, 49.

[6] For a detailed analysis of the debates within the founding of the museum, see Edward Linenthal, *Preserving Memory: The Struggle to Create America's Holocaust Museum* (New York: Viking, 1995).

[7] In the spring of 1995, I delivered a lecture at the museum that raised the subject of Palestinians. My lecture was published in 1997 by *European Judaism* with the title, "Restoring the Ordinary: An Inquiry into the Jewish Covenant at the End of Auschwitz." The controversy that resulted from my lecture is detailed in Jonathan Mahler, "Museum Blasted Over Speech: Critics Say *Shoah* Showcase is No Place for Politics," *Forward*, April 22, 1995.

[8] These policies and responses to them are detailed in a series of books I have written over the last decade. See Marc H. Ellis, *Toward A Jewish Theology of Liberation* (Maryknoll, NY: Orbis, 1987), *Beyond Innocence and Redemption: Confronting the Holocaust and Israeli Power* (San Francisco: HarperCollins,

1990), *Ending Auschwitz: The Future of Jewish and Christian Life* (Louisville, KY: Westminster/John Knox, 1994), *Unholy Alliance: Religion and Atrocity in Our Time,* (Minneapolis: Fortress Press, 1997), and *O'Jerusalem: The Contested Future of the Jewish Covenant* (Minneapolis: Fortress Press, 1999). Material explored in these books will not be footnoted in the text.

[9] This journey to Auschwitz provides the framework for *Ending Auschwitz.*

[10] There was even a controversy about whether or not to invite the president of Israel to the dedication ceremonies of the museum as it might "link itself too closely with Israel." See Linenthal, *Memory,* 258.

[11] For a harsh condemnation of the Oslo Accords from a Palestinian perspective, see Edward Said, *Peace and Its Discontents: Essays on Palestine in the Middle East Process* (New York: Random House, 1995). Responding to the banning of his writings by the Palestinian Authority, Said responded with an essay in *The Guardian* of August 23, 1996. This essay was reprinted under the title "He Won't Gag Me," in *News From Within* (September 1996): 8-10.

[12] Rabin's speech was reprinted in the *New York Times,* February 26, 1994. For the banner see Thomas Friedman, "How About You?" *New York Times,* November 8, 1995.

[13] Elias Davidsson, "War Crimes Record of Rabin," *Inquiry* 2 (March/April 1993): 17-18.

[14] On the killing of the Egyptian prisoners of war, see Serge Schmemann, "After a General Tells of Killing P.O.W.'s in 1956, Israelis Argue Over Ethics of War," *New York Times,* August 21, 1995. Dayan's words are quoted by Edward Said, *The Question of Palestine* (New York: Random House, 1980), 14. For the question of torture in Israel, see an interview with Stanley Cohen by Yifat Suskind, "Torture in the Only Democracy in the Middle East," *News From Within* 12 (August 1996): 26-30.

[15] Quoted in Michael Palumbo, *The Palestinian Catastrophe: The 1948 Expulsion of a People from Their Homeland* (London: Quartet Books, 1987), 126-127. For the massacre at Deir Yassin, see Palumbo, *Catastrophe,* 47-56. Palumbo refers to the emptying of Lydda with the chapter heading "Lydda Death March"; see pp. 126-138.

[16] Goldhagen, *Hitler,* 55.

[17] This exchange is quoted in Alan Cowell, "Author: Nazis Weren't Only Cause of Holocaust," *New York Times,* September 8, 1996.

[18] *Report on Israeli Settlements in the Occupied Territories* 6 (July 1996): 3,4.

[19] The report on the pope's visit to Germany can be found in Alan Cowell, "Pope Extolls Church's Nazi Resistance, But With a Sidestep," *New York Times,* June 23, 1996, and Alan Cowell, "Demonstrators and Devout Greet the Pope in Germany," *New York Times,* June 24, 1996. For the comment on the bishops, see Goldhagen, *Hitler,* 110.

[20] John Paul II, "The Almighty Has Done Great Things," *L'Osservatore Romano,* October 21, 1992; Goldhagen, *Hitler,* 114.

Notes to Chapter 15:
Edward Said and the Future of the Jewish People

[1] For an analysis of Wiesel with regard to the 1967 War, see Marc H. Ellis, *Beyond Innocence and Redemption: Confronting the Holocaust and Israeli Power* (San Francisco: HarperCollins, 1990), 9-12.

[2] Fackenheim enunciates this commandment in a series of lectures he delivered at New York University in 1968. These lectures were published as *God's Presence in History: Jewish Affirmations and Philosophical Reflections* (New York: New York University, 1970).

[3] While this shadow of another holocaust can be found in Wiesel and Fackenheim, it also features prominently in the work of the Holocaust theologian Irving Greenberg. Even as late as 1988, in a long essay responding to the Palestinian uprising, Greenberg evokes this possibility. See Irving Greenberg, "The Ethics of Jewish Power," *Perspectives* (New York: National Jewish Center for Learning and Leadership, 1988).

[4] Nathan Perlmutter and Ruth Ann Perlmutter, *The Real Antisemitism in America* (New York: Arbor House, 1982); Elliot Abrams, *Faith or Fear: How Jews Can Survive in a Christian America* (New York: Free Press, 1997).

[5] The most recent chronicler of the scope and use of Jewish power in the United States is J. J. Goldberg, *Jewish Power: Inside the American Jewish Establishment* (New York: Addison-Wesley, 1996).

[6] This is what I consider to be the eighth Jewish culture in Jewish history, a concept I develop in *O' Jerusalem: The Contested Future of the Jewish Covenant* (Minneapolis: Fortress Press, 1999). For the first seven cultures, see Efraim Shmueli, *Seven Jewish Cultures: A Reinterpretation of Jewish History and Thought* (Cambridge: Cambridge University Press, 1990).

[7] John Murray Cuddihy, *The Ordeal of Civility: Freud, Marx, Levi-Strauss, and the Jewish Struggle with Modernity* (New York: Dell, 1974).

[8] John Murray Cuddihy, "The Holocaust: The Latent Issue in the Uniqueness Debate," in Philip Gallagher, ed., *Christians, Jews and Other Worlds: Patterns of Conflict and Accommodation* (New York: University Press of America, 1988), 73, 63. Cuddihy writes as part of his introduction: "I cried, —from sadness, from joy that the *Diary* and its testimony had survived in triumph, that a Pole had been its custodian, and that Kaplan had had the last word, for here was I, now, reading those very words, and crying"(63).

[9] John Murray Cuddihy, "The Elephant and the Angels; or, The Incivil Irritatingness of Jewish Theodicy," in Robert Bellah and Frederick Greenspahn, eds., *Uncivil Religion: Interreligious Hostility in America* (New York: Crossroad, 1987), 24-25, 28, 35.

[10] Edward Said, *The Question of Palestine* (New York: Vintage, 1979), xvii, xiv. Also see Edward Said, *Orientalism* (New York: Vintage, 1979).

[11] Said, *Orientalism*, 307; Said, *Palestine*, 86.

[12] Said, *Palestine*, 88, 99. Said writes with reference to Zionists: "Both in theory and practice their effectiveness lies in how they Judaize territory coterminous-

ly with de-Arabizing it"(99).

[13]Said, *Palestine,* 113.

[14]Said, *Orientalism,* 316; Edward Said, "Michael Walzer's 'Exodus and Revolution': A Canaanite Reading," *Grand Street* 5 (Winter 1986): 105. Also see their responses to each other in "An Exchange: 'Exodus and Revolution,'" *Grand Street* 5 (Summer 1986): 247-259.

[15]Edward Said, "An Ideology of Difference," in *The Politics of Dispossession: The Struggle for Palestinian Self-Determination, 1969-1994* (New York: Vintage, 1994), 84-106. The essay was originally published in *Critical Inquiry* 12 (September 1985).

[16]Said, "Ideology," 88, 99.

[17]Said, "Ideology," 105, 93, 87, 89-90, 106. For an interesting early recognition of Chomsky's work see Edward Said, "Chomsky and the Question of Palestine," in *The Politics of Dispossession,* 323-337. This essay was originally published in the *Journal of Palestine Studies* 4 (Spring 1975).

[18]Edward Said, "An Exchange on Edward Said and Difference III: Response," *Critical Inquiry* 15 (Spring 1989): 629, 631, 632, 627; Daniel Boyarin and Jonathan Boyarin, "An Exchange on Edward Said and Difference II: Toward a Dialogue with Edward Said," *Critical Inquiry* 15 (Spring 1989), 627.

[19]Boyarin, "Dialogue," 627, 633; Said, "Response," 635, 635-636, 636.

[20]See a collection of his dissents from the Oslo process in Edward Said, *Peace and Its Discontents: Essays on Palestine in the Middle East Peace Process* (New York: Vintage, 1996).

[21]Said, "An Exchange: 'Exodus and Revolution,'" 259.

[22]Said, "Response," 637; Said, "Ideology," 106.

[23]Said, "A Canaanite Reading," 106.

[24]Edward Said, *The World, the Text, and the Critic* (Cambridge, MA: Harvard University Press, 1983), 27, 291-292, 30.

Notes to Chapter 16:
Dorothy Day, the Jews, and the Future of Ecumenical Religiosity

[1] For an important study of Christian anti-Semitism, see Gavin I. Langmuir, *History, Religion, and Antisemitism* and *Toward a Definition of Antisemitism,* 2 vols. (Berkeley: University of California Press, 1990).

[2] Richard Rubenstein's statement of his views about God and human solidarity are found in his classic text *After Auschwitz: Radical Theology and Contemporary Judaism* (Indianapolis: Bobbs-Merrill, 1966). For William Miller's analysis of the Catholic Worker movement, see his introduction to *A Harsh and Dreadful Love: Dorothy Day and the Catholic Worker Movement* (New York: Liveright, 1973), 3-16.

[3] Miller, *Harsh and Dreadful,* 138.

[4] For a description of Rayna, see William Miller, *Dorothy Day: A Biography* (New York: Harper and Row, 1982), 31-54. For Dorothy's early relationship with

Michael Gold, see pp. 64-68.

5 Miller quotes from Day's statement in *Harsh and Dreadful,* 150-151. For the report of the forming of the committee see "Catholics to Fight Against Anti-Semitism," *Catholic Worker,* June 1939. The previous month there was a strong open letter to Coughlin penned by "the Gladfly." See "Open Letter to Father Coughlin," *Catholic Worker,* May 1939.

6 Peter Maurin, "Let's Keep the Jews for Christ's Sake," *Catholic Worker,* July-August 1939; Ade Bethune, "Son of God," *Catholic Worker,* December 1939.

7 Maurin, "Keep the Jews."

8 Maurin, "Keep the Jews."

9 Peter Maurin, "Salvation is of the Jews," *Catholic Worker,* July/August 1942. For Maurin's essays "Why Pick on the Jews" and "Judaism and Catholicism," see *Catholic Worker* January 1940 and February 1940, respectively. For Jacques Maritain's understanding of Jews and Judaism, see Robert Royal, ed., *Jacques Maritain and the Jews* (Notre Dame, IN: University of Notre Dame Press, 1994).

10 Maurin, "Why Pick."

11 Peter Maurin, "Unpopular Front," *Catholic Worker,* September 1937.

12 Dorothy Day, "Day by Day," *Catholic Worker,* March 1934; "Catholic Church Has Defended Jews During Times of Stress," *Catholic Worker,* December 1938; "Archbishop Decries Slander and Untruths About Jews," *Catholic Worker,* July-August 1939; "Anti-Semitism Decried by Father Rice," *Catholic Worker,* September 1939; "Hospitality To Immigrants And Own Poor Jews," *Catholic Worker,* May 1940.

13 "Peace Now Without Victory Will Save Jews," *Catholic Worker,* May 1943; Dorothy Day, "Where is Sanctuary," *Catholic Worker,* June 1943. Below this column is a review of a book published by the Jewish Agricultural Society which describes the ability of Jews to contribute to rural life in the tradition of the Catholic Worker. See "Room on the Land," *Catholic Worker,* June 1943.

14 Robert Ludlow, "The Jews," *Catholic Worker,* September 1948.

15 Hector Black, "Community in Action," *Catholic Worker,* July-August 1951.

16 Michael Harrington, "Paths in Utopia," *Catholic Worker,* July-August 1951.

17 Peter Maurin, "The Race Problem," *Catholic Worker,* May 1938.

Notes to Chapter 17:
Questioning Conversion: Gillian Rose, George Steiner, and Christianity

1 John Milbank, *The Independent,* December 13, 1995; Margaret Archer, *Warwick University Newsletter,* January 1996.

2 Rowan Williams was quoted in the *Tablet,* January 6, 1996.

3 Marina Warner, *Daily Telegraph,* December 14, 1995.

4 I recall this and other stories of my travel to Auschwitz in *Ending Auschwitz: The Future of Jewish and Christian Life* (Louisville, KY: Westminster, 1994).

5 See Gillian Rose, *The Melancholy Science: An Introduction to the Thought of Theodor W. Adorno* (London: Macmillan, 1978).

[6] George Steiner, *Language and Silence: Essays on Language, Literature and the Inhuman* (New York: Atheneum, 1970), viii, 159.

[7] George Steiner, "The Long Life of Metaphor: An Approach to the Shoah," in *Writing and the Holocaust*, ed. Berel Lang (New York: Holmes and Meier, 1988), 155. For an extended discussion of Steiner's understanding of Judaism as a hunt for truth, see "Our Homeland, the Text," in his collection of essays, *No Passion Spent, Essays 1978-1995* (New Haven, CT: Yale University Press, 1996), 304-327.

[8] Steiner, *Language and Silence*, 39.

[9] Steiner's analysis of this contribution and confrontation can be found in his essay, "The Long Life of Metaphor," in *Writing*, 154-174.

[10] Steiner, *No Passion Spent*, 388.

[11] George Steiner, "A Responsion," in *Reading George Steiner*, ed. Nathan Scott and Ronald Sharp (Baltimore: Johns Hopkins University Press, 1994), 280-281.

[12] Steiner, *No Passion Spent*, 36, 38

[13] Steiner, *No Passion Spent*, 36-39.

[14] This is the burden of Steiner's essay "Long Life of Metaphor," in *Writing*.

[15] Steiner, *No Passion Spent*, 345.

[16] Steiner, *No Passion Spent*, 346, 347.

[17] Viktor Frankl, *Man's Search for Meaning* (New York: Simon and Schuster, 1972).

[18] For a fascinating portrait of Simone Weil's Jewishness, see Thomas Nevin, *Simone Weil: Portrait of a Self-Exiled Jew* (Chapel Hill: University of North Carolina Press, 1991).

[19] See the diary of Anne Frank in its definitive edition: *Anne Frank, The Diary of a Young Girl: The Definitive Edition*, ed. Otto Frank and Miriam Pressler (New York: Doubleday, 1995) and Etty Hillesum, *The Diaries of an Interrupted Life* (New York: Pocket Books, 1985).

[20] Lawrence Langer, *Holocaust Testimonies: The Ruins of Memory* (New Haven, CT: Yale University Press, 1991), 43, 37, 2.

[21] Langer, *Holocaust Testimonies*, 99.

[22] Rachel Feldhay Brenner, *Writing as Resistance: Four Women Confronting the Holocaust* (Philadelphia: Pennsylvania State University Press, 1997), 100.

[23] Brenner, *Writing*, 101.

[24] Brenner, *Writing*, 175.

[25] Brenner, *Writing*, 175-176.

[26] Quoted in Brenner, *Writing*, 60.

[27] Brenner, *Writing*, 63.

[28] Quoted in Brenner, *Writing*, 108, 113, 109.

[29] Brenner, *Writing*, 111.

[30] Brenner, *Writing*, 113.

[31] Quoted in Brenner, *Writing*, 136.

Notes to Chapter 19:
On Revolutionary Forgiveness: Practicing the Covenant
in a Time of Colonization and Evangelization

1 These thoughts were brought together for the first time in my book *Toward a Jewish Theology of Liberation* (Maryknoll, NY: Orbis, 1987). A second edition was published after the Palestinian uprising began and with a new final chapter, "The Palestinian Uprising and the Future of the Jewish People."

2 *Toward a Jewish Theology of Liberation* was followed by two subsequent books that dealt with the unfolding difficulties facing Jewish identity. See *Beyond Innocence and Redemption: Confronting the Holocaust and Israeli Power* (San Francisco: HarperCollins, 1990) and *Ending Auschwitz: The Future of Jewish and Christian Life* (Louisville, KY: Westminster/John Knox, 1994).

3 Carter Heyward and Anne Gilson, *Revolutionary Forgiveness: Feminist Reflections on Nicaragua* (Maryknoll, NY: Orbis, 1987), 108.

4 Richard Rubenstein, *After Auschwitz: Radical Theology and Contemporary Judaism* (Indianopolis: Bobbs-Merrill, 1966). Also see his second edition with a somewhat changed emphasis; *After Auschwitz: History, Theology and Contemporary Judaism* (Baltimore: Johns Hopkins University Press, 1992).

5 Richard Rubenstein, *The Cunning of History: Mass Death and the American Future* (New York: Harper and Row, 1975). Also see Hannah Arendt, *The Origins of Totalitarianism* (New York: Harcourt, Brace and Co., 1951.

6 Hannah Arendt, *The Human Condition: A Study of the Central Dilemmas Facing Modern Man* (Garden City, NY: Doubleday, 1959), 214, 215.

7 Arendt, *Human Condition,* 218.

8 Arendt, *Human Condition,* 220, 216.

9 Adi Ophir, "Between Eichmann and Kant: Thinking on Evil after Arendt," *History and Memory: Studies in Representation of the Past* 8 (Fall1996): 96, 93.

10 Ophir, "Eichmann and Kant," 99.

11 Ophir, "Eichmann and Kant," 126-127.

12 Johannes Baptist Metz, *The Emergent Church: The Future of the Christianity in a Post- Bourgeois World* (New York: Crossroad, 1981), 19.

13 Patrick Hart, ed., *The Other Side of the Mountain: The End of the Journey* in *The Journals of Thomas Merton, vol. 7* (San Francisco: HarperCollins, 1998).

14 Quoted in Marc H. Ellis, *Unholy Alliance: Religion and Atrocity in Our Time* (Minneapolis: Fortress Press, 1987), 122.

15 These ideas are discussed in more detail in Marc H. Ellis, *O'Jerusalem: The Contested Future of the Jewish Covenant* (Minneapolis: Fortress Press, 1999).

16 These understandings of Jesus can be found in John Dominic Crossan, *The Historical Jesus: The Life of a Mediterranean Jewish Peasant* (San Francisco: HarperCollins, 1991), and John Dominic Crossan, *The Birth of Christianity: Discovering What Happened in the Years Immediately After the Execution of Jesus* (San Francisco: HarperCollins, 1998).

17 See John E. Hare, *The Moral Gap: Kantian Ethics, Human Limits, and God's Assistance* (Oxford: Oxford University Press, 1996).

Index